My H

A N N A
A K H M A T O V A
My Half Century
S E L E C T E D   P R O S E
EDITED BY RONALD MEYER

NORTHWESTERN UNIVERSITY PRESS
EVANSTON, IL

Northwestern University Press
Evanston, Illinois 60208-4210

First published in 1992 by Ardis Publishers, Ann Arbor. Copyright © 1992 by Ardis
Publishers. Northwestern University Press edition published 1997 by arrangment with
Ardis Publishers. All rights reserved.

"Dante" by Anna Akhmatova is translated by Judith Hemschemeyer, and is reprinted
from volume II of *The Complete Poems of Anna Akhmatova* (Zephyr Press, 1990),
with the permission of the publisher. Translation copyright © 1989 by Judith
Hemschemeyer.

The editor gratefully acknowledges permission to quote from Walter Arndt's translations of Anna Akhmatova, *Selected Poems* (Ardis, 1976) and Alexander Pushkin,
Collected Narrative and Lyrical Poetry (Ardis, 1984).

Printed in the United States of America

ISBN 0-8101-1485-2

Library of Congress Cataloging-in-Publication Data

Akhmatova, Anna Andreevna, 1889–1966.
    [Selections. English. 1997]
    My half century : selected prose / Anna Akhmatova ; edited
by Ronald Meyer.
        p. cm.
    Originally published: Ann Arbor : Ardis, 1992.
    Includes bibliographical references and index.
    ISBN 0-8101-1485-2 (alk. paper)
    I. Meyer, Ronald. II. Title.
PG3476.A324A14 1997
891.78'4208—dc21   97-14774
                                                            CIP

The paper used in this publication meets the minimum requirements of the American
National Standard for Information Sciences—Permanence of Paper for Printed
Library Materials, ANSI Z39.48-1984.

To Emma Gershtein,
with respect and affection

Contents

Afterword

List of Illustrations

PREFACE

IN A 1962 INTERVIEW Akhmatova states: "I am hard at work on a volume of prose. This will be something in the way of an autobiography. I want to tell about the people I had occasion to meet during the course of half a century. I am beginning my narration with how my girlfriend met Dostoevsky. I remember all the details of her story."[1] Elsewhere, Akhmatova characterizes the prose work-in-progress as the story "of my life and the fate of my generation." Unfortunately, Akhmatova did not live to complete the book that she alternatively titled *My Half Century, Pages from a Diary,* or simply *Prose,* although several plans are extant in her notebooks. (A partial outline is recorded in her diary for February 6, 1966, translated in the present volume.)

Akhmatova's archives contain a number of notes regarding memoirs as a genre and her goal in particular:

> However, a book, a cousin to *Safe Conduct* and *The Noise of Time,* must come about. I'm afraid that in comparison with its elegant cousins it will seem like a grubby child, a simpleton, a Cinderella, and so forth. Both of them (Boris and Osip) wrote their books when they had just barely come of age, when everything was not a fairy tale away. But to see the 1890s from the altitude of the middle of the twentieth century is almost impossible without becoming dizzy.

Akhmatova draws the lines of kinship of her autobiographical book to Boris Pasternak's *Safe Conduct* (1931) and Osip Mandelstam's *Noise of Time* (1922-23), prose narratives that describe their background and creative genesis at the turn of the century. Although Akhmatova embarks on her autobiography more than

two decades later, the plans and fragments indicate that she intended to focus on her adolescence and the early years of her literary career—it was never conceived as a full-scale chronicle.
Besides subject and setting, Akhmatova most likely planned to
follow the lead of her fellow poets in their choice of narrative
composition. Both *Safe Conduct* and *The Noise of Time* have been
characterized as loosely connected episodes or fragments, rather
than continuous and flowing narratives. In the late 1920s
Pasternak referred to his work as "autobiographical fragments."
It is ultimately futile to speculate what shape Akhmatova's work
would have taken upon completion, but it may not have differed
significantly from the style of the fragments collected and translated in this volume.

Akhmatova's history and defense of Acmeism and its founder,
Nikolai Gumilyov, represents a subsection within the autobiography. Akhmatova's authoritative and indignant voice me-
thodically corrects the misperceptions (largely emanating from
the West, since Acmeism was practically a forbidden subject in
the Soviet Union) regarding her poetic career and the times in
which she lived. As Akhmatova's friend Nadezhda Mandelstam
writes in her memoir *Hope Abandoned*:

> In her last years Akhmatova "put on her phonograph record" for
> each visitor, that is, told him or her the story of Acmeism and her
> own life, hoping that they would commit it to memory and pass it
> on in the only permissible version—hers. In Moscow these
> "records" were soon erased from people's minds, but it is said
> that in Leningrad they were carefully noted down by Naiman.[2]

As the recent explosion of memoir literature attests, Akhmatova's
literary secretary, the poet and translator Anatoly Naiman, was
not alone in taping these "records." Akhmatova, however, realized the importance of a printed document, and also entered
these statements into her notebooks.

Akhmatova was particularly incensed by the memoirs and literary studies of emigré Russians who, in her opinion, deliberately falsified her place in the history of Russian letters. The primary target in this case is the poet Georgy Ivanov, whose book
Petersburg Winters, in Akhmatova's opinion, belongs to the genre
of pseudo-memoirs for its invention of dialogue. Injured justice
and invective are the order of the day when Akhmatova reaches
the subject of Ivanov's *Petersburg Winters*: "Justice demands that

we register that (as is the case with all of Ivanov's writings) there is not a single word of truth in it." Uncompromising as she is with fellow Russians, Akhmatova occasionally exhibits more tolerance toward Westerners of non-Russian descent, acknowledging that to understand the complexities and absurdities of life in the Soviet Union was all but impossible. Lidia Chukovskaya, Akhmatova's Boswell, records the following anecdote as told to her by Akhmatova:

> I received a letter from a Swedish professor who is writing a book about me. He wrote that he was coming to see me. And he did come, but I was in the hospital, so he went there to see me. A fine fellow and he knows a lot, but the most amazing thing was the blinding whiteness of his shirt. It was as white as the wing of an angel. While we had two bloody wars and a lot of other blood, the Swedes were washing and ironing that shirt.[3]

Reading Akhmatova's diatribes against what she perceived as malicious misrepresentation, perhaps fueled by envy, as well as simple, honest mistakes, it is important to remember that most of this material dates from the 1950s and 60s, when Slavic studies in the West were at an embryonic stage and the situation in the Soviet Union did not allow discussion of Gumilyov or Acmeism. The difficulties can be better appreciated if we consider that many of the items from Akhmatova's autobiography, as well as the portraits of her contemporaries, waited thirty years for publication in uncensored form.

Akhmatova as prose writer is best known for her studies on the life and works of Russia's greatest poet, Alexander Pushkin. Akhmatova's turn to prose, and the study of Pushkin in particular, may be compared with a similar phenomenon in the work of Marina Tsvetaeva, who began to devote her energies to prose because the conservative tastes of the Russian emigration found her verse to be too idiosyncratic and unpoetic. Akhmatova's Pushkin studies have been acclaimed as classics, but it is not mere coincidence that she begins these studies in the mid-1920s, precisely when she was banned from publication. The comparison of Akhmatova and Tsvetaeva, the two great women poets of twentieth-century Russia, has become clichéd and yields varying results. Pushkin occupies a major place in the prose (and poetry) of both poets. At first glance their treatment of Pushkin would seem to have little in common. Akhmatova's studies are masterpieces of interpretation, while such works as Tsvetaeva's *My Pushkin* are lyrical evocations of her intimate relationship with Pushkin's life and works, without pretense or claim to literary scholarship. Indeed, Akhmatova's disapproval of Tsvetaeva's works on Pushkin is well documented. The differences, however, are not as great as they may seem, for the autobiographical subtext in Akhmatova's Pushkin studies is striking.

Consider the opening lines of Akhmatova's "A Word about Pushkin":

> My predecessor, Pavel Shchegolyov, concludes his work on Pushkin's duel and death with a series of speculations about why society and its spokesmen hated the poet and ejected him like an alien being from its midst. The time has now come to turn this question around and to speak aloud not about what *they* did to him, but what *he* did to them. After the ocean of filth, deceit, lies, the complacency of friends, and the plain foolishness....

The invective continues for another paragraph. The sharp change in tone from scholarly formula (recognizing the works of one's predecessors) to passionate outburst is a rhetorical device that Akhmatova utilizes in other Pushkin studies. Pushkin as national poet and his tragic fate are emblematic of the role of the poet in Russia. It is difficult not to substitute the name of Akhmatova (or Gumilyov, or Mandelstam), who, like Pushkin, was under constant scrutiny by the State. Similarly, when Akhmatova, in "Pushkin and the Banks of the Neva," analyzes how Pushkin reproaches Nicholas I for not allowing the families of the Decembrists to bury their dead, it is difficult not to recall the many victims of the purges buried in unmarked graves—for example, Mandelstam.

Akhmatova's Pushkin studies are not disguised political pamphlets or Aesopian defenses of poetry. The research in her study of Benjamin Constant's *Adolphe* and Pushkin's work and her commentary on Pushkin's tale, *The Golden Cockerel,* are acknowledged masterpieces of Pushkin criticism. Yet, even in the essay on *The Golden Cockerel* one sees contemporary political implications. Writing in the 1930s, one of the bleakest decades in Russian history, Akhmatova is the first to identify the source of Pushkin's tale as Washington Irving's "The Legend of the Arabian Astrologer." Akhmatova, however, proceeds to interpret Pushkin's use of

Irving's tale as a device for political satire, marshalling formidable evidence to prove that the fairy-tale Tsar is based on Nicholas I.

Akhmatova made her debut in prose in 1914 with a review of Nadezhda Lvova's posthumously published book of verse. The combined circumstances of Lvova's suicide and Valery Bryusov's patronage may have influenced Akhmatova's sympathetic review. Apart from the discerning assessment of Lvova's strengths and weaknesses, this short piece is noteworthy for Akhmatova's statement on the particular merits of Russian women's lyric poetry: "Of course, women are also capable of achieving an elevated mastery of form..., but their strength lies elsewhere, it lies in their ability to express fully the most intimate and wonderfully simple things in themselves and the world around them." We should note that this appraisal of women's lyric verse was penned by the author of *Evening*, on the eve of the publication of her second book, *Rosary*, to some degree prompting the critics of her own work. But Akhmatova did not cultivate the genre of the literary review as Gumilyov and Mandelstam had done—her next review did not appear for fifty years. For the most part, the handful of reviews and occasional pieces collected in this volume represent the poet's public aspect, and range from Akhmatova's moving appeal to the women of wartime Leningrad to her appreciation of Dante, which marked her last public appearance (1965).

Akhmatova remarked both in conversation and in letters that she was rarely visited by the epistolary muse. To be sure, she did not devote herself to the epistolary genre to the degree achieved by Marina Tsvetaeva in her celebrated correspondence with Pasternak and Rilke. In general, Akhmatova's correspondence, at least that which has survived and has been published, sets its aims at more purely prosaic concerns, often revealing an intimate glimpse of the poet genuinely concerned about the fate of family and friends. Although there are chronological gaps in Akhmatova's correspondence, the letters collected in this volume provide in outline her biography from a young schoolgirl suffering unrequited love (the letters to Sergei von Shtein), the beginning poet (the letters to Alexander Blok, Valery Bryusov, and Fyodor Sologub), wife (the letters to Nikolai Gumilyov and Vladimir Shileiko), and the poet during her last years (the letters to Joseph Brodsky in exile). But perhaps the most telling letters are not those written to fellow poets, but to the friends with whom Akhmatova shared her life and troubles over many years (for example, Nadezhda Mandelstam, Emma Gershtein, and Nikolai Khardzhiev).

For many years Akhmatova's claim that she did not write letters was taken at face value, and it was believed that correspondence represented a very minor part of her work. This assumption was reinforced by the fact that many letters were deliberately destroyed, while others had not yet surfaced. In her letter to Emma Gershtein, Akhmatova alludes to another reason for the relative meagerness of her correspondence:

> Where is Marusya [the poet Maria Petrovykh] and how is her health? I'm not writing her because in general I can't write, and also because she can't open letters (that's the next stage in our shared illness), but I love her and think about her constantly.

This letter, written in relatively "vegetarian times" (1958), documents the lingering fear of correspondence due to the consequences that could be meted out to the sender, addressee, or their families, for even the most perfunctory letter. And we should bear in mind that few people would voluntarily risk correspondence with an officially censured poet, moreover the ex-wife of a poet executed for treason. The Akhmatova correspondence stands as a testament not only to her stature as a poet and friend, but also serves to acknowledge some of the people who played such an important role in Akhmatova's life.

R. M.

Acknowledgments

I wish to acknowledge the individuals who contributed translations to this volume: Anna Lisa Crone, Christopher Fortune, Uliana Gabara, Helena Goscilo, Sharon Leiter, Edith Stevens, Mary Ann Szporluk, Janet Tucker, and Nicholas Tyrras.

Ellendea Proffer of Ardis Publishers provided the encouragement, guidance, and financial support that enabled me to bring this project to completion.

For their help with translation, identification, and annotation, as well as less tangible problems, I particularly wish to thank Walter Arndt, Andrei Bitov, Eugenia Gavrilova, Helena Goscilo, David Lowe, and the late Inna Varlamova.

Finally, I wish to thank Emma Gershtein, Akhmatova's friend of many years and one of the major editors of the Russian edition of her prose works, for our ten years of friendship.

R. M.

A Note on the Text

The study of Akhmatova the prose writer is relatively new, not because the prose does not merit investigation, but for lack of reliable and accurate texts in either Soviet or Western editions, not to mention the numerous texts that remain unpublished to this day. The Moscow Central Archive holds 21 notebooks that date from Akhmatova's last decade, but only short excerpts have so far been made public. Akhmatova's Pushkin studies, as collected and edited by Emma Gershtein in the volume *About Pushkin,* represent the major exception to the textological problems that Akhmatova scholars must yet address.

The Akhmatova jubilee in 1989, coupled with the literary rehabilitation of her first husband, Nikolai Gumilyov, and the repeal of the onerous 1946 Resolution condemning her, brought forth a wealth of new texts and filled in the lacunae and ellipses in previously censored ones. Mr. X. is now revealed to be Gumilyov, for example, which was patently clear from the start, and Akhmatova's diatribes against the injustices of the Stalinist literary establishment are reinstated. A major difficulty in compiling this translation hinges on the fact that in many cases there is no canonical text, since Akhmatova did not prepare a final version for publication. A prime example is the memoir of Mandelstam to which Akhmatova attached particular importance: two versions appeared in 1989 and a third in 1990–all three differ from previously published redactions.

The present translation represents the most complete collection of Akhmatova's prose in any language. At the time of the project's inception, the two-volume edition of Akhmatova's *Works* (Sochineniia, Moscow, 1986) best presented the entire spectrum of the prose, but included no letters. This edition has served as the primary text for the translations, but has been substantially supplemented and revised. In all cases sources are indicated in the notes to the separate pieces. The bibliography lists all the editions consulted.

R. M.

A BIOGRAPHICAL SKETCH

And fame came sailing, like a swan
From golden haze unveiled,
While you, love, augured all along
Despair, and never failed.

— From "To My Verses" (1910s)
Translated by Walter Arndt

ANNA AKHMATOVA BELONGS TO the magnificent quartet of Russian poets whose fellow members are Osip Mandelstam, Boris Pasternak and Marina Tsvetaeva. Like her fellow poets, Akhmatova suffered a bitter fate. Mandelstam died en route to a labor camp (1938); Tsvetaeva hanged herself (1941); Pasternak, ostensibly the "luckiest" of the four, fell victim to a vicious campaign after the publication of *Doctor Zhivago*, followed by the Nobel Prize for Literature, and in the midst of unbearable pressures died at home in 1960. After the brilliant success of her first books, Akhmatova was forcibly silenced in the mid-1920s and was unable to publish any verse until 1940. But the rehabilitation was short-lived. In August 1946, the Central Committee passed a resolution (rescinded only in 1988) that condemned the "half-nun, half-harlot" Akhmatova, along with Mikhail Zoshchenko, one of the most remarkable satirists of the time. It was only in the 1960s that Akhmatova began to receive the homage due her.

Akhmatova's publishing record, however, represents only a small fraction of her personal tragedy. In 1921, the poet Nikolai Gumilyov, her former husband and the father of her only child, was arrested and executed on the false charge of counterrevolutionary conspiracy. Their son Lev was arrested three times and spent years in exile. All this unfolded against the background of two world wars, revolution, civil war, the Great Terror, the 900-day Leningrad blockade, and evacuation in Central Asia.

Until quite recently the vast majority of memoir literature about Akhmatova has been devoted to the postwar years. Virtually every account refers to the poet's grandeur, regal bearing, and stately demeanor. The adjective *velichavaya* (stately, majestic, regal) functions as a code word for Akhmatova. That this should be the case in the years when Akhmatova was lionized as the greatest living poet in Russia is not surprising, since she represented much more than the sum of her poetry. Akhmatova, however, did not adopt this imposing posture in her later years, when sickness and age inflated her figure to grandmotherly proportions. Rather, Akhmatova consciously developed this aspect of her personality while still a young woman and novice poet. One eyewitness describes Akhmatova at the beginning of her literary career, when she began to attend the major Petersburg literary salon of the 1910s, Vyacheslav Ivanov's Tower:

> Among the poetesses who read their poetry at the Tower, Anna Akhmatova stands out most vividly in my memory. She was captivating both as a woman and as a poet.
>
> Lithe, tall, svelte, her head wrapped in a floral shawl. The aquiline nose, her dark hair with the short bangs in front and held in place in back with a large Spanish comb. The small, slender mouth that seldom laughed. Dark, stern eyes. It was impossible not to notice her. You couldn't walk past her without admiring her. The young people went crazy when Akhmatova appeared on stage at literary readings. She was a good and skillful reader, who was fully aware of her feminine charm, and she possessed the regal self-assurance of an artist who knew her worth.[1]

The eminent literary critic Lidia Ginzburg ironically notes Akhmatova's majesty in her description of their first meeting a decade later: "[Akhmatova] is gifted with an absolutely natural and to a large extent convincing majesty. She holds herself like a queen in exile at some bourgeois spa."[2] Significantly, in 1927 Ginzburg already intuits that Akhmatova had assumed the role of guardian of Russian poetry:

Akhmatova clearly has taken on the responsibility for an era, for the memory of those who have died and for the reputations of the living. Those who are not inclined will naturally find this irritating—it's a matter of historical taste. Akhmatova sits very quietly and looks at us with a puzzled gaze. This is not because she doesn't understand our culture, but rather because she doesn't need it. It's not even worth discussing whether our culture needs her, since she's a part of it.[3]

That the responsibility for an era should be shouldered by a lyric poet in her thirties points to Akhmatova's unique position in twentieth-century Russian letters.

Akhmatova's carefully choreographed system of gestures (Ginzburg's observation) not only created the image of the Poet, but also partially bridled her impulsive and headstrong nature. In her autobiography Akhmatova recalls with obvious relish how she was called the wild girl for deliberately flaunting the etiquette of provincial society and how she crawled out onto the ledge of a St. Petersburg apartment, an event that also appears in her verse ("Epic Motifs").

The marked tendency towards hagiography in Russian biographical and memoir literature on Akhmatova, which many Westerners have adopted as well, obscures an important facet of Akhmatova's character. Although many people were permitted to view only the *grande dame* of Russian literature, some intimate friends were privy to Akhmatova's lively sense of humor and wit that triumphed even during the darkest times. One anecdote from Ginzburg is typical:

> In February 1933 Mandelstam came to Leningrad to read his poetry. Akhmatova invited me and Boris to her place to see Mandelstam. As it happened, we were both arrested then (and later soon released).
>
> Akhmatova said to the Mandelstams: "Here's the cheese, and there's the sausage, but the guests, I'm afraid, have been arrested."[4]

And the same majestic Akhmatova, according to another friend, the literary scholar Emma Gershtein, could quaff down a tankard of beer at a stand on the street, drinking in the admiration of the onlooking workers.[5] That, too, constituted a performance.

Anna Andreyevna Gorenko was born near Odessa on June 23, 1889 (June 11, Old Style), to Inna Stogova and Andrei Gorenko, a retired naval engineer. She was the third of five children. Before Anna celebrated her first birthday, the Gorenko family moved north, first to Pavlovsk and then to Tsarskoe Selo, both summer residences of the Tsar's family, located outside of St. Petersburg. Tsarskoe Selo, renamed Pushkin in 1937 in honor of its most illustrious resident, provides the background of much of Akhmatova's early life, and she lovingly evokes the setting in her poetry and prose. For Akhmatova, Tsarskoe Selo was inseparable from Pushkin. Famed for its parks, Tsarskoe Selo had changed little physically since the time of Pushkin's residence and the place held a special importance in her psychological geography. (The changes would come later, when Akhmatova visited Tsarskoe and barely recognized the town.)

The Gorenko family was not literary and there were few books in the house. Nonetheless, the young Anna penned her first poems at the age of eleven. Rather than receiving encouragement from her family to pursue poetry, Papa Gorenko worried that his daughter would sully the family name with her bohemian endeavors. Accordingly, Anna chose the pseudonym Akhmatova, the Tatar name of her maternal greatgrandmother. As her protégé Joseph Brodsky writes:

> The five open *a*'s of Anna Akhmatova had a hypnotic effect and put this name's carrier firmly at the top of the alphabet of Russian poetry. In a sense, it was her first successful line.... This tells you a lot about the intuition and quality of the ear of this seventeen-year-old girl who soon after her first publication began to sign her letters and legal papers as Anna Akhmatova.[6]

But Akhmatova was not destined to be long under the protection of her father, of whom she would write: "I cannot respect my father, I never loved him, why should I obey him?" The Gorenkos separated in 1905. Andrei Gorenko, who had a reputation as a womanizer, moved in with the widow of a former colleague, and his wife and children left for the South, first to Yevpatoria on the Black Sea and then to Kiev.

Akhmatova's letters written in 1906-7 to her brother-in-law, Professor Sergei von Shtein, are the few documents we have of her life during this period. The seventeen-year-old girl graduates from the gymnasium in Kiev in 1907, and goes on to enroll in Law

School, but yearns for Tsarskoe Selo and Petersburg: "Suddenly I am seized with a desire for Petersburg, for life, for books. But I am an eternal wanderer through foreign, crude, and dirty towns" (March 13, 1907). The letters chronicle a tale of unrequited love, courtship, and marriage. A persistent refrain throughout these romantic and impetuous letters is her request that von Shtein send her a photograph of Vladimir Golenishchev-Kutuzov, then a student at St. Petersburg University, who evidently did not reciprocate Akhmatova's adoration. Thanking von Shtein for the photograph, Akhmatova continues:

> I can't tear my soul away from him [Golenishchev-Kutuzov]. I am poisoned for my whole life; bitter is the poison of unrequited love! Will I be able to live again? Certainly not! But Gumilyov is my Fate, and I obediently submit to it. Don't condemn me, if you can. I swear by all that is holy to me that this unhappy man will be happy with me. (February 11, 1907)

Nikolai Gumilyov (1886-1921) met Anna Gorenko in 1903, while he was a student at the Tsarskoe Selo Lycée. Though Akhmatova states in 1907 that she will obediently become Gumilyov's wife, the wedding did not take place until three years later, on April 25, 1910, after Akhmatova declined a number of Gumilyov's proposals, and then finally acquiesced. Soon afterwards the young couple set off for Paris, a journey that is celebrated in Akhmatova's memoir of Amedeo Modigliani. By this time Gumilyov had become obsessed with travel, seeking in foreign spaces "the golden door." Gumilyov had earlier lived in Paris, where he studied French literature at the Sorbonne, pined for Akhmatova while being quite the ladies' man, and organized a journal that claims the first publication of a poem by Akhmatova. From Paris Gumilyov made his first of several trips to Africa and Egypt. Married life did not quench Gumilyov's thirst for travel. The Gumilyovs returned from Paris in June 1910, settling in Tsarskoe Selo with Gumilyov's mother, and just a few months later in September the young husband embarked on a six-month trip to Africa. During this period Akhmatova composed many of the poems that would later make up her first book, *Evening* (1912).

Some critics have attempted, rather unsuccessfully, to construct a mentor-pupil relationship in the Gumilyov-Akhmatova marriage, but, as Akhmatova writes, she "did not marry the founder of Acmeism, but a young Symbolist poet who was the author of *Pearls* and reviews of poetry collections." Although there is evidence that Gumilyov acted as a sounding board for Akhmatova, he did not encourage his wife to become a poet, but instead believed that she should seek an artistic outlet in some other medium, perhaps dance. Akhmatova herself admits that her early poems were weak and that Gumilyov did not bother to conceal his low opinion of them. In the several prose fragments regarding the beginning of her literary career, Akhmatova cites not the influence of Gumilyov ("...there is no trace of Gumilyov's influence on my poetry"), but the discovery of Innokenty Annensky and his posthumous collection, *The Cypress Chest:*

> I read... the proofs of *The Cypress Chest* (when I traveled to Petersburg in early 1910) and understood something about poetry.... I was absolutely mad about *The Cypress Chest*. Poems came at an even flow—nothing like it had ever happened before. I searched, I found, I lost. I sensed (rather vaguely) that I was beginning to succeed.

Annensky is the only teacher Akhmatova ever acknowledged and in this instance Gumilyov fulfilled the role of conduit. It was Gumilyov who showed Akhmatova the proofs of the book written by his mentor, the former headmaster of the Tsarskoe Selo Lycée. Akhmatova's maturation as a poet took place during her husband's absence. While Gumilyov was away, Akhmatova was received into literary Petersburg society, where she read her poems, and secured her first important publication in *Apollon*, the leading literary and art journal of the period. Recalling her poetic debut, Akhmatova carefully underscores this independence from Gumilyov:

> Gumilyov returned from his journey to Africa (Addis Ababa) on March 25, 1911 (Old Style). In the course of our first conversation he asked me, in passing, "Did you write any poetry?" Secretly rejoicing, I answered, "Yes." He asked me to read some, listened to several poems, and said, "You're a poet—you need to put a book together."

Evening appeared the following year in an edition of 300 copies, published by the fledgling literary association known as the

Poets' Guild, which had come into being as an alternative to Russian Symbolism.

The Poets' Guild was founded in November 1911 by Gumilyov and Sergei Gorodetsky, a promising young poet who was destined to remain the author of one book *(Spring Corn)*. Nadezhda Mandelstam in her *Hope Abandoned* describes the origins of the guild:

> Gumilyov, who had been more deeply involved with the Symbolists than either Akhmatova or Mandelstam, gradually drifted apart from them because the work of his younger friends—including his wife's—began to bring home to him the inner emptiness of Vyacheslav Ivanov's theories. Gumilyov's "The Prodigal Son" ("Kolya's first Acmeist poem," as Akhmatova called it) was read in the Academy of Verse, where Vyacheslav Ivanov, surrounded by respectful acolytes, reigned supreme. Ivanov made a devastating attack on "The Prodigal Son," and his tone was so scathing and rude ("We had never heard anything like it," in Akhmatova's words) that Gumilyov's friends left the Academy and set up the Poets' Guild in opposition to it.[7]

In her history of Acmeism and elsewhere, Akhmatova details, often sarcastically, the split with Vyacheslav Ivanov, one of the leading poets and theoreticians of Russian Symbolism, and host to the influential Petersburg literary salon, nicknamed the Tower. In Akhmatova's version, Ivanov is a vastly overrated poet and a somewhat ridiculous figure. Ivanov, however, is merely a concrete metonym for Russian Symbolism as a whole, which beginning in 1910 was undergoing a well-publicized crisis. The inception of the Poets' Guild may have been prompted by Ivanov's overbearing tactics and rudeness, but just as much at play was the familiar scenario of fathers and sons. Akhmatova takes pains to distance herself (and her fellow Acmeists) from Symbolism, in particular Vyacheslav Ivanov and Valery Bryusov.

The one exception among the Symbolist poets for Akhmatova was Alexander Blok, now generally acknowledged as the finest poet of that movement. For Akhmatova, Blok represented not simply a poetic school, but something much larger:

> I consider Blok to be not only the greatest European poet of the first quarter of the twentieth century (I bitterly mourned his un-

timely death), but also the essence of his era, that is, the most characteristic representative of his time.[8]

Akhmatova's portrait of Blok is one of the few finished pieces in *My Half Century*. The aim of the memoir is to record Akhmatova's few encounters with Blok, in part to dispel the "provincial" rumors about an affair between the "last romantic poet" and the leading woman poet of the following generation. In the opinion of many readers and critics, after Blok's death Akhmatova became the foremost poet. The reading public surmised an extra-literary intimacy based on the publication in Vsevolod Meyerhold's *Love for Three Oranges* of Blok's poem "To Anna Akhmatova" and Akhmatova's "I visited the poet." Akhmatova in private conversation characterized her memoir as being "about how [she] didn't have an affair with Blok," and emphasizes that the majority of their meetings were brief and in public. And just as Akhmatova singled out Blok from his Symbolist confederates, Blok made an exception for Akhmatova among the Acmeists in his attack on the young Acmeist school.

Acmeism, the poetic school that grew out of the Poets' Guild, produced three genuine poets: Gumilyov, Mandelstam, and Akhmatova. The January 1913 issue of *Apollon* printed two Acmeist manifestoes, followed two months later by programmatic poems, intended to serve as illustrations of the tenets expounded in the theoretical pieces. On one level, Acmeism called for a retreat from the Symbolist preoccupation with mysticism and meditation on the unknowable. Gumilyov writes: "The first thing that Acmeism can answer... is to point out that the unknowable, by the very meaning of the word, cannot be known."[9] Nadezhda Mandelstam's account of "The Three," however, emphasizes not the poetics of the new movement, but a literary brotherhood that came into being out of a shared philosophy:

> Three poets—Akhmatova, Gumilyov, and Mandelstam—referred to themselves as Acmeists to the end of their lives. I have often asked what it was that united three such different poets, so unlike each other, each with a different understanding of poetry, and why the bond was so strong that none of them ever renounced the youthful alliance which lasted so briefly.... It is my considered opinion that the Acmeists were brought together as a group not just by their attitude toward poetry, but by a common philosophy of life in general....[10]

The solidarity shared by these three very different and strong personalities weathered divorce and even death. In a letter to Akhmatova, written on the seventh anniversary of Gumilyov's death, Mandelstam writes: "My dialogue with Kolya [Gumilyov] has never been broken off and never will be."[11]

In her autobiography Akhmatova repeatedly returns to the 1910s, no doubt prompted by the spurious myth that the 1920s witnessed an unparalleled flowering of the arts in Russia:

> Not long ago I heard someone say that "the teens was one of the most colorless decades." That is probably what one is supposed to say nowadays, but I nevertheless answered that "apart from everything else it was the period of Stravinsky and Blok, Anna Pavlova and Scriabin, Rostovtsev and Chaliapin, Meyerhold and Diaghilev."

Akhmatova was at the center of Petersburg artistic society, which often gathered at the infamous cabaret, The Stray Dog, immortalized by Akhmatova in her poem "We are all carousers and loose women here." The poet Georgy Adamovich describes seeing Akhmatova at the cabaret:

> Now they sometimes refer to her in memoirs as a great beauty. No, that she wasn't. She was more than beautiful, something better. I have never seen another woman so expressive, with her ability to capture attention. Later something of the tragic surfaced in her. Rachel in *Phaedra*, as Mandelstam said in his famous poem after one of her readings at The Stray Dog when... she seemed to ennoble and exalt everything around her... but my first impression was different. She smiled, laughed, was merry, slyly whispering to her neighbor. But then they asked her to read something, and she suddenly changed, as if turning pale, and in the "mocker" and "gay little sinner of Tsarskoe Selo" (as Akhmatova later characterized herself at the end of her life in *Requiem*) flashed the future Phaedra. But only for a moment.[12]

Contemporary music, theater, and poetry found a home at the bohemian cabaret, whose performers included Vladimir Mayakovsky, Mikhail Kuzmin, Osip Mandelstam, and Alexander Blok's wife, Lyubov Mendeleyeva. The actress, singer, dancer, and great beauty, Olga Glebova-Sudeikina, who frequently appeared at The Stray Dog, became one of Akhmatova's most intimate friends and the model for the heroine of Akhmatova's *A Poem without a Hero.*

In Akhmatova's cosmogony the year 1914 marked the beginning of the "real twentieth century," both in broad political terms (the war) and more personal ones (for example, the publication of her second collection of verse, *Rosary*). One of the best-known expressions of Akhmatova's personal calendar is to be found in *A Poem without a Hero,* where in the description of Petersburg in 1913 we read the lines:

> While along the legendary quay
> Approached not the calendar
>   But the real Twentieth Century.

The year 1914 crops up repeatedly in the autobiography as well:

> In March 1914 my second book, *Rosary,* was published. It was allotted a life of approximately six weeks. In early May the Petersburg season was beginning to die down; little by little everybody was leaving. This time the parting with Petersburg turned out to be forever. We returned not to Petersburg but to Petrograd; from the nineteenth century we suddenly found ourselves in the twentieth; everything had changed, beginning with the city's appearance. It seemed that a little book of love lyrics written by a beginning author should have been lost in world events. Time decreed otherwise.

Despite the usual identification of love as the primary subject of women's poetry, Akhmatova's "little book of love lyrics" marked a significant innovation in Russian poetry. *Rosary* produces the illusion of an intensely autobiographical lyrical diary that traces the course of love from first meeting to disillusion and separation. Writers of different critical bents commented on Akhmatova's laconicism, the introduction of prosaic or non-poetic vocabulary and imagery, and the conversational intonation. Lines such as "I put on a tight skirt/To make myself look thinner" could not fail to jar the reader accustomed to Symbolist poetics. Akhmatova's readers knew her poetry by heart and it became fashionable "to say the *Rosary.*"

Rosary met with incredible success, and as is often the case with success, it inspired flocks of imitators. In "Epigram" (1958)

Akhmatova ironically bemoans her plight as model for hapless, lovesick poetesses:

> Could pretty Trixie have composed like Dante,
> Or Laura lauded Love's perfervent pain?
> I taught girls speech, *but* Lord of the *quo ante!*
> How can I ever shut them up again?

The jest is very near the truth. Russian Symbolism to a large extent was an all-male fraternity—women were delegated the role of divine inspiration, Zinaida Gippius representing the major exception. However, Gippius, who published her criticism under the masculine pseudonym of Anton Krainy, has never been celebrated for her femininity. Compare Léon Bakst's famous portrait of Gippius, where she lounges dressed à la George Sand in male attire, with any photograph or artistic rendering of Akhmatova and the difference becomes immediately apparent. By the time of the publication of *Rosary*, Akhmatova was already a well-known figure in Petersburg artistic circles, and as Viktor Zhirmunsky notes, her fame rested not only on her poetry, but also on her striking looks:

> Her early lyrics (in particular *Rosary*) enjoyed unrivaled success, both with the critics and literary circles, as well as with the reader; the numerous reviews, for the most part positive, attest to this success. In those years she was lavished with universal acclaim not only as a poet, but also as a beautiful woman. Her portrait was drawn many times, her famous bangs and classic shawl were ingrained in the memory of her contemporaries. Not only the female readers and the countless female imitators learned to love "according to Akhmatova"—even the young Mayakovsky, according to the memoirs of people close to him, always read her poetry, which he knew by heart, when he was in love.[13]

Akhmatova spent the summer of 1914 at Slepnyovo, her mother-in-law's country estate, with her infant son Lev (born October 1, 1912). Gumilyov had enlisted in the Imperial Army soon after the Russian declaration of war. According to Akhmatova, she and Gumilyov began to grow apart during this period. In Akhmatova's words, Gumilyov "was always a bachelor, I cannot picture him married," and she went so far as to claim that her union with Gumilyov had never been a real marriage:

> With the Bloks the infidelities started early on—on both sides....
> But at least it was a *marriage,* and not what you got with N.S.
> [Gumilyov]. Can you really consider that he was married to Anna
> Nikolayevna?[14] Or to me? Was *that* really a *marriage?*[15]

If fate brought Gumilyov and Akhmatova together, it alone
proved powerless to forge a marriage. Several memoirists maintain that Gumilyov's love for Akhmatova was genuine, but that
Akhmatova never reciprocated that love. Apart from Gumilyov's
frequent and prolonged absences, there were affairs and infatua-
tions (as with the Bloks, on both sides). Akhmatova and Gumilyov formally separated only four years later, in 1918, but they
retained cordial relations. After Gumilyov's death, Akhmatova,
and not Gumilyov's disciples, undertook the task of collecting his
manuscripts, letters, and other materials.

Among the dozens of reviews of *Rosary,* Akhmatova especially prized the analysis of her poetry by the literary critic and
poet Nikolai Nedobrovo (1882-1919).[16] In the 1960s Akhmatova
still considered Nedobrovo's essay one of the finest works ever
written about her verse. Nedobrovo and Akhmatova became acquainted in 1913. Akhmatova's attachment to Nedobrovo was
very real, but did not cross the "sacred boundary" from Platonic
to physical. The final quatrain of the lyric "All year you've been
inseparable from me" (1914-15) more than likely hints at the nature of the Akhmatova-Nedobrovo relationship:

> Gentle, gentle, he doesn't ask to be caressed,
> Only gazes at me
> And endures with a smile of bliss
> The frightful ravings of my semi-consciousness.[17]

Early in his friendship with Akhmatova, Nedobrovo writes
his friend, the artist Boris Anrep (1883-1969), about his visits
with Akhmatova, recommending her both as a poet and a
woman.[18] Anrep soon replaced Nedobrovo in Akhmatova's affections and more deeply than had been the case with anybody
previously, including Gumilyov. Though the romance was cut
off in 1917 by Anrep's emigration to England and had been limited to his leaves from the front during wartime, the intensity rivals any other in Akhmatova's biography. The relationship left
its mark on Akhmatova's poetry as well—Anrep is the addressee

of more poems than any other and her only acrostic spells "Boris Anrep." Of the poems dedicated to Anrep, "The Tale of the Black Ring" (1917-36) takes pride of place. Akhmatova and Anrep had exchanged talismans: she presented him with an heirloom ring, which had belonged to her grandmother, Anrep gave her a wooden crucifix. When Gumilyov heard that Akhmatova had parted with her ring, he supposedly joked: "I'll cut off your hand and you take it to Anrep and tell him that if he doesn't want to give the ring back, then he can have the hand that goes with the ring."[19]

The Nedobrovo-Anrep period roughly corresponds to the composition of the poems that were published as *White Flock,* which appeared in September 1917, on the eve of the Bolshevik Revolution. By this time Akhmatova and Gumilyov had separated, leaving their son in the care of Gumilyov's mother, though Akhmatova insisted that she have custody of Lev. Akhmatova moved to Petersburg, where she lived with Valeria and Vyacheslav Sreznevsky. Valeria Sreznevskaya, a friend of Akhmatova's from childhood in Tsarskoe Selo, had witnessed Gumilyov's courtship and the marriage's gradual dissolution. This period begins Akhmatova's "homelessness," which continued for the rest of her life, only partially remedied when in 1955 she was given a summer dacha outside of Leningrad that was all her own. From 1917 on Akhmatova lived with friends, husbands (even after the domestic situation had become intolerable and there was no real relationship left), and relatives.

During this period, Akhmatova frequently met with Osip Mandelstam:

> Mandelstam and I met particularly often in 1917-18, when I lived on the Vyborg Side at the Sreznevskys (Botkinskaya Street), not in the mental hospital, but at the apartment of the head physician, Vyacheslav Sreznevsky, the husband of my friend Valeria.
>
> Mandelstam often came to take me out for rides in a horse-drawn cab past the incredible potholes of the revolutionary winter, amidst the celebrated bonfires that burned almost until May, and we would listen to the gunfire wafting from who knows where. That's how we drove to readings at the Academy of Arts, where they held benefits for the wounded and where we both read several times.

According to Akhmatova, in early 1918 she suggested to Mandelstam that they see less of each other, lest the nature of their friendship be misinterpreted. Nadezhda Mandelstam rather acidly comments on Akhmatova's newly-discovered sense of decorum. The dates seem to suggest that rather than worrying about Gumilyov, Akhmatova may have been concerned about how Mandelstam's visits would be interpreted by her future husband, the Assyriologist Vladimir Shileiko (1891-1930). Pavel Luknitsky recorded Akhmatova's version of the divorce from Gumilyov and the marriage to Shileiko:

> In 1918 Gumilyov returned and was staying in furnished rooms.... She [Akhmatova] stayed until the morning. She left for the Sreznevskys. Later when Gumilyov came to the Sreznevskys, Akhmatova took him to another room and said, "Give me a divorce...." He didn't ask her to stay with him or even question her. He just asked, "Will you remarry? Are you in love?" Akhmatova answered, "Yes." "Who is he?" "Shileiko." Gumilyov didn't believe her: "That can't be true. You're hiding something, I don't believe that it's Shileiko."[20]

Gumilyov and Akhmatova soon set out to visit their son in Slepnyovo:

> Akhmatova: "He was very reserved.... Sometimes he didn't show anything, sometimes he got angry, but it always took a very restrained form. Of course, he was very upset."
> Akhmatova said that he only touched on the subject once, when they were sitting in the room, watching Lyova in front of them play with his toys. Gumilyov suddenly kissed Akhmatova's hand and said to her sadly, "Why did you make all this up?"[21]

The marriage between Akhmatova and Vladimir Shileiko was registered in December 1918. Akhmatova's acquaintance with Shileiko, a scholar with an international reputation as well as a published poet, most likely predates 1913. Though an Assyriologist and translator by profession, Shileiko was a member of Akhmatova's circle, who had published his poetry in *The Hyperborean* and *Apollon*, and had read his poetry at The Stray Dog. In fact, Akhmatova credits Gumilyov and her close friend Mikhail Lozinsky with bringing Shileiko to her notice: "It was Kolya and Lozinsky. They kept singing a tune for two voices, 'The Egyptian,

the Egyptian!...' So, I... well, I accepted."[22] Apart from his scholarly research, for which Akhmatova assumed secretarial duties,
Shileiko served on the editorial board of Maxim Gorky's World
Literature Publishing House and the affiliated Translation
Workshop. The publishing enterprise had the ambitious aim to
translate the classics, but on a more practical level provided income for needy writers in the lean post-Revolutionary years. The
almost incestuous nature of Petersburg literary life is highlighted
by the publication in 1919 of *The Epic of Gilgamesh*, translated
(from the French) by Gumilyov, with an introduction by Vladimir
Shileiko.

Akhmatova and Shileiko first lived in a room in the House on
the Fontanka (later immortalized in Akhmatova's *A Poem without
a Hero*), and then moved to rooms in the Marble Palace, which
looked out onto the Field of Mars. Akhmatova's life had changed
irrevocably. The rations Shileiko received as an academic allowed the couple to survive, but it meant that Akhmatova had to
stand in line, while her husband conducted his research in the library. And then she was expected to take Shileiko's dictation,
sometimes hours at a time. Looking back on the marriage,
Akhmatova explained to Luknitsky: "I went to him of my own
free will.... I felt so impure and thought I would be cleansed."[23]
The headstrong and willful Akhmatova experienced a need to
serve somebody else, but she ultimately realized that this servi-
tude would be at the expense of her poetry:

> Three years of hunger. Vladimir was sick. He could get by with-
> out anything except tea and smokes. We rarely cooked meals—we
> didn't have any food and nothing to cook it in. If I had lived with
> Shileiko any longer I would also have forgotten how to write po-
> etry. He simply was an impossible person to live with.[24]

The couple parted in 1921, after only three years of marriage, but
their mutual respect for each other continued. Akhmatova's note
to Shileiko, dated November 26, 1928, bears witness to her continuing high regard for her former husband:

Dear Friend,

    I am sending you my poems. If you have time tonight, take a look at them. I've already deleted a lot—they were very bad. Note on a separate piece of paper the ones you think don't merit publication. I'll drop by tomorrow. Forgive me for bothering you.

Yours,
Akhmatova

After leaving Shileiko, Akhmatova moved in with her friends, Olga Glebova-Sudeikina and the composer Artur Lourié. The relative barrenness of the previous years with Shileiko becomes apparent with the burst of creativity Akhmatova experiences in 1921. The ménage à trois, perhaps sexual, certainly fulfilled artistic needs. During this time Akhmatova penned a ballet libretto based on Alexander Blok's *Snow Mask*, for which Lourié composed the music. Unfortunately, the libretto has not survived.

    Today Sudeikina is best remembered as the heroine of *A Poem without a Hero*, where in the Second Dedication she is described as "Confusion-Psyche,/Fluttering a fan of black and white." Akhmatova characterizes the heroine in a way that unmistakably points to Sudeikina as the prototype, yet does not limit the heroine to that biography. In discussing with Chukovskaya the correspondence between Sudeikina and the heroine, Akhmatova stated that "it's not completely she herself, merely her physical appearance; she is a heroine of the period, and not she." Nadezhda Mandelstam found the great beauty to be already somewhat of an anomaly in the new Soviet era:

> It may be that I was less impressed than I should have been with Olga's beauty. Perhaps she really was a "fair-haired marvel." But one should not forget that tastes change and the ideal for womanhood for my generation was similar to the one still in fashion.[26]

Nadezhda Mandelstam, a mere ten years younger than Akhmatova, was bemused by Akhmatova's (and Sudeikina's) outmoded sense of feminine wiles:

> Akhmatova regarded Olga as the embodiment of all the feminine qualities and was always giving me some tip or other about how to manage various domestic problems, or how to look my

best in the way recommended by the goat-legged heroine of the *Poem* which has no hero....

One of the secrets for preserving one's good looks and youth was: dark hair must be worn smooth and plain, while light hair was to be fluffed up or curled. Then there was the secret (à la Kseshinskaya) about how to be a success with men: never take your eyes off them, always look straight at their mouths—that's how "they" like it.... These were typical Petersburg fads of the beginning of the century. I told Akhmatova that it was all old hat, but she wouldn't listen to me—though her own way of charming people was quite different.[27]

The fall of 1921 brought the deaths of two people close to Akhmatova: Alexander Blok and Nikolai Gumilyov. The two deaths became permanently linked in Akhmatova's memory: "I learned of N.S.'s arrest at Blok's funeral. 'The odor of decay is sickeningly sweet' in my poem 'Terror,' written on the night of August 25, 1921, is connected with that funeral." Akhmatova did not learn of Gumilyov's execution by firing squad until September 1st, but "Terror" is dated the day of his execution. With these two deaths, the literary polemics surrounding Symbolism and Acmeism became moot. In a poem dated September 1921, Akhmatova addresses the personal tragedy of these deaths, and mourns the passing of an era:

Tear-sodden autumn, like a widow sheathed
In weeds of black, all happy vision blearing,
And idly shuffling over words bequeathed,
Forever sobbing, never clearing...

Anno Domini MCMXXI, Akhmatova's fifth collection of verse, appeared in 1922. She did not publish another book until 1940. It was the final book to appear as the author intended. For the next fifty years Akhmatova would be severely constrained by censorship, publishing, and then only after overcoming numerous obstacles, volumes to which she referred as her *"Poorly Selected Works."* *Anno Domini* reflects the productivity of the post-Shileiko period, as the majority of the poems are dated 1921.

The early 1920s witnessed the gradual erosion of Akhmatova's public stature as leading poet, culminating in 1925 with vicious attacks in the press and a Party Resolution banning her from publication. The critics who had been hostile remained so in their reviews of *Anno Domini*: "It's even more sad when a poet repeats herself and these repetitions are infinitely more pale" (Valery Bryusov). On the other hand, Akhmatova had ardent supporters, particularly among the young Formalist critics, Boris Eikhenbaum, Viktor Vinogradov, and Viktor Zhirmunsky.[28] However, promotion by the Formalists became a mixed blessing with the political rout of Formalism. But the true danger emanated from an entirely new source—the revolutionary zealots who quickly were transformed into Party sycophants, thus rendering literary criticism unrecognizable. As Akhmatova notes in her humorously titled "Akhmatova and the Struggle Against Her":

> Normal criticism also ceased to exist in the early 1920s.... Its place was taken by something perhaps unprecedented, but in any case unequivocal. To survive in the face of the press of that period seemed completely improbable. Little by little, life was transformed into a constant wait for death.

The descent in Akhmatova's fortunes was swift. In a 1922 review of Akhmatova's poetry, published in *Pravda*, Akhmatova is named "a first-class lyric poet," who "without question is the best Russian poet since Blok's death." By 1924 the critic G. Lelevich writes that Akhmatova's poetry is nothing more than a "small, pretty sliver of gentry culture." Akhmatova was criticized for her apoliticalness, for ignoring the great events, while focusing on her petty love life. Well-intentioned criticism was deliberately misinterpreted. In his lecture "Akhmatova and Mayakovsky" (1921) Kornei Chukovsky declares Akhmatova to be the rightful heiress to the riches of pre-Revolutionary Russian culture, which others misinterpreted as yet another proof of her indifference to contemporary life.

Sudeikina and Lourié emigrated to Paris in 1924. The years had turned lean, and publishing became more and more difficult for Akhmatova. The critic Lidia Ginzburg recounts an anecdote that dates from the final period of Akhmatova's life at Sudeikina's:

> When Anna Andreyevna was living with Olga Sudeikina, they had an eighty-year-old woman to do the housekeeping.... The old woman was constantly troubled that her mistresses didn't have any money: "Olga Afanasievna isn't earning anything at all. Before Anna Andreyevna used to hum, but now she's not humming. She lets her hair down and walks around like a deer...."[29]

Sudeikina and Lourié, like many others, encouraged Akhmatova to leave Russia with them. Akhmatova never wavered in her decision against emigration, viewing that act as abandonment:

> I am no kin to those who left you,
> My Land, to preying foemen's wrongs.
> Their coarse enticements I am deaf to,
> Nor will I give them of my songs.
>
> The outcast, though, I sorrow over
> As one shut in, confined to bed.
> For darkness shades your path, poor rover,
> Of wormwood tastes the exile's bread.

After Sudeikina's departure, Akhmatova returned to the Marble Palace, since she had no place of her own. Shileiko was frequently away in Moscow for long periods, and somebody had to take care of Tapa, the St. Bernard.

Akhmatova was frequently ill, plagued by tuberculosis, the disease that had afflicted other members of her family. In 1925 Akhmatova lived for a time in a pension in Tsarskoe Selo, in part to build up her strength. Nadezhda Mandelstam, whom she had met a few years earlier, was staying in the same pension and describes their first encounter:

> She found me alone.... I was wearing those same striped pajamas that Georgy Ivanov had taken for a man's suit. I suddenly realized we had run out of cigarettes, but, not wanting to change in order to go out and get some, I sent her instead: "You go, Anna Andreyevna, while I make the tea." She never forgot this incident; years later in Tashkent she was still telling people how I had spoken to her: "And I trotted out as meekly as a little calf." Though she had tired of the simpering adulation of all the woman admirers who danced attendance on her, she was so used to it by then that she could never forget how I sent her out for cigarettes.[30]

While convalescing in Tsarskoe Selo, Akhmatova was visited by Nikolai Punin (1888-1953), a gifted art historian and critic, who earlier had been associated with *Apollon* and now lectured at the Institute of Art History. The following year Akhmatova moved into Punin's apartment in the south wing of the House on the Fontanka (the rooms in which the Akhmatova Museum is now housed). Their marriage was never registered, even after Akhmatova received a formal divorce from Shileiko. Life in the apartment was difficult, since Punin's ex-wife and daughter continued to stay on there because of the housing shortage—an uncomfortable situation for all concerned. The Akhmatova-Punin relationship lasted for fifteen years, a fact to which Akhmatova makes reference in the "Second Northern Elegy," where she writes that the fifteen years seemed like "fifteen granite centuries." To some degree Akhmatova's relationship with Punin duplicated the one with Shileiko, in that she again offered herself as a servant to Punin by translating and helping him prepare lectures. But whereas Akhmatova characterized her marriage to Shileiko as a "dismal understanding," Punin made her miserable by insulting her and flaunting his affairs. Akhmatova herself admitted to Anatoly Naiman that she "lived with Punin several years longer than was necessary," adding that the "institution of divorce was the best thing mankind ever invented."

In the mid-1920s attacks in the press against Akhmatova were crowned with success: Akhmatova was officially banned from publication. The resolution, however, was never made public or printed and Akhmatova learned of it only through an acquaintance:

> After my readings in Moscow (Spring 1924) the resolution regarding the cessation of my literary activity was put into effect. I was no longer published in journals or almanacs, or invited to literary evenings. I met Marietta Shaginyan on Nevsky Prospect. She said: "You're such an important person—the Central Committee passed a resolution about you—not to be arrested, but not to be published either."

Akhmatova professionally undertook the study of the life and works of Alexander Pushkin during this period, though without the benefit of any institutional affiliation.

The 1930s find Akhmatova in relative isolation, excluded from the literary establishment. She once complained to the critic Viktor Shklovsky that she sat at home all day alone: "People who don't respect me don't visit because they're not interested; and the people who respect me don't visit me out of respect because they're afraid that they'll bother me."[31] The dilemma of not being able to publish was soon dwarfed by the Great Terror, engineered by Joseph Stalin, as it began to touch Akhmatova's family and friends. Akhmatova was staying at the Mandelstams when Osip Mandelstam was arrested on May 13, 1934, ostensibly for a lampoon on Stalin. Reprieved this first time, Mandelstam was released and sentenced to exile in Voronezh, where Akhmatova was one of the first to visit. Nadezhda shared her husband's fate, for which Akhmatova nicknamed her the "Decembrist's wife," alluding to the political exiles of a century earlier. Mandelstam was not spared, but arrested a second time in 1938 and died en route to a labor camp.

Mandelstam's first arrest was soon followed by the arrests of Akhmatova's son Lev and Nikolai Punin. The two were released after Akhmatova petitioned Stalin on behalf of her son. Lev was arrested a second time on May 10, 1937 and sentenced to exile, after being held in a Leningrad prison for seventeen months. Lev Gumilyov lived in exile until 1944, when he volunteered to serve at the front. Looking back on happier days, Akhmatova would refer to the former "vegetarian times."

Akhmatova composed *Requiem*, the harrowing record of her son's imprisonment during the years 1935-40:

> In the terrible years of Yezhov's reign of terror, I spent seventeen months in the prison queues in Leningrad. Somehow, one day, someone "identified" me. Then a woman standing behind me, whose lips were blue with cold, and who, naturally enough, had never even heard of my name, emerged from that state of torpor common to us all and, putting her lips close to my ear (there, everyone spoke in whispers), asked me:
> "And could you describe *this?*"
> And I answered her:
> "I can."
> Then something vaguely like a smile flashed across what once had been her face.

Too dangerous to commit to paper, the cycle was memorized by the most trusted of Akhmatova's friends so that it would survive, even if its creator did not. *Requiem* was not published in the Soviet Union until 1988.

The resolution banning Akhmatova was temporarily eased in 1940 with the appearance of her collection *From Six Books*. According to Akhmatova, this sign of grace came from Stalin himself, who had inquired about her the previous year. The authorities, however, soon realized the error of their decision, and the magnanimous gesture was overruled. *From Six Books* was withdrawn from circulation in libraries and public sale only a few months after it appeared. Vilified in the press, anxious about the fate of her son, and concerned for the future of Europe, which was defending itself against Hitler's advancing armies, Akhmatova gradually developed a new poetic voice: "A return to my former style was impossible.... The apogee was 1940."

The long poem *The Way of All the Earth*, dated March 1940, heralded this new style, and the year ended with the inception of Akhmatova's masterwork, *A Poem without a Hero:* "It came to me for the first time in the House on the Fontanka on the night of December 27, 1940." Akhmatova composed and revised *A Poem without a Hero* over a span of more than twenty years. The poem is dedicated "to its first listeners—my friends and countrymen who perished in Leningrad during the siege." A symphonic construction of literary and historical allusions, the poem is Akhmatova's longest and most complex work and has engendered scores of interpretations. One of the focal points of the work is the suicide in 1913 of Vsevolod Knyazev, a young cadet who was spurned by Olga Sudeikina and whom Akhmatova had loved. These shades from the past (and many others) visit the poet on New Year's Eve and prompt a meditation on the poet's past and present, as well as the history of her country and culture.

World War II found Akhmatova in Leningrad. In September 1941, at the beginning of the 900-day German blockade of Leningrad, Akhmatova was evacuated to Tashkent via Moscow. Strangely enough, not long before her departure from Leningrad, the same Akhmatova whose book had been pulled from circulation was invited to deliver a patriotic address to her fellow citizens. The invitation came from Georgy Makogonenko, a well-known scholar of eighteenth-century Russian literature, who was then in charge of the literary department of Leningrad Radio. Makogonenko explains his choice: "Of course, she didn't have many readers. But as paradoxical as it may seem, she was well known. Her name was firmly ensconced in history—the history of Russian literature. Her name was linked with Leningrad."[32] The ailing Akhmatova immediately agreed to Makogonenko's request.

Akhmatova spent the war years in Tashkent at a hotel that had been assigned to the evacuated writers. She lived poorly, was often ill, dependent upon the good will of friends and strangers, and lived for news from Leningrad. Akhmatova was particularly anxious about Vladimir Garshin (1887-1956), who had become the object of Akhmatova's romantic affections. Akhmatova and Garshin, a medical doctor and professor (and the nephew of the writer Vsevolod Garshin), met when Akhmatova was hospitalized, after which he began to call on her at the House on the Fontanka. It was her relationship with Garshin that finally allowed Akhmatova to leave Punin. Garshin seldom wrote to Akhmatova in Tashkent and when he did the letters were often far from what she could have wished—he would report, for example, that his estranged wife was the most important person in his life. With good reason, Akhmatova feared not only for Garshin's life, but also for his mental health. Yet, she sent him a copy of *A Poem without a Hero* through a common friend and considered him a hero for continuing to work through the blockade. The degree of Akhmatova's attachment to Garshin can be fully appreciated by the fact that Garshin's proposal of marriage stipulated that she bear his name and that Akhmatova assented to this condition.

Akhmatova set off for home from Tashkent on May 15, 1944. The years in evacuation yielded the publication in Tashkent of a heavily censored volume of *Selected Poems* (1943), the completion of the first redaction of *A Poem without a Hero* and numerous lyrics, and Akhmatova's first and only drama, *Enuma elish*, which the author destroyed in 1944 and partially reconstructed during her last years. Her first stop on her way home was Moscow, where she stayed with her friends the Ardovs at their apartment on the "legendary Ordynka," a refuge that Akhmatova frequently sought whenever she was in Moscow. She gave a reading while in Moscow at the Polytechnic Museum. The reading was nothing short of a triumph. Finally, everything seemed to be right—she would soon be back in her native Leningrad, Lev Gumilyov had survived the war, and she had informed Moscow friends of the impending marriage to Garshin. Met by her fiancé at the train station, Akhmatova learned that he had married in her absence. The apartment in the House on the Fontanka was unlivable and Akhmatova again was forced to live on the charity of friends, this time Olga Rybakova.[33] Though relieved to be back in her city, Akhmatova found it to be unrecognizable, a "specter pretending to be my city."

Publishing fairly regularly in journals, Akhmatova read her poetry at two important evenings: in April 1946 she was a member of the Leningrad delegation invited to perform at the House of Columns in Moscow and in August she participated in an evening in commemoration of Alexander Blok at the Bolshoi Dramatic Theater in Leningrad. On both occasions she received standing ovations. The relative normalcy of Akhmatova's literary career took a sudden—and final—turn for the worse on August 14, 1946, when the Central Committee approved a resolution engineered by Andrei Zhdanov, which censured the journals *The Star* and *Leningrad* for publishing the works of Akhmatova and Mikhail Zoshchenko. A brief extract from Zhdanov's report suffices to convey the imbecilic ravings of the Secretary of the Central Committee:

> Anna Akhmatova is one of the representatives of this empty reactionary literary swamp. She belongs to the so-called literary group of Acmeists, who emerged from the ranks of the Symbolists, and is one of the standard-bearers of an empty, aristocratic, drawing-room poetry, which is totally alien to Soviet literature....
>
> The thematics of Akhmatova's poetry are personal through and through. The scope of her poetry is wretchedly limited, it is the poetry of a lady foaming at the mouth, constantly dashing from the drawing room to the chapel. Her basic theme is erotic love.... She is neither a nun, nor a harlot, but really both....[34]

The Party resolution remained in force even after Stalin's death, a fact with which Akhmatova had to contend for the rest of her life. When Stalin's crimes were being partially rectified in the 1950s and 60s, allowing the release of thousands of unjustly sentenced individuals and the literary rehabilitation of wrongly accused writers, the Party resolution was not overturned. As Akhmatova remarked to Chukovskaya: "So that's how it is! Stalinism has been repealed, but Zhdanovism is still in effect! You barely have a chance to be happy about the ray of light in the kingdom of darkness before you're once again plunged into the familiar darkness."[35]

Akhmatova ascribed the resolution to two causes, the first being the success of her readings. Showing a photograph taken in 1946 of her and Pasternak, she ironically remarked: "That's me earning the resolution." The second cause she believed to be not only responsible for her censure, but also a major factor in setting the Cold War in motion, namely, her meeting in 1945 with Sir Isaiah Berlin, at the time a temporary First Secretary at the British

Embassy in Moscow, now known for his many works on Russian history and literature.

Like most Soviet citizens, Akhmatova had been effectively isolated from the West since World War I—the only other foreign citizen Akhmatova had met was the Polish artist Joseph Czapski. Akhmatova immediately experienced an unusual warmth and respect for Berlin, who was able to inform Akhmatova about friends that had seemingly disappeared forever, for example, Artur Lourié, Boris Anrep, Salomea Andronikova-Halpern. The extent of Akhmatova's immediate liking and trust for Berlin can be understood by the fact that she read him both *Requiem* and *A Poem without a Hero*, though she understandably did not allow him to copy them.[36] That Akhmatova attributed great significance to their meeting is evident from *A Poem without a Hero*, where Berlin, the "Guest from the Future," is addressed in the Third Dedication. Akhmatova firmly believed that not only did the meeting with Berlin act as a catalyst for the 1946 Resolution, but, as she told Berlin in Oxford in 1965, they "inadvertently, by the mere fact of [their] meeting, had started the Cold War and thereby changed the history of mankind." Akhmatova, who elsewhere appears so politically astute and sensible, remained firmly convinced of the political repercussions of their meeting, saying that Stalin himself was outraged that "the little nun was receiving foreign visitors." Berlin, sensitive to Akhmatova's self-image, notes that this interpretation of the apparently innocuous events suited Akhmatova's "tragic image of herself as Cassandra," and that he felt powerless to object. Whatever the reasons for the resolution, the result was expulsion from the Writers' Union. Akhmatova laconically summarizes the situation: "Zoshchenko and Akhmatova were expelled from the Writers' Union, that is, they were doomed to starvation."

The decade ended with the arrest of Nikolai Punin on September 30, 1949 and Lev Gumilyov a few months later on November 6th. Akhmatova's ex-husband died in a Siberian camp in 1953, Lev Gumilyov was not released until 1956, after the Twentieth Party Congress that paved the way for the rehabilitation of thousands of wrongly accused and sentenced.

The 1950s open with one of the bleakest moments in Akhmatova's literary career, namely the publication of the cycle "In Praise of Peace," political doggerel written in the vain hope of securing her son's release. If we consider what this prostitution of her poetic talents cost the proud Akhmatova, we can begin to sense the degree of her desperation. To make matters worse, the despondent gesture went unrewarded and yielded only self-humiliation.

Joseph Stalin died on March 5, 1953, a date that Akhmatova and friends hereafter would heartily celebrate. Stalin's death signalled the gradual return to a state of affairs resembling a greater degree of normalcy, commonly referred to as The Thaw.

During this time Akhmatova earned her living through literary translation, a career she had begun in the 1930s with the French verses of Alexander Pushkin for the Academy edition of Pushkin's works and the letters of the Flemish painter Peter Paul Rubens, in addition to the translation work she did for Shileiko and Punin. During the last two decades of her life, translation became practically a daily occupation—she translated approximately 150 poets from 30 languages, in most cases basing her work on a literal translation. Akhmatova in general regarded translation as a way to earn a living and not a part of her poetic work: "For a poet, translation is not a creative endeavor and is not representative of his work; I don't attach much significance to it. By and large one has to translate out of material considerations." Justifiably pleased when her translations were praised, Akhmatova nevertheless told Lidia Chukovskaya that for a poet, the process of translation during a period of poetic creativity amounted "to eating your own brain." Akhmatova appeared in the twin guise of poet and translator in her next published collection, *Poems* (1958), a small brick-red volume that was compiled to please the censor, rather than the reader (or author).

The death of Boris Pasternak in 1960 came as a blow to Akhmatova, who was convalescing from a heart attack. Akhmatova's personal relationship with Pasternak was often strained, largely because she believed that Pasternak did not really know her poetry, but also because she thought that he was too actively concerned about his career. In any case, she steadfastly maintained that Pasternak was a great poet, and begins her poem written on his death with the line: "Now has the voice which has no equal faltered."

The 1960s witnessed a dramatic increase in Akhmatova's literary fortunes. She finally received the recognition which had been withheld for so many years. Dependent on others for so long, she was now in a position that allowed her to offer limited patronage and protection to others, both old friends (for example, Nadezhda Mandelstam and Emma Gershtein) and new ones (Anatoly

Naiman and Joseph Brodsky). Beginning poets sought her out, hoping to earn approval. Akhmatova, who had been so regularly abused, rarely attacked the feeble poems, but resorted to an arsenal of non-commital responses that have become legendary:

> If there was a description of a landscape in what she read, Akhmatova would say, "Your poems have a feeling for nature." If she came upon dialogue, "I like it when direct speech is introduced into poetry." If the verse was unrhymed, "It is harder to write blank verse than rhymed." Anyone who after this asked her to look at "a few recent poems" would hear her say, "This is very much you." And finally, the universal "In your poems the words stand in their proper place" was always in reserve.[37]

Akhmatova came to be identified with four young poets, often referred to ironically as "Akhmatova's little boys"— Yevgeny Rein, Dmitry Bobyshev, Anatoly Naiman, and Joseph Brodsky. Naiman, who fulfilled the duties of literary secretary from 1962 on, worked as co-translator with Akhmatova, which perhaps saved him from the fate of his friend Brodsky, who was arrested and sentenced for "parasitism." Akhmatova's joke about herself—"I'm Madame Larousse now—I get questions about everything"—hints at the special position she held in her last years. She was not only the last surviving great poet of her generation, but also a living thread with the pre-revolutionary Petersburg past. Akhmatova keenly desired that the thread not be broken.

Akhmatova's reputation at home became more secure with the publication of two more volumes of her verse, *Poems 1909-1960* (1961), nicknamed "the frog" for its green cover, and *The Flight of Time* (1965). There had been constant battles with the censor, and of course there was no possibility of printing *Requiem* or the complete *A Poem without a Hero*. Akhmatova writes without any sense of hyperbole: "The contemporary reader does not know my poems, either the new ones or the old ones."

In 1963 *Requiem* was published in Russian by an emigré press in West Germany and was quickly translated into several languages. International recognition soon followed. Akhmatova traveled to Italy to receive the Taormina Prize in 1964, the first time she had been abroad since 1912. The following spring she was in England to receive an honorary doctorate from Oxford University, where she was reunited with Isaiah Berlin. Stopping in Paris on the way home, Akhmatova received calls from old friends, Boris Anrep and Georgy Adamovich, among others.

During her last years, Akhmatova divided her time between her dacha at the writers' colony in Komarovo, located outside Leningrad, the Leningrad apartment she shared with Irina Punina and her step-granddaughter Anna Kaminskaya, and Moscow, where the Ardovs often served as the main base, but where a succession of women friends offered her hospitality. These are the years of the well-documented *Akhmatovka:*

> She brought into currency the concept of the "Akhmatovka" for the rush of visitors who called on her. At times it was no easy matter to schedule those who wished to call on her: visits ran into each other, arriving and departing visitors bumped into each other in the doorway or in the hall, A must not coincide with B, X was jealous of Y's relationship with Z. In short, it was like a railway station with a tight schedule and inevitable accidents.[38]

Akhmatova died on March 5, 1966, the anniversary of Stalin's death. The autobiography section of the present volume closes with Akhmatova's last diary entries. Hospitalized in Moscow after a heart attack, Akhmatova was full of plans for her prose book. She was buried in Komarovo, following Orthodox services in Leningrad at St. Nicholas Church.

Ronald Meyer

October 1991
New York City

My Half Century

Pages from a Diary

PAGES FROM A DIARY

The Hut

I WAS BORN IN the same year as Charlie Chaplin, Tolstoy's *Kreutzer Sonata*, the Eiffel Tower, and, it seems, T. S. Eliot.[1] That summer Paris celebrated the one-hundredth anniversary of the fall of the Bastille—1889. The ancient festival of St. John's Eve (Midsummer Night) was—and is still—celebrated on the night of my birth, June 23rd. I was named Anna in honor of my grandmother, Anna Yegorovna Motovilova.[2] Her mother, a descendant of Genghis Khan, was the Tatar princess Akhmatova, whose name I took for my literary name, not realizing that I was about to become a Russian poet. I was born in Sarakina's dacha (Bolshoi Fontan, the 11th railroad stop) near Odessa. This little dacha (more like a hut) was situated at the bottom of a very narrow and steep tract of land next to the post office. The seashore there is steep and the railroad tracks went along the very brink.

When I was fifteen years old and we were living in the dacha at Lustdorf, we were traveling through this area for some reason, and my mother suggested that we go and see Sarakina's dacha, which I had never seen. At the hut's entrance I said, "Some day they'll put up a memorial plaque here." I wasn't being vain. It was just a silly joke. My mother was distressed. "My God," she said, "how badly I've brought you up."

1957

***

... No matter how hard you search, you will find no one in my family who wrote poetry, except for the first Russian poetess, Anna Bunina, who was the aunt of my grandfather Erazm Ivanovich Stogov.[3] The Stogovs, landowners of modest means in the Mozhaisk region of Moscow Province, had been resettled there for their participation in the revolt led by Martha, the Burgomaster's Wife.[4] They had been wealthier and more distinguished in Novgorod.

My forefather, the Khan Akhmat, was killed in his tent during the night by a Russian assassin who had been bribed, and as Karamzin tells it, with that act the Mongol yoke on Russia came to an end.[5] A religious procession took place on that day in the Sretensky Monastery in Moscow to commemorate the happy event. As everybody knows, this Akhmat was a descendant of Genghis Khan.

In the eighteenth century one of the Akhmatova princesses—Praskovya Yegorovna—married Motovilov, a wealthy and distinguished landowner in Simbirsk. Yegor Motovilov was my great-grandfather. His daughter, Anna Yegorovna, was my grandmother. She died when my mother was nine years old, and I was named Anna after her. Several diamond rings and one emerald ring were made from her coronet, but even though I had slender fingers, I could not use her thimble.

Shukhardina's House

THE HOUSE WAS 100 years old. It belonged to the merchant widow, Evdokiya Ivanovna Shukhardina, whose strange clothes I had admired as a child. This house was located on the corner of Shirokaya Street and Bezymyanny Lane (the second one from the station). It was believed that at one time, before the railroad, there had been some sort of eating house or wayside inn in the building. I used to peel off the wallpaper in my yellow room (layer by layer) and the very last one was an unusually bright red. "That's the wallpaper that was in that inn 100 years ago," I thought. The cobbler B. Nevolin lived in the basement. Nowadays this would be a still from a documentary film.

That house is more memorable for me than any other house in the world. My childhood (the ground floor) and early youth (the upper floor) were spent there. Approximately one-half of my dreams take place there. We left it in the spring of 1905. It was later rebuilt and lost its old-fashioned look. It has been gone for a long time now, and a park for the station or something of that sort was put in on that site. (The last time I visited Tsarskoe Selo was June 1944.) Gone, too, is Tur's dacha (Joy or New Khersones), three miles from Sevastopol, where I spent every summer from the age of seven to thirteen and where I earned the nickname "wild girl." And Slepnyovo[6] of the years 1911 to 1917 is gone, too. The only thing that still remains is that name beneath my poems in *White Flock* and *Plantain*, but that is probably all in the order of things....

1957

***

... And sometimes on that same Shirokaya Street a funeral procession of unbelievable splendor would pass by coming from or going to the station: a boys' choir would sing with angelic voices, and you couldn't see the coffin for all the fresh greenery and flowers, which were dying from the frost. People carried lanterns, the priests burned incense, the blindered horses stepped slowly and solemnly. Behind the coffin walked the guardsmen, who always somewhat reminded you of Vronsky's brother with their "drunken, open faces,"[7] and then the gentlemen in their top hats. The carriages with formidable old women and their dependents followed the catafalque as if they were awaiting their turn, and everything resembled the description of the countess's funeral in "The Queen of Spades."[8]

And it always seemed to me (later, when I would recall those spectacles) that they were a part of some grandiose funeral for the entire nineteenth century. That was how the last of Pushkin's younger contemporaries were buried in the 1890s. This spectacle in the blinding snow and the bright Tsarskoe Selo sun was magnificent, but the same thing in the yellow light and thick fog of those years, which oozed out from everywhere, could be terrifying and even somewhat infernal.

***

I was ten years old when we lived (for one winter) in Daudel's building (the corner of Srednyaya and Leontievskaya Streets in Tsarskoe Selo). A Hussar officer who lived nearby drove out in his red and fantastic-looking automobile, went a block or two—and his car broke down. The shamed driver towed it back home. Nobody believed then in the possibility of automobile, let alone air, transportation.

***

In sum, I lived in Tsarskoe Selo from the age of two to sixteen.[9] During that period my family spent one winter (when my sister Iya[10] was born) in Kiev (Institutskaya St.) and another in Sevastopol (Sobornaya, Semyonov's building). The main place in Tsarskoe Selo was the house that belonged to the merchant's wife Yelizaveta Ivanovna Shukhardina[11] (Shirokaya St., the second house from the station on the corner of Bezymyanny Lane). But the first year of the century, 1900, my family lived (during the winter) in Daudel's house (the corner of Srednyaya and Leontievskaya Streets). That is where I had the measles and maybe even the chickenpox, too.

***

The smells of Pavlovsk Station. I'm destined to remember them all my life, like a person who is blind, deaf and dumb. The first smell is the smoke from the antediluvian train that would bring me to Tyarlevo, the park, the *salon de musique* (which was called the "salty moujik"). Second, the polished parquet and some scent from the barbershop. Third, the strawberries in the station store (Pavlovsk strawberries!). Fourth, the mignonette and roses (the coolness in the stuffiness) from the fresh, damp boutonnieres that were for sale in the flower stall (on the left), and then the cigars and the restaurant's greasy food. And the specter of Nastasya Filippovna, too.[12] Tsarskoe Selo was always a *weekday*, because you were *at home*, and Pavlovsk was always a holiday, because you needed to go somewhere, because you were far from home.

***

My generation is not threatened with a melancholy return, because there is nowhere for us to return to.... Sometimes (when it's so deserted and fragrant in the parks) it seems to me that you could get in a car and drive to the days of the opening of Pavlovsk Station, to those places where a shadow inconsolably searches for me, but then I begin to realize that this is not possible, that one shouldn't bury oneself (never mind in a gasoline tin can) in memory's mansions, that I would not see anything and that I would only blot out what I see so clearly now.

A Counterfeit Biography

TSARSKOE SELO WAS WINTER, the Crimea (Tur's dacha) was summer, but it's impossible to convince anybody of that, because everyone takes me for a Ukrainian. First, because my father's name was Gorenko, and second, because I was born in Odessa and graduated from Fundukleyevskaya School, and third, the main reason, because Nikolai Gumilyov wrote: "From the Serpent's lair / from the city of Kiev / I took not a wife, but a sorceress...." (1910).[13]

But I lived in Kiev a shorter period than I did in Tashkent (1941-44, during the evacuation)—one winter, when I was finishing Fundukleyevskaya School, and two winters, when I was attending the Women's College. But people's lack of consideration for one another knows no limits. And the reader of this book should get used to the idea that nothing was the way he thinks it was, or when, or where. It's awful to say, but people see only what they want to see, and hear only what they want to hear. They speak to themselves "in general" and almost always answer themselves, without listening to the person with whom they are speaking. This characteristic of human nature explains ninety percent of the monstrous rumors, false reputations, and sacredly-guarded gossip. (We still keep alive Poletika's serpentine hissing about Pushkin!!![14]) I ask those who disagree with me only to remember what they have heard about themselves.

The Wild Girl

A PAGAN CHILDHOOD. IN the neighborhood of that dacha (Joy, Streletsky Bay, Khersones) I was nicknamed the "wild girl," because I went barefooted, walked around without a hat, jumped off the boat in the open sea, swam when it was storming, and sunbathed until my skin peeled. And all this shocked the provincial young ladies of Sevastopol.

***

My childhood was just as unique and wonderful as the childhood of every other child in the world....

It's both easy and difficult to speak about childhood. Thanks to its static quality, it's very easy to describe, but all too often this description is permeated by a saccharine sweetness that is entirely alien to such an important and profound period of life as childhood. Moreover, some people want to appear to have been too unhappy in childhood, while others want to appear to have been too happy. Usually both are nonsense. Children have nothing with which to compare and they simply do not know whether they are happy or not. As soon as consciousness appears, a person finds himself in a completely settled and fixed world and the most natural thing is to believe that this world was never any different. This initial picture will remain in a person's soul forever, and there are some people who believe only in it, though they somewhat disguise this peculiarity. Others, on the contrary, do not at all believe in the authenticity of this picture and rather lamely repeat, "Was that really me?"

...Somewhere close to the age of fifty the whole beginning of life returns. This explains some of my poems from 1940 ("Willow," "Fifteen-Year-Old Hands"), which, as is well known, elicited reproaches for my being drawn to the past.

***

Anna's room:[15] a window that looks out onto Bezymyanny Lane..., which in winter was covered in deep snow and in summer was magnificently overgrown with weeds: thistle, sumptuous nettles, and giant burdock. A bed, a small table for preparing my lessons, a bookshelf. A candle in a bronze candlestick (there wasn't any electricity). An icon in the corner. No attempt was made to relieve the severity of the decor (knickknacks, needlework, picture postcards).

***

In Tsarskoe Selo she did everything expected at the time of a well-brought-up young lady. She knew how to fold her hands, curtsey, answer an old woman's questions politely and concisely in French, and fasted in the school church during Holy Week. From time to time her father would take her (in her school uniform) with him to the opera at the Mariinsky Theater (a box). She frequented the Hermitage and the Alexander III Museum. Spring and summer there were music concerts in Pavlovsk—at the station.... Museums and art exhibitions.... In winter there was often skating in the park.

There is a sort of ancient feeling in the Tsarskoe Selo parks too, but it's completely different (the statues). She read a lot and constantly. The then dominant influence, Knut Hamsun, had, in my opinion, a great influence on her (*Mysteries*); *Pan* and *Victoria* to a lesser extent. Ibsen was another influence... She studied poorly in the lower grades, but did well later on. School was always a burden (she didn't have many friends).

***

I wrote my first poem when I was eleven years old (it was terrible), but even before that my father for some reason called me a "decadent poetess".... Because my family had moved to the South, I did not graduate from the Tsarskoe Selo School, but the Kiev (Fundukleyevskaya) School, where I studied for all of one year. Then I studied for two years at the Kiev Women's College.... All this time (with rather long breaks) I continued to write poetry and for some unknown reason numbered each poem. Just for fun I can report that judging from the surviving manuscript, "Song of the Last Encounter" was my two-hundredth poem.[16]

***

I returned to the North in June 1910. Tsarskoe Selo seemed dead to me after Paris. There's nothing surprising about that. But where did my Tsarskoe Selo life vanish to in five years? I did not find even one of my fellow students from school and did not cross the threshold of one Tsarskoe Selo home. The new life in Petersburg had begun. In September Nikolai Gumilyov set out for Africa. I wrote the poems that made up the book *Evening* during the winter of 1910-11. Gumilyov returned from Africa on March 25th and I showed him those poems....

***

Those naive poems by a frivolous girl for some reason were reprinted thirteen times (if I've seen all the pirated editions). And they came out in several translations. The girl herself (as far as I recall) did not foresee such a fate for them and used to hide the issues of the journals in which they were first published under the sofa cushions "so that she wouldn't get upset." She even went to Italy (1912), because she was distressed that *Evening* had been published. Sitting in the streetcar and looking at her fellow passengers, she thought to herself: "What lucky people—they don't have books coming out."

Slepnyovo

I WORE A GREEN malachite necklace and a cap made of fine lace in those days. In my room (which faced north) hung a large icon—Christ imprisoned. The narrow bed was so hard that I'd wake up in the night and sit for a long time to rest.... A small portrait of Nicholas I hung over my bed, not like the Petersburg snobs did to achieve an almost exotic touch, but simply and genuinely as Onegin had done ("Portraits of the Tsars on the wall").[17] I've forgotten whether there was a mirror in the room. The remnants of an old library, which even included *Northern Flowers*,[18] and Baron Brambeus[19] and Rousseau, stood on the shelves. The war of 1914 found me there, and I spent the last summer (1917) there.

...The trace horse would squint and arch its neck in a classic manner. My poems came with an easy, free gait. I waited for a letter that did not come—and never came. I often saw that letter in my dreams; I would unseal the envelope, but either it was written in some incomprehensible language or I was going blind....

The peasant women went out to work in the fields dressed in homespun sarafans, and the old women and clumsy girls seemed more graceful than any ancient statue.

In 1911 I arrived in Slepnyovo straight from Paris and the hunchbacked servant in the ladies' room at the station in Bezhetsk, who had known everybody in Slepnyovo for years, refused to recognize that I was a lady and she said to someone: "A French girl has come to visit the Slepnyovo masters." And the Zemstvo superintendent, Ivan Yakovlevich Derin, a bespectacled and bearded bumpkin who turned out to be my neighbor at dinner, was so embarrassed that he couldn't find anything better to ask me than: "You probably find it very cold here after Egypt." The fact of the matter is that he had heard that on account of my unbelievable thinness and (so it seemed to them) mysteriousness, the local young people called me the famous London mummy that brings everyone bad luck.

Nikolai Stepanovich [Gumilyov] couldn't bear Slepnyovo. He would yawn, be bored, and go off on unexplained trips. He wrote "such boring and not golden olden times" and filled the Kuzmin-Karavayevs'[20] album with a lot of mediocre poems. He did, however, understand something and learned a few things.

I did not go horseback riding and did not play tennis, but just gathered mushrooms in both of the Slepnyovo gardens, while Paris still glowed behind me in a sort of final sunset (1911)....

Once I was in Slepnyovo during the winter. It was magnificent. Everything was somehow transposed into the nineteenth century, almost back to Pushkin's time. The sleds, felt boots, bearskin rugs, enormous fur coats, the ringing quiet, the snowdrifts, the diamond-like snow. I greeted the year 1917 there. After gloomy wartime Sevastopol, where I was short of breath because of my asthma and would freeze in a cold, rented room, it seemed that I had found myself in some Promised Land. But in Petersburg Rasputin had already been murdered and they were waiting for the Revolution which had been set for January 20th (the same day that I had dinner with Natan Altman).[21] He made me a present of a drawing, which he inscribed: "On the day of the Russian Revolution." Another drawing that has survived is inscribed: "To the wife of the soldier Gumilyov, from the drafts-man Altman."

***

For me Slepnyovo is like an arch in architecture.... It's small at first, but then gets bigger and bigger. And finally—complete freedom (if you exit).

***

No one really knows what era he is living in. That is why we did not know in the early 1910s that we were living on the eve of World War I and the October Revolution.

[1957?]

The 1910s

NINETEEN HUNDRED AND TEN was the year of Symbolism's crisis—and the deaths of Leo Tolstoy and Komissarzhevskaya.[22] Nineteen-hundred-eleven is the year of the Chinese revolution that changed the face of Asia, and the year of Blok's *Notebooks,* so full of foreboding.[23] *The Cypress Chest....* Not long ago I heard someone say that "the 1910s were one of the most colorless decades." That is probably what one is supposed to say nowadays, but I nevertheless answered that "apart from everything else, it was the period of Stravinsky and Blok, Anna Pavlova and Scriabin, Rostovtsev and Chaliapin, Meyerhold and Diaghilev."[24]

Of course, during this period, like all others, there were a lot of people without any taste (Severyanin, for example)....[25] In comparison with the tastelessness of the first decade, however, the 1910s were a composed and graceful period. Fate clipped off the second half and let loose a lot of blood in the process (the war in 1914)....

***

The twentieth century began with the war in the fall of 1914, just as the nineteenth century began with the Congress of Vienna.[26] Dates on the calendar have absolutely no meaning. Our revolt against Symbolism was entirely legitimate, because we thought of ourselves as people of the twentieth century and did not wish to remain in the previous century....

The City

THE WORLD OF ART artists had a sense of Petersburg's "beauty" and it was they, incidentally, who discovered mahogany furniture.[27] I remember Petersburg from very early on—beginning with the 1890s. It was essentially Dostoevsky's Petersburg. It was Petersburg before streetcars, rumbling and clanking horse-drawn trams, boats, signs plastered from top to bottom, unmercifully hiding the buildings' lines. I took it in particularly freshly and keenly after the quiet and fragrance of Tsarskoe Selo. Inside the arcade there were clouds of pigeons and large icons in golden frames with lamps that were never extinguished in the corner recesses of the passageways. The Neva was covered with boats. A lot of foreign conversation on the street.

Many of the houses were painted red (like the Winter Palace), crimson, and rose. There weren't any of these beige and gray colors that now run together so depressingly with the frosty steam or the Leningrad twilight.

There were still a lot of magnificent wooden buildings then (the houses of the nobility) on Kamennoostrovsky Prospect and around Tsarskoe Selo Station. They were torn down for firewood in 1919. Even better were the eighteenth-century two-story houses, some of which had been designed by great architects. "They met a cruel fate"—they were renovated in the 1920s. On the other hand, there was almost no greenery in Petersburg of the 1890s. When my mother came to visit me for the last time in 1927, she, along with her reminiscences of the People's Will, unconsciously recalled Petersburg not of the 1890s, but of the 1870s (her youth), and she couldn't get over the amount of greenery. And that was only the beginning! In the nineteenth century there was nothing but granite and water.

***

I was astonished to read in *The Star* (Lev Uspensky's article) that Maria Fyodorovna rode about in a golden carriage.[28] What nonsense! True, there were golden carriages, but they were used only for highly ceremonial occasions: coronations, weddings, christenings, the first reception of an ambassador. Maria Fyodorovna's equipage was distinguished only by the medals on her driver's chest. Isn't it strange what nonsense can be invented after only forty years? What will happen after 100 years?

[1957]

More about the City

YOU CAN'T BELIEVE YOUR eyes when you read that Petersburg staircases always smelled of burnt coffee. There would often be tall mirrors and sometimes carpets. But not in one single Petersburg home did one ever smell anything on the staircase but the perfume of the ladies who had passed through and the cigars of the gentlemen who had passed through. The fellow probably had in mind the so-called "black" entrance (that is the back entrance, nowadays, generally, the only one) and there it really could smell of anything at all, because the doors from all the kitchens opened out onto that stairway. For example, bliny for Shrovetide, mushrooms and fast-day oil during Lent, and smelt from the Neva in May. When they were cooking something pungent, the cooks would open the door onto the back staircase "to let out the fumes" (that's how they termed it), but nevertheless, the back staircase, alas, more often than not smelled of cats.

The sounds in the Petersburg courtyards. First of all, the sound of firewood being thrown into the cellar. Organ-grinders ("Sing, my little sparrow, sing, soothe my heart..."), grinders ("I grind knives, scissors..."), secondhand-clothes dealers ("Dressing gowns, dressing gowns..."), who were always Tatars. Tinsmiths. "I've got Vyborg pretzels." The reverberation in the courtyards and wells.

Smoke over the rooftops. The Petersburg Dutch ovens. The Petersburg fireplaces—an ineffective offensive. The Petersburg fires during bitter frosts. The peal of bells that would deafen the city with their sound. The drum roll that always made one think of an execution. The sleds that collided with all their might against the curbstones of the humpbacked bridges, which now have nearly lost their humpbackedness. The last branch-line on the islands always reminded me of a Japanese print. The horse's muzzle, frozen with icicles, almost touching your shoulder. And then there was the smell of damp leather in the horse-drawn cab when it rained. I composed almost all of *Rosary* in conditions like these, and at home would merely write down the finished poems.

***

...I started to write again in 1936, but my handwriting had changed, and my voice sounded differently. Life was leading by the bridle a Pegasus that in some way reminded one of the White Horse of the Apocalypse or the Black Horse from poems not yet born.... A return to my former style was impossible. It is not for me to judge which is better, which is worse. The apogee was 1940. Poems came without a break, stepping on each other's heels, in a hurry and breathless, and occasionally there were probably some bad ones.

From a Letter to ***
(Instead of an Introduction)[29]

IN EARLY MARCH 1940 totally unconnected lines began to appear in the margins of my drafts. This in particular concerns the draft of the poem "Vision,"[30] which I wrote the night of the storming of Vyborg and the announcement of the armistice.

The sense of these lines seemed vague to me and, if you like, even strange. For quite some time they were just stray lines that did not show any promise of being transformed into something unified. Then their time came and they took their place in the forge and came out as you see them here.

In the fall of the same year I wrote three non-lyrical pieces as well. At first I wanted to group them together with "The Kitezh Woman"[31] and write a book called *Short Narratives*, but one of them, *A Poem without a Hero*, broke loose, ceased to be short, and, most importantly, would not suffer any neighbors. The other two poems, "Dostoevsky's Russia"[32] and "Fifteen-Year-Old Hands,"[33] suffered another fate: they evidently perished in Leningrad during the blockade and what I have reconstucted from memory here in Tashkent is hopelessly fragmentary. Therefore, "The Kitezh Woman," as our fathers would have said, has remained in proud solitude.

***

I wrote "The house was one hundred years old"[34] in the state of an evacuee's melancholy in Tashkent, where in a typhus-induced delirium I kept hearing my heels tapping along Tsarskoe Selo's arcade. That's me going to school. The snow around the cathedral has darkened, the ravens are cawing, the bells are ringing, somebody is being buried.

***

Everything was so long ago. The first day of the war, which until recently was so close, and Victory Day, which seems like just yesterday, and August 14, 1946....[35] But that's all history. Not long ago there were translations, some of which I submitted, others that I did not, and Moscow life and the pine trees that are pitching so angrily now on this white night.

Last year I wrote "Here is the essence of north—and it's autumn / I've chosen as this year's friend"[36]—and that is already so far away now. And I was getting ready to write about the 1890s!

1957

***

A book, which I will never write,[37] but which nevertheless exists and which people have earned. In the beginning I wanted to write all of it, but now I've decided to insert several segments from it into the narrative of my life and the fate of my generation. This book was conceived long ago and my friends know individual episodes.

I started to write my biography several times, but, as they say, with mixed results. I was eleven years old the first time I set out to write my biography in my mother's red, ruled notebook, which had been used to record household expenses (for the year

1900). When I showed my notes to the grownups, they said that I remembered practically back to when I was a two-year-old infant (the Pavlovsk Park, the puppy Ralph, etc.). The last time was in 1946. Its only reader turned out to be the investigator who had come to arrest my son and searched my room at the same time (November 6, 1949).[38] The next day I burned the manuscript with the rest of my archive. As far as I recall, it was not very detailed, but it did have my impressions of 1944—"Leningrad after the Blockade" and "Three Lilacs"—about Tsarskoe Selo and a description of my trip at the end of July to Terioki, where I read my poetry to the soldiers at the front. It's difficult to reconstruct them now. The remainder, however, has become so ingrained in my memory that it will only disappear with me.

X., who wrote the introduction to Kropotkin's celebrated memoirs, characterizes this literary genre rather well (Rousseau, Goethe). However, even he, of course, does not say the main thing: every attempt at a continuous narration in memoirs is a falsification. Not a single human memory is so constructed that it remembers everything in order. Letters and diaries often turn out to be poor aids....

1957

***

And who would have believed that I was fated to live so long and why didn't I know it? My memory has become unbelievably sensitive. I'm surrounded by the past and it is demanding something from me. But what? The dear shades of the distant past are practically talking to me. Perhaps for them it's the last chance for bliss, which people call oblivion, to pass by. Words spoken a half century ago, which I did not recall once during these fifty years, are surfacing from somewhere. It would be strange to explain away all of this as merely my summer solitude and the nearness to nature, which, for a long time now, has reminded me only of death.

***

I've been tinkering with the biographical book for several days. I've noticed that it's very tedious to write about yourself and very interesting to write about people and things (Peters-burg, the smell of Pavlovsk Station, the boats in Gungerburg,[39] the Odessa port after the forty-day strike).[40] You should write about yourself as little as possible.

***

...I'm afraid that everything I'm writing here belongs to the gloomy genre of "Faust's Daughter" (cf. Daudet's *Jacques*),[41] that is, all of this simply does not exist. And the more that people praise this wretched, paltry muttering, the less I believe them. This is because I myself see and hear so much behind these words that it completely erases the words themselves.

November 22, 1957
Moscow

***

To manage to write one-hundredth of what I would like would be happiness....

***

...However, a book, a cousin to *Safe Conduct* and *The Noise of Time,* must come about.[42] I'm afraid that in comparison to its elegant cousins it will seem like a grubby child, a simpleton, a Cinderella, and so forth.

Both of them (Boris and Osip) wrote their books when they had just barely come of age, when everything they were remembering was not a fairy tale away. But to see the 1890s from the altitude of the middle of the twentieth century without becoming dizzy is almost impossible

***

I have no intention of resurrecting the genre of the "physio-logical sketch" and cramming my book with innumerable unim-portant details.[43]

***

As far as memoirs in general are concerned, I should warn the reader that twenty percent are counterfeit in one way or another. The willful introduction of direct speech ought to be recognized as an act punishable by law, because it so easily moves on from memoirs to respectable works of criticism and biographies. Continuity is a deception as well. The human memory is constructed so that it works like a projector that throws light on individual moments, while leaving the rest in impenetrable darkness. One can and should forget something, even with a splendid memory.

***

It makes absolutely no difference where you begin: the middle, end, or beginning. For instance, I want to begin now with the fact that these little green houses with the glassed-in terraces (I'm living in one of them) were constantly before my (closed) eyes in 1951 in the Fifth Soviet Hospital (Moscow), where I was recovering from a heart attack and was probably under sedation. These houses didn't exist then—they were built in 1955—but when I saw them I immediately remembered where I had seen them before. And that's why I wrote in "Epilogue":

> I live as in someone else's house, one I've dreamed,
> Where, it may be, I died...[44]

***

Pro domo mea [about myself] I will say that I never fled or skulked away from Poetry, although repeated and powerful blows of the oars on my numbed hands, which clung to the side of the boat, were an indication that I should let myself sink to the bottom. I confess that at times the air around me lost its moisture and its ability to conduct sound, that the bucket being lowered into the well brought forth a dry thump on stone rather than a joyful splash, and that, in general, I was unable to breathe for several years. "To introduce words" and "to bring words together" has now become the usual practice. What was daring at the time sounds commonplace after thirty years. There is another path—precision—and it's even more important that each word in a line be in its proper place, as if it had been there for one thousand years, but the reader is hearing it for the first time in his life. This is a very difficult path, but when it's successful, people say: "That's about me. It's as if I had written it." I myself (very rarely) also experience this sensation when reading or listening to other people's poems. It's something akin to envy, but a bit more noble.

X. asked me whether it was difficult or easy to write poetry. I answered that when somebody dictates it to you, it's quite easy, but that when there is nobody dictating—it's simply impossible.[45]

1959

***

A poet has a secret relationship with everything that he has ever written and this often is at odds with what the reader thinks about one poem or another.

For example, in my first book, *Evening* (1912), I really only like the lines:

> Becoming intoxicated by the sound of a voice,
> That resembles yours.[46]

I even think that a lot of things in my poetry came out of those lines.

On the other hand, I very much like a somewhat dark and not at all typical poem of mine: "I came to take your place, sister," which has remained without sequel. I like the lines:

> And the tambourine's beat is no longer heard,
> And I know, the silence is frightening.[47]

What the critics still mention often leaves me completely indifferent.

For the author poems are also divided into those the poet remembers writing and those that seemed to be generated spontaneously of their own accord. In some the author is doomed to hear the sound of a violin that once helped him to compose, and in others the rumble of a traincar which prevented him from writing them. Poems can be associated with the scent of perfumes and flowers. The wildrose in the cycle "Wildrose in Bloom" really did emit the intoxicating fragrance at some moment connected with this cycle.

This, however, applies not just to my own poems. In Pushkin I hear the waterfalls of Tsarskoe Selo ("those living waters"[48]), the end of which I myself witnessed.

From a Diary

December 24, 1959 (European Christmas Eve)
...A light snowstorm. A peaceful, very quiet evening. T. left early—I have been alone the whole time, the telephone has been silent. Poems are coming all the time. I, as always, chase them away until I hear a genuine line. All December was poetry, despite the constant heart trouble and the frequent attacks, but "Michal" still won't yield, that is, something that seems secondary to me dimly shows itself.[49] But I will nevertheless master it.

Attempts to write my reminiscences unexpectedly call forth deep layers from the past, my memory is becoming almost painfully acute: voices, sounds, smells, people, the bronze cross on the pine tree in Pavlovsk Park, etc., there's no end to it. I remembered, for example, what Vyacheslav Ivanov said when I read my poems at his house for the first time, and that was in 1910, that is, fifty years ago.[50]

I must guard my poetry from all of that.

Lately I constantly have the additional sense that somewhere something is going to happen to me. It's still unclear from which direction. Maybe in Moscow, or some place else, something is drawing me like the hot air from an enormous oven or a ship's propeller.

On the 29th Irina[51] and I go to the Writers' House in Komarovo—for just ten days. Maybe I'll rest up, but most likely not.

...Everybody knows that there are people who can sense spring from Christmas on. Today it seemed to me that I sensed it, although winter hasn't set in yet. So many wonderful and joyful things are connected with it that I'm afraid of spoiling everything if I tell anybody. And it also seems to me that I am somehow connected to my Korean rose and the demonic hydrangea, and the entire silent dark life of their roots. Are they cold now? Is there enough snow? All of this moves me deeply and I don't forget them even when I'm asleep.

The Birches

FIRST, I HAVE NEVER seen birches like those. I'm scared to recall them. It's a hallucination. Something threatening, tragic, like the Pergamum altar,[52] magnificent and unique. And it seems that there should be ravens. And there's nothing better on earth than those birches, so enormous, mighty, as ancient as the Druids and even more ancient. Three months have passed and I still haven't come to my senses, like yesterday, but I still don't want this to be a dream. I need them to be real.

1959-1961

***

It's common knowledge that everyone who left Russia took his last day with him. I recently happened to verify this by reading Di Sarra's article about me.[53] He writes that all of my poetry is influenced by Mikhail Kuzmin.[54] Nobody has thought that for forty-five years. But Vyacheslav Ivanov, who left Petersburg for good in 1912, took with him the impression that I was somehow connected with Kuzmin and that was the only reason Kuzmin wrote the introduction to my *Evening* (1912). That was the last thing that Vyacheslav Ivanov could remember and, of course, when he was asked about me abroad, he said I was Kuzmin's pupil. That is how this half-double, half-werewolf, which had peacefully lived in somebody's conception of me all these decades, and which had no contact with me or my real fate, was put into motion.

One unwittingly asks the question how many doubles or werewolves like this are wandering around the world and what will their ultimate role be.

***

Among these not-altogether-honest devices one is striking: the desire to separate the first book *(Rosary)* from everything else, to declare it her *livre de chevet* [favorite book] and then and there trample underfoot everything else, that is, to make me into something in between Sergei Gorodetsky *(Spring Corn)*, that is, a poet with no career as a writer, and Françoise Sagan, a "darling, honest" girl.[55]

The fact of the matter is that *Rosary* came out in 1914 and it was allotted a life of two-and-one-half months. The literary season then came to a close at the end of May. When we returned from the country we were greeted by the war. A second edition with a run of 1000 copies was ordered within a year.

It was almost the same thing with *White Flock.* It came out in September 1917 and because of the lack of transit it was not even shipped to Moscow. However, a second edition was ordered within a year, that is, exactly as had been the case with *Rosary.* Alyansky[56] printed the third edition in 1922. Then the Berlin edition appeared (the fourth edition). That was the last one, because after my trips to Moscow and Kharkov in 1924 [...] I was not published any more. And that continued until 1939. [...]

The two-volume collection that Gessen had printed was destroyed. The abuse that had been episodic became systematic and calculated (Lelevich in *On Guard*, Pertsov in *The Life of Art*, etc.),[57] at times reaching 12 points on the scale, that is, a life-threatening storm. I was not allowed to translate (with the exception of Rubens' letters—1930). However, my first Pushkin study ("Pushkin's Last Tale") was published in *The Star.* And this is what I find out about myself in the foreign press. It turns out that I quit writing poetry altogether after the Revolution and that I did not write again until 1940. But why weren't my books reprinted and why was my name mentioned only in the context of vulgar abuse? Evidently the desire to irrevocably immure my name in the 1910s has an irresistible power and some temptation that I fail to comprehend.

***

I was listening to the dragonfly waltz from Shostakovich's ballet suite. It's a marvel. It's as if grace itself were dancing. Is it possible to do with words what he does with sound?

November 1961

A Sketch[58]

April 19, 1962
Leningrad-Moscow

THIS IS WRITTEN FOR you, it was you who for some reason that splendid March of 1962 thought to show me in the unrelenting sunlight the terrible landscape of my life and my poetry (perhaps for the last time): from the pillaged, iconless dining room in Peter's little house[59] and the monstrous grave of Tsarevich Alexei[60] underneath the staircase in the Peter-and-Paul Cathedral to the pond into which they threw Rasputin's body in 1917. And the deserted windows of the Marble Palace[61] ("There I am drinking with you golden wine...") and the corner of the Field of Mars, which my poem does not wish to leave and does not; and the gates we used to pass through at one time in order to walk down the narrow basement staircase that led to the motley, smoke-filled, and always somewhat mysterious Stray Dog;*[62] and on Zhukovsky Street the "design of the horse's head," which I saw for the last time on the day of Mayakovsky's death.[63] The wall of the former stable has been torn down and a gray, two-story house has been added on. And the most terrifying building in the city (on the corner of Sadovaya, kitty-corner from Nikolsky Market)—where Raskolnikov murdered the old woman.[64] That house was recently razed and a potbellied monster was erected in its place.

The first (lower) layer for me is Petersburg of the 1890s, Dostoevsky's Petersburg. It was covered from head to toe in tasteless signs (underwear, corsets, hats), there was absolutely no greenery, grass, or flowers; the beat of the drums that always reminded you of the death sentence, the good French you associate with the capital, grandiose funeral corteges, and the imperial processions, which Mandelstam described.

I don't think we drove by the House on the Fontanka.[65] That would have been too much....

The inscriptions that used to adorn the pediments were taken down long ago: "This house is consecrated to Our Lord God for

*See "The Last Half-Hour in The Stray Dog." This is how it happened: B.V. Tomashevsky came by to take me to the janitor Moses in the bomb shelter on Griboyedov Canal (September 1941). We had gotten off the streetcar on Mikhailovsky Square. The alarm was sounded—everybody was being ordered to go somewhere. We go. One courtyard, a second, and a third. A narrow staircase. We've arrived. We sit down and at the same time pronounce: "The Dog."

all its days" on the Engineer's Palace, and "Pray to the Lord in His Holy House" on the Vladimirov Cathedral.

The gigantic money-box at the church (where I heard "Andrei Kritsky's Canon")[66] and on which was written: "Where your treasure is, that is where your heart is," had taken its place once again.

...And the two windows in the Mikhailovsky Palace, which had remained just as they were in 1801,* so that it seemed they were still murdering Paul on the other side of them,[67] and the Semyonov barracks and Semyonov Square, where Dostoevsky waited for his death,[68] and the House on the Fontanka—an entire symphony of horrors: ranging from the very quietest ("The Sheremetiev lime trees / the house spirits' roll call")[69] to one that resonated throughout the world on August 14, 1946:

> I was with all of them,
> With these and with those,
> But now I remain
> All by myself, alone.[70]

And the office of the military prosecutor on Nevsky Prospect next to the famous shop "Death to Husbands"; and the seagulls by Liteiny Bridge, which I crossed on my way to the lines at Kresty Prison[71] (Prison No. 1)—"and the three-hundredth woman in line with a parcel";[72] and the Arch of the General Staff, where the military court was located and where my son was tried; and the Summer Garden—the first time fragrant and frozen in the July quiet, the second time under water in 1924,[73] and once again the Summer Garden, gashed by the stinking trenches (1941); and the Field of Mars—the parade ground— where in 1915 the recruits were trained at night (the drum), and the Field of Mars—dug up for a vegetable garden and left half-neglected (1921) "under the clouds of raven wings";[74] and the gates from which the members of the People's Will were led to their execution; and, not far from the gates, Muruzi's house (on the corner of Liteiny), where I saw Nikolai Gumilyov for the last time (the day Yury Annenkov sketched me).[75]

...And the friends who have turned into memorial plaques (Lozinsky)[76] and Solovyovsky Lane, where we did not move to because of the war in 1914 ("The sidestreet is nothing more than a black crack"); and the furnished rooms in the New York Building (across from the Winter Palace), where Natan Altman

---

*The room was locked until 1917.

painted me,* and from where I went out through the window on the seventh floor "to see the snow, the Neva, and the clouds,"[77] and walked along the ledge to visit Venya and Vera Belkin.

All this is my Leningrad.

***

And if it was destined that Poetry should flourish in the twentieth century, namely in my Homeland, I will be so bold as to say that I have always been a cheerful and trustworthy witness... And I am certain that even now we do not truly know what a magical chorus of poets we possess, that the Russian language is young and supple, that we have only recently begun to write poetry, and that we love and believe in it.

---

*Grandi (an Italian artist who lived next door) stopped by to look at Altman's portrait when it was nearly finished. He uttered an immortal phrase that Mandelstam liked to repeat: "There will be big loaf." (He evidently meant to say *laugh*.)

BRIEFLY ABOUT MYSELF

I WAS BORN ON June 11 (23, Old Style), 1889, near Odessa
(Bolshoi Fontan). My father at the time was a retired naval
mechanical engineer.[1] I was taken to the North—Tsarskoe
Selo—as a one-year-old infant. I lived there until I was sixteen.

My first memories are of Tsarskoe Selo: the lush, verdant
splendor of the parks, the common, where my nanny took me,
the hippodrome, where little, dappled ponies galloped, the old
station, and a few other things, which later found their way into
my "Tsarskoe Selo Ode."[2]

I spent each summer near Sevastopol, on the shore of Strelets
Bay, and there I made friends with the sea. My most vivid impression from those years is ancient Khersones which was near
where we lived.

I learned to read with Leo Tolstoy's primer. When I was five I
listened to how the teacher worked with the older children,[3] and
I, too, began to speak French.

I wrote my first poem when I was eleven years old. Poetry for
me began not with Pushkin and Lermontov, but with Derzhavin
("On the Birth of a Porphyrogenite Child") and Nekrasov (Red-
Nosed Frost).[4] My mother knew these pieces by heart.[5]

I studied at the Tsarskoe Selo girls' school. At first, poorly,
later much better, but always unwillingly.

In 1905 my parents separated, and mother took the children
South. We spent an entire year in Evpatoria, where I completed
the next to last year of school at home, pined for Tsarskoe Selo
and wrote a great number of incompetent poems. Muted echoes
of the 1905 Revolution reached the isolated world of Evpatoria. I
attended my last year of school in Kiev at the Fundukleyevskaya
School, from which I graduated in 1907.

I entered the Law School of the Higher Womens' Courses in Kiev. I was content as long as we were studying the history of law and I particularly enjoyed Latin; I lost interest in the courses when we began the purely legal subjects.

In 1910 (April 25th, Old Style) I married Nikolai Gumilyov, and we left for a month in Paris.[6]

The construction of the new boulevards on the living body of Paris (as described by Zola) had not yet been completely finished (Boulevard Raspail). Werner, a friend of Edison's,[7] pointed out two tables in the Taverne de Panthéon and said: "And those are your Social Democrats—the Bolsheviks sit here, the Mensheviks over there." With varied success women either tried to wear pants (*jupes-culottes*) or practically swaddled their legs (*jupes-entravées*). Poetry was in complete decline and was only purchased on account of the designs of more or less famous artists. Even then I understood that Parisian art had devoured French poetry.

After moving to Petersburg, I studied at Rayev's Higher Historical-Literary Courses. At this time I was already writing the poems that went into my first book.

I was overwhelmed when I was shown the proofs of Innokenty Annensky's *The Cypress Chest*, and I read it as if the world had ceased to exist.[8]

In 1910 the crisis of Symbolism became clearly apparent and beginning poets were no longer joining that movement. Some went the way of Futurism, others—Acmeism. I became an Acmeist with my colleagues from the First Poets' Guild—Mandelstam, Zenkevich, and Narbut.[9]

I spent the spring of 1911 in Paris, where I witnessed the first triumphs of the Russian ballet. In 1912 I traveled through northern Italy (Genoa, Pisa, Florence, Bologna, Padua, Venice). Italian art and architecture made an enormous impression: it was like a dream that you remember for the rest of your life.

In 1912 my first collection of poetry, *Evening*, was published. All of 300 copies were printed. The critics received it favorably.

On October 1, 1912, my only son, Lev, was born.

In March 1914 my second book, *Rosary*, was published. It was allotted a life of approximately six weeks. In early May the Petersburg season was beginning to die down; little by little everybody was leaving. This time the parting with Petersburg turned out to be forever. We returned not to Petersburg but to Petrograd; from the nineteenth century we were suddenly transported to the twentieth; everything had changed, beginning with the city's appearance.[10] It seemed that a little book of love lyrics written by a beginning author should have been lost in world events. Time decreed otherwise.

I spent each summer in what used to be Tver Province, ten miles from Bezhetsk. This is not a picturesque spot: fields plowed in regular squares on the hilly terrain, mills, quagmires, dried-out swamps, grain, and more grain.... I wrote a good number of the poems from *Rosary* and *White Flock* there. *White Flock* was published in September 1917.

Readers and critics treat this book unfairly. For some reason people think that it enjoyed less success than *Rosary*. This collection appeared under even more ominous circumstances. Transportation was coming to a standstill—it was impossible to ship the book even to Moscow; it was all sold in Petrograd. The journals were closing down, as well as the newspapers. Therefore, unlike *Rosary*, *White Flock* did not have a sensational press. Hunger and ruin were mounting with each day. Curiously enough, all these circumstances are not taken into account nowadays.

After the Revolution I worked in the library of the Agriculture Institute. In 1921 a collection of my poetry, *Plantain*, was published, and the book *Anno Domini* in 1922.

Approximately in the mid-1920s I began to study very seriously and avidly the architecture of old Petersburg and Pushkin's life and works. The result of my Pushkin studies were the three essays on *The Golden Cockerel*, Benjamin Constant's *Adolphe*, and *The Stone Guest*. All these were published in due course.

The studies "Alexandrina," "Pushkin and the Shores of the Neva," and "Pushkin in 1828," which I have been working on for almost twenty years, will apparently be published in my book *Pushkin's Death*.

Beginning in the mid-1920s they practically ceased publishing my new poems or republishing the old ones.

World War II of 1941 found me in Leningrad. At the end of September, during the blockade, I was evacuated to Moscow by airplane.

I lived in Tashkent until May 1944, eagerly devouring the news about Leningrad and the front. Like other poets, I frequently made public appearances in the hospitals and read my poems to the wounded soldiers. In Tashkent I learned for the first time what the shade of a tree and the sound of water can mean in scorching heat. And I also learned what human kindness is—I was often seriously ill in Tashkent.

In May 1944 I flew into springtime Moscow, which was already overflowing with joyous hopes and expectations of imminent victory. I returned to Leningrad in June.

The terrifying specter pretending to be my city so shocked me that I described this reunion in prose. The sketches "Three Lilacs" and "Death's Guests"—the latter about a poetry reading at the front in Terioki—came into being at this time. Prose always seemed to me to be both a secret and a temptation. From the very beginning I knew everything about poetry—I never knew anything about prose. Everybody praised my first attempt very highly, but, of course, I did not believe them. I invited Zoshchenko[11] over. He suggested that some things should be cut and said that he agreed with the rest. I was happy. Later, after my son's arrest, I burned it with the rest of my archive.[12]

I have been interested in the problems of literary translation for a long time. I translated a great deal in the postwar years. And I am translating now.

In 1962 I completed *A Poem without a Hero*, which I had been writing for twenty-two years.[13]

Last winter, on the eve of the 700th anniversary of Dante's birth, I once again heard the sounds of Italian speech—I visited Rome and Sicily.[14] In the spring of 1965 I traveled to Shakespeare's homeland, saw the British sky and the Atlantic Ocean, met with old friends and became acquainted with new ones, and I visited Paris once again.[15]

I have never stopped writing poetry.[16] For me it is my connection with time and with the new life of my people. When I wrote poetry, I felt the rhythms that were resounding in the heroic story of my country. I am happy that I lived during this time and have seen events that have had no equal.

1965

REVIEWING THE PAST

I CONSIDER IT NOT only relevant but also vitally important to return to the year 1946 and Stalin's role in the Resolution of August 14th. Nobody in the press has written about this yet. I think that a comparison of what was said about Zoshchenko and Akhmatova with what was said about Churchill is a good start. It's absolutely inexcusable to cite exact quotations from the report by Zhdanov which swept us into the atmosphere of a communal-apartment quarrel. On one hand, the young people (of the post-Stalin era) do not remember it, and there's no reason to teach it to them, and the petty bourgeoisie who have not read my books still speak of "Akhmatova's pornographic poetry" (quoting Zhdanov), and there's no need to warm up their favorite dish. An objective tone and quotations are entirely out of place. One should sense the author's indignation (something like: "We cannot believe our eyes," "It's impossible to explain why a woman poet who has never written one erotic line...") concerning the fact that somebody who considers himself to be a critic is writing obscenities. There were denunciatory articles not only in *Culture and Life* (Alexandrov's[1] national newspaper), but also in all the national and regional press—reaching a four-digit number in the course of many years. And all this in the course of many years was proffered to our young people for their edification. It was an examination question in all institutions of higher education throughout the country.

Zoshchenko and Akhmatova were expelled from the Writers' Union, that is, they were doomed to starvation.

ON THE OCCASION OF THE FIFTIETH ANNIVERSARY OF MY LITERARY CAREER

LECTURES
Akhmatova and the Struggle against Her

I

"And the swan—for Akhmatovitis."

M Y POEMS PUBLISHED IN *Apollon* in the spring of 1911. Burenin's swift response in *New Time*. He supposed that he had annihilated me with his parodies, though he did not even mention my name.[1]

In 1919 I was annihilated by Bunin in Odessa (the epigram "The Poetess")[2] and by Bryusov in Moscow[3] (in honor of Adelina Adalis[4]).* After that, beginning in 1925, I remained completely unpublished and was systematically and consistently attacked in the current press (Lelevich in *On Guard*, Pertsov in *The Life of Art*, Stepanov in *Leningrad Pravda*, and many others). (The role of Kornei Chukovsky's article "Two Russias.")[5] You can imagine just what kind of life I was leading then.† And so it continued

---

*See Tsvetaeva's *Prose* (The Evening of Nine Poetesses).

†After the Central Committee's first Resolution (1925?), about which M. Shaginyan informed me on Nevsky Prospect and which was never published, they naturally stopped inviting me to read. This is obvious from the list of public readings. After a considerable break, I read my poetry for the first time at an evening commemorating Mayakovsky (the 10th anniversary of his death) in the House of Culture in Vyborg, with Zhuravlyov.[6]

This (1st) Resolution was evidently not as comprehensive as the infamous Resolution of 1946, because I was allowed to translate Rubens' *Letters* for the Academia Publishing House and two of my essays on Pushkin were published, but they had stopped asking me for poetry.

Moreover, out of sympathy for Pilnyak and Zamyatin I left the Union.[7] I did not complete the application and therefore did not enter the Union of Soviet Writers, which was then being organized.

until 1939, when Stalin inquired about me at a reception held in connection with the awarding of prizes for writers.

A handful of my poems were printed in the Leningrad journals and then the publishing house Soviet Writer received instructions to publish my poems. That is how the very winnowed-down collection *From Six Books,* which was allotted a life of six weeks, came into being.* Contrary to references published abroad, there was never a separate edition of *Willow.*[8]

After that, as everybody knows, I, who had already been thoroughly annihilated innumerable times, was again subjected to annihilation in 1946 by the concerted efforts of certain people (Stalin, Zhdanov, Sergiyevsky,[9] Fadeyev,[10] Yegolin[11]), the last of whom died yesterday, but my poetry has more or less survived, though my name is not mentioned in print (perhaps in deference to an old and venerable tradition) and there was not one mention of my book *Poems,* which was published in 1958.[12]

II

"That is how it was on the ice-covered Neva"[13] and on the Moscow River, but as everyone knows, examples are infectious.

"... And the struggle against her" was borne beyond the borders of our homeland. My position there was even more hopeless, because my only defense, that is, my poetry, was missing, and its place was taken by monstrous and meaningless literal translations (for example, the Italian Einaudi and French Laffitte editions)[14] and the no less monstrous rumors about my hopeless passion for Alexander Blok, which for some reason still suits everyone.†[15] Moreover, I've been reproached for a good number of

---

*The following circumstance affected the fate of this book: Sholokhov nominated it for the Stalin Prize (1940). He was seconded by A. N. Tolstoy and Nemirovich-Danchenko. N. Aseyev was supposed to receive the prize for his poem "Mayakovsky Begins." Then the denunciations and everything else one expects in these situations began. *From Six Books* was banned and removed from all bookstores and libraries. The Italian Di Sarra for some reason believes this collection to be a complete collection of my poetry. Foreigners believe that I stopped writing poetry, although, if nothing else, I wrote *Requiem* during the period 1935-1940.

†I repeat once again that this provincial rumor gained currency in the 1920s, i.e., after Blok's death, and that in the 1910s everybody knew only too well with whom he was having a love affair, they talked about Delmas openly, nobody doubted that she was Carmen, etc.

things. One reproaches me because I'm not a Symbolist. Another compares me to the "innovators" and keeps shelving me in the archive. Shatsky[16] claims that Gumilyov considered my poetry to be the "hobby of a poet's wife" (despite all of Nikolai Stepanovich's published judgments). Georgy Ivanov has spent his whole life, at Odoeyevtseva's bidding, trying to wound me somehow, beginning with his vulgar *Petersburg Winters*.[17]

In his *Dictionary of Russian Literature*, Harkins, I do not know at whose bidding or with what aim, writes about me so indecently that when I try to tell my acquaintances about it they simply do not believe me.[18] What were his sources!? Pierre Seghers puts on the cover of a book of my poems in translation (1959)[19] the alluring fact that I have been divorced twice (and this is on the cover!), moreover, that the first time I was forced into it, and that it took place before the Revolution. My poor little divorce! (Early August 1918.) Who would have thought that in forty years' time it would have the great honor of appearing to have been a scandalous proceeding of international proportions? I did not even go anywhere, I did not speak with anybody, I absolutely do not know how it was done. I simply received a piece of paper that I was divorced from so-and-so. There was famine and terror—everybody was leaving for somewhere (many of them forever), everyday life as such didn't exist, everybody was getting divorced. Everybody was so used to seeing us apart and nobody was interested in other people's business. As if anyone were up to that! And now forty years have gone by and I discover that before the Revolution I was forced to divorce. Why "before," why "forced"? Whom do I have to thank for this information? Most likely, after relaying such sumptuous pieces of information, the individual wishes to remain anonymous, as they said in the old days.*

(Upon taking a book at random from the shelf at friends—the Rozhanskys[20]—I learn that I am an *amie intime* of—can you guess?—Pasternak. Payne's discovery, which most likely nobody will bother to dispute.)[21]

---

*In a fit of pique I determined the following: I am the only one about whom Harkins writes in the connection of divorce, although almost all the people he writes about were divorced, and many more than once (Tolstoy, Simonov, Berggolts, etc.).

A Footnote to the Essay
"Akhmatova and the Struggle against Her"[22]

Normal criticism also ceased to exist in the early 1920s (the attempts by Osinsky and Kollontai were met with an immediate and harsh rebuff).[23] Its place was taken by something perhaps without precedent, but in any case unequivocal. To survive in the face of the press of that period seemed completely improbable. Little by little, life was transformed into a constant wait for death. It was pointless to attempt to find any kind of work because after the articles by Pertsov, Lelevich, Stepanov, etc.,* any work would have been pulled out from under me on the spot.

Another Note

Two poets gave birth to entire flocks of disciples—Gumilyov and Mandelstam. The first one immediately after his death (Tikhonov, Shengeli, Bagritsky). All of literary southern Russia raved about him. The second—right now (1961); almost all of the young beginners in Moscow and Leningrad rave about him.

---

*For some reason among the titles I remember: "Lyric Poetry and Counter-Revolution" (?!).

RANDOM NOTES

THE POETS' GUILD WAS conceived in the fall of 1911 as a counterbalance to the Academy of Verse, where Vyacheslav Ivanov reigned supreme. Before that N. S. [Gumilyov] was not well acquainted with Gorodetsky, who in general was much older than all of us and who was already trying out Chulkov's[1] "mystical anarchism" and "conciliarism," and who for some reason very quickly went out of style and ceased to be the "sunny boy," Seryozha Gorodetsky, and was searching for the next "lifesaver." The first meeting of the Guild (a very splendid one) with Blok[2] and the Frenchmen, took place at Gorodetsky's; the second at Elizaveta Yurievna Kuzmina-Karavayeva's on Manège Lane. That was the day I met Lozinsky.

It was not long before discussions arose about the necessity to distance ourselves from Symbolism, which, incidentally, had announced the year before (in 1910) that it was in a state of crisis.[3] During this period N. S. wrote the poems that make up the collection *Foreign Skies*.[4] He, therefore, considered *Foreign Skies* to be his first Acmeist collection. *Pearls* appeared in the spring of 1910, that is, well before the beginning of talk about a new movement. (In his article-obituary [1921] Georgy Ivanov—in his review of *The Pillar of Fire*—maintains that the real Gumilyov begins with *Foreign Skies*, but even he does not detect the unity of Gumilyov's work from the first book to *The Pillar of Fire*.)

There is a very interesting note in the new edition of Blok: "We were right when we fought the pseudo-realists, but are we right to fight with, perhaps, our *own* Gumilyov"[5] (my italics—A.A.).

Time will judge or, rather, has already judged them, but it is terrible that this literary enmity was brought to an end by the death of both of them at the same time.

I learned of N. S.'s arrest at Blok's funeral. The line "The odor of decay is sickeningly sweet" in my poem "Terror," which was written on the night of August 25, 1921, is connected to that funeral.[6]

I learned about N. S.'s death (I read about it in a newspaper at the station) on September 1st in Tsarskoe Selo, where I was living (across from Kitayeva's house) in something halfway between a hospital, and a sanatorium, and I was so weak that I did not go to the park even once. On September 15th I wrote "Tear-sodden autumn, like a widow sheathed...."[7] That summer the forests near Petersburg burned—the streets were filled with overpowering yellow smoke (the same as in 1959). In the autumn the Field of Mars was an enormous, ravaged vegetable garden and there were clouds of ravens. After I arrived from Tsarskoe Selo, I set out on foot (everybody walked then) to Shileiko's at the Marble Palace (by way of the Field of Mars)—and he was crying.[8] (I notice that what I'm writing isn't quite right: I have almost ten subjects on two pages and everything is very inconsistent, as they like to put it nowadays.)

ON THE HISTORY OF ACMEISM

I T IS SIMPLY IMPOSSIBLE to understand the origins of Acmeism without knowing the facts and ideas that will be set forth here. The last time I spoke with Mikhail Zenkevich on this subject, he drew my attention to the fact that the Acmeists never had patrons, which cannot be said of the Symbolists. That is true, but it is far from the main thing. We even subsidized issues of *The Hyperborean* ourselves, and the journal was run almost single-handedly by Lozinsky. Zhirmunsky[1] admits that he made a mistake with Kuzmin and his "beautiful clarity" (see Kuzmin's article that appeared several weeks after N. S.'s [Gumilyov] death).

In order to discuss Acmeism it is necessary to know exactly when it appeared and not to quote Gumilyov in 1910 as Gleb Struve[2] does ("We cannot be anything else but Symbolists"). Gumilyov was hoping that Bryusov *(Russian Thought)* would support him to spite Vyacheslav Ivanov, who was immediately openly hostile (see his letter),[3] but what would Bryusov have left, if he were to renounce Symbolism? And Bryusov came down hard on Acmeism, and in his article N. Gumilyov was transformed into Mr. Gumilyov, which in the language of the time signified something outside of literature.[4]

But all these bits of information, though essential, are secondary. Above all it is necessary to understand Gumilyov's personality and the most important thing in this personality was that as a boy he believed in Symbolism, like people believe in God. It was an inviolable, sacred object, but as he drew nearer to the Symbolists, in part to the Tower (V. Ivanov), his faith wavered and and he began to sense that something had been profaned.

Andrei Bely states somewhere that he gave Gumilyov the program for Acmeism, which he had carelessly jotted down on a piece of paper and that Gumilyov took it, saying that it suited him.[5] I have never heard a more desperate and senseless fabrication. On my part, I can add that when Gumilyov invited Bely and his wife to our place in Tsarskoe Selo, Bely was practically rude when he declined. And he places Acmeism in 1910 (see...) [sic]. And why would Bely, one of the pillars of Symbolism and the author of the primary work on Symbolism,[6] overthrow himself?

An internal split within the Guild took place in 1914. Gumilyov and Gorodetsky quarrelled. The letters they exchanged have survived, that is, I have in mind Gorodetsky's letters to Gumilyov, which somebody recently procured from Rudakov's widow, to whom I entrusted them for safe-keeping, but who, as is well known, is selling everything that was entrusted to her.[7] But that is not the point now. In 1915 an attempt at reconciliation took place and we visited the Gorodetskys at their new apartment (near the mosque) and we even spent the night there. But the split was evidently too deep and a return to the former relationship was impossible.

Later various guilds came into being, some of which invited me, while others did not, but none of them have the slightest significance for the history of Acmeism.[8]

Mandelstam's essay "The Morning of Acmeism" was most likely written in 1913 and not when it was published in *Sirena* (1919).[9] The term Acmeism itself was not passed on to future generations by us or our friends (there were no friends, just enemies).

I remember when Osip and I were in the editorial offices of *Northern Notes* and we pestered the syndicate, saying that the time had come to end the Guild (the first one). We wrote a petition in my notebook and I forged all the signatures on the spot. (S. Gorodetsky appended the following instructions: "Everyone is to be hanged, and Akhmatova is to be incarcerated for life." All this was a joke, but...).

It was there as well, I remember, that Gorodetsky made me uncomfortable by viciously attacking Blok's poem, "The reed pipe began to sing...."[10]

It was at the same meeting that N. Klyuyev publicly disowned us, and when the surprised N. S. [Gumilyov] asked him what it meant, he answered: "Fish look for a deeper place, man for a better place. "[11]

Indeed, at the time it was not at all comfortable to be an Acmeist.

And, as could be expected, a decisive battle at the Academy of Verse took place. I returned from my mother's in Kiev and came down with a fever.

During the winter of Acmeism's *Sturm und Drang* we made public appearances as a group several times. Gumilyov and Gorodetsky lectured, and I remember how old Radetsky (?)[12] with his gigantic beard would shake his fists and shout: "Those Adams and that skinny Eve" (that is, me).

***

That group had plans to withdraw me from circulation, because they had a willing candidate for the vacancy. And that is why Georgy Ivanov describes those public appearances in his vulgar memoirs *(Petersburg Winters)* the way he does:

> Not even a tenth of those who wanted to hear Akhmatova managed to get a seat in the small auditorium in the House of Literature.[13] Later the reading was repeated at the university. But even the enormous university facility proved to be too small. You would think that it had been a triumph.
>
> But, no. The majority of the audience was disappointed.
>
> "Akhmatova has written herself out."
>
> Well, of course.
>
> They had not heard or read her for five years. They were expecting the Akhmatova they loved—new gloves for the left hand put on the right one.[14] But they heard something completely different:

> > All is looted, betrayed, past retrieving,
> > How on earth did this splendor appear?
> >
> > Oh, the wondrous draws closer ever
> > To the hovels of rubble and grime,
> > Known to no one and witnessed never,
> > But sought out from the onset of time.[15]

The audience did not know what to make of it—"some kind of Bolshevism."* They applauded out of habit, but thought to themselves: "Of course, she's written herself out."

The critics gladly took up this "voice of the people." Now every schoolboy who follows the literary scene knows that Akhmatova has nothing to offer.

Absolutely nothing. The general public, which once had made Akhmatova famous, and it was a clamorous and lightning-quick fame that was out of the ordinary for a poet, had been deceived by Akhmatova. All the schoolgirls of Russia who had issued her a "mandate" to be the ruler of their souls were deceived.

One has to admit that this short passage has enjoyed unusual success. I've seen it both in English† and in Italian.‡

However, justice requires that one note that (as is the case with all of Georgy Ivanov's writings) there is not a single word of truth in it.

My books *Plantain* and *Anno Domini* (published by Alyansky at Alkonost and Blokh at Petropolis) appeared in the early 1920s—at first in large print runs (5,000 copies), and 15,000 copies were quickly sold.

But neither the English nor the Italian version prints the end of the paragraph, where on the contrary, my supposed "degradation" was seen as final and irreversible. I supposedly realized this myself (in 1932)[17] and ceased writing poetry until 1940, when for some reason a "complete" collection of my works appeared at the same time as some book entitled *Willow*. *Willow* is the title of the first section of the collection *From Six Books;* it was never published as a separate book and contained a handful of the poems that I had written from 1922 to 1940 (the title is taken from the first poem "Willow"; this in actual fact is *Reed).* As far as the completeness of the collection goes, the title itself disputes that claim. But for some reason foreigners want to immure me in the 1910s, and nothing, not even the print runs of my books can dissuade them. From 1940 to 1961 *95,000* copies of my books were printed in the USSR and it was still *impossible* to buy a collection of my poetry. As far as the early 1920s are concerned (the so-called NEP years), after Kornei Chukovsky compared me

*See A. Surkov's afterword to my book (1961) to ascertain the type of Bolshevism.[16]

†Strakhovsky (Shatsky).

‡Commentary to an anthology of twentieth-century poetry (Einaudi, 1961).

with Mayakovsky ("Two Russias"), Viktor Vinogradov wrote the well-known article "Akhmatova's Stylistics" and Boris Eikhenbaum an entire book (1922), the Formalists began to study my poetry, and gave lectures about it, etc.[18] Indeed, all this (as so much in my life) ended rather sadly. In 1925 the Central Committee passed a resolution (which did not appear in print), regarding my withdrawal from circulation. The two-volume collection of my works (to be published by Gessen at Petropolis) was banned and I was no longer published.

In particular, I believe that poetry (especially lyric poetry) should not flow like water over a waterfall and be a poet's daily occupation. In fact, from 1925 until 1935 I did write little, but my contemporaries (Pasternak and Mandelstam) also had intermissions. But even those few poems could not appear because of the pernicious cult of personality. Moreover, during this period I wrote the Tsarskoe Selo narrative poem *The Russian Trianon*, which has not survived, because I detected an *Onegin* intonation in it (independent stanzas have been published).[19]

***

April 4, 1963

... And so, I did not guess until today in what way I am guilty before mankind, what crime I have committed for which they will not cease trying to exact revenge: I wrote poetry that people liked and continue to like. Evidently, this cannot be forgiven. Take a look at how carefully and delicately S. K. Makovsky speaks of my contemporaries.[20] Vera Nevedomskaya is a beauty and Kardovsky's pupil, etc.[21] Tanya Adamovich is simply camouflaged and is called Tatyana Alexandrovna A.[22] She is also a beauty and, moreover, is intelligent. Gumilyov was hopelessly in love with her, etc. But as soon as I appear the tone changes. It turns out that I introduced Gumilyov to her out of jealousy and even gave up my bed at Tsarskoe Selo to her, while I slept in some passageway (!).

This person, in unbearably familiar tones, does not hesitate to accuse a Russian poet of vulgar pandering, even though he has no grounds whatsoever for doing so. This is worthy of our Samarin, who assured Georgy Shengeli that he had proof of an affair between me and Nicholas II.[23]

Of course, both Vera and Tanya are right there on the spot and somebody could defend their honor, but that is not the point. Neither of them wrote the books *Rosary*, *Triptych*, and *Requiem*. There is no reason to exact revenge from them—may they live in peace and prosper. And again I hear the serpentine rustle of my epigraph: "What a resemblance there is between slander and truth."[24]

July 12, 1963
When Innokenty Fyodorovich Annensky was informed that the brother of his *belle-fille* Natasha (Shtein) was marrying the elder Gorenko, he replied: "I would marry the younger one."[25] This fairly restrained compliment was one of Anna's most prized possessions.

Incidentally, the departure of Anna's family from Tsarskoe Selo (1905) saved her from the more or less open persecution on the part of the brutalized Tsarskoe Selo residents that Gumilyov was forced to endure. In this terrifying place everything that was above a certain level was subject to annihilation. In his unpublished memoirs N. N. Punin writes eloquently on this subject, Vsevolod Rozhdestvensky, now unmasked for what he is,[26] says almost nothing about it and evidently neither Gollerbakh[27] nor Otsup[28] even suspected its existence.

Of such an enormous, complicated and important phenomenon at the end of the nineteenth and beginning of the twentieth century as Symbolism, the residents of Tsarskoe Selo knew only: "O, cover your pale legs"[29] and *Let's Be Like the Sun.*[30]

That is why Otsup (in his introduction to Gumilyov's *Selected Works*),[31] repeating one of the innumerable legends about Gumilyov, states that N. S. said to some young lady, as they were riding in a carriage: "Let's be like the sun." It is obvious to anybody who lived in Tsarskoe Selo at the time that this is a lie and that to write that is the same thing as writing that Gumilyov said it to a young lady as they were sitting together in the bathtub. But Otsup left Tsarskoe Selo practically a child and did not belong to "society" of the time. The long years of Paris life have effaced the distant childish memories, but malicious gossip and the desire to make a poet an object of ridicule have remained intact. So!

NIKOLAI GUMILYOV
AND ACMEISM

I MARRIED N. S. GUMILYOV on April 25, 1910 and returned to Tsarskoe Selo after an absence of five years. (See my poem "The First Return.")[1]

It is also necessary, finally, to clarify N. S.'s attitude towards my poetry, because to this day I come across in print (in the foreign press) incorrect and absurd facts. For instance, Strakhovsky writes that Gumilyov considered my poetry to be simply the "hobby of a poet's wife," and [...][2] (in America again) that Gumilyov began to teach me how to write poetry after we married, but that the pupil soon surpassed..., etc. This is all absolute nonsense! I had been writing poetry since I was eleven years old completely independently of N. S. When the poems were bad, he, with his innate integrity and directness, would tell me so. Then the following happened: I read (in the Bryullov room at the Russian Museum) the proofs of *The Cypress Chest* (when I traveled to Petersburg in early 1910) and understood something about poetry. In September N. S. went to Africa for half a year, and during this period I wrote roughly what became my book *Evening*. I, of course, read these poems to many of my new literary acquaintances. Makovsky accepted several for publication in *Apollon*, etc. (See *Apollon*, 1911, No. 4, April.)

When N. S. returned on March 25th he asked me whether I had written any poetry. I read him everything I had written and he gave his opinion, which he evidently never retracted (see his review of the collection *Orion*).[3] At the same time I would like to add a parenthetical reminder, again in answer to Di Sarra and Lafitte, that I did not marry the founder of Acmeism, but a young Symbolist poet, who was the author of *Pearls* and reviews of poetry collections *(Letters about Russian Poetry)*.

Acmeism came into being in late 1911. In 1910 Gumilyov was still an orthodox Symbolist. The split with the Tower evidently began with Gumilyov's review of *Cor ardens* that was published in *Apollon*.[4] I have written many times elsewhere about everything that followed (the essay "The Fate of Acmeism"). Vyacheslav Ivanov never forgave him for something in that review. When N. S. read his "Prodigal Son" at the Academy of Verse, Vyacheslav attacked him in a tirade which was practically obscene. I remember that when we were making our way back to Tsarskoe Selo we were absolutely crushed by what had happened, and later N. S. always regarded Vyacheslav Ivanov as an unqualified enemy.

It was more complicated with Bryusov. N. S. had hoped that he would support Acmeism, as is evident from his letter to Bryusov. But how could a person who considered himself to be the pillar of Russian Symbolism and one of its originators, renounce it in the name of anything else? Bryusov's rout of Acmeism followed in *Russian Thought*, where Gumilyov and Gorodetsky are even referred to as "Misters," that is, people without any connection to literature whatsoever.

1910

EVERYBODY, PARTICULARLY THOSE ABROAD, wants to believe that Vyacheslav Ivanov "discovered" me. I do not know who the father of this legend is. Maybe Pyast, who frequented the Tower (see his *Meetings*).[1]

In reality, the situation was that N. S. Gumilyov took me to Ivanov's after our return from Paris (summer, 1910). He indeed did ask me whether I wrote poetry (there were just the three of us in the room) and I read "And when we had cursed each other" (1909, the Kiev notebook) and something else ("They came and said...," I think),[2] and Vyacheslav very indifferently and ironically pronounced: "What lush Romanticism!" At the time I did not completely understand his irony. In the autumn, after he had managed to incur Ivanov's eternal disfavor with his review of *Cor ardens* (see *Apollon* and Ivanov's letter to Gumilyov), N. S. went to Africa, to Addis Ababa, for half a year. Vyacheslav ran into me at the Rayevsky courses, where he was lecturing, and he invited me to his Mondays (not Wednesdays anymore). There I did indeed read my poetry several times and he indeed did praise it, but by then everybody (Tolstoy, Makovsky, Chulkov, etc.) was praising my poetry, which had been accepted and published in *Apollon*, but the very same Ivanov hypocritically urged me to see Zinaida Gippius.[3] Alexandra Nikolayevna Chebotaryevskaya[4] took me to the next room and said: "Don't go to see her: She's evil and will insult you terribly." I answered: "I'm not planning to go see her." Moreover, Vyacheslav Ivanov tried very hard to talk me into leaving Gumilyov. I remember his words: "You'll make a man out of him by doing that." Ivanov would cry tête-à-tête over poems and then lead the way to the "salon," where he would quite caustically tear them to pieces, but I've told this story so often and over such a long period of time now that it's boring to even write it down.

Vyacheslav was neither Magnificent nor Tauridic (the latter he came up with himself), but a "fisher of men," and Berdyayev has written about him better than anybody (*Autobiography*).[5]

Nikolai Nedobrovo, who enjoyed unconditional favor at the Tower, and Blok, whom Vyacheslav called Nightingale to his face, both knew him well and did not believe a single word he said. Today's young people, that is, descendants in the true sense, read *Cor ardens*, are at a loss, and say: "Second-rate Balmont."

You can find out how Vyacheslav Ivanov "wished" to present himself if you take the time to read about him in Einaudi's anthology, where, incidentally, he comes first (Blok is second).

We (the young people of the time) were amused by how this absolutely healthy forty-four-year-old man, who was destined to live until 1949, was fussed over by gray-haired ladies: Maria Zamyatina[6] once ran down from the Tower to wrap the Teacher's legs in a blanket (in April) when he and I were riding to the Moika—to the Academy. He was *playing* somebody who never existed and in my opinion should not exist. I found his *playing* the *self-lover*, as he liked to call himself, particularly unpleasant, because I pitied and liked poor Vera.[7]

What X. has recounted about his family "amusements" is horrible. I've never read Kuzmin's "A Female Corpse in the House."[8]

CLEARING UP
A MISUNDERSTANDING

AND NOW IT'S MAKOVSKY'S turn. I have just read in Driver (page 71)[1] that the Makovskys for some reason became my confidants and that Sergei Konstantinovich [Makovsky] published my poems in *Apollon* (1911) against Gumilyov's will. I will not allow the tragic shade of the poet to be insulted by this absurd and laughable gossip, and the person who printed this nonsense should be ashamed.

In the beginning, I indeed did write very feeble poems, a fact which N. S. did not even think of hiding from me. Indeed, he advised me to take up some other form of art, for example, the dance ("You are so lithe"). In the autumn of 1910 Gumilyov left for Addis Ababa. I stayed behind alone at the Gumilyov home (Bulvarnaya St., Georgiev's house), and, as always, I read a lot, frequently went to Petersburg (mainly to see Valya Sreznevskaya, who then was still Tyulpanova), visited my mother in Kiev and was absolutely mad for *The Cypress Chest*. Poems came at an even flow—nothing like it had ever happened before. I searched, I found, I lost. I sensed (rather dimly) that I was beginning to succeed. And then they began to praise me. And you know what praise was like on the Parnassus of the Silver Age! To this exorbitant and shameless praise I replied rather coquettishly: "But my husband doesn't like them." This is what they have remembered and exaggerated. Finally, it got into somebody's memoirs and a half–century later is used to support the vile and malicious rumor which seeks to serve the "noble cause" of depicting Gumilyov either as a base and envious person or as a person who did not understand anything about poetry. The Tower would have been overjoyed.

Gumilyov returned from his journey to Africa (Addis Ababa) on March 25, 1911 (Old Style). During our first conversation he casually asked me, "Did you write any poetry?" I, secretly rejoicing, answered, "Yes." He asked me to read, listened to several poems and said, "You are a poet—you need to make a book." The poems in *Apollon* (1911, No. 4) appeared soon afterwards.

ROSARY

*R*OSARY—MARCH 15, 1914. Lozinsky read the proofs. When we were discussing the print run, Gumilyov said thoughtfully: "But maybe it will have to be sold in every small shop." The print run of the first edition was 1,100 copies. It was sold out in less than a year. The main article was by Nikolai Nedobrovo.[1] There were two negative reviews by S. Bobrov and Talnikov.[2] The rest were positive.

"We are all carousers..."[3] is a poem that was written by a bored and capricious young girl and not a description of debauchery, as is commonly thought today....

***

In a year *Rosary* will be half a century old.

Rosary (continuation).

The book was published on March 15, 1914 (Old Style) and it was allotted a life of approximately six weeks. In early May the Petersburg season was beginning to die down; little by little *everybody* was going away. This time the parting with Petersburg turned out to be forever. We returned not to Petersburg, but to Petrograd; from the nineteenth century we suddenly found ourselves transported to the twentieth, everything had changed, beginning with the city's appearance. It seemed that a little book of love lyrics by a beginning author should have been lost in world events. That did not happen with *Rosary*....

And later it would resurface many more times both from the sea of blood and from the polar ice; it spent some time on the executioner's block and graced the list of banned literature (Index librorum prohibitorum), became an item among stolen goods

(Efron's Berlin edition)[4] and also appeared in a pirated edition in Odessa when the Whites were in power (1919).

Habent sua fata libelli.

June 24, 1963

***

Dmitry Maximov maintains that *Rosary* played a very special role in the history of Russian poetry: it was destined to be the tombstone on the grave of Russian Symbolism.[5] (See also B. Mathesius.[6]) To some extent he is repeating what I recently was told by Viktor Zhirmunsky and Mikhail Zenkevich (the first a scholar, the second a witness).

***

Rosary, as I have already stated, appeared on March 15, 1914, that is, soon after the campaign to destroy Acmeism came to an end. Everybody and everything had rushed to strangle the new movement with unusual fervor and an uncommon unanimity. Everybody—from Suvorin's *New Time* to the Futurists, the Symbolist salons (the Sologubs[7] and Merezhkovskys[8]), literary societies (the so-called Fiza) the former Tower, that is, V. Ivanov's circle, etc., etc.—pitilessly tore the *Apollon* manifestoes to shreds.[9] The Symbolists occupied the command posts, so the battle was a hopeless affair. They possessed enormous experience in literary politics and battles, whereas we did not know anything about all of that. It reached the point where we were forced to announce that *The Hyperborean* was not an Acmeist journal.[10] The titles alone of the anti-Acmeist articles give some idea of the polemic's general tenor ("Freezing Parnassus," "At the Feet of the African Idol," "Without Divinity, Without Inspiration," etc.).[11] In the influential *Russian Thought*, Bryusov called N. S., Mr. Gumilyov, which in the language of the time was used to designate somebody outside of literature.

...I am writing all this in connection with my reminiscences about *Rosary*, because the word Acmeism is not to be found in any of the several dozen positive reviews of the collection. It was practically a swear word. Zhirmunsky's "Symbolism's Successors" (December 1916) was the first genuine treatment of Acmeism.

Zhirmunsky's reminiscences go here.

Half a century has passed. Grandsons have become grandfathers. One comes across a first reader of *Rosary* less often than bison outside the Belovezhskaya Forest. All this, it goes without saying, is quite natural. The orthography has changed (give examples), as has the reckoning of time (the old and new styles, not March 15th, but...), and the name of the city, where this book appeared (not Petersburg, but Leningrad) and the country (not Russia, but the USSR).

At this point the reader (not without some irritation) is preparing himself to learn that only the poetry has not changed. That would be wonderful! However, I think that the poetry has changed as well, that the predictions (Kuzmin in his introduction, Khodasevich)[12] that have been realized force one to interpret differently this or that place, that what in 1914 was stunningly new now seems ordinary after the countless imitations. The same way that the hundredth kiss must inevitably blot out the first one.

***

The publisher of *Northern Notes*, the Social Revolutionary Chatskina, invited us to her home when *Rosary* was published. (I wore the blue dress in which Altman painted me.) An enormous crowd of guests had gathered. Around midnight they began to take their leave. The hostess bade farewell to some and asked others to stay. Then everybody went into the dining room, where a festive table was laid out and we found ourselves at a banquet in honor of some members of the People's Will, who had just been released from Shlisselberg. I sat next to L. K.,[13] across from German Lopatin.[14] Later, I often recalled with horror what L. K. said to me: "If they would give me *Rosary* to read, I'd agree to spend as much time in prison as the person sitting opposite us."

Somebody introduced me to Stepun.[15] He at once said: "Take your glass, walk around the table and clink glasses with German Lopatin. I want to witness that historic moment." I went up to the old man and said: "You don't know me, but I wish to drink to your health." The old man answered something halfway between a compliment and a rude remark, but that's not interesting.

June 26, 1963. Leningrad

WHITE FLOCK

T HIS COLLECTION APPEARED UNDER even more ominous circumstances than *Rosary*. It came out in September 1917. If *Rosary* was tardy, then *White Flock* simply missed the bus. Transportation was coming to a standstill—it was impossible to ship the book even to Moscow, it was sold entirely in Petrograd. The paper was coarse—practically cardboard.

The journals were closing down, as well as the newspapers. Therefore, unlike *Rosary*, *White Flock* did not have a sensational press. Hunger and ruin were mounting with each day. Curiously enough, all these circumstances are not taken into account nowadays and it's generally accepted that *White Flock* enjoyed less success than *Rosary*.

Within a year Mikhailov (Prometheus Publishing House) bought the rights from me for a second edition. That was in 1918, when Petersburg was already completely without food and was half-deserted. In 1918 an abridged pirated edition came out in Tbilisi; then Blokh and Alyansky printed *White Flock* at Petropolis Publishing House (with an additional printing in Berlin) and Alyansky published it by himself at Alkonost (1922). As was the case with *Rosary*, *White Flock* has had its place in one-volume collections of my verse (*From Six Books*, 1940, Soviet Writer; an American edition in 1952, Chekhov Publishing House;[1] and the green volume in 1961).[2] It provided the name for the Czech one-volume collection of my verse translated by Marčanová with a very sensible afterword by Mathesius. (Two editions appeared, one before the war.) I have never noticed that *White Flock* was not successful.

White Flock's old shoes are still present in the book *From Six Books*, as was the case incidentally with *Rosary*. For example: the poem "I have a certain smile" (1913)[3] was excluded because of the word *pulpit*. This, of course, is true of the 1961 collection as well. Thus, the contemporary reader does not know my poems, either the new ones or the old ones.

ANNO DOMINI

The matter is more complicated as far as my third collection, *Anno Domini*, is concerned. A second edition came out in 1923 in Berlin (Petropolis and Alkonost) and was not allowed to be shipped to Russia. The print run, which was large by the standards of the time, remained abroad.

The fact that there were poems in it which had not been printed in the USSR would form one-third of the basis for my guilt, and provoked the first resolution about me (1925); the second third was Kornei Chukovsky's "Two Russias (Akhmatova and Mayakovsky)"; the final third was that I read "A New Year's Ballad"[1] at an evening organized by *The Russian Contemporary* (April 1924) at the Conservatory (Moscow). It was printed (without the title) in the first issue of *The Russian Contemporary*; Zamyatin, who had always been kindly disposed towards me, showed me a bundle of press cuttings and said with unexpected irritation: "You've ruined the entire issue for us." ("Lot's Wife"[2] was also printed in the same issue.)

Pertsov (*Life of Art*) recalls my reading at the Conservatory in Moscow in his article "Literary Watersheds" (1925). Somebody took my copy of the article, but I remember very well one sentence: "We cannot sympathize with a woman who does not know when to die...." Moreover, he was mildly baffled that just a year earlier Akhmatova had filled the Moscow Conservatory with young girls.

ON *PETERSBURG WINTERS*

T HE FEELING WITH WHICH I read the passage from *Petersburg Winters* regarding my public readings (House of Literature, 1921) can only be compared with the final chapter of Kafka's *The Trial*, where the character is simply led to slaughter in front of everybody and everybody finds this to be a natural thing. There is not one word of truth in that passage. The author presents the poem

> All is looted, betrayed, past retrieving,
> Death's black wing has been flickering near,
> All is racked with a ravenous grieving...[1]

as a model of a fallen woman's lyric poetry and as an example of how I had written myself out. The audience supposedly "clapped out of habit." Nobody claps out of habit, they just slam the door as they leave. To this day people remember those readings with excitement and write to me about them.

And here we have Georgy Ivanov and Otsup, who back then were already hard at work discrediting my poetry any way possible. They knew certain details of my biography and thought that my place was vacant and decided to give it to Irina Odoyevtseva.

I was not even asked to contribute to *The Dragon* or the almanacs put out by the Poets' Guild. An absolutely indecent review of *Plantain* appeared there (by N. Otsup); Georgy Ivanov and Adamovich wrote in the same manner about Irina Odoyevtseva in *The House of Art*, No. 2.

I would not bother to recall these matters of "bygone days," if this little page from Georgy Ivanov's memoirs did not enjoy such unusual success in the foreign press. It has become the canvas of my post-revolutionary biography for the entire world. Strakhov-sky translated and published it in his book *(Gumilyov, Akhmatova, Mandelstam,* 1949), and I detect it in the writings of Harkins, Di Sarra, and Ripellino.[2] Friends tell me: "Don't draw attention to it." Maybe I am reluctant, but the advice is strange. If in the fifty years of my literary career I have never objected to anything, then my objection now should be taken seriously.

It's completely understandable why the foreigners have taken this bait. It was too tempting to proclaim that the Revolution had finished off a young talent, particularly since after 1924 my po-etry ceased to appear in print (i.e., it was banned), mainly for re-ligious reasons.

But the foreigners are ultimately of no consequence. What is incomprehensible to me is how a Russian writer, who knew the real situation, could so quickly go to rack and ruin.

Georgy Ivanov could not help knowing that during NEP my books sold out very quickly (15,000 copies at Alyansky's Alkonost), that Boris Eikhenbaum's work (a book) about my po-etry appeared during that period; Vinogradov's lengthy essay "Akhmatova's Stylistics" was published in the first issue of *Literary Thought,* as well as chapters in books by Chulkov *(Our Fellow Travelers),*[3] Aikhenvald,[4] etc. Chukovsky read his lecture "Two Russias." I won't even mention the public readings. My poetry was studied by the Formalists, which Vinogradov and Zhirmunsky can corroborate on their own.

This prosperity came to an end with my trip to Moscow (April 1924), where at an evening organized by *The Russian Contemporary* I read "A New Year's Ballad," after which my works were re-moved from circulation by decision of the Central Committee until 1939.

During the period of the personality cult my name was banned, abuse flowed like water over a waterfall,* my portraits were removed from the walls during searches,† and Pasternak barely managed to persuade the editorial board of *New World* to allow my name to be printed over his poem that was addressed to me—"It seems to me I am collecting words..." (1930?).[5]

And it seems to me that the time has come to expose uncondi-tionally these stinking "memoirs" by Georgy Ivanov‡ and not to

* For example, Pertsov, Malakhov, Lelevich, etc.
† And they were removed from exhibitions (Della-Vos-Kardovskaya).
‡ It's enough to recall what he writes about Gumilyov and Mandel-stam! Now, it seems, that the entire group has renounced Gumilyov, that is, Peter renounces and Judas betrays.

write about them with patent sympathy as Signor LoGatto does in his recently published book.[6]

He probably does so because there is nothing else. But, in my opinion, better nothing than acknowledged slander.

Dixi.

August 13, 1961. Komarovo

***

After my readings in Moscow (Spring 1924) the resolution regarding the cessation of my literary activity was put into effect. I was no longer published in journals or almanacs or invited to literary evenings. I met Marietta Shaginyan on Nevsky Prospect. She said: "You're such an important person—the Central Committee passed a resolution about you—not to be arrested, but not to be published either."

In 1929 after *We* and "Mahogany" I left the Writers' Union.

. . . .

In May 1934, when applications for membership in the new union were sent round, I did not fill out the application. I have been a member of the union only since 1940, which is plain to see from my membership card.

They stopped publishing me altogether from 1925 to 1939 (see the criticism, beginning with Lelevich, 1922-33). I was witness to my civic death for the first time then. I was thirty-five years old....

***

After the 1946 Resolution I worked on the topics "Pushkin and Dostoevsky" and "Pushkin's Death." The first topic is enormous. There is no end to the material. At first I simply reeled, I could not believe it. Irina Tomashevskaya[7] has always said that it was the best thing I have ever done. (I burned it with the rest of my archive when Lyova was arrested on November 6, 1949.)

***

None of the places where I grew up and lived in my youth exist any longer: Tsarskoe Selo, Sevastopol, Kiev, Slepnyovo, Gungerburg (Ust-Narova).

The following have survived: Khersones (because it is eternal), Paris—by somebody's oversight, and Petersburg-Leningrad, so that there would be a place to lay my head. By offering refuge to what remained of me in 1950, Moscow proved to be a kind dwelling place for my almost posthumous existence.

PSEUDO-MEMOIRS

L ITERARY CRITICISM TODAY IS impossible without a
critique of the sources. It is time to learn to distinguish the
senile (Makovsky) and ranting (Nevedomskaya) gibber-
ish from the conscientious work of memory. Due to circumstances in the twentieth century, an enormous number of people
have been left completely without archives and have learned to
do without them splendidly. Remember Rousseau, who said: "I
only lie when I cannot remember."

***

I'm somewhat anti-Browning. He always spoke in another
character, for another character. I do not let anybody else speak a
word (in my poetry, it goes without saying). I speak myself and
for myself everything that is possible and that which is not.
Sometimes I unconsciously recall somebody else's phrasing and
transform it into a line of poetry.

***

Nevertheless, some kind of poison is hidden in these journeys,
and in general I was the "happiest" when I lived on Konnitsa[1]
and was laid low by some neverending and rather pernicious
flu, and missed Friday after Friday (sixteen-year-old Anya's[2]
only free day—she was to be my *Wegleiterin* in Moscow). That
was probably in 1956. I was so certain that not one line of mine
would ever be printed, and this certainty dwelt so comfortably
and easily in my consciousness that it did not cause me the least

bit of disappointment. And how easily and freely I told the three young men from *Literature and Life* who had come to me for poems: "You won't print them anyway...." That is how a respectable person should live! And now... Then I gave them the completely new "Summer Sonnet" and something else.[3] That means it's ten years now that I've been publishing again. And the fetters of this....

EXCERPTS FROM
THE LAST DIARY ENTRIES

February 6, 1966 (The Hospital, Moscow).[1]

I felt poorly all day yesterday. Two doses of oxygen, I swallowed something and they injected me with something (morphine?). The most terrifying thing is that they cannot find the cause. But somehow they have suppressed the attack. Today everything seems to be in order. Irina[2] called yesterday, everything there is all right. Unrelenting cold and there is no end in sight. I think that I've written everything about Lozinsky. It will go in the book of portraits (Modigliani, Mandelstam, and others). It would be good to have two sections: poetry and prose. Marusya[3] was here this morning—she brought a letter from Tolya.[4] His interesting translations of Eliot (from *The Four Quartets*).

Poetry[5]

V.S.S. (To Valya) 2.
1913 and 1964.
To Pasternak (three).
Ante (...)
To Bulgakov (1940).
To Marina (1940).
The Teacher (To Annensky).

Prose

Gumilyov (Amanda's[6] dissertation—collect the finished sections and continue).
+ Modigliani (Paris).

+ Mandelstam (Acmeism, Poets' Guild, Sturm und Drang).
Lozinsky (almost ready).
Blok (almost ready).
Pasternak.
Bulgakov.

February 7. Monday.

An X-ray this morning. They say they didn't find anything. But would they really tell me if they had found something? Yulya[7] is coming.

Yulya was here.

Last evening I listened to Prokofiev's "Hallucination." Richter performed. It was marvelous, I still haven't come to my senses. No words (of any kind) can even remotely convey what it was like. It is almost impossible that such a thing occurred. A gigantic symphony orchestra, directed by an otherworldly force (moreover, with Satan himself as the first violinist) enveloped the entire space as it streamed towards the blue, frosty window.

February 8. Tuesday.

The moon continues. I became ill after the X-ray. A sleepless night. Ira will call this evening. My health is not coming back. Was it like this that January in the Harbor in 1961 (?).[8] I think about a sanitarium (any one) with horror. In the Harbor I wrote "Native Land"[9] and something else, but here it's just asphyxia and silence! The 10th is the day of Pushkin's death and Pasternak's birth. I know that after I finish writing about Lozinsky I should write about Boris [Pasternak]. *C'est compliqué,* as the scoundrel Tolstoy said about luring Tsarevich Alexei from Italy.[10]

They're reading Pushkin's poem on the radio ("The Country").

February 10.

Today makes three months that I've been in the hospital. Now I can definitely write down the following: there exists a law whereby after a lengthy stay every hospital slowly turns into a prison . And after six days they declare a quarantine to make the picture complete. "Parcels" are delivered in pillowcases, the entrance is locked (like in a madhouse), the doctors, nurses, and orderlies wear masks, and there is unrelenting boredom.

Remember Pushkin's lines: "Or to die from boredom / Somewhere in quarantine..."[11]

They stop allowing the recovering patients to go out for a walk. The pigeons we are so sternly forbidden to feed, drone on in their own prison on the other side of the windows.

February 14 (The Hospital).

Larisa Alexandrovna has been taken ill and there's nobody to discharge me from the hospital.

Tolya yesterday at 5. A lot about Leningrad. He's in good shape, as the athletes put it. We will continue our talk today.

A Moscow snowstorm like in the days of Alexei Mikhailovich.[12] You can picture the low, wide sleds, the tall fur hats and the menacing rumble of the Moscow bells.

Anya[13] for some reason isn't coming. Has she arrived?

I may translate a Bulgarian epic.

They've asked me for an essay on Shostakovich. Me—about music? I find it amusing.... I'll speak with Tanya Aizenman.[14] Maybe a few kind words. Something on the order of what they are broadcasting now about Dmitry Dmitrievich's "1905."[15]

Don't forget:

(1) To give Tolya the letter in reply to the proposal about publishing my book in a deluxe edition.

(2) To find out whether the television broadcasts about Lozinsky and Blok remain intact.[16] *(Show the Lozinsky.)* To ask the author of the poem "Destruction"[17] about Blake.

(3) The royalties for Dzhalil (Lipkin,[18] maybe).

***

I've just read Yevtushenko's poems in *Youth* (No. 1).[19] Why does nobody see that this is simply very bad Mayakovsky? "I'm not censuring the animal" (as Remizov[20] used to joke)—one can probably come to some important conclusions based on that observation.

Lenin's letter about Stalin is staggering. The references to Kamenev and Zinoviev were their death sentences.[21]

***

Yesterday they talked about nighttime London on the radio. I regret that I never saw it.

February 16 (Anna Sretenskaya).[22]
Wednesday. I'm to be discharged on Saturday. Am I happy? I don't know. Anya is here. It turns out that M. I.[23] is in the USA. Friends visited and brought wonderful flowers. I recalled that day in the 1910s. N. V. Nedobrovo.

In the evening they declared a quarantine in the hospital. I've found myself in quarantine before (in Leningrad at the former Mariinsky Hospital).

***

17. They're playing and singing *Khovanshchina*.[24] Tolya called.
18. *The last day.* At noon tomorrow they'll take me to Ordynka. I look all right, but in actual fact I'm not fit for anything.

Yesterday I heard on the radio a poem set to music. Very archaic language, Slavonicisms and a high style. Who is it? Derzhavin, Batyushkov? No, in a minute it's announced that it's just Yesenin. That troubled me a bit. I have always regarded Yesenin somewhat coolly. What's going on here? Can it really be that what we hear and read nowadays is so much worse that Yesenin seems to be a great poet?? What we hear and read is so often done dilletantishly, always skillfully, but there's the inevitable aftertaste of a margarine-saccharine lisping. That is an inevitable part of the program.

Tomorrow will be a *folle journée*—Saturday is Shrovetide.

Prokofiev's "*Suggestion diabolique*" is still with me. Arseny[25] has a recording, but I'm too weak to go to his place.

The Last Sunday before Lent
Yesterday I returned to Ordynka. It was very pleasant to be going for a drive after a hundred-day confinement in the hospital.

In the evening Nika[26] and Yulya. Tolya.

L'année dernière à Marienbad[27] has proven to be the assassin of my "Prologue."[28] That's both good and bad. My heart ached as I read it. My God. It also has a theater. Who will believe that I wrote "A dream within a dream" without knowing this book? And where do these sinister coincidences come from? I will ask them to find "Prologue" in the depths of my suitcases and I will compare it with the Frenchman.

I'm still carrying the prison of the hospital with me. I still see an almost black pigeon at the window who seems ready to deliver a letter to any address whatsoever and who is pecking at the glass with his beak. And the front door is locked, like in a madhouse.

They say that someplace far away a memorial service was held for me... as a victim (1946).

Tomorrow—First Monday in Lent

("Lord, Master of my life..."[29] and the pealing of bells that I've remembered since childhood.)

...On the other hand, the Frenchman (Alain Robbe-Grillet) does not portray the era—it could have happened at any time at all. It's simply the story of how one person skillfully walks off with another's wife. She's inert, lacks personality, in general, she's nobody special. The rape scene *(viol)* is completely unnecessary, and the fact that he sticks a rag in her mouth is simply vile. The ending is disappointing. Whereas I don't even have an ending—just the prohibition of the performance and the iron curtain.

...Domodedovo (March 3, 1966).

I came to the sanatorium with Nina.[30] A big, empty house that is somewhat reminiscent of *L'année passée à Marienbade* [sic].[31]

The night in Moscow was horrible. I took something for my asthma twice and was still short of breath. Larisa Alexandrovna reported that the sanatorium probably would not admit me and that Krylova stated that I was a hospital case, and she started such a fuss that I lost heart. Everything, as always, turned out fine.

March 4

I stayed in bed until 8:00 (as the local doctor ordered). It is simply so nice and so enchantingly quiet here. I'm completely absorbed by the Qumran news.[32] I read in *Ariel* (an Israeli journal) about the latest discoveries. I'm astounded, as probably everyone is. Instead of the third century (see Brockhaus and Efron on the New Testament), the time is set before the year 73 A.D. (that is, before the war). There cannot be any mistake. The Apocalypse with editorial headings is described exactly, as well as the conduct of the first martyrs. For some reason, the Jews (but not the Christians) were not persecuted by the Romans. They (the Romans) were geniuses at colonization and the procurator, Pontius Pilate himself, went outside to speak with Annas and Caiaphas, because if they had entered his palace they would have defiled themselves and would not have been able to celebrate Passover; and the Roman emperors ordered that if the day (once a year) of the distribution of presents should fall on a Friday, the presents were to be left for the Jews (see Mommsen,[33] vol. —, page —). Why did the Romans persecute so horribly the meekest Christians even before 73 A.D., that is, immediately after Christ's death (33 A.D.).

We have such detailed information about the lives of the first Christians.*

Translated by Ronald Meyer

---

* The Roman matrons were still wearing their customary attire and jewelry, so the executioner did not know how to cut off the head in such a way that the pearls and emeralds on the necks of the first martyrs would not be damaged.

My Half Century

REMINISCENCES OF ALEXANDER BLOK

I N PETERSBURG IN THE fall of 1913, on the day when Verhaeren's[1] arrival in Russia was celebrated in some restaurant, a large, private reception (for students only) was held at the Bestuzhev Institute.[2] One of the organizers was thoughtful enough to invite me. I was supposed to pay tribute to Verhaeren, whom I dearly loved, not for his celebrated urbanism, but for the short poem "On the Little Wooden Bridge at the End of the World."

But after I pictured to myself the splendor of a celebration in a Petersburg restaurant, which for some reason always resembled a wake with its tailcoats, good champagne, and the bad French and toasts, I opted for the students.

The lady patronesses, who had devoted their whole lives to the struggle for equal rights for women, came to this reception as well. One of them, the writer Ariadna Vladimirovna Tyrkova-Vergezhskaya,[3] who had known me since childhood, said to me after my reading: "Anichka has won equality for herself."

I met Blok in the greenroom.

I asked him why he was not taking part in the Verhaeren celebration at the restaurant. The poet answered with a winning directness: "Because they'll ask me to speak and I don't speak French."

A student came up to us with a list and said that I would read after Blok. I begged him: "Alexander Alexandrovich, I cannot read after you." He—with a reproach in his voice—replied: "Anna Andreyevna, we are not tenors." He was Russia's most famous poet of the period. For the previous two years I had been reading my poetry fairly often at the Poets' Guild, at the Society of Lovers of the Artistic Word[4] and at Vyacheslav Ivanov's Tower, but this was completely different.

If the theatrical stage is capable of hiding a person, then reading alone on stage can mercilessly expose him. The stage is similar to an executioner's block. Perhaps, I experienced that for the first time then. The audience begins to look like a many-headed hydra to the performer. It's very difficult to command the hall— Zoshchenko was a genius at that. And Pasternak was good on stage as well.

Nobody knew me and when I came out there was a cry of "Who's that?" Blok had advised me to read "We Are All Carousers Here."[5] I started to resist: "They laugh when I read 'I put on a tight skirt.'"[6] He replied: "They laugh too when I read 'And the drunkards with their rabbit eyes.'"[7]

I think that it was at some literary evening or other, not that one, when Blok returned to the greenroom, after listening to Igor Severyanin read, and said: "He has a voice like a sleazy lawyer."

On one of the last Sundays of 1913[8] I brought Blok copies of his books so that he would inscribe them for me. In each one he simply wrote: "To Akhmatova From Blok." (Here is *Verses on a Beautiful Lady.*[9]) But in the third volume he wrote out his madrigal dedicated to me: "Beauty is frightening, they'll tell you."[10] I have never had the Spanish shawl in which Blok portrays me, but at the time Blok was mad about Carmen and made a Spaniard out of me, too.[11] And it goes without saying that I never wore a red rose in my hair. It is not accidental that this poem is written in the Spanish stanzaic form known as the romancero. At our last meeting, backstage at the Bolshoi Dramatic Theater in 1921, Blok came up to me and asked: "But where is your Spanish shawl?" Those were the last words that I ever heard him say.

***

The one time that I visited Blok at his home, I mentioned in passing that the poet Benedikt Lifshits[12] had been complaining that he, Blok, interfered with his writing just by his very being. Blok did not break out into laughter, but replied completely seriously: "I understand that. Leo Tolstoy interferes with my writing."

In the summer of 1914 I was at my mother's in Darnitsa, near Kiev. In early July I set off for home, to the village of Slepnyovo, by way of Moscow. In Moscow I got on the first mail train that came along. I was smoking on the open platform. Somewhere near an empty platform the engine slowed down and they threw on a bag of mail. Suddenly Blok appeared before my amazed eyes. I shout, "Alexander Alexandrovich!" He looks around and, since he was not only a great poet but also a master of the tactful question, he asks: "Who are you traveling with?" I manage to answer: "I'm alone." And the train pulls out.

Today, fifty-one years later, I open Blok's *Notebook* and under July 9, 1914, I read: "Mother and I went to look over the sanatorium near Podsolnechnaya. —A demon is teasing me. —Anna Akhmatova riding a mail train."[13]

Blok writes elsewhere that Delmas, Yelizaveta Kuzmina-Karavayeva, and I had worn him out with our telephone calls.[14] I think I can shed some light on this.

I had called Blok. Alexander Alexandrovich with his typical straightforwardness and habit of thinking out loud asked me: "You probably are calling because Ariadna Vladimirovna Tyrkova told you what I said about you." Dying of curiosity, I went to Ariadna Vladimirovna's on one of her at-home days and asked her what Blok had said. But she was implacable: "Anichka, I never tell one of my guests what others say about him."

Blok's *Notebook* offers small gifts by wresting dates from the depths of oblivion and returning them to half-forgotten events. Once again I see the burning wooden St. Isaac's Bridge as it floats out to the mouth of the Neva, and my companion and I watch this unprecedented sight with horror. And this day has a date, as recorded by Blok: July 11, 1916.

And once again after the Revolution (January 21, 1921), in a theater cafeteria I meet an emaciated Blok with crazed eyes, who says to me: "Everybody meets here as if they were in the other world."

And here the three of us (Blok, Gumilyov, and myself) are having dinner (August 5, 1914) at the Tsarskoe Selo train station during the first days of the war (Gumilyov is in a soldier's uniform). Blok then was making the rounds of the recruits' families in order to offer them assistance. When the two of us were left alone, Kolya said, "Can it really be that he will be sent to the front? That's the same thing as roasting nightingales."

And a quarter of a century later in that very same Dramatic Theater—an evening to commemorate Blok (1946)—I read the poem that I had just written:

> He was right—again the street lamp, the drug store,
> The Neva, silence, granite...
> Like a monument to the century's beginning,
> There this man stands—
> When he, bidding farewell
> To Pushkin House, waved his hand
> And accepted mortal weariness
> As undeserved peace.[15]

Translated by Ronald Meyer

MIKHAIL LOZINSKY

I MET MIKHAIL LOZINSKY in 1911, when he came to one of the first meetings of the Poets' Guild. That was the first time I heard the poems that he read.

I am proud that to my lot has fallen the bitter happiness of making my small offering to the memory of this unique and wonderful individual, who combined fantastic powers of endurance, a most refined wit, nobility, and loyal friendship.

Lozinsky was an indefatigable worker. Struck down by a severe illness that undoubtedly would have broken another person, he continued to work and help others. When I visited him in the hospital back in the thirties, he showed me the X-ray of his hypophysis and said in an absolutely calm voice: "They'll tell me when I'm going to die."

He did not die then and the terrible illness that tormented him proved to be powerless in the face of his superhuman will. It's dreadful even to think that it was precisely at this time that he undertook the great achievement of his life—the translation of Dante's *The Divine Comedy*.[1] Mikhail Leonidovich said to me: "I would like to see *The Divine Comedy* illustrated in a very particular way so that Dante's famed expansive similes would be depicted, for example, the return of the happy gambler, surrounded by the crowd of flatterers. The Venetian hospital and so on can be somewhere else." Probably, all these scenes passed before his educated eye as he translated, captivating him with their immortal liveliness and splendor, and it grieved him that they were not being fully conveyed to the reader. I think that not everyone here realizes what it means to translate *terza rima*. That may be the most difficult task for the translator. When I spoke to

Lozinsky about it, he answered: "You need to understand right away when you look at a page how the translation will take shape. That is the only way to cope with *terza rima*; it's simply impossible to translate it line by line."

I would like to cite yet one more typical example of the translator Lozinsky's advice to me. He said: "If you are not the first one to translate something, don't read your predecessor's work until you have finished your own, otherwise your memory can play nasty tricks on you."

Only those who do not understand Lozinsky at all can repeat that his translation of *Hamlet* is obscure, heavy, and unintelligible. Mikhail Leonidovich's task in this instance was to convey the age of Shakespeare's language and the complexity about which even the English complain.

Lozinsky translated *Hamlet* and *Macbeth* simultaneously with the Spaniards,[2] and his translation is simple and clear. When we saw *The Widow of Valencia* together, I just gasped: "Mikhail Leonidovich, it's a miracle! Not one banal rhyme!" He just smiled and said: "Yes, you may be right." And it's impossible to escape the feeling that the Russian language has more rhymes than it seemed to have before.

In the difficult and noble art of translation Lozinsky was for the twentieth century what Zhukovsky was for the nineteenth.[3]

All his life Mikhail Leonidovich was extremely devoted to his friends. He was always ready to help people in any way—loyalty was Lozinsky's most characteristic trait.

When Acmeism came into being and there was nobody closer to us than Mikhail Leonidovich, he nevertheless did not want to renounce Symbolism, though he served as editor of our journal *The Hyperborean*, was one of the founding members of the Poets' Guild, and a friend to all of us.

In closing, I would like to voice the hope that today's evening will become only a first step in studying the legacy of him whom we rightly value as a person, friend, teacher, helper, and incomparable translator of poetry.

In the spring of 1940, when Mikhail Leonidovich was reading the proofs of my collection *From Six Books*, I wrote him a poem in which this is all expressed:[4]

> From a shade almost beyond Lethe's banks
> At the hour when worlds are destroyed,
> Accept this gift of springtime

In response to your better gifts,
So that the gift which knows no season,
Indestructible and true,
The exalted freedom of the soul
That is named friendship—
Will smile at me as meekly
As it did thirty years ago...
And the grilles of the Summer Garden
And snowcovered Leningrad
As in this book would arise
From out of the mists of magical mirrors,
And the reed, come to life,
Would sing out over thoughtful Lethe.

Translated by Ronald Meyer

AMEDEO MODIGLIANI

I FIRMLY BELIEVE THOSE who describe Modigliani differently from the way I knew him, and this is why. I could only have known one aspect of his nature (the radiant aspect)—I was simply a stranger, for the most part, a not too intelligible woman of twenty, and a foreigner at that. But even I noticed a big change in him when we met again in 1911; he had become somber and a little thinner.

In 1910 I saw him only rarely, a few times in all. Nevertheless, he wrote to me all winter. He did not tell me he was writing poetry.

As I realize now, he was surprised, most of all, by my ability to guess people's thoughts, to see their dreams, and other trifles to which those who know me have long been accustomed. He would say repeatedly: "*On communique.*" Often he would tell me: "*Il n'y a que vous pour réaliser cela.*"

It is likely that neither of us understood one essential thing: that everything that was happening was the pre-history of both our lives: his—very short, mine—very long. The breath of art had not yet charred, not yet transformed our two existences; this should have been the light, bright hour that precedes the dawn. But the future, which as we know casts its shadow long before it appears, knocked at the window, hid behind lampposts, cut through our dreams, and threatened with the terrible Baudelairian Paris concealed somewhere nearby. And all that was divine in Modigliani only sparkled through a sort of gloom. He was not at all like anyone in the world. Somehow I have always remembered his voice. I knew him when he was poor, and I did

not understand how he survived—he didn't possess even a
shadow of recognition as an artist.

He lived at the time (1911) at Impasse Falguière. He was so
poor that in the Luxembourg Gardens we always sat on a bench
and not, as was customary, on the chairs for which one had to
pay. On the whole he complained neither about his quite obvious need, nor about his apparent lack of recognition. Only once,
in 1911, did he say that during the winter he had been so unwell
that he couldn't even think about what was dearest to him.

He seemed to be surrounded by a dense ring of solitude. I
don't recall that he exchanged greetings with anyone in the
Luxembourg Gardens or the Latin Quarter, where everyone
more or less knew one another. I didn't hear him mention the
name of any acquaintance, friend, or artist, nor did I hear him tell
a single joke. I never saw him drunk, and he never smelled of
wine. He evidently started drinking later, but hashish already
figured somewhat in his stories. At that time there was no one
woman in his life. He never talked about former love affairs
(which, alas, everyone does). With me he never spoke about anything mundane. He was courteous, but this was not the result of
his upbringing, but of his exalted spirit.

At that time he was devoting himself to a sculpture, and he
worked in the little courtyard behind his studio; you could hear
the knock of his mallet in the deserted alley. The walls of his studio were hung with unbelievably tall portraits (from floor to ceil-
ing as I recall). I haven't seen any reproductions of them—have
they survived? He named his sculpture *la chose*, and apparently
it was exhibited at the Salon des Indépendants in 1911. He asked
me to go and have a look at it, but he didn't come up to me at the
exhibition because I wasn't alone, but with friends. A photograph that he gave me of this piece disappeared during the period of my great losses.

At that time Modigliani was raving about Egypt. He took me
to the Louvre to see the Egyptian section; he was convinced that
everything else (*tout le reste*) was not worth looking at. He made
a drawing of my head in the attire of Egyptian queens and
dancers, and he seemed totally captivated by the great art of
Egypt. Obviously, Egypt was his latest passion. Very soon his
work became so original that you could not distinguish the influences when gazing at his canvases. Now this period of Modigliani's is called *le période nègre*.

He used to say: *"les bijoux doivent être sauvages"* (apropos my African beads), and he drew me wearing them. He took me to see *le vieux Paris derrière le Panthéon*, at night by moonlight. He knew the city well, but all the same, we got lost once. He said: *"J'ai oublié qu'il y a une île au milieu (L'île St-Louis)."* It was he who showed me the *real* Paris.

On the subject of the *Venus de Milo*, he said that beautifully proportioned women who are worth sculpting and drawing always appear awkward in dress.

During a drizzle (a frequent occurrence in Paris) Modigliani would carry an enormous, old black umbrella. Sometimes we would sit under this umbrella on a bench in the Luxembourg Gardens, a warm summer rain would be falling, and nearby slumbered *le vieux palais à l'Italienne*. Together we would recite Verlaine, whom we knew well by heart, and we were glad that we could remember the same things.

I read in some American monograph that Modigliani was probably influenced, to a large extent, by Beatrice Hastings,[1] the one who called him *"perle et pourceau."* I can testify—and feel obliged to do so—that Amedeo was just as cultivated long before his acquaintance with Beatrice Hastings, that is in 1910. And a lady who calls such a great artist a "swine" could hardly enlighten anybody.

The first foreign visitor[2] who saw Modigliani's portrait of me in my apartment in the house on the Fontanka in November 1945 said something about the portrait which "cannot be remembered, nor forgotten," as a famous poet once said about something completely different.

People who were older than we would point out where Verlaine used to walk along an avenue of the Luxembourg Gardens, accompanied by a throng of admirers from "his café," where he held forth so eloquently each day, to "his restaurant" to have dinner. But in 1911 along this avenue walked not Verlaine, but a tall gentleman in an impeccable frock coat and top hat, and with the ribbon of the Legion of Honor—and our neighbors whispered: *"Henri de Régnier!"*

For both of us this name meant nothing. As for Anatole France, Modigliani (like many other cultivated Parisians) did not even want to hear about him. He was glad that I didn't like him either. But in the Luxembourg Gardens, Verlaine existed only in the form of a statue that was unveiled that same year. And about Hugo, Modigliani said simply: *"Mais Hugo c'est déclamatoire."*

***

Once, when I went to call on Modigliani, he was out; we had apparently misunderstood one another, so I decided to wait several minutes. I was clutching an armful of red roses. A window above the locked gates of the studio was open. Having nothing better to do, I began to toss the flowers in through the window. Then, without waiting any longer, I left.

When we met again, he was perplexed at how I had gotten into the locked room, because he had the key. I explained what had happened. "But that's impossible—they were lying there so beautifully...."

Modigliani loved to wander around Paris at night, and often, hearing his footsteps in the sleepy stillness of the streets, I would go to the window and, through the Venetian blinds, watch his shadow lingering below....

By the early 1920s the Paris of that time was already called *vieux Paris* or *Paris d'avant guerre*. Horse cabs still thronged the streets then and the coachmen had their own taverns known as *Rendez-vous des cochers*. My young contemporaries, those who were soon to die on the Marne or at Verdun, were still alive. All the artists of the "left," except for Modigliani, were recognized. Picasso was as famous then as he is today, but at the time everyone spoke of "Picasso and Braque." Ida Rubinstein was playing Scheherazade, and Diaghilev's Ballets Russes was becoming an elegant tradition—Stravinsky, Nijinsky, Pavlova, Karsavina, Bakst.

We now know that Stravinsky's fate did not remain tied to the 1910s, and that his creative work became the highest musical expression of the spirit of the twentieth century. We did not know it then. On June 20, 1910, *The Firebird* premiered, and on June 13, 1911, Diaghilev presented Fokine's *Petrouchka*.

The laying of the new boulevards onto the living body of Paris (which Zola has described) was still not yet finished (Boulevard Raspail). Werner, a friend of Edison, pointed out two tables to me in the Taverne de Panthéon and said: "And these are your social democrats—the Bolsheviks here, and the Mensheviks over there." Women, with varying degrees of success, tried wearing trousers (*jupes-culottes*) and practically swaddled their legs (*jupes entravées*). Poetry was in a state of total neglect, and people bought it only for designs by the more or less famous artists.

Even then I understood that in Paris painting had swallowed up French poetry.

René Ghil was advocating "scientific poetry," and his so-called students were exceedingly reluctant to visit the master.

The Catholic Church canonized Jeanne d'Arc.

> *Et Jehanne la bonne Lorraine*
> *Qu'Anglois brûlèrent à Rouen...*
>   (Villon)

I recalled these lines from the immortal ballad while looking at the statuettes of the new saint. They were in extremely dubious taste and were being sold in shops dealing in religious wares.

***

Modigliani regretted that he couldn't understand my poems, and he suspected that there was something miraculous lurking in them; but they were only my first uncertain attempts. (For example, those published in *Apollon* in 1911.[3]) He openly laughed at the Apollonian illustrations (*The World of Art*).

I was amazed at how Modigliani could find a certain man handsome who was known for his plainness, and how he would insist on it. Even then I thought that he really did not see things as we did.

In any case, what passed for *fashion* in Paris, a word adorned with splendid epithets, didn't concern Modigliani at all.

I didn't pose for his drawings of me; he did them at home and gave them to me later. There were sixteen in all, and he asked me to mount and hang them in my room in Tsarskoe Selo. They vanished in that house during the first years of the Revolution. The one that survived bears the least resemblance to his future nudes....

We talked about poetry more than anything. We both knew a great many French poems—by Verlaine, Laforgue, Mallarmé, and Baudelaire. Later, I met another artist—Alexander Tyshler[5]—who, like Modigliani, loved and understood poetry. This is such a rarity among artists!

He never read Dante to me. Probably because at the time I did not know Italian.

One time he said: *"J'ai oublié de vous dire que je suis juif."* He told me that he was born near Livorno, and also that he was twenty-four, but he was really twenty-six.

He also told me that he used to be interested in aviators (nowadays: pilots), but when he got to know one of them, he was disappointed: they turned out to be merely sportsmen (what did he expect?).

At that time the early light airplanes (see Gumilyov: "To pierce the thunder-clouds / In heavy and droning machines"), which, as everyone knows resembled book-cases on legs, circled round my rusting and twisted contemporary (1889), the Eiffel Tower.

To me it resembled an enormous candlestick holder, forgotten by a giant in the capital of the dwarves. But this is something out of Gulliver.

***

...And around us still seethed the recently triumphant Cubism, which remained alien to Modigliani.

Marc Chagall had brought his enchanting Vitebsk to Paris, and along a Parisian boulevard strolled Charlie Chaplin in the guise of an unknown young man whose star had not yet ascended—(*Le Grand Muet*, as the cinema was then called, still kept eloquently silent).

***

"And far to the north..." in Russia, Leo Tolstoy, Vrubel, and Vera Komissarzhevskaya had died; the Symbolists declared themselves in a state of crisis; and Alexander Blok was prophesying:

> O, my children, if you only knew
> The cold and gloom of days to come...

Three leviathans on which the twentieth century now rests— Proust, Joyce, and Kafka—lived like men and had not yet become myths.

***

In the years that followed, when I would ask those returning from Paris about Modigliani, certain that such a person must have achieved fame, the answer was always the same: we don't know, we haven't heard of him. Neither A. Ekster[6] (an artist from the school which produced all the "left" artists of Kiev), B. Anrep[7] (a well-known mosaicist), nor N. Altman[8] (who painted my portrait during the years 1914-15) knew of him.

The only time Gumilyov mentioned the name Modigliani was when we went together for the last time to visit our son in Bezhetsk in May 1918,[9] and he called him a "drunken monster" or something to that effect. Apparently, they had clashed in Paris because Gumilyov was speaking in Russian in the company of certain people and Modigliani objected. And to think they both had barely three years to live....

Modigliani had little regard for travelers. He considered our travels a substitute for genuine activity. In his pocket he always carried a copy of *Les chants de Maldoror*,[10] which at the time was a bibliographic rarity. He recounted to me how he had gone into a Russian church at the midnight Easter service to watch the procession, since he loved magnificent ceremonies, and how some "probably very important gentleman" (perhaps an ambassador) exchanged the Easter kiss with him. Obviously Modigliani did not understand what this meant.

For a long time it seemed I would not hear anything more about him... But I did hear a great deal...

***

At the beginning of NEP,[11] when I was on the board of what served at the time as the Writers' Union, we would meet in the office of Alexander Tikhonov[12] (in the Leningrad publishing house World Literature). Postal service had been resumed with other countries, and Tikhonov used to receive a lot of foreign books and magazines. Once during a meeting, someone handed me a copy of a French art magazine. I opened it, and there was a photograph of Modigliani... and a little cross.... The long article was an obituary. From it I learned that he was a great artist of the twentieth century (as I recall, they were comparing him to Botticelli), and that there were already monographs about him in

English and Italian. Later, in the 1930s, Ilya Ehrenburg told me a great deal about Modigliani; he had known him in Paris later than I, and had dedicated some poems to him in his book *Poems about the Eves*. I also read about him in Francis Carco's book *From Montmartre to the Latin Quarter*,[13] and in a popular novel in which the author placed him with Utrillo. I can say with certainty that this hybrid of Modigliani's life during the years 1910-11 is in no way accurate, and that what the author has done belongs in the category of impermissible devices.

And even quite recently Modigliani was made the hero of an extremely vulgar French film *Montparnasse 19*.[14] It is so bitter!

Bolshevo 1958—Moscow 1964

Translated by Christopher Fortune

OSIP MANDELSTAM

I

July 28, 1957[1]

AND LOZINSKY'S[2] DEATH SOMEHOW broke the thread of my reminiscences. I no longer dare to recall things that he cannot corroborate (about the Poets' Guild, Acmeism, the journal *The Hyperborean*, and so forth). In recent years we rarely saw each other because of his illness and I didn't get a chance to have a real talk with him about some important matters or to read him my poems from the 1930s (*Requiem*). Probably that accounts for the fact that he continued to think of me to some degree as the same poet he had known long ago in Tsarskoe Selo. This became clear when we were both reading the proofs of my collection *From Six Books* in 1940.

***

Something similar happened with Mandelstam, who of course knew all my poems, but in a different way. He did not know how to reminisce, rather it was a different sort of process for him that I don't have a name for now, but something doubtless akin to creativity. (For example, Petersburg in *The Noise of Time*[3] seen through the bright eyes of a five-year-old boy.)

Mandelstam was one of the most brilliant conversationalists. He didn't just listen to himself and answer himself, which is what almost everyone does nowadays. In conversation he was polite, quick to react, and always original. I never heard him repeat himself or "play the same old record." He learned foreign languages with unusual ease. He could recite pages of *The Divine Comedy* in Italian.[4] Shortly before his death he asked Nadya[5] to teach him English, which he didn't know at all. The way he spoke about poetry was stunning: he was passionate and sometimes monstrously unfair, about Blok, for instance.[6] He said of Pasternak: "I think about him so much that it makes me tired" and "I'm sure he hasn't read a single line of mine."[7] And about Marina: "I am anti-Tsvetaeva."[8]

Osip was at home with music and this is a very rare trait. What he feared most was becoming mute, he called it asphyxia.[9] He was horror-struck when it seized him and he would think up absurd reasons to explain the disaster.[10] A second and frequent disappointment was his readers. He always thought that the wrong kind of reader liked his poetry. He knew and remembered other people's poetry well, would often become fascinated by a single line, and easily memorized what was read to him.

> The white garment of Brother Snow
> Falls onto the mud, still hot from the horses' hooves.

I remember this only as he read it. Whose is it?[11]

He liked to talk about his so-called "dumbness." Sometimes he would tell silly stories to amuse me. For example, when he was still a young boy he had supposedly translated the Mallarmé line *"La jeune mère allaitait son enfant"* as: "And the young mother was feeding from dream."[12] We used to make each other laugh so hard that we would fall off the couch with the singing springs at Tuchkov Lane,[13] and we giggled until we almost fainted, like the confectionary girls in Joyce's *Ulysses*.

I met Osip Mandelstam at Vyacheslav Ivanov's Tower in the spring of 1911.[14] He was a wiry boy then, with a lily of the valley in his lapel, his head thrown way back, with fiery eyes and lashes that reached almost halfway down his cheeks. The second time I saw him was at the Tolstoys[15] on Old Nevsky. He didn't recognize me, and Alexei Nikolayevich [Tolstoy] began to ask him what Gumilyov's wife looked like. Mandelstam gestured with his hands to show what a big hat I wore. I got frightened that something irreparable would happen and introduced myself.

That was my first Mandelstam, the author of the green *Stone* (published by Acme)[16] with the inscription: "To Anna Akhmatova—flashes of consciousness in the forgetfulness of days. Respectfully, the Author."

With his peculiarly charming self-irony Osip liked to tell the story of how an old Jew, the owner of the print shop where *Stone* was printed, congratulated him on the book's publication, shook his hand, and said: "Your writing will only get better and better, young man."[17]

I see him now through the sparse smoke and fog of Vasilyevsky Island, and where the Kinshi Restaurant used to be on the corner of the second line and Bolshoi Prospect (a hairdresser's salon is there now), where once, according to legend, Lomonosov drank away his governmental watch, and where we (Gumilyov and I) used to go for breakfast when we lived on Tuchkov Lane. There weren't any gatherings at the Tuchkov apartment, nor could there have been. It was just Nikolai Stepanovich's student lodgings and there was hardly room to sit down. Georgy Ivanov's description of five o'clock meetings there (see his "The Poets") is a fabrication from beginning to end.[18] Nikolai Nedobrovo never crossed the threshold of the Tuchkov apartment.[19]

This Mandelstam was a generous contributor, if not co-author, to the "Anthology of Ancient Stupidity," which the members of the Poets' Guild would compose during dinner (almost all of them, except me): "Lesbos, where are you?" and "Leonid's son was a tightwad."[20]

> "Whence comest thou, wanderer?" "I was at Shileiko's.[21]
> Wondrously lives the man, he dines on goose,
> If he touches a knob with his finger, the light comes on
>   by itself.
> If such people live on Fourth Rozhdestvensky Street,
> Say, wanderer, I beseech you, who lives on Eighth?"

I recall this as being Osip's, and Zenkevich[22] agrees with me.
An epigram on Osip:

> Ash on his left shoulder, and be still—
> Goldtooth—the terror of his friends!

(This is "the terror of the seas—Onetooth.")[23]

Gumilyov may even have written this. Osip always tried flicking the ashes over his shoulder when he smoked, but a little mountain of ash would pile up there.

Perhaps it is worth preserving some fragments of the Guild's parody on Pushkin's famous sonnet, "Severe Dante did not scorn the sonnet":

Valère Bryussof did not scorn the sonnet,
Ivanov wrote them in wreathes,
Aneta's husband[24] liked their meters,
Voloshin did not jabber any worse.

And many poets were captivated by it,
Kuzmin chose it as his hack,
When, forgetting flounces and rockets,
He galloped after Blok, but didn't catch him.

Vladimir Narbut, a regular wolf,[25]
(I forget—) wrapped himself in a metaphysical jacket
And Zenkevich neglected
Moravskaya's[26] diamond dewdrops for it.

Here are verses (triolets) about those Fridays (by V. V. Gippius,[27] I think):

1.
On Fridays at *The Hyperborean*[28]
Literary roses bloom
....
Mikhail Lozinsky emerges,
Joking and smoking,
Caressing his infant journal
With his giant hand.

2.
Nikolai Gumilyov has
His leg raised high,
As he tosses out pearls[29]
For romantic sowing.
Who cares if Lyova[30] is bawling in Tsarskoe,
Nikolai Gumilyov has
His leg raised high.

3.
Akhmatova peers at everyone
With a sad and beckoning gaze.

Her sweetsmelling fur
Was real muskrat.[31]
She looks into the eyes of the silent guests.
. . . .
. . . .
4.
. . . Mandelstam, Joseph
After taking his seat in the Acmeist landau...

Osip Emilyevich's letters to Vyacheslav Ivanov were found recently.[32] They are letters written by a participant in the ProAcademy (the Tower).[33] This is the Symbolist Mandelstam. Ivanov's replies have not yet surfaced. The letters were written by an eighteen-year-old boy, but you would swear that their author was forty. There are a great number of poems. They are good, but lack what we call Mandelstam.[34]

The memoirs of Adelaide Gertsyk's sister maintain that Ivanov didn't acknowledge us.[35] In 1911 Mandelstam did not hold any pietistic reverence for Vyacheslav Ivanov.[36] The Poets' Guild was boycotting the Academy of Verse. For example:

Vyacheslav, Veslav Ivanov,
Strong of body, like a nut,
Let loose an Academy of sofas,[37]
Like a wheel, on the Guild.

When Ivanov came to Petersburg in 1914, he visited the Sologubs on Razyezzhaya Street. It was an unusually festive evening with a magnificent dinner. Mandelstam came up to me in the drawing room and said: "I think that one maestro is a marvelous sight, but two is a bit ridiculous."[38]

Naturally, we would run into each other everywhere in the 1910s: in editorial offices, at the homes of acquaintances, at *The Hyperborean* on Friday, that is, at Lozinsky's, at The Stray Dog, where Lozinsky, by the way, introduced me to Mayakovsky. Once at the Dog, when everyone was eating loudly and the dishes were clanking, Mayakovsky took it into his head to recite poetry. Osip went over to him and said: "Mayakovsky, stop reciting poems. You're not a Romanian orchestra." I witnessed this in 1912 or 1913. The sharp-witted Mayakovsky was at a loss how to respond and he later told the whole story to Khardzhiev[39] very amusingly. We would likewise meet at the Academy of Poetry (The Society of Zealots of the Artistic Word), where Vyacheslav Ivanov was king, and at the meetings of the Poets' Guild, which was hostile to the Academy. Mandelstam very soon became concertmaster at the Guild. It was then that he wrote the enigmatic (and not very successful) poem "A black angel in the snow."[40] Nadya claims that it refers to me.

The story of this black angel is rather complicated, I think. For the Mandelstam of that period it was a weak and incomprehensible poem. It seems that it was never published. Apparently it was prompted by conversations with Vladimir Shileiko, who had said something like that about me. But Osip did not then "know how" (his expression) to write poems "to a woman and about a woman." "The black angel" is probably his first attempt, which explains its closeness to my lines:

> The wings of black angels are sharp,
> But the Last Judgment will soon come,
> And raspberry-colored bonfires
> Will grow like roses in the snow.[41]

Mandelstam never read "Like a black angel" to me. We know that conversations with Shileiko inspired his poem "The Egyptian."[42]

Gumilyov had a deep appreciation for Mandelstam's poetry very early.[43] They became acquainted in Paris. (See the end of Osip's poem about Gumilyov, where he's described as being powdered and wearing a top hat: "But an Acmeist in Peter is dearer to me / Than a romantic Pierrot in Paris.")

The Symbolists never accepted him.

Osip used to come to Tsarskoe, too. I was his confidante several times when he fell in love, which was fairly often. As far as I remember his first love was Anna Mikhailovna Zelmanova-Chudovskaya, a great beauty and an artist. She painted him on Alexeyevsky Street on a blue background with his head thrown back (1914?). He didn't write any poems for her and complained bitterly to me that he didn't yet know how to write love poetry. His second love was Tsvetaeva, the addressee of his Crimean and Moscow poems. The third was Salomea Andronikova (née Andreyeva, now Halpern), whom Mandelstam immortalized in *Tristia*: "When Solominka, you lie awake in your huge bedroom."[44] I remember Salomea's magnificent bedroom on Vasilyevsky Island.

Osip really did travel to Warsaw and was shocked by the ghetto there (Mikhail Zenkevich remembers this as well), but even Nadya has never heard anything about the attempted suicide that Georgy Ivanov reports, nor about a daughter named Lipochka, whom she supposedly gave birth to.

In the early years after the Revolution (1920), when I was living in total solitude and didn't even meet with Mandelstam, he for a time he was in love with Olga Arbenina,[45] an actress at the Alexandrinsky Theater, later the wife of Yury Yurkin,[46] and he wrote poems to her: "I could not keep your hands in my own," etc.).[47] The manuscripts were supposedly lost in the blockade, but I recently saw them at X.'s.

Many years later Mandelstam would call all these prerevolutionary ladies (me included, I'm afraid) "gentle European women":

> and from those days' beautiful women, gentle European women,
> what anguish I consumed, what torment![48]

There are marvelous poems addressed to Olga Vaksel and to her shade: "In a cold Stockholm bed" and also "If you wish, I'll take off my felt boots."[49]

In 1933-34 Osip was briefly, wildly, and unrequitedly in love with Maria Sergeyevna Petrovykh.[50] He dedicated, or rather addressed, to her what in my opinion is the best love poem of the twentieth century, "The Turkish Woman" (my title)—"Seamstress of bewitching glances."[51] Maria Sergeyevna says there was one other absolutely magical poem about the color white. The manuscript has apparently been lost. Maria Sergeyevna knows several lines by heart.

I hope it is unnecessary to say that this Don Juan list does not represent a catalogue of the women with whom Mandelstam was intimate.

The lady who "glanced over her shoulder" was known as Byaka (Vera Arturovna), then the wife of Sergei Sudeikin and now married to Igor Stravinsky.[52]

In Voronezh Osip was friendly with Natasha Shtempel.[53]

There is no basis for the legend that he was infatuated with Anna Radlova.[54]

> The commander entered the iconostasis...
> In the still of night it smelled of Valerian[55] drops

The commander asks me
Why do you have braids?...
And shining satin shoulders?...

This is a parody of Radlova's poem, which Osip wrote as a playful tease, but not *par dépit* [out of annoyance]. At someone's house he whispered to me in feigned horror: "The commander has arrived!" That is, someone had told Radlova about his poem.

The 1910s are a very important period in Mandelstam's development as a writer, and there's still a lot to be considered and written about this. (Villon, Chaadayev, Catholicism....[56]) See Zenkevich's memoirs about Mandelstam's connection with the Hylea[57] group.

Mandelstam rather diligently attended the meetings of the Poets' Guild, but during the winter of 1913-14 (after the rout on Acmeism) we began to think of the Guild as a burden and even submitted a petition to Gumilyov and Gorodetsky[58] to have it shut down. Osip and I wrote it. Gorodetsky passed a resolution: "Hang everyone and imprison Akhmatova. Malaya Street, No. 63." This took place in the editorial offices of *Northern Flowers.*

A souvenir of Mandelstam's visit to Petersburg in 1920, in addition to his amazing poems to Olga Arbenina, are the lively posters of the period (faded, like Napoleonic banners) announcing evenings of poetry, where the name of Mandelstam stands alongside Nikolai Gumilyov and Alexander Blok. The old Petersburg signboards were still all in place, but behind them there was nothing but dust, darkness, and yawning emptiness. Typhus, hunger, execution by firing squad, dark apartments, damp wood, and people swollen beyond recognition. You could pick a large bouquet of wildflowers in Gostiny Dvor. The famous Petersburg wooden pavement was rotting. The smell of chocolate still wafted from the basement windows of Kraft. All the cemeteries had been pillaged. The city had not just changed, it had turned into its exact opposite. But people still loved poetry (mainly the young people) almost the same way as they do now, that is, in 1964.

In Tsarskoe Selo, renamed Detskoe Selo by then, almost everyone kept goats, and for some reason almost all of them were named Tamara.

Tsarskoe Selo in the 1920s was something unimaginable. All the fences had been burned. Rusty beds from World War I field hospitals stood over the open drains of water pipes, the streets were overgrown with grass, roosters of all colors wandered around crowing... The gates of Count Stenbock-Fermor's house, which not long before had been noted for its magnificence, sported an enormous sign: Mating Center. But in autumn the oaks on Broad Street, witnesses to my childhood, still smelled as tart as ever, and the crows on the cathedral's crosses cawed the same way they had when I listened to them on my way to school through Cathedral Square, and the statues in the parks looked exactly as they had in the teens. I would sometimes recognize residents of Tsarskoe Selo in the tattered and frightening figures. The arcade was closed.

> All the stone protractors and lyres...

It always seemed to me that Pushkin wrote that about Tsarskoe Selo. And the even more startling line: "Into the darkness of some-one else's garden"—the most daring line I've ever read or heard (although, "the sacred twilight" isn't bad either).

A Sketch from Nature

THIS IS THE STORY about the poem "Half-turned...."[59] In January 1914 Pronin[60] organized a big event at The Stray Dog, not in the usual basement location, but in a large hall on Konyushennaya Street. The habitués became lost among the crowds of "aliens" (that is, alien to any art whatsoever). It was hot, crowded, noisy and pretty pointless. We (twenty or thirty of us) finally grew tired of it and went to The Dog on Mikhailovsky Square, where it was dark and cool. I was standing on the stage talking to someone. Several people in the audience asked me to recite some poems. And I recited something without changing my pose. Osip came up to me and said: "I can't get over how you read, how you just stood there!" and something about my shawl. (Read about Mandelstam in Valeria Sreznevskaya's memoirs.[61]) A similar sketch from nature is the quatrain "The facial features are distorted." Mandelstam and I were at Tsarskoe Selo Station in the 1910s. He watched me talking on the telephone through the glass of the telephone booth. When I came out he recited those four lines to me.

About the Poets' Guild

THE POETS' GUILD HELD meetings from November 1911 to April 1912 (that is, until we departed for Italy), approximately fifteen meetings (three a month). From October 1912 to April 1913, approximately ten meetings (two a month). (Not bad material for a *Works and Days*, which it seems no one is working on.) It was I (the secretary?!) who sent the notices; Lozinsky had made me a list of addresses of the membership (I gave it to the Japanese Narumi in the 1930s). Each notice had a lyre on it. The same lyre is on the cover of my *Evening*, Zenkevich's *Wild Porphyry*, and Yelizaveta Kuzmina-Karavayeva's *Scythian Potsherds*.

The Poets' Guild (1911-14)

GUMILYOV AND GORODETSKY WERE the founders; Dmitri Kuzmin-Karavayev, the scrivener; Anna Akhmatova, secretary; Osip Mandelstam, Vladimir Narbut, M. Zenkevich, N. Bruni, G. Ivanov, Adamovich, Vasily Gippius, M. Moravskaya, Yelizaveta Kuzmina-Karavayeva, Chernyavsky, M. Lozinsky, the members.[62] The first meeting was held at the Gorodetskys on the Fontanka. Blok and some Frenchmen were there.... The second meeting was at Liza's place on Manège Square, and later we met at our place in Tsarskoe Selo (Malaya, 63), at Lozinsky's on Vasilyevsky Island, and at Bruni's in the Academy of Arts. Acmeism was resolved upon at our place in Tsarskoe Selo.

II

MANDELSTAM GREETED THE REVOLUTION as a fully-formed and well-known poet, albeit in a limited circle.

He was totally absorbed by the events taking place.

Mandelstam was one of the first to write poems on civic themes. The Revolution was a tremendous event for him, and the word "the people" *(narod)* appears in his poetry for a reason.

Mandelstam and I met particularly often in 1917-18, when I was living on Vyborg Side at the Sreznevskys (Botkinskaya Street, 9), not in the mental hospital but in the apartment of the head physician, Vyacheslav Sreznevsky, the husband of my friend Valeria.

Mandelstam would often come to take me out for rides in a horse-drawn cab past the incredible potholes of the revolutionary winter, amidst the celebrated bonfires that burned almost until May, and we would listen to the gunfire wafting from who knows where. That's how we would drive to readings at the Academy of Arts, where they held benefits for the wounded and where we both read several times. Osip was also with me at Butomo Nazareva's concert at the Conservatory when she sang Schubert ("They sang Schubert to us...").[63]

All the poems Mandelstam addressed to me date from this period: "I did not seek in blossoming moments" (December 1917). The strange, partially realized prophecy there refers to me:

> Some day in the mad capital,
> At a wild celebration on the shores of the Neva,
> To the strains of a loathsome ball,
> They will rip the kerchief from your lovely head.[64]

"Your marvelous pronunciation..."[65]

In addition, at different times he wrote four quatrains to me:

(1) "You want to be toylike" (1911).
(2) "Facial features are distorted" (1910s).
(3) "Bees grow accustomed to their keeper" (1930s).
(4) "Our friendship is in decline" (1930s).

After some hesitation, I have decided to record here the fact that I had to explain to Osip that we shouldn't be meeting so often, because it could give people ground for misconstruing the nature of our relationship.[66] After I did this, roughly in March, Mandelstam disappeared. However, at the time everything was so chaotic and amorphous—people were disappearing, some forever, and everyone for some reason felt that he was on the periphery (of course not in the present-day meaning of the word)— and there was no center (Lozinsky's observation), so Osip's disappearance did not surprise me.

Osip Mandelstam at Zachatyevsky Lane.[67]

***

In Moscow Mandelstam became a regular contributor to *The Banner of Labor*. His mysterious poem "Telephone" probably dates to this period.

Telephone

On this wild terrible earth
You, friend of midnight funerals,
In the high severe office
Of the suicide—the telephone!

Black eyes of asphalt
Dug up by hooves in rage,
And soon will come the sun: soon
The insane rooster will crow.

But there is the oaken Valhalla
And the old feasting dream;
Fate had ordered, the night had decided,
When the telephone awoke.

The heavy curtains drank in all the air,
It was dark on the theatrical square.
A ring—and spheres began to whirl:
Suicide was resolved.

Where to run from hollow life,
From this stony life to go?
Silence, damned casket!
On the sea bottom flowers: Forgive me!

And only a voice, a voice—a bird
Flies to the feasting dream.
You—are deliverance and summer lightning
Of suicide—the telephone![68]

Moscow. June 1918.

I saw Mandelstam again in passing in Moscow in 1918. In 1920 he visited me once or twice on Sergiyevsky Street (in

Petersburg), when I was working in the library of the Institute of Agronomy and was living there. (I had a government apartment in Prince Volkonsky's mansion). That was when I learned that he had been arrested by the Whites in the Crimea and by the Mensheviks in Tiflis. In 1920 Mandelstam visited me on Sergiyevsky to tell me about Nikolai Nedobrovo's death in Yalta in December 1919. He had learned of this tragedy from Voloshin when he was in Koktebel. *Nobody* has *ever* been able to tell me any more details. That was what it was like then!

In the summer of 1924 Osip Mandelstam brought his young wife to meet me (Fontanka, 2). Nadyusha was what the French call *laide mais charmante* [homely but charming]. My friendship with Nadyusha began then and continues to this day.

Osip's love for Nadya was extraordinary and unbelievable. When she had her appendix taken out in Kiev, he didn't leave the hospital, but stayed the whole time in the hospital porter's room. He wouldn't let her out of his sight, didn't let her work, was insanely jealous, and asked her advice on every word in his poems. In general, I have never seen anything like it in my life. The letters that have survived from Mandelstam to his wife fully confirm my impression.[69]

In 1925 the Mandelstams and I lived in the same wing in Zaitsev's boarding house in Tsarskoe Selo. Both Nadya and I were very ill. We stayed in bed, took our temperatures, which were always high, and for that reason, it seems, we never took a stroll in the nearby park. Osip went to Leningrad every day, trying to find work and somehow get some money. There he read me in complete secrecy his poems to Olga Vaksel, which I memorized and secretly wrote down ("If you wish, I'll take off my felt boots").[70] It was there that he dictated to me his memoir of Gumilyov.

The Mandelstams spent one winter in Tsarskoe Selo in the Lycée building (because of Nadya's health). I visited them several times—I came to ski. They wanted to live in the semicircle of the Great Palace, but the stoves smoked and the roofs leaked. That's how they ended up at the Lycée. Osip didn't like living there. He fiercely hated the so-called Tsarskoe Selo lispers, Gollerbakh and Rozhdestvensky, and the way they cheapened Pushkin's name.

Mandelstam had a strange, almost frightening, attitude towards Pushkin, in which I sensed a crown of superhuman chastity. He strongly disliked any "Pushkinism." Neither Nadya nor I knew that the line "The sun of yesterday is borne on a black stretcher" referred to Pushkin, and it didn't become clear until we read the drafts in the 1950s.[71] He picked up "Pushkin's Last Tale" from my desk, my article about *The Golden Cockerel*, and said: "It's just like a game of chess."

> The sun of Alexander shone
> One hundred years ago, it shone on all (December 1917).[72]

This, of course, is also Pushkin. (That is how he conveys my words.)

In general, there is not and should never be a study of "Mandelstam and Tsarskoe Selo." It was not his element.

I visited the Mandelstams in the Chinese Village one summer when they were staying with the Lifshitses. There was absolutely no furniture in their rooms and there were gaping holes in the rotted floors. Osip was not at all interested that Zhukovsky and Karamzin had once lived there. I am sure that he purposely would say, when he would ask me to go out with them for cigarettes or sugar: "Let's go to the European part of the city," as if this were Bakhchisarai or something equally exotic. There was the same pronounced disinterest in his line "The Uhlans smile there." From the very beginning there had never been Uhlans in Tsarskoe Selo, but there were Hussars, yellow cuirassiers, and a convoy.[73]

In 1928 the Mandelstams were in the Crimea. This is Osip's letter, dated August 25th (the day of Gumilyov's death):

> Dear Anna Andreyevna,
> Pavel Luknitsky[74] and I are writing you from Yalta, where the three of us are leading the harsh life of labor.
> We would like to be home and see you. You should know that I am able to conduct an imaginary conversation with only two people—Nikolai Stepanovich [Gumilyov] and you. My talks with Kolya have not been interrupted and never will be.[75]
> We'll be back in Petersburg for a short time in October. Nadya is forbidden to spend the winter there. We were selfish and convinced P.N. [Luknitsky] to stay in Yalta. Write to us.
> Yours,
> O. Mandelstam.

He needed the South and the sea almost as much as he needed Nadya.

> Oh, give me an inch, a needle's
> eyeful of blue sea.[76]

His attempts to secure employment in Leningrad were unsuccessful. Nadya didn't like anything connected with the city and was always drawn to Moscow, which was where her favorite brother Yevgeny lived. Osip thought that people knew and appreciated him in Moscow, but in fact the opposite was the case. There is one particularly striking detail in his biography. At the time (1933), when Osip was greeted in Leningrad as a great poet, a *persona grata*, etc., and all of literary Leningrad went to pay its respects to him at the Yevropeiskaya Hotel (Tynyanov, Eikhenbaum, Gukovsky)[77] and his arrival and readings were real events, which people recalled for many years and still remember even now (1962),[78] no one cared to know about him in Moscow, and except for two or three young natural scientists, he had no friends there. (His acquaintance with Bely took place in Koktebel.[79]) Pasternak was somewhat hesitant and avoided him, caring only about his Georgians and their "beautiful wives." The leaders in the Union of Writers conducted themselves with suspicious restraint.[80]

Among contemporary writers Mandelstam held Babel and Zoshchenko in high esteem. Mikhail Mikhailovich [Zoshchenko] knew this and was very proud of it. For some reason Mandelstam hated Leonov most of all.[81]

Someone reported that N. Ch.[ukovsky?] had written a novel. Osip didn't believe it. He said that for a novel one needs at least a term of hard labor like Dostoevsky's or the estate of a Tolstoy. In Leningrad in the 1930s Mandelstam ran into Fedin in some editorial office and said to him, "Your novel (*The Rape of Europe*) is Dutch cocoa on a rubber sole, and the rubber is Soviet." (He told the story the same day it happened.[82])

In the fall of 1933 Mandelstam finally received an apartment (which he immortalized in verse), two rooms, a fifth-floor walk-up (no gas stove or tub) on Nashchokin Lane ("The apartment is as quiet as paper"). It seemed his wandering life had come to an end. There for the first time Osip had books, mainly old editions of Italian poets (Dante, Petrarch).

In actual fact nothing had ended. He constantly had to be phoning somewhere, waiting for something, hoping for something. And nothing ever worked out. Osip was an enemy of verse translation. At Nashchokin I witnessed him tell Pasternak: "Your complete collected works will be comprised of twelve volumes of translation and one of your own poetry." Mandelstam knew that translation saps a poet's creative energies, and it was almost impossible to force him to translate. A lot of people started to come around, but it was often quite hard to figure out what they were about, and almost all of them were superfluous.

Though the times were relatively vegetarian, the shadow of misfortune and doom hovered over that house. Once we were walking down Prechistenka (February 1934); I don't remember what we were talking about. We turned onto Gogol Boulevard and Osip said, "I'm ready for death." Twenty-eight years have gone by and I recall that moment every time I pass that spot.

I didn't see Osip and Nadya for quite a long time. In 1933 somebody invited the Mandelstams to Leningrad[83] and they stayed at the Yevropeyskaya Hotel. Osip had two public readings. He had just learned Italian, raved about Dante, and would recite entire pages from memory.[84] We began talking about *The Purgatory* and I quoted a section from Canto XXX (the appearance of Beatrice):

> a lady came in view: an olive crown
>> wreathed her immaculate veil, her cloak was green,
>> the colors of live flame played on her gown.

> My soul—such years had passed since last it saw
>> that lady and stood trembling in her presence,
>> stupefied by the power of holy awe—[85]

(I'm quoting from memory.)

Osip burst into tears. I became frightened: "What's wrong?" "No, nothing. To hear those words and in your voice." It's not my place to reminisce about this. Nadya can if she wants to.[86]

Osip recited to me from memory parts of Nikolai Klyuyev's poem "The Blasphemers of Art," the cause of poor Nikolai Alexeyevich's death.[87]

When I said something disparaging about Yesenin, Osip objected that he could forgive Yesenin absolutely everything for the line, "I did not shoot the wretched in dungeons."

In a word, there was nothing for them to live on—some semi-translations, semi-reviews, semi-promises. His pension was

barely enough to pay for the apartment and his ration. By this
time Mandelstam's physical appearance had changed drasti-
cally. He had put on weight, turned gray, and had trouble
breathing. He looked like an old man (he was forty-two years
old), but his eyes sparkled as before. His poetry got better and
better, and his prose did too.

A few days ago I was reading *The Noise of Time* (I hadn't
opened the book since 1928) and I made an unexpected discovery. In addition to his sublime and original poetic achievements,
he also managed to be the last chronicler of Petersburg. He is
precise, lucid, objective, and unique. In his book those streets,
half-forgotten and much maligned, come to life in all their fresh-
ness of the 1890s and 1900s. They'll say that he wrote it five
whole years after the Revolution, in 1923, that he was out of
touch with the times, but absence is the best cure for forgetting
(I'll explain later). The best way to forget something forever is to
see it every day. (That's how I forgot the House on the Fontanka,
where I lived for thirty-five years.) But his theater and
Komissarzhevskaya, about whom he doesn't say the final word:
she's the Queen of the Moderne; and Savina, a lady exhausted
from shopping at Gostiny Dvor; and the smells of Pavlovsk
Station, which will pursue me all my days. And the martial capital in all its splendor seen through the shining eyes of a five-year-
old boy, and the feeling of Judaic chaos, and the bewilderment
the boy feels with the man in the cap (at the table)....[88]

Sometimes this prose reads like a commentary to his poetry,
but Mandelstam never presents himself as a poet, and if you
didn't know his poetry, you'd never guess that this was a poet's
prose. Everything he wrote about in *The Noise of Time* lay very
deep within him. He never spoke about it and was a bit put off
by the *World of Art* infatuation with old (and not so old) Petersburg.

Moreover, the details about the political demonstrations that
took place near the Kazan Cathedral are interesting in that they
testify to his very keen interest in these events and force us to recall what Osip himself prepared for the book *Writers of the Soviet
Epoch* (quote).[89]

This prose, so unprecedented and forgotten, is only now beginning to find its reader. Yet, on the other hand, I constantly
hear, mainly from young people who are crazy about it, that
there has never been prose like this in all of the twentieth century. (The so-called *Fourth Prose*.[90])

I remember very well one of the conversations we had about poetry then. Osip, who very painfully endured what is now called the "personality cult," said to me: "Poetry must be civic now," and he recited "Our lives no longer feel ground under them."[91] It was roughly at the same time that he came up with the theory of "introducing words to each other."[92] Much later he claimed that poetry is written *only* as a result of strong shocks, which could be joyful or tragic. About his poem praising Stalin, where he says, "I feel like saying not Stalin, but Djugashvili" (1935?),[93] he said to me: "I now understand that I was ill when I wrote it."

When I read Osip my poem "It was dawn when they took you. I followed" (1935),[94] he said: "Thank you." That poem is from *Requiem* and refers to the arrest of Nikolai Punin in 1935.[95]

Mandelstam rightfully took the last lines in the poem "A Little Geography" to refer to him:

> This city, celebrated by the first poet,
> By us sinners and by you.[96]

On May 13, 1934 he was arrested. On the same day, after a torrent of telegrams and phone calls, I left Leningrad (where shortly before he had had his confrontation with Alexei Tolstoy) for the Mandelstams. We were all so poor then that I took with me to sell for the return ticket my Order of the Monkey Chamber Charter,[97] the last one Remizov awarded in Russia (it was delivered to me after Remizov fled in 1921), and the statuette by Danko (my portrait, 1924).[98] (S. Tolstaya bought them for the Writers' Union Museum.)

Yagoda himself had signed the order for Mandelstam's arrest. The search of the apartment lasted all night. They looked for poems, they walked on manuscripts that had been thrown out onto the floor from the small suitcase. We all sat in one room. It was very quiet. You could hear someone playing a ukulele next door at Kirsanov's.[99] An investigator unearthed "Wolf" in my presence ("For the sake of the future's trumpeting heroics") and showed it to Osip.[100] He nodded silently. He kissed me as he was leaving. They took him away at 7:00 a.m. It was completely light outside. Nadya set off for her brother's and I went to the Chulkovs on Smolensk Boulevard, No. 8, and we agreed to meet somewhere. We returned home together, cleaned up the apartment, and sat down to breakfast. Again there was a knock on the door, it was them again, another search. Yevgeny Khazin said: "If they come again they'll take you with them." Pasternak, whom I had visited that same day, went to see Bukharin at the *Izvestiya* offices to petition on Mandelstam's behalf; I went to the Kremlin to see Yenukhidze. (At the time it took practically a miracle to get into the Kremlin. Ruslanov, an actor at the Vakhtangov Theater, arranged it for me through Yenukhidze's secretary.) Yenukhidze was polite enough, but immediately asked: "Maybe there were some poems?" Through these efforts we accelerated and probably mitigated the outcome. The sentence was three years in Cherdyn, where Osip jumped out of a hospital window and broke his arm, because he thought they were coming for him (see "Stanzas," stanza 4). Nadya sent a telegram to the Central Committee. Stalin ordered a review of Mandelstam's case and permitted him to choose another place of exile. It was then that he telephoned Pasternak.[101] The rest has all been told too many times.

Pasternak and I were together at Usiyevich's, where we found the bosses of the Writers' Union and a lot of the Marxist young people of the time. I was also at Pilnyak's, where I saw Baltrushaitis, Shpet, and S. Prokofiev.

It was during this period that the former founder of the Poets' Guild, Sergei Gorodetsky, uttered the following immortal phrase in the course of a public appearance somewhere: "These are lines by the Akhmatova who has become a counterrevolutionary." Even *The Literary Gazette* (May 1934),[102] which ran a report on the meeting, softened the orator's actual words.[103]

At the close of his letter to Stalin, Bukharin wrote: "And Pasternak is worried as well." Stalin stated that an order had been issued so that everything would be put right for Mandelstam. Stalin asked Pasternak why he hadn't exerted himself on Mandelstam's behalf, saying, "If my friend were in trouble, I would do everything possible to help him." Pasternak replied that if he hadn't done anything, Stalin would not have found out about the matter. "But why didn't you turn to me or to the writers' organizations?" "The writers' organizations haven't been involved in matters like this since 1927." "But, isn't he your friend?" Pasternak hesitated and after a brief pause Stalin continued his question, "But he's a master, isn't he?" Pasternak answered, "That's beside the point."

Pasternak thought that Stalin was testing whether he knew about the poems and that was his explanation for his shaky answers.

"...Why are we spending all our time talking about Mandelstam? I've wanted to have a chat with you for a long time."

"About what?"

"About life and death." And Stalin hung up.

Nadya never went to Pasternak or ever pleaded with him for anything, as Robert Payne has reported.[104]

The only man to visit Nadya was Perets Markish. Many women came that day. I remember that they were all dressed up and looked lovely in their bright spring dresses: Sima Narbut, as yet untouched by misfortune; the beauty we called "the captive Turkish woman," Zenkevich's wife; and clear-eyed, svelte, and unusually calm Nina Olshevskaya. Nadya and I, yellow and numb, sat in rumpled sweaters. Emma Gershtein and Nadya's brother were with us.[105]

Early in the morning fifteen days later, they called Nadya and suggested that if she wanted to accompany her husband she should be at Kazan Station that evening. It was all over, and Nina Olshevskaya and I went to collect money for the trip. People were generous. Elena Sergeyevna Bulgakov burst into tears and emptied her purse into my hands.

Nadya and I went to the station together. We stopped at the Lubyanka for the documents. It was a bright, clear day. Out of every window loomed the "huge cockroach whiskers" of the man responsible for this "celebration."[106] They didn't bring Osip for a long time. He was in such bad shape that even they couldn't get him to sit in the prison cart. My train (at Leningrad Station) was going to leave, so I didn't wait for him to come. The brothers, Yevgeny Khazin and Alexander Mandelstam, saw me off and returned to Kazan Station, and only then did they bring Osip, though it was forbidden to speak with him. It was very bad that I didn't wait for him and that he didn't see me, because in Cherdyn he began to think that I must certainly have perished. (They traveled in a convoy led by "fine lads from the secret police's iron gates" who were reading Pushkin.[107])

Preparations for the First Congress of the Union of Writers were underway at the time (1934) and they sent me application to fill out. Osip's arrest had affected me so that I couldn't lift a finger to do so. At the congress Bukharin proclaimed Pasternak to be the leading Soviet poet (to the horror of Demyan Bedny),[108] he reprimanded me, and most likely said nothing about Osip.

In February 1936 I visited the Mandelstams in Voronezh and learned all the details of his "case." He described how he had run around Cherdyn in a fit of delirium, looking for my bullet-ridden corpse, how he had talked about this openly with whomever he met; and he thought that the arches honoring the Chelyuskins had been erected to commemorate his arrival.

Pasternak and I went to the Supreme Public Prosecutor to petition on Mandelstam's behalf, but the Terror had already begun and it was pointless.

It's striking that space, breadth, and a deep breathing appeared in Mandelstam's verse precisely in Voronezh, when he was not free at all.

> When I get my breath back, you can hear
> In my voice the earth, my last weapon...[109]

After I returned from the Mandelstams, I wrote my poem "Voronezh." Here is the ending:

> And in the disgraced poet's room
> Fear and the Muse stand guard in turn.
> And there is a night,
> Which knows no dawn. (*The Flight of Time*, 1965)

Osip wrote of himself in Voronezh: "I am an expectant person by nature. That makes it all the harder for me here."

In the 1920s Mandelstam twice attacked my poetry very harshly in the press (*Russian Art*, nos. 1, 2-3). We never discussed this. Nor did he ever speak of how he had praised my poetry, and I read it only recently (the review of the 1916 *Almanac of the Muses* and his "Letter about Russian Poetry," Kharkov, 1922).[110]

In Voronezh they employed not altogether aboveboard tactics to force Osip into giving a lecture about Acmeism. We should not forget what he said in 1937: "I do not disown the living or the dead." Asked to define Acmeism, he answered: "Nostalgia for world culture."

Sergei Rudakov was with Mandelstam in Voronezh, and unfortunately, he turned out to be not as good a person as we thought. He obviously suffered from some sort of delusion of grandeur if he thought that he—and not Osip—was writing the poetry. Rudakov was killed in the war and I don't want to go into details about his conduct in Voronezh. However, everything he says should be taken with great caution.[111]

Everything Georgy Ivanov writes in his cheap memoir *Petersburg Winters*—Ivanov who left Russia in the early 1920s and did not know the mature Mandelstam at all—is shallow, empty, and irrelevant. It's easy enough to write memoirs like that. You don't need memory, or attention to detail, or love, or a feeling for the era. Anything goes, and the undiscerning consumer gratefully accepts it. What's even worse, of course, is that sometimes this makes its way into serious literary scholarship. That is what Leonid Shatsky (Strakhovsky) did with Mandelstam. He has handy two or three volumes of rather "piquant" memoirs— Georgy Ivanov's *Petersburg Winters*, Benedict Lifshits's *One-and-a-half Eyed Archer* and Ilya Ehrenburg's *Portraits of Russian Poets* (1922). Strakhovsky uses these books for all they're worth. His factual material is taken from Kozmin's very early reference book *Contemporary Writers* (Moscow, 1928). Then he takes the poem "Music at the Train Station" from Mandelstam's collection *Poems* (1928), not even the most recent poem in the book, and says that it's the poet's final work.[112] The date of Mandelstam's death is arbitrarily established as 1945 (seven years after the actual date— December 27, 1938). The fact that Mandelstam published in several journals and newspapers, if nothing more than his great cycle "Armenia" in *New World* in 1930 doesn't interest Shatsky at all.[113] He very blithely announces that Mandelstam ceased to write after "Music at the Train Station," that he became a poor translator, went to pieces, and wandered around from tavern to tavern. This is probably based on some word-of-mouth information from some Parisian Georgy Ivanov or other. And instead of the tragic figure of the rarest of poets, who during his Voronezh exile continued to write poems of ineffable beauty and power, we are left with a "city madman," a rogue, a degraded being. And all this is in a book published under the imprint of Harvard University, the best and oldest university in America, which deserves our heartfelt congratulations.[114]

***

An eccentric? Of course, he was. For instance, he threw out a young poet who came to complain that he wasn't getting published. The embarrassed youth descended the stairs, while Osip shouted at him from the upper landing: "Did they publish André Chénier? Or Sappho? Or Jesus Christ?"

To this day Semyon Lipkin and Arseny Tarkovsky readily share their stories of how Mandelstam criticized their early poetry.[115]

Artur Lourié,[116] who knew Mandelstam intimately and wrote a very worthwhile piece about Mandelstam and music, told me in the teens the story of how once he and Mandelstam were walking down Nevsky Prospect and they met an unusually magnificent lady. Osip, never at a loss for words, remarked: "Let's take everything she has and give it to Anna Andreyevna." (The accuracy of this can be verified by Lourié.)

He really disliked it when young women liked my *Rosary*. There's a story about how once he visited the Katayevs and had a pleasant conversation with the lovely mistress of the house. Towards the end of his visit he wanted to test the lady's taste in literature and asked: "Do you like Akhmatova?" To which she naturally replied: "I haven't read him." And Osip flew into a rage, said something rude, and left in a huff. He didn't tell me about this himself.

In the winter of 1933-34, when I was staying with the Mandelstams in Nashchokin Lane, the Bulgakovs invited me to a party (February 1934). Osip got upset: "Do they want to introduce you to the Moscow literary world?!" Although I was trying to calm him down, I unfortunately said: "No, Bulgakov is a pariah himself. There will probably be someone there from the Moscow Art Theater." Then Osip got really angry, ran from room to room and shouted: "How can we save Akhmatova from the Moscow Art Theater?"[117]

Once Nadya brought Osip to meet me at the train station. He had gotten up early, and was cold and out of sorts. When I stepped off the train, he said, "You arrived with the speed of Anna Karenina."

Osip nicknamed the room where I stayed in their apartment the "heathen temple" (it would later be turned into a kitchen). He called his room "Behind Pyast," because Pyast lived in the room in front of it. He called Nadya "Mamanas" (our mama).

Was he an eccentric? But that's hardly the point. Why do memoirists of a certain ilk (Shatsky, E. Mindlin, S. Makovsky, G. Ivanov, Benedict Lifshits) so carefully and lovingly collect and preserve all kinds of gossip and nonsense, which basically presents a philistine view of the poet, instead of bowing their heads before so great and incomparable a phenomenon as the birth of a poet, whose very first poems amaze us with their perfection and which seemingly come forth out of nowhere.

Mandelstam has no teacher. That is something worth thinking about. I don't know a similar case in all of world poetry. We know Pushkin's and Blok's sources, but who can show us the source of this divine new harmony, which we call the poetry of Osip Mandelstam?[118]

***

In May 1937 the Mandelstams returned to Moscow, back "home" to Nashchokin Lane. At the time I was staying with the Ardovs in the same building. Osip was already ill and spent a good deal of time in bed. He read me all his new poems, but he wouldn't let anyone copy them down. He talked a lot about Natasha (Shtempel) with whom he had been friendly in Voronezh. (Two poems are addressed to her: "The buds smell of a viscous vow" and "Falling involuntarily to the empty earth.")

The Terror had been gaining momentum for a year now and was raging all around us. One of the Mandelstams' two rooms was occupied by a man who wrote false denunciations about them and soon they weren't even able to show themselves in the apartment. Osip had failed to get permission to remain in the capital. X. told him, "You are too nervous." There was no work to be had. They would come in from Kalinin and sit on the boulevard. It was probably then that Osip said to Nadya: "One has to know how to change professions. We are beggars now. It's always easier for beggars in summer."

> You're still alive, you're not alone yet—
> she's still beside you, with her empty hands,
> and a joy reaches you both across immense plains
> through mists and hunger and flying snow.[119]

The last poem I heard Osip read was "Through Kiev, through the streets of the monster" (1937).[120] This is the story. The Mandelstams had nowhere to spend the night. I left them at my place (the House on the Fontanka). I made up the couch for Osip. I went out for some reason and when I came back Osip was already falling asleep. But he woke up and recited the poem. I repeated it. He said "Thank you," and fell asleep.

At this time the so-called House of Popular Science was housed in the Sheremetyev mansion. You had to walk through that dubious institution to get to our rooms. Osip asked me with concern: "Isn't there perhaps another 'popular' exit?"

At this time we were both reading read Joyce's *Ulysses*, Osip in a good German translation and I in the original. Several times we were on the verge of discussing *Ulysses*, but we were no longer up to books.

They spent a year that way. Osip was already seriously ill, but kept demanding with inexplicable obstinacy that the Union of Writers organize a reading for him. The date for the reading was even set, but they apparently "forgot" to send out the announcements and nobody came. Osip invited Aseyev by phone. "I'm going to *The Snow Maiden*," he said. And when Osip ran into Selvinsky on the street and asked him for money, Selvinsky gave him three rubles.

I saw Mandelstam for the last time in the fall of 1937. He and Nadya had come to Leningrad for two days. It was an apocalyptic time. Misfortune was at all our heels.[121] They had absolutely nowhere to live. Osip had great difficulty breathing and gasped at the air with his lips. I went to see them, but I don't remember where they were staying. It was all like a terrible dream. Someone who arrived after me said that Osip's father ("Grandpa") didn't have any warm clothing. Osip took off the sweater he was wearing under his jacket, so that it would be given to his father.

My son says that during his interrogation they read Osip's depositions about him and about me and that they were irreproachable. Alas, that can be said of few of our contemporaries.

They arrested him the second time on May 2, 1938 in a rest sanatorium near Cherusti Station (at the height of the Terror).[122] My son at that time had already been imprisoned for two months on Shpalernaya Street (since March 10th). Everyone was talking openly about how they were torturing the prisoners. Nadya came to Leningrad. You could see the fear in her eyes. She said, "I won't rest until I know that he's dead."

Early in 1939 I received a short letter from a woman friend in Moscow which read: "Our friend Lena gave birth to a baby girl, and our friend Nadyusha lost her husband."[123]

Komarovo

P.S. There was only one letter from Osip (to his brother Alexander) from the place (...) where he died.[124] Nadya has the letter. She showed it to me: "Where is my Nadinka?" he wrote, and asked for warm clothing. A parcel was sent. But it was returned, because it didn't reach him while he was still alive.

Vasilisa Shklovskaya was a true friend to Nadya through all those difficult years, as was her daughter Varya.

Now Osip Mandelstam is a great poet, acknowledged by the entire world. Books are written about him—dissertations are defended. It is an honor to have been his friend and a disgrace to have been his enemy. A scholarly edition of his works is in preparation. Unearthing one of his letters is a literary event.

For me he is not only a great poet, but also the person who after learning (probably from Nadya) how bad things were for me at the House on the Fontanka, told me as we were saying goodbye at the Moscow Station in Leningrad: "Annushka (he had never called me that before), always remember that my house is your house." That can only happen right before death....

July 8, 1963. Komarovo

Translated by Anna Lisa Crone and Ronald Meyer

INNOKENTY ANNENSKY

I

WHEREAS BALMONT AND BRYUSOV brought what they had started to a completion themselves (even though they continued to confuse provincial graphomaniacs for a long time), Annensky's work came alive with exceptional vigor in the next generation. And if he had not died so early, he would have seen his cloudbursts pour down onto the pages of Pasternak's books, his half-*zaum* "Dedu Lidu ladili"[1] in Khlebnikov, his *rayoshnik*[2] ("Balloons") appear in Mayakovsky, and so on. I don't mean to imply that they all imitated him. But he traveled so many paths at the same time! He had so much that was new in him that all innovators seemed related to him....

Boris Leonidovich Pasternak... affirmed categorically that Annensky played a large role in his work....

Osip and I spoke about Annensky several times. He also spoke of Annensky with true piety.

I don't know whether Marina Tsvetaeva knew Annensky.

There is love and admiration for his Teacher in both Gumilyov's poetry and prose.

II

In recent times Innokenty Annensky's poetry has begun to resound especially strongly. I find this completely natural. Let us recall that Alexander Blok, citing lines from *Quiet Songs*, wrote to the author of *The Cypress Chest*: "This will be in my memory forever. Part of my soul has remained in this."[3] I am convinced that Annensky should assume a place of honor in our poetry alongside Baratynsky, Tyutchev, and Fet.

...It is not because they imitated him that Annensky is the teacher of Pasternak, Mayakovsky, and Gumilyov—no... these poets were already "contained" in Annensky. Let us recall, for instance, Annensky's poem from "Sideshow Trefoil":

> Buy my balloons, kind sirs!
> Hey, fox fur coat, if you have some to spare,
> Don't begrudge five little kopecks:
> I'll let them go right up to the sky—
> Two hours later, get an eyeful, with both your eyes![4]

Compare "Children's Balloons" with the verse of the young Mayakovsky, with his declamations in "Satyricon" that are filled with a lexicon that is markedly that of the common people.

If an inexperienced reader comes across:

> Chatterbox-bells
> Chatterbox-bells
> Clanked and clashed,
> The further, the more...
> Clanked and clashed,
> Chatterbox-bells.
> Tin bells flew past,
> Added their jabber,
> Clattered, babbled,
> Clattered, blabbered,
> Quit their chatter.[5]

he will think this is Velimir Khlebnikov's poetry. In the meantime I read Annensky's "Sleigh Bells." We shall not be mistaken if we say that in "Sleigh Bells" was cast the seed from which Khlebnikov's sonorous poetry later grew. The lavish Pasternakian cloudbursts already pour down on the pages of *The Cypress Chest*. The sources of Nikolai Gumilyov's poetry are not in the poems of the French Parnassians, as is usually thought, but in Annensky. I find my own "origin" in Annensky's poems. His work, in my view, is marked by a tragic element, by sincerity, and artistic integrity.

Translated by Mary Ann Szporluk

NIKOLAI GUMILYOV
(A Poet Still Unread)

November 6, 1962. Moscow.

I. The two acrostics of 1911.[1] The same thing in Adam's dream about Eve.[2] She is split in two. But always alien. That is part of the general scheme, but already has reference to Akhmatova. A constant struggle. Compare *Pearls*. (Quotations.)

II. The dedication of "Rusalka." The autograph.[3]

III. He burned the manuscript of the play *King Batinvol's Jester* at Schmidt's dacha, because I did not want to listen to it.

IV. The subject of Gumilyov and the Tsarskoe Selo group (Rozhdestvensky, Otsup, etc.).[4]

V. Late reminiscences ("Ezbekieyeh" and "Memory").[5]

VI. My first letter to Paris.

> What is this—again a threat
> Or a plea for mercy?[6]

VII. The deaf-and-dumb are not demons,[7] but literary scholars; they do not understand at all what they are reading and see Parnassus and Leconte de Lisle,[8] when a poet is pouring out his life's blood (Vyacheslav Ivanov and Bryusov).[9] I agree that it is difficult in the "Giants' Palace"[10] to make out the Tsarskoe Selo tower from which we (Kolya[11] and I) watched the cuirassier's chestnut steed kick, and how the horseman skillfully calmed him; that you do not immediately detect the yellow water lilies in the pond situated between Tsarskoe Selo and Pavlovsk in the *nénuphar* of "The Lakes,"[12] that only when speaking of Annensky does Gumilyov, by this time an Acmeist poet, dare to utter the name of his own city, which he thought seemed too prosaic and ordinary for poetry (see *The Path of the Conquistadors* and *Romantic*

Flowers), but this feeling, the tragedy of love, permeates all of Gumilyov's early poetry. The heroine, like the landscape, is encoded—it could not have been any other way. This is her first portrait:

> That wife who was always sad
> Had eyes that shone in twilight.[13]

And later on:

> And the essence is robed in the sun,
> This magnificent sacred object...

And it is she who is the maiden's corpse in the singer's song, and it is she who refuses to follow the magician, and "The Devil's Betrothed" is the one who is given the magic ring—"for the flickering radiance of her dishevelled braids." It is she whom he promises to take to the summit and show the world's grandeur ("You, for whom I gathered in the East..."). And the dishevelled twilight hair ("Anna Comnenus")[14] is terrifying. And she is the Rusalka of *The Path of the Conquistadors* ("The rusalka has an enchanting glance/The rusalka has *sad eyes*..." Cf. "Anna Comnenus": "But the *eyes* are *doleful*/Like a grave at twilight...").

In 1910 he brought me "Ballad" as a present:[15]

> To you, my friend, I give this song,
> I always believed in your steps,
> When you, soothing and chastising, led the way.

(Cf. the poem "She": "to study the radiant pain."[16])

The terrifying poems in *Foreign Skies* belong to the next period: "And melting in your eyes..." (which he sent me on the way to Africa)...

Later "The Tightrope Walker," "Margarita," "The Poisoner."[17]

In the beginning he was only healing his soul with travel and later he became a true traveler (1913). Everything (the good and the bad) arose from this feeling—both travel and his Don Juanism. In 1916, when I was regretting that everything had turned out so strangely, he said, "No, you taught me to believe in God and to love Russia."

***

Gumilyov

(1) The autograph of "Rusalka" (1904).

(2) Why it is not mentioned that the Paris edition of *Romantic Flowers* was dedicated to me (a quotation from the letter to Bryusov). This same dedication was repeated in *Pearls* (1910).

(3) Why regret the absence of memoirs by enemies (Voloshin, Kuzmin) and not ones by friends (Lozinsky, Zenkevich...).[18]

(4) How can one dignify or allow the petty and cretin A. A. Gumilyova even to approach the sacred shade [of Gumilyov]; she remembers nothing either about N. Gumilyov, or even about her own husband. The only person in the Gumilyov family who was close to N.S. [Gumilyov] was his mother. He never spoke of his father at all, and openly laughed at Mitya, and just as openly despised him. [...][19]

(5) About the joys of earthly love (dedicated to me).[20]

(6) Why have all of N.S.'s trips from Paris and Petersburg to see me (Kiev, Sevastopol, Schmidt's dacha, Lustdorf) been left out?

(7) Why have the following people been left out: Tanya Adamovich (1914-16), Larisa Reisner (1916-17), Arbenina (1920), etc.?[21]

But there is no reason to be surprised when this lively band has succeeded in excising even me from N.S.'s biography. In this instance, I feel sorry for Gumilyov as a poet. All his early work turns out to be a Parisian fabrication ("one is struck by the lack of individuality," and so forth. And this is seriously quoted by a supposedly genuine biographer in 1962).[22] But these poems are vital and terrifying, it is from them that a great and splendid poet arose. The *terrifying* and burning love of those years is made out to be Leconte de Lisleism (see the reviews of Gumilyov by Bryusov and Ivanov) and half a century later a biographer presents this as an indisputable fact. Is it really possible that the entire history of literature is fashioned this way?

(5)[23] I did not take part in any circus performances (1911-12; Gumilyov was in Africa during the summer of 1913), I did not ride a horse (I was carrying my child to term in 1912), but while everybody in Podobino or Dubrovok was lying about in the hayloft, maybe I demonstrated my litheness once or twice. Vera Nevedomskaya[24] apparently had a rather protracted flirtation with N.S., I remember that I found her letter to Kolya which did not leave much to the imagination, but even then that was so uninteresting that it's simply not worth remembering.

(6) *He did not know how to ride a horse.* Of course, he did not know how to ride a horse in 1911-12, but, nevertheless, he apparently learned to do so while in the reserves of the Uhlan regiment in the fall of 1914 (in the village of Navoloki, near Novgorod), since he spent almost all of World War I in the saddle and at night in his sleep would shout: "Mount your horses!" He evidently was dreaming about night alerts, and he was awarded a second Order of St. George for something accomplished on horseback....

***

Why have I never read anywhere that I asked for a divorce when N. S. returned from abroad in 1918 and I had already promised V. K. Shileiko[25] that I would be with him. (I told M. A. Zenkevich about this on Sergievsky St., No. 7. See his 1921 novel.)[26]

Why hasn't it occurred to these supposed scholars to mention the rather noteworthy fact, in my opinion, that there is no trace of Gumilyov's influence on my poetry, despite the fact that we were so involved, and that Acmeism as a whole grew out of his observations based on my poetry of those years as well as Mandelstam's poetry. Georgy Ivanov even takes the liberty of inventing Gumilyov's own words on this subject *(Petersburg Winters).*[27]

It is true that N. S. did not like my early poetry. What was there to like! But when he returned from Addis Ababa on March 25, 1911, and I read him what subsequently would be called *Evening,* he immediately said, "You are a poet, you need to make a book." And if he had had any doubts about that, would he really have allowed me to become an Acmeist? You simply do not understand Gumilyov at all to entertain that idea for a second. But that's how it is. Approximately half of this worthy gang (Struve...) honestly cannot imagine what Gumilyov was really like; others, like Vera Nevedomskaya, adopt an idiotic and patronizing tone when they speak about Gumilyov; a third group consciously and deftly distort (Georgy Ivanov). [...] And, taken together all this is probably known as fame. And wasn't it the same with Pushkin and Lermontov? Gumilyov is still an unread poet. A visionary and a prophet. He foretold his own death in detail, including even the autumn grass. It was he who said: "On heavy and lumbering vehicles..."—and even more terrifying ("The Eagle"), "All *forbidden labors* for the elders...," and, finally, "Land, why do you play with me...."[28]

***

Tsarskoe Selo is ostensibly absent from N.S's poetry. He once used it as the background to his poem "Annensky" ("The last of the Tsarskoe Selo swans." He did not wish to be a Tsarskoe Selo swan himself).[29]

However, that's not quite the case. Even in the poems in *The Path of the Conquistadors* you can glimpse the sketchy outlines of the Tsarskoe Selo landscape and the architecture in the parks (the pavilion in the shape of ancient temples), though they were rendered by a still inexperienced hand. But none of this is named and was supposedly seen by the author in his dreams: isn't it easier to recognize in "the palace of giants"—simply the tower in ruins by the Orlov gates? From that tower we really did watch a golden steed (a cuirassier's) "rear up on its hind legs."

And Gumilyov told me of another reminiscence of Tsarskoe Selo:

> The evening was still. The earth silent,
> The flowerbeds scarcely breathed,
> And from the green canal,
> May bugs soared and flew.[30]

And this is somewhere near The Big Folly, and does not look much like the Gobi Desert.

A third reminiscence is in the poem "The Lakes." I am the "sad girl." It was written during one of our protracted quarrels. N.S. later pointed the place out to me. The *nénuphar*, of course, is a yellow water lily, and there really were willows. For N.S. Tsarskoe Selo was doleful, base prose.

Two photographs of me in Tsarskoe Selo Park (one in winter and one in summer) in the 1920s were taken on the same bench where N.S. first said that he loved me (February...).

***

Margarita

WHEN I WAS YOUNG I had a strange dream in which somebody said to me (true, I don't remember who): "Faust never existed— Margarita made it all up... There was only Mephistopheles..." I do not know why we dream such terrifying dreams, but I told my dream to N.S. He made a poem out of it. He needed the theme of a death caused by a woman—in this case, the sister.[31]

***

Now, as the reader can see, I am not touching upon that special, exceptional relationship, that incomprehensible union, which has nothing to do with being in love or marital relations, where I am called "That Other One" ("And he is like a criminal, stern") who "puts down the staff, smiles and simply says, 'We've arrived.'"[32] The time has truly not yet come for a discussion of this kind of relationship. But a feeling, precisely of this sort, compelled me over the course of several years (1925-30) to devote myself to the collection and organization of materials related to Gumilyov's legacy. This was not done by his friends (Lozinsky), or his widow, or his son when he was grown, or the so-called disciples (Georgy Ivanov). I saw N.S. three times in my dreams in a twenty-four-hour period and he asked me to do this (1924, Kazanskaya, No. 2).

***

I saw X. [Gumilyov] in my dreams three times in a row in 1924. For six years I collected his *Works and Days* and other materials: letters, drafts, memoirs. In general, I've done everything possible to preserve his memory. It is astounding that nobody else took this on. His so-called disciples have behaved disgracefully. Georgy Ivanov's role. Abroad they have all renounced him.[33]

***

May 9 [1963]. Victory Day.

I completed a long and terrifying journey through this poetry, both with a lamp and in complete darkness, with the sureness of a sleepwalker stepping along the very edge. I did not write about this myself at the time or even later (except for two poems—one of which was even published[34]), but one of the seven "Leningrad Elegies"—1921 ("It was dreadful to live in that house") —describes the domestic nighttime fears of the Tsarskoe Selo house.[35]

I know Gumilyov's main themes. And the main thing is his cryptographic writing.

In the latest edition Struve allows him to be torn to shreds by two individuals, one of whom (Bryusov) did not understand him, while the other (V. Ivanov) hated him. People say that he (G. Struve) should be forgiven, because he does not know anything. I, too, do not know a lot of things, but in those instances I avoid publishing material that I do not understand [...].

***

A Poet Still Unread
(Continuation)

August 5, 1963

The inattention of the critics (and the readers) knows no bounds. What do they find in early Gumilyov besides Chad, a giraffe, captains, and other theatrical junk in the same vein?[36] Not one of his themes is analyzed, illuminated or named. What did he live for, where was he going? How did it happen that out of all those things I listed above a great and remarkable poet was formed, the creator of "Memory," "Sixth Sense," "The Streetcar," and similar poems?[37] Remarks like "I only like *The Pillar of Fire*," or attributing the poem "The Worker"[38] to the revolutionary period, etc., drive me to despair, but you hear them every day.

***

[July 1965]

[...] Gumilyov sought refuge in travel not only from an unhappy love (as we saw above), but also from literary failures and disappointments. Unfortunately, even such obvious things are not within the reach of our scholars. But, nevertheless, when you write about poetry you should also study the elementary subtext, and not just stupidly repeat that Gumilyov was Bryusov's pupil and an imitator of Leconte de Lisle and Hérédia.

The fact of the matter is that for Gumilyov both poetry and love were always tragic. That is why "The Magic Violin" develops into *Gondla*.[39] And that is why countless love lyrics end with death (almost all of *Romantic Flowers*), and the war was an epos—Homer—for him. And when he went to prison, he took the *Iliad* with him.

And, in general, more than anything, travel was a drug for all ailments ("Ezbekieyeh," quotation). And still he apparently lost faith in travel (temporarily, of course). He told me countless times about the "golden door" that must open up before him somewhere in the depths of his wanderings, but when he returned in 1913, he confessed that the "golden door" did not exist. That was a terrible blow for him (see "Iambic Pentameters").[40]

[...] It goes without saying that one could make a sizable book out of the two pages that I've written today, but I leave that to others, for example, the authors of dissertations on Gumilyov who are still subsisting on conversations about his apprenticeship with Bryusov and the imitations of Leconte de Lisle and Hérédia. But where have they seen that a poet with such a sorry past should become the author of "Memory," "Sixth Sense," "Streetcar Gone Astray," as well as a very shrewd expert on poetry *(Letters about Russian Poetry)*[41] and an invariable *best-seller*,[42] since his books are more expensive than any other and are the most difficult to obtain. And it's not at all a matter of his being banned—he's hardly alone there.[43]

I am firmly convinced that Gumilyov is a poet who still has not been read and who through some peculiar misunderstanding has remained the author of "Captains" (1909), which he himself, to put it bluntly, hated.

Translated by Ronald Meyer

BORIS PASTERNAK

SECOND BIRTH[1] ENDS THE first period in his lyric poetry. Evidently, that path did not lead any further... A long (ten years) and excruciating intermission ensued, when he really could not write even one line.[2] I witnessed this with my own eyes. I can still hear his dismayed intonation: "What's wrong with me?!" Then came the dacha (Peredelkino), at first a summer one and later one for the whole year. For all practical purposes he left the city forever. His meeting with *Nature* took place there, outside of Moscow. All his life nature was his only legitimate Muse, his secret confidante, his Bride and Beloved, his Wife and Widow—she was for him what Russia was for Blok. He remained true to her to the end and she rewarded him like a queen. The asphyxia was cured. When I arrived in Moscow in June 1941 he said to me over the telephone: "I've written nine poems. I'm coming over right away to read them." And he came. He said: "That's only the beginning—I'll write a lot."

Translated by Ronald Meyer

MARINA TSVETAEVA

I

OUR FIRST AND LAST two-day meeting took place in June 1941 on Bolshaya Ordynka, No. 17, in the Ardovs' apartment (the first day) and on Marina Grove at Nikolai Khardzhiev's (the second and last).[1] It is frightening to think how Marina would have described these meetings herself, if she had remained alive and I had died on August 31, 1941.[2] It would have been a "sweet-smelling legend," as our forefathers put it. Perhaps it would have been the lamentation of a twenty-five-year-old love, which turned out to be in vain, but in any case, it would have been magnificent. Now, when she has returned to her Moscow such a queen and forever (not like the one with whom she was so fond of comparing herself, that is, with a Negro child and a monkey in French dress, that is, *décolleté grande gorge*), I simply wish to remember those *Two Days* "without any legends."

II

In June 1941, when I read Marina Tsvetaeva a part of the poem[3] (the first draft), she rather caustically said: "One has to possess a great deal of courage to write about Harlequins, Columbines, and Pierrot in 1941," evidently assuming that the poem was a *World of Art* stylization in the spirit of Benois and Somov, that is, the old-fashioned rubbish with which she had perhaps struggled in emigration. Time has shown that this is not so.

III

Marina went off into *zaum*.[4] Cf. *The Poem of the Air*.[5] She became cramped within the boundaries of Poetry. She is dolphin-like, as Shakespeare's Cleopatra says of Antony.[6] One element alone was too small for her and she withdrew into another or other ones. Pasternak was the opposite: he returned (in 1941— the Peredelkino cycle) from his Pasternakovian *zaum* to the boundaries of traditional Poetry (if poetry can be traditional). Mandelstam's path was more complicated and mysterious.

1959

Translated by Ronald Meyer

TITSIAN TABIDZE

PAOLO YASHVILI

I BECAME ACQUAINTED WITH Titsian Tabidze and Paolo Yashvili in the early 1930s at Boris Pasternak's.[1] Titsian and Paolo—those two names represented Georgia for us Russian poets then. The two of them often came to Moscow and Leningrad together.

Individual moments of our meetings remain with me: at Boris Pasternak's, at Mikhail Lozinsky's, the well-known poet and translator, at the banquet in 1935 in Moscow, held to celebrate Titsian's birthday. During these meetings there were endless conversations about poetry and literature, and poems and translations were read.

On one of these evenings Paolo Yashvili read his first poem "Nita the Captain," dedicated to Titsian's daughter Tanit Tabidze. I remember the conversation that arose immediately about the little girl's desire to become a navigator on an ocean-liner no matter what.

Titsian Tabidze always read his poems in Georgian. Sometimes he would read them to me and I would try to plumb their depths to better grasp their sound in the poet's language.

We all loved Titsian very much. He was a very warm, sincere person who was devoted to poetry with all his soul and who lived art; moreover, he possessed a rare ability to behave in society. We Leningrad poets, and the nation at large, very bitterly mourned his death.

Through the examples of their lives, work, and tireless activities Titsian Tabidze and Paolo Yashvili nourished friendship between our literatures, between the poets of Georgia and Russia.

Translated by Ronald Meyer

Prose about the Poem

PROSE ABOUT THE POEM

I T IS IMPOSSIBLE TO determine just when I began to hear the Poem within me. It may have been when I was standing with my companion on Nevsky Prospekt (after a dress rehearsal of *The Masquerade*,[1] February 25, 1917) and a Cossack cavalry charged down the road, or once when I was standing alone on Liteiny Bridge and it was raised suddenly, in broad daylight (an unprecedented incident), to let a minesweeper proceed to the Smolny in support of the Bolsheviks (October 25, 1917). I really don't know!

***

The Poem is a peculiar revolt of things. Olga's[2] things, among which I had lived for a long time, suddenly demanded their place under the poetic sun. They came to life for a moment, as it were, but the sound that was left continued to vibrate over many long years. The rhythm born from these shock waves, abating at times, then rising again, accompanied me during periods of my life that were completely unlike. The Poem proved to be more capacious than I first thought. It imperceptibly assumed events and feelings from different layers of time, and now that I have finally rid myself of it, I see it as a complete and single entity. And I am not bothered by what I had said in Tashkent: "With this one there goes another..."

Red Cavalry Street, Leningrad, Sunday, March 1959

***

...I immediately heard and saw the whole Poem as it exists now (with the exception of the war, of course), but it took twenty years for the whole Poem to emerge from the first outline.

For months, for years, it lay as if hermetically sealed; I would forget it, I didn't like it, I waged an internal battle with it. Work on it (whenever it let me approach) reminded me of developing a photograph. Everything was already there. The Demon was always Blok, the Milepost—the Poet in general, the Poet with a capital "P" (something like Mayakovsky), and so on. The characters were developing, changing; life was casting new players. Someone departed. Conflict with readers went on all the time. But there was help from them as well, especially in Tashkent. There it seemed that we were all writing it together.

Sometimes the Poem aspired to become a ballet (on two occasions), and then nothing could hold it back. I thought that it would stay put there forever. I wrote something that resembled a ballet libretto, but then the Poem returned again and everything continued on as before. The first shoot (the first impetus), which I concealed from myself for decades, was, of course, a note by Pushkin: "Only the first lover leaves an impression on a woman, like the first casualty in a war!"[3] Vsevolod was not the first casualty and never was my lover, but his suicide was so similar to another catastrophe that they have merged forever for me.[4] The second scene, which the projector of memory has snatched from the darkness of the past, is of Olga and me after Blok's funeral looking for Vsevolod's grave in the Smolensk Cemetery (where he was buried in 1913). "It's somewhere by the wall," Olga said, but we couldn't find it. For some reason I will remember that moment forever.

Leningrad, 17 December 1959

***

I started the Poem in Leningrad (in 1940, my most productive year), and continued it first in "the paupers' Constantinople"—Tashkent—which was like a magical cradle for it, and then, in the last years of the war, back in the House on the Fontanka among the ruins of my city, in Moscow, and amid the little pines of Komarovo. Alongside this Poem, so florid (despite the absence of colorful epithets) and awash in music, proceeded the mournful *Requiem*, whose sole accompaniment could only be Silence and the occasional distant tolling of a funeral bell. In Tashkent it had still another companion—the play *Enuma Elish*, comical and prophetic at the same time, of which not even ashes remain.[5] Lyric poetry did not disturb it, and it did not interfere with lyric poetry.

***

(From a Letter to N N)[6]

...KNOWING THE CIRCUMSTANCES OF my life during that time, you are able to judge this better than others.

In the autumn of 1940, while sorting out my old papers (which later perished during the siege), I came across some poems and letters which I had had for a long time but had not yet read ("The Devil made me rummage in the packing-case"). They concerned the tragic events of 1913 that are related in *A Poem without a Hero*.

I then wrote the verse fragment "To Russia you came out of nowhere," in connection with the poem "The Contemporary Woman." Perhaps you may even recall how I read you these poems in the House on the Fontanka, in the presence of the old Sheremetiev maple ("and a witness to everything in the world...").

During that sleepless night of December 26-27, this fragment unexpectedly started to grow and turn into the first sketch of *A Poem without a Hero*. The history of the Poem's subsequent growth is set forth to some extent in the mutterings entitled "In Place of a Foreword."

You cannot imagine how many wild, absurd, and ridiculous rumors this "Petersburg Tale" has given birth to.

Strange though it may seem, my contemporaries were its harshest critics, and in Tashkent their accusations were formulated by X.[7] when he said that I was settling some old accounts with the era (the 1910s) and with people who were either dead or could not answer back. Moreover, those who didn't know some of the "Petersburg circumstances" would find the poem incomprehensible and uninteresting.

Others, especially women, considered *A Poem without a Hero* a betrayal of some former "ideal" and, what is even worse, an unmasking of my old poems in *Rosary*, which they "so love."

So, for the first time in my life, instead of a sweet stream, I encountered the frank indignation of readers; naturally I was inspired by this. Then... I completely stopped writing poetry, but nevertheless, in the course of fifteen years the Poem would unexpectedly overtake me again and again, like an attack of some incurable disease (it happened everywhere—during the music at a concert, in the street, even in my sleep). More than anything, it tormented me in Leningrad in December 1959, turning again into a tragic ballet, which is obvious from my diary entries (December 13th) and the stanzas about Blok. I could not tear myself away from it, and was continually adding to and revising something that was to all appearance finished.

> (But that theme was for me,
> Like a chrysanthemum crushed on the floor,
> After the coffin has passed.
> I drank it in with every drop,
> And, stricken by a devilish black thirst,
> Did not know how to get rid
>   Of this thing possessed)

It's no wonder that X., as you know, said to me: "Well, you're done for, it will never let you go."

But... I see that my letter is longer than it should be, and I still have to...

May 27, 1955, Moscow

***

Second Letter[8]

August 22, 1961
Komarovo

...HAVING BECOME ABSORBED in reporting the latest events of 1955, I really strung out my last letter somewhat, and then it seems I lost it, because you never mentioned it during our many meetings in Moscow. Since that time something unexpected and grand has happened—my poetry returned to the world. In that letter, among other things, I wrote to you about my Poem. Now I can add that it really was behaving very badly, so much so that at one point I fully intended to deny that it was mine, like the owner of a dog that has bitten someone in the street who assumes an air of ignorance and strolls off without quickening his pace. But nothing came of that either[9] (from the very beginning it seemed that it might be better if it were anonymous, and to attribute it to a deceased poet would be quite unconscionable): (a) because no one would want to acknowledge it as theirs, and (b) because everyone with whom I talked on this subject insisted that their relatives had copies of my work done in my hand, complete with spelling mistakes (which is a lie, of course).

However, the above mentioned letter has not been lost to a grateful posterity, and if the same fate is in store for this one too, then don't lose hope of seeing it published in Los Angeles or Timbuktu with the sacred inscription: ALL RIGHTS RESERVED. Even I am obliged to admire such an inscription on my unceded writings... But these are details. What the Poem is doing on its own is far worse. Rumor has it that it is trying to overpower other works of mine that are in no way related to it, and, in this manner, to distort both my literary development (such as it is) and my biography.

Moreover, I am once again persuaded that it is better for a woman to play the coquette when she is *du bon côté de la quarantaine*[10] than the other way round. But, sinner that I am, and out of sheer coquettishness, I lovingly related to you in detail in that ill-fated letter all the occasions when my Poem was *under attack*. Apparently, it is tempting to believe such "frankness" on the part of an author.

It is, of course, possible (and essential) to interpret every work of art, no matter how significant, in various ways (this is especially true of a masterpiece). Take, for example, Pushkin's "The Queen of Spades," which is a society tale of the 1830s, a kind of bridge between the eighteenth and nineteenth centuries (right down to the furnishings in the Countess's room), a biblically inspired "Thou shalt not kill" (hence all of *Crime and Punishment*), a tragedy of old age, a new kind of hero (the *raznochinets*), the psychology of a gambler (evidently a merciless self-observation), as well as a study of language (each person speaks differently, and the old woman's pre-Karamzinian Russian is especially interesting—presumably she does not speak that way in French). Excuse me, I'm beginning to babble; I musn't get started on Pushkin... But when I hear that the Poem is a "tragedy of conscience" (Viktor Shklovsky in Tashkent), an explanation of why the Revolution took place (I. Shtok in Moscow), a "Requiem for all of Europe" (a voice from the mirror), a tragedy of atonement, and God knows what else, I become uneasy... (In Komarovo in 1960, Viktor Zhirmunsky called it: "the fulfillment of the Symbolists' dream.") Many imagine it to be a tragic ballet (however, Lidia Ginzburg considers that its magic is an impermissible device — "why?").

> Can't live to the century's end...
> The twenty first, the twenty third...
> Like shavings flying from a lathe!

These lines are, if you'll excuse me, from a most sober and renowned atomic physicist.[11] But enough of this—I'm afraid that in a third letter I will have to apologize for these quotations, as I now apologize for those of 1955.

But what am I to do with the old shaman woman who protects herself from the music and the fire with "incantations" and "Dedications." It is she who forces me to experience feelings that are very flattering to an author's pride—those of a mother hen who has hatched a swan's egg and is helplessly flapping her wings on the shore after the cygnet has swum far away. Because you are an old friend, I shall not conceal from you the fact that distinguished foreigners have asked me whether I am truly the author of this work. To the honor of our homeland, I must admit that on this side of the border there are no such doubts. People simply come in off the streets and complain that the Poem has tormented them. And it occurs to me that someone did indeed dictate it to me, and what's more, kept the best lines till last. I am especially convinced of this because of the demoniacal ease with which I wrote the Poem. The rarest of rhymes simply hung on the tip of my pencil and the most intricate turns of phrase appeared by themselves on the page.

***

Most of all I will be asked who the "Prince of Darkness" is (I've already been asked about the Milepost...); he is, very simply, the devil. He is also in "Tails": "That most elegant Satan." I don't really want to speak about it, but for those who know the entire history of 1913 it is no secret. I will say only that he was probably born under a lucky star; he is one of those for whom everything is possible. I won't begin now to list everything that was possible for him; if I were to do so the hairs of today's reader would stand on end.

The one mentioned in the title, and the one whom I so desperately sought [...], is not actually in the Poem, but much is based on his absence.

One need not see him in the hero of the "Tsarskoe Selo Lyrical Interlude" (part I, chapter 3); nor should the completely guiltless Count Komarovsky[12] be brought into the Poem only because he lived in Tsarskoe Selo, his initials were V. K., and he committed suicide in the autumn of 1914 in an insane asylum.

The mysterious "Guest from the Future" will probably prefer to remain unnamed, and since he alone of all the others "does not breathe with Lethe's chill," he is not in my charge.

But surely this is necessary only for the musical description, as in Schumann's *Carnaval*, or else for completely idle curiosity.

Someone "without face or name" (the "Superfluous Shade" from chapter 1) is, of course, no one—the constant companion of our life and the perpetrator of so many woes.

Thus the sixth page of my Poem became, quite unexpectedly and for no known reason, the receptacle of my secrets. But who is obliged to believe the author? And why should one think that future readers (if there are any) will be interested in these details? On such occasions I am reminded, for some reason, of Blok, who recorded the story of the *Song of Fate* in his diary with such enthusiasm. We learn the names of everyone who heard the first reading in the author's home, and who said what and why.

Apparently, Alexander Alexandrovich attached a great deal of significance to this play. But for almost half a century I have not heard anyone say a kind word about it, or, for that matter, any word at all (criticizing Blok just isn't done).

***

The attempts "to ground" the Poem (as the late S. Z. Galkin[13] advised) ended in complete failure. It categorically refused to go into the suburbs. There isn't a single gypsy woman on a spit-covered road or any steam train going to Skorbyashchaya or Goryachoe Pole—it wanted nothing to do with any of this. It did not go to the fatal bridge with Mayakovsky, or into a five-kopeck bathhouse smelling of birch twigs, or into Blok's enchanting taverns with ships on the walls and the secrets and myth of Petersburg all around: it stubbornly remained on the fateful corner of the house that the Adamini[14] brothers had built at the beginning of the nineteenth century, from which one could see the windows of the Marble Palace and the snub-nosed soldiers of the Pavlov Institute returning to their barracks to the beat of a drum. At that time when bits of a hundred May Day parades flashed through a soft, wet, New Year's snowstorm falling on the Field of Mars and

> All the mysteries of the Summer Garden —
> The floods, the assignations, the siege...

***

Komarovo, August 26, 1961

Beside an attempt to lead the Poem into the suburbs (the Vyazemsky Monastery, second-hand bookshops, churchyard fences, and so on), the process of grounding it also entailed an attempt to give the dragoon some sort of biography, some sort of pre-history (his fiancée from the Smolny Institute, the cousin who entered a nunnery—"The Grand Investiture," and the gypsy woman who stabbed herself because of his betrayal). Both of them came from the ballet, and they were not allowed back into the Poem ("Two Dear Shades").[15] Perhaps they will reappear in one of the pieces of music. But these two girls turned out to be completely superfluous to the Poem itself. I did not know enough about another part of his *real* biography, and all of it would have been based on a collection of his poetry (Mikhail Kuzmin).

The biography of the heroine (half Olga, half Tatyana Vecheslova)[16] is written down in one of my notebooks. There you'll find the ballet school (Tatyana's), the polonaise with Nijinsky, Diaghilev, Paris, Moscow, carnival shows, *the artist*, "la danse russe"[17] in the Palace at Tsarskoe Selo, and so on. The Poem didn't want any part of this. It's curious to think what it might still want.

***

The Poem overflows into my reminiscences, which at least once a year (often in December) demand that I do something with them.

> It is a revolt of things,
> It is Kashchei himself
> Sitting on my decorated trunk...[18]

***

Another quality of the Poem: a magic potion being poured into a vessel suddenly thickens and turns into my biography, as if seen by someone in a dream or in a row of mirrors ("And I am happy or sad that I am going with you..."). Sometimes it looks transparent and gives off an incomprehensible light (similar to light during the White Nights, when everything shines from within); unexpected galleries open up, leading nowhere; a second step is heard, an echo, which considers itself the main sound, speaks on its own, not repeating the other; the shades pretend to be those who have cast them. Everything doubles and trebles—down to the very bottom of the casket.

And suddenly this *Fata Morgana* gives way. On the table there are just verses, rather elegant, well-crafted, and audacious. There is no longer a mysterious light, no second footstep, no rebellious echo, no shades that have taken on a separate existence. And then I begin to understand why it leaves so many readers cold. Generally, this happens when I read it to someone who doesn't comprehend, and it comes back to me like a boomerang (forgive the trite comparison), but in such a way (!?) that it wounds me, too.

Komarovo, May 17, 1961

***

It wasn't until today that I was finally able to formulate the peculiarity of my method (in the Poem). Nothing is said straight-forwardly. The most complex and profound things are not expressed in a dozen pages, as is their wont, but in two lines, yet they are intelligible to everyone.

***

This poem is accompanied by *The Other*, which almost from the very start was a hindrance (in any case, in Tashkent). There simply were omissions, incomplete gaps ("There was no Romeo, but of course there was an Aeneas"),[19] from which it was some-times possible to grasp something almost miraculously and in-sert it into the text.

***

Again the Poem doubles. A second step is audible the whole time. Something going alongside—another text, and it's impossi-ble to discern which is the voice and which the echo, and which is the shadow of the other, because the Poem is so capacious, not to say fathomless. Not once has a torch cast within illuminated its bottom. Like the rain I penetrate into the narrowest cracks, ex-panding them—that's how new stanzas appear. Sometimes I imagine the Petersburg period of Russian history in these words:

"Let this place be damned"[20] —

and then Suzdal—the Pokrovsky Monastery—Eudoxia Lopu-khina. The Petersburg horrors: the death of Peter, and Paul, Pushkin's duel, the flood, the blockade. All of this should resound in music that is not yet realized. It's December again, and again the Poem is knocking on my door, swearing that this will be the last time. Again I see it in an empty mirror.

***

The feeling of New Year's Eve and Christmas Eve is the *axis* on which the whole thing revolves, like a magical carousel.... It is the breath that sets all the details in motion and stirs up the surrounding air. (The wind of tomorrow.)

***

The plan of "Prose about the Poem." (Perhaps it will be a new "In Place of a Foreword").

1. Where and when I wrote it.
2. How it pursued me.
3. About the Poem itself. The failed attempt to ground it (an entry from the colored notebook). Its digressions into ballet. The boomerang. The carousel. The Poem of New Year's Eve. (Examples.)
4. Its connection with the Petersburg Hoffmanniana.
5. The subtext. *The Other*—mourning—its fragments in *Triptych*.

Write broadly and freely. A symphony.

***

In our time the cinema has supplanted both tragedy and comedy, just as pantomime did in Rome. The classical works of Greek drama were transformed into libretti for the pantomimes (during the Roman Empire). Perhaps this is not a chance analogy! Is it not the same with *Romeo and Juliet* (Prokofiev) and *Othello* (Khachaturian), which were turned into ballets?

***

If it is possible to transform Shakespeare's tragedy *Romeo and Juliet* and Pushkin's poem *Mavra*[21] into ballets, then I see no reason for not doing the same with *A Poem without a Hero* (that is to say, not into a classical ballet, but into some kind of choreographic performance with singing offstage, etc.). For fifteen years now I have been told that there is music in this piece by almost everyone who has read it.

***

November 25... While I was working away at what was sometimes a ballet and sometimes a screenplay, I still couldn't figure out what exactly I was doing. The following quotation clarified the matter for me: "This book may be read as a poem or verse play," writes Peter Viereck in *The Tree Witch* (1961),[22] who then goes on to explain the technique of how the poem is transformed into a play. At the same time I was doing the very thing with *Triptych*. His work is a contemporary of my Poem and, it's possible, such a similarity....

[1961]

Translated by Christopher Fortune and Nicholas Tyrras

THE BALLET LIBRETTO
for
A Poem without a Hero

I.

A TABLE WITH two place settings is lit on a dark stage. Candles. X., in a long black shawl, is sitting with her elbows on the table, her back to the audience. A clock. Five minutes before midnight. A conversation with someone not present. (He is a portrait, a bust or a *shade*.) A bell rings. Everything changes. A table takes up the whole stage—an enormous banquet hall. A crowd in costume. Everyone is dancing: The Demon, Don Juan with Donna Anna shrouded in mourning, Faust (in old age) with the dead Gretchen, The Milepost (alone), the Goat-Footed Girl leads a Bacchic procession, as on a black-figured vase. X. disowns them all and above all herself, the youngest one, in the much-celebrated shawl. The "Guest from the Future" steps out from one of the mirrors, *traverse la scène*, and steps into another. Everyone is terrified. The most banal dance by Columbine, Harlequin, and Pierrot. A false sense of conviviality. A Chiromancer or Rasputin (the "Superfluous Shade") and everyone around him. (He limps, dressed in a frock coat.) He reveals to everyone their future. *Suddenly* a man appears, head and shoulders above everyone, in a black cloak and mask. He throws off his cloak, takes off his mask—it is the boy-dragoon. The Superfluous Shade refuses to tell his fortune, but the dragoon insists. At the back of the stage there is a fleeting scene of a suicide...

Later on there should be scenes characterizing Petrograd in 1920. [The last entry]: "No, it is not 1920 but 1941; the first bombing has begun. Everyone died long ago."

II. (The dragoon's dream: the past and the future.) At Columbine's. The *intérieur* of Olga's room. A corner is lit. On the walls are portraits of Olga, which periodically come to life and exchange glances, without leaving their frames. Verka—a diminutive lady's maid. She dresses Columbine and puts on her shoes. A mirror. In the mirror the Superfluous Shade is reflected. Notes and flowers are delivered. A dining room. The dragoon arrives. An intimate breakfast. His jealousy. He takes away a letter and the roses. Her pledge. Complete accord. *Pas de deux*. A small chamber. She cuts off "a blonde curl" and gives it to him. (A rendezvous in the Maltese Chapel.) Mozart's *Requiem*. Two harlequins—he chases away both of them. A reception. The bedroom again. The altar of Venus. But the dragoon is already forgotten. Olga, reclining in a lace cap and chemise, is receiving guests. Candles burn in tall glass candlesticks. "And in a circular mirror the bed is reflected." And the youth is almost forgotten...

> You are to him as a magnet is to steel.
> Turning pale, he watches through tears
> As roses are brought to you,
> And how his foe is celebrated.

The guests, Klyuyev and Yesenin, dance a wild, Russian, almost Khlystian, dance. The Demon. She greets him unreservedly. Black roses. The first scene of the dragoon's jealousy. His despair. A cold frost looks in through the window... The clock chimes "How glorious is..." The Lame and Courteous One tries to console the dragoon, tempting him with something very dark. Vyacheslav Ivanov's "Tower"—the Lame and Courteous One is at home. Antiquity. The altar of Pergamum[1] comes to life. Oedipus and Antigone. A curse. Pagan Rus (Gorodetsky, Stravinsky, *The Rite of Spring*, Tolstoy, early Khlebnikov).[2] Out in the street. The Tauride Gardens in snow, a blizzard. Specters appear in the blizzard. (Perhaps even Blok's *Twelve*, but in the distance and unreal.)...

III. The dragoon by a streetlamp. Assignations: Vera with a malicious note. A general, two whores take leave of him, they call to the dragoon—he does not come. He imagines her in a window behind tulle curtains, in various guises, like death. (*One moment!*) Psyche. The Noise of time! A snowstorm. The Field of Mars. The specters' ball. The apparition of a military parade.

(Martial music.) Marches. A procession. A lyrical interlude. Everything is intertwined, as in a dream. (Olga watches a fragment of my ballet *The Snow Mask* in a theater box.) The dragoon composes verses beneath the streetlamp. Torches. The general again, in the greatcoat of Tsar Nicholas's regiment. The dragoon, who is lost in thought, doesn't notice him. At the back of the stage a second curtain rises—a fearful flight of stairs, illuminated by gaslight (a bluish color).... Olga returns from the masquerade, accompanied by the Stranger. A scene before the door. The dragoon stands motionless in the niche. Their farewell leaves no doubt. A kiss. Olga goes in. The dragoon's suicide.... A shot. The light goes out. A musical dirge. Olga comes out and kneels over the body. The door is left wide open and through it everything that will happen is visible—everything that we know and the unknown Future beyond that.

Red Cavalry Street, December 18, 1959

A Second Variant of the Finale

A DOOR IS FLUNG open (it widens and lengthens). Columbine (with a candle) comes out in a long black dress and kneels by the body. Another figure in the same dress and with the same candle ascends the staircase to stand by the body. Strains of Chopin.

December 24, 1959

***

The Superfluous Shade appears at the ball in the *first scene*. He is dressed in a white domino and a red mask and carries a lantern and spade. He has a retinue behind the scenes, which he summons with a whistle; he dances with them. They all disperse. In the *second scene* he looks through the window of Columbine's room and is reflected in the mirror, doubling, trebling, etc. The mirror shatters into pieces, presaging misfortune.

In the *third scene* he climbs out of a carriage dressed in a beaver coat and top hat and invites the dragoon to accompany him.... Stars, and the branches in the Mikhailovsky Garden. The dragoon shakes his head and reveals the blonde curl. The

Superfluous Shade tries to snatch the curl with his white-gloved hand. The dragoon grabs the Shade by the hand—but there is no hand, only a glove. In a rage he tears the glove.

***

The Stray Dog—an evening with Tamara Karsavina[3]—she is dancing in the mirror. A masquerade—the large fireplace is ablaze. Suddenly all the masks turn into Superfluous Shades (they exchange glances and laugh)....

***

...*Everyone* was at this masquerade. No one sent their regrets. Osip Mandelstam, with not a single love poem to his name yet but already famous ("Ashes on the Left Shoulder"),[4] and Marina Tsvetaeva, who had arrived from Moscow for her "Otherworldly Evening"[5] and who got everything in this world confused... The shade of Vrubel—from whom all the demons of the twentieth century arose, he being the first... The enigmatic, rustic poet Klyuyev, the great Stravinsky who compelled the entire twentieth century to sound the way he heard it, the demoniacal Doctor Dapertutto,[6] and Blok (the tragic tenor of the age), immersed for the past five years in a hopeless malaise, and Velimir I[7] who walked in as if it were *The Stray Dog.* And Faust—Vyacheslav Ivanov, and Andrei Bely who ran in with his dance-like gait and with the manuscript of his *Petersburg* under his arm, and the legendary Tamara Karsavina. And I won't swear that those aren't Rozanov's[8] spectacles gleaming in the corner, or that that isn't Rasputin's flowing beard. And at the back of the hall, the stage, or hell (I don't know which) a sound rings out from time to time, half mountain echo and half the voice of Chaliapin. And there, floating past at times, is something like the Tsarskoe Selo swan or Anna Pavlova, and Mayakovsky, before he met the Briks,[9] is probably smoking by the fireplace... (but in the depths of the "dead" mirrors, which begin to come to life and to shine with a kind of suspicious, dull luster, and in their depths the one-legged, old organgrinder (as Fate is depicted) reveals to all assembled their future—their end). Nijinsky's last dance,[10] Meyerhold's departure.[11] The only one who is absent is the one who definitely should be there, and not just be there, but stand on the landing and greet the guests... But still:

> We must drink to him,
> Who is not yet with us.

January 6-7, 1962

Translated by Christopher Fortune and Nicholas Tyrras

About Pushkin

A WORD ABOUT PUSHKIN

M Y PREDECESSOR, PAVEL SHCHEGOLYOV,[1] con-
cludes his work on Pushkin's duel and death with a
series of speculations about why society and its
spokesmen hated the poet and expelled him as an alien being
from its midst. It is now time to turn this question around and
speak aloud not about what *they* did to him, but what *he* did to
them.

After an ocean of filth, deceit, lies, the complacency of friends
and the plain foolishness of the Poletikas and non-Poletikas,[2] the
Stroganov clan,[3] the idiot horseguardsmen, who made the
d'Anthès affair *une affaire de régiment* (a question of the regiment's honor), the sanctimonious salons of the Nesselrodes, et
al.,[4] the Imperial Court, which peeked through every keyhole,
the majestic secret advisors—members of the State Council—
who had felt no shame at placing the great poet under secret
surveillance—after all of this, how exhilarating and wonderful it
is to see the prim, heartless ("swinish" as Alexander Sergeyevich
himself put it) and, to be sure, illiterate Petersburg watch as
thousands of people, upon hearing the fateful news, rushed to
the poet's house and remained there forever with all of Russia.

"*Il faut que j'arrange ma maison* (I must put my house in
order)," said the dying Pushkin.

In two days' time his house became a sacred place for his
Homeland, and the world has never seen a more complete or
more resplendent victory.

Little by little, the entire era (not without reluctance, of
course) came to be called the Pushkin era. All the beauties,
ladies-in-waiting, mistresses of the salons, Dames of the Order of
St. Catherine, members of the Imperial Court, ministers, aides-
de-camp and non-aides-de-camp, gradually came to be called

Pushkin's contemporaries, and were later simply laid to rest in card catalogues and name indices (with garbled birth and death dates) to Pushkin's works.

He conquered both time and space.

People say: the Pushkin era, Pushkin's Petersburg. And there is no longer any direct bearing on literature; it is something else entirely. In the palace halls where they danced and gossiped about the poet, his portraits now hang and his books are on view, while their pale shadows have been banished from there forever. And their magnificent palaces and residences are described by whether Pushkin was ever there or not. Nobody is interested in anything else. The Emperor Nikolai Pavlovich in his white breeches looks very majestic on the wall in the Pushkin Museum; manuscripts, diaries, and letters are valuable if the magic word "Pushkin" is there. And, the most terrifying thing for them is what they could have heard from the poet:

> You will not be answerable for me,
> You can sleep peacefully.
> Strength is power, but your children
> Will curse you for me.

And in vain do people believe that scores of handcrafted monuments can replace that one *aere perennius* (stronger than bronze) not made by hand.[5]

May 26, 1961
Komarovo

Translated by Ronald Meyer

PUSHKIN'S LAST TALE

I

PUSHKIN'S *TALE OF THE GOLDEN COCKEREL* has attracted relatively little scholarly attention.

The historical and literary articles and commentaries contain very meager and inaccurate information about Pushkin's last tale (1834).

It was thought to have a literary source, since the plot of *The Golden Cockerel* is not to be found in Russian or foreign folklore.

However, none of the investigations of the past twenty or thirty years has scored any success.[1]

Attempts to find the source of *The Golden Cockerel* in the tales of *The Arabian Nights* have also failed.

I have succeeded in locating the source of *The Golden Cockerel*. It is "The Legend of the Arabian Astrologer" in Washington Irving's book *The Alhambra*.

Washington Irving's book *The Alhambra* was published in Paris in 1832.[2]

A rather accurate French translation of the book was published simultaneously in Paris.[3]

The French two-volume edition of *Les contes de l'Alhambra* is among the seven books by Irving in Pushkin's library.[4]

Critics had noted the influence of Washington Irving on the author of *The Tales of Belkin* during his lifetime (N. Polevoi in *The Moscow Telegraph* and an anonymous reviewer in *Literary Supplements to The Russian Invalid* in 1831).

The extent of Irving's direct influence on Pushkin still remains an open question.[5]

Pushkin himself refers to Irving only once—in his retelling of John Tanner's biography (1836).

II

Washington Irving was very popular in Russia in the 1820s and 30s. Innumerable translations of his works can be found in all of the better known journals of the period: *The Moscow Telegraph, The Messenger of Europe, Atheneum, Son of the Fatherland, The Telescope,* and *The Literary Gazette.* Therefore, *The Alhambra* became a topic of discussion in the Russian journals soon after it was published in Paris.

The first review of *Les contes de l'Alhambra* appeared in the July issue of *The Moscow Telegraph,* which came out in October 1832.

> W. Irving has previously written *The Life and Voyages of Christopher Columbus* and *The Conquest of Granada.* He now describes his journey to Granada; he sees Alhambra as a symbol of the Moors' dominion and presence in Spain and relates the superstitious legends that the Spanish imagination carried off from the ruins of the Moorish palace. In the beginning you read of W. Irving's journey through southern Spain; then a detailed description of Alhambra. The author temporarily takes up residence in Alhambra, and various incidents and various encounters give occasion for stories about the old legends or, to be more precise, tales about Alhambra. There are seven stories in all: "The Arabian Astrologer"; "Legend of the Three Beautiful Princesses"; "Legend of Prince Ahmed el Kamel, or, The Pilgrim of Love"; "The Moor's Legacy"; "The Rose of the Alhambra"; "Governor Manco and the Soldier"; "Two Discreet Statues." What can one say about them? They are all clever and many of them are entertaining; but it would be the same if a Frenchman were to start telling our *Russian* tales: that is how W. Irving tells his *Moorish* tales. One of them was translated for *The Telescope,* but very poorly, moreover, it's the worst one. The best ones in our opinion are: "The Arabian Astrologer"; "The Pilgrim of Love"; "Two Discreet Statues"; "The Rose of the Alhambra" and "The Moor's Legacy." We shall try to translate one of these for *The Telegraph's* readers from the English original. (pp. 250-51)

A translation of one of the *Alhambra* tales, which the critic in *The Moscow Telegraph* reviewed negatively, was placed in *The*

Telescope's ninth issue (September): "Governor Manco. From *The Alhambra,* A New Composition by Washington Irving."

In a special note the publisher characterizes this piece as a "Spanish folk tale, retold by W. Irving."

The translation from the cycle of the *Alhambra* tales that was promised by the *The Moscow Telegraph's* reviewer was printed in issues 21 and 22 (November). The translation of "Legend of Prince Ahmed al Kamel" was accompanied by the following note:

> We received this tale with a letter, in which the translator writes, among other things: "In the 14th issue of *The Moscow Telegraph* you note your intention to translate one of the *Alhambra* tales for your readers. Perhaps you would like to place in *The Telegraph* the tale I am sending you from that book, which I have translated in its entirety? I should like to know tentatively whether my translation merits publication."

Thus, *The Alhambra* was translated in its entirety into Russian soon after the appearance of the English and French editions. However, for some reason that remains unknown to us, this translation went unpublished.[6]

Finally, in the ninth issue of *Library for Reading* (1835), where *The Tale of the Golden Cockerel* was first published, an article entitled "Washington Irving" appeared, which was a translation from *Revue Britannique* (1834, XII). It gives this characterization of the *Alhambra* tales:

> The *Alhambra* tales belong more directly to invention [the author is comparing *The Alhambra* with *The Conquest of Granada*]; but romantic legends are interspersed with travel notes that have the same freshness and charm as the descriptions in *The Sketch Book*.

The majority of the *Alhambra* tales are novellas about Moorish treasures.

In Irving's letters from Alhambra he frequently mentions his guide Mateo Ximenez, whose stories he recorded.[7]

However, Irving himself exposes his method of "creating" folk legends:

> Having... made the reader in some degree familiar with the localities of the Alhambra, I shall now launch out more largely into the

wonderful legends... which I have diligently wrought into shape
and form, from various legendary scraps and hints picked up in
the course of my perambulations; in the same manner that an anti-
quary works out a regular historical document from a few scat-
tered letters of an almost defaced inscription. (See the chapter
"Local Traditions.")[8]

In addition to the cycle of novellas about treasure, the book contains the following: "Legend of the Three Beautiful Princesses"
and two parodies of magic tales: "Legend of Prince Ahmed al
Kamel" and "Legend of the Arabian Astrologer."

III

The plot of the parody "Legend of the Arabian Astrologer" is
extraordinarily complicated with its miraculous events and all
the accoutrements of a pseudo-Arabian fantastic tale, which
Irving characterizes as "the style of Harun al Rashid."

This legend is prefaced by a short prologue, entitled "The
House of the Weathercock," in which Irving attempts to ground
his tale to a specific place—the ancient Moorish palace in
Granada, which the author supposedly had searched out. The
palace is called La Casa del Gallo de Viento, which in Irving's
opinion, translates as House of the Weathercock (a weathercock
in the shape of a Moorish horseman that used to decorate one of
the towers). Professor B. A. Grzhevsky has explained to me that
there is no such Moorish palace in Granada, that weathercock in
Spanish is *jiralda* (and not Gallo de Viento) and that in the eighth
century, which is the period Irving indicates, Arabian architecture is an impossibility.

The legend is rather long, so I will limit myself here to the
shortest possible summary.

Enemies attack the old Moorish king, Aben Habuz, "a retired
conqueror."

The Arabian astrologer, the venerable old man Ibrahim, a con-
fidant of the king, tells him about a talisman that warns of invad-
ing enemies (a bronze cock and ram) and constructs another talisman for the same purpose (a bronze horseman).[9]

The enemies of Aben Habuz are destroyed.

The talisman begins to work again.

Scouts find a Gothic princess in the mountains.

The king falls in love with the princess and ransacks Granada in order to carry out her whims. Insurrection breaks out.

The astrologer demands the maiden as his reward for services rendered to the king.

The king, who had given his word to reward the astrologer, refuses.

A quarrel between the astrologer and the king ensues.

The astrologer and the princess vanish into the astrologer's underground residence, where they remain to this day (a denouement similar to *Barbarossa*).

The talisman stops functioning. With the passage of time it is transformed into an ordinary weathercock.

Enemies again attack "the retired conqueror" Aben Habuz.

In this legend Irving makes use of material from the historical writings on which he was working at the time of his stay in Alhambra. These works are: *The Conquest of Granada* (1829), *The Conquest of Spain* (1835), and *Mahomet and His Successors*, which did not appear until 1850.

Irving is a great literary hoaxer in the tradition of Addison.

Three years before the appearance of *The Alhambra* he published *The Conquest of Granada*. This book belongs to the genre of historical chronicles, which was very popular at the time. The narrative is told by the fictitious author of the cycle, the monk Antonio Agapida.

I will not go into the complicated issue of "Legend of the Arabian Astrologer" and its links with Spanish folklore and the so-called frontier romance,[10] an issue that requires a separate study, but I will note that the primary characters in "Legend of the Arabian Astrologer" are taken from the chronicle. The biography of Aben Habuz in many particulars repeats the biography of Muley Aben Hassan, Boabdil's father, the last king of the Moors. The astrologer Ibrahim is a nameless Arabian magician who took part in the defense of Malaga. The Gothic princess is the captive Christian girl, one of the wives of King Muley Aben Hassan.

We can date Pushkin's acquaintance with Irving's *The Alhambra* to 1833. Although Pushkin could have read reviews of *The Alhambra* in 1832 in *Journal des Débats*.

The rough draft of "The Tsar saw before him" (Tsar uvidel pred soboi) dates from this period.[11] The first ten lines of this sketch, which until now have eluded commentary, represent, as we have established, a verse "retelling" of a piece from "Legend of the Arabian Astrologer," which Pushkin did not make use of in *The Golden Cockerel*.

I will cite the parallel texts:

The tsar saw before him
A small table with a chessboard.
And on the chessboard
He set out in an orderly row
A host of little soldiers made of wax.
The dolls sit menacingly,
On their horses, arms akimbo,
With calico gloves,
In plumed helmets,
And broadswords on their shoulders...

and before each window was a table, on which was arranged, as on a chessboard, a mimic army of horse and foot, with the effigy of the potentate that ruled in that direction, all carved of wood.

The king... approached the seeming chess-board, on which were arranged the small wooden effigies, when, to his surprise, he perceived that they were all in motion. The horses pranced and curveted, the warriors brandished their weapons, and there was a faint sound of drums and trumpets...[12]

These statuettes are a magical depiction of enemy forces, which at the touch of the magic wand either retreated or began to wage war among themselves and destroyed each other. And then the same fate would befall an enemy on the attack.

Just how close the plot of Pushkin's "folk tale" is to Irving's legend becomes clear when the texts are compared:

In the realm of Threeteenseventy,
Commonwealth of Thriceleventy,
Lived the famous Tsar Dadon.
Fierce he was from boyhood on,
And when scarcely more than twenty
Wrought his neighbors wrongs aplenty.
Aging now, he changed in mind,
Would give up the warlike grind
For a life serene and festive.

In old times... there was a Moorish king named Aben Habuz... He was a retired conqueror, that is to say, one who having in his more youthful days led a life on constant foray and depredation, now that he was grown feeble and superannuated, "languished for repose," and desired nothing more than to live at peace with the world, to husband his laurels, and to enjoy in quiet the possessions he had wrested from his neighbors.

But his neighbors, growing restive,
Caused the grizzled Tsar alarm,
Dealing him a world of harm.
To protect the tsardom's borders
From the raids of bold marauders,
He was forced to raise and post
An unconscionable host.
Field commanders, never drowsing,
Still would scarce have finished
    dousing
Flames at left when, ho! at right
Hostile banners hove in sight.
These fought off, some visitation
Came by sea. The Tsar's frustration
Drove him wild enough to weep
And forgo the balm of sleep.
Who could thrive when thus
    infested?[13]

It so happened, however, that this most reasonable and pacific old monarch had young rivals to deal with... Certain distant districts of his own territories, also, which during the days of his vigor he had treated with a high hand, were prone... to rise in rebellion... Thus he had foes on every side... the unfortunate Aben Habuz was kept in a constant state of vigilance and alarm, not knowing in what quarter hostilities might break out.

It was in vain that he built watchtowers on the mountains, and stationed guards at every pass... Was ever peaceable and retired conqueror in a more uncomfortable predicament?

The situations are absolutely identical. All that is missing is the motif of rebellion in the provinces. The "biographies" of Tsar Dadon and King Aben Habuz coincide. Let me note that the heroes in Pushkin's other tales (Saltan, Yelisei and others) are not supplied with biographies.

So he pondered and requested
Succour from a gelding sage,
Planet-reckoner and mage;
Sent a runner to implore him
And the magus, brought before him,
From beneath his ample frock
Drew a golden weathercock.
"Let this golden bird," he chanted,
"High atop the spire be planted,
And my clever Cockerel
Be your faithful sentinel.
While there's naught of martial riot,
He will sit his perch in quiet;
Let there be on any side
Signs of war to be espied,
Of some squadron border-poaching,
Or some other ill approaching,
Straight my bird upon the dome
Will awaken, perk his comb,
Crow and veer, his ruff a-fluffing,

...an ancient Arabian physician arrived at his court... In a little while the sage Ibrahim became the bosom counsellor of the king... Aben Habuz was once inveighing against the injustice of his neighbors, and bewailing the restless vigilance he had to observe... the astrologer remained silent for a moment and then replied, "Know, O King... I beheld a great marvel... on a mountain... was a figure of a ram, and above it a figure of a cock, both of molten brass, and turning upon a pivot. Whenever the country was threatened with invasion, the ram would turn in the direction of the enemy, and the cock would crow; upon this the inhabitants of the the the city knew of the danger, and of the quarter from which it was approaching and could take timely means to guard against it."

Point where harm is in the offing."
Rapt, the Tsar allowed the sage
Heaps of gold for ready wage.
"Such momentous boon afforded,"
He rejoiced, "shall be rewarded
By a wish, to be fulfilled
Like my own as soon as willed."

"God is great," exclaimed... Aben Habuz, "what a treasure would be such a ram to keep an eye upon these mountains around me; and then such a cock to crow in time of danger!... how securely I might sleep in my palace with such sentinels on the top!"

"Give me such a safeguard, and the riches of my treasury are at thy command."

In Irving's tale the astrologer only tells the king about the talisman in the shape of a bronze cock (he constructs a bronze horseman).

It is generally accepted that the cock in Pushkin's tale is "alive." However, the line "Then a tiny ringing was heard" (the flight of the golden cockerel) apparently contradicts that.

Cockerel atop the spire
Started guarding march and shire,
Scarce a danger reared its head,
Up he perked as though from bed,
Slewed about, his collar ruffled,
To that side and, wings unshuffled,
Crew aloud, "Keeree-kookoo!
Reign abed, your guard is true."
Kings, the Tsar's domains investing,
Henceforth never dared molest him:
Tsar Dadon on every hand
Hurled them back by sea and land!

... and [Aben Habuz] even taunted and insulted his neighbors, to induce them to make incursions; but by degrees they grew wary from repeated disasters, until no one ventured to invade his territories.

In Irving, the magic talismans do not speak (the bronze cock and bronze horseman). In Pushkin, the golden cockerel speaks ironically about the Tsar.

One year, two, the shrewd informant
Had been roosting all but dormant,
When one morning they broke in
On Dadon with fearful din.
"Tsar of ours! The realm's defender!"
Cries the household troop's
        commander.
"Majesty! Wake up! Alert!"
"Eh?... what's up?... Is someone hurt?"
Drawled the Tsar amid a double
Yawn, "who is this? What's the
        trouble?"
Answered him the Captain thus:

For many months the bronze horseman remained on the peace establishment....

Tidings were brought early one morning, by the sentinel appointed to watch the tower, that the face of the bronze horseman was turned towards the mountains of Elvira....

"Hark, the rooster's warning us;
Look below and see the people
Mill in fear, and on the steeple
See the rooster, ruffle-fleeced,
Crowing, pointing to the East."
"Up! No time to lose!" their Master
Spurred them on, "Mount
        horses! Faster!"
Eastward thus a force he sped,
With his eldest at its head.

"Let the drums and trumpets sound to arms, and all Granada be put on the alert," said Aben Habuz.

The dialogue between the Tsar and the captain belongs to the plane of the grotesque. The analogous episode in Irving's tale, despite the generally ironic tone of the narration, does not have similar undertones.

The Pushkin tale continues with the inserted episode about the Tsar's sons and the Tsar's campaign, which is absent in Irving's legend.

In Irving the warriors set off for the mountains, the place indicated by the talisman, where they do not encounter even one enemy, but do find the Gothic princess. They bring her to Aben Habuz.

... The prize of maidens,
Queen of Shamakhan, in radiance
Lambent like the morning star,
Quietly salutes the Tsar...
....
Thus full seven days he lavished,
All enslaved by her and ravished,
On delight and merriment
In the royal maiden's tent.

The beautiful damsel was accordingly conducted into his presence... Pearls of dazzling whiteness were entwined with her tresses; and jewels sparkled on her forehead, rivalling the lustre of her eyes... The flashes of her dark refulgent eyes were like the sparks of fire on the withered, yet combustible, heart of Aben Habuz... Aben Habuz resigned himself to the full sway of passion.

The situation in Pushkin is much more complicated than in Irving. The Tsar falls in love with the Shamakhanian queen over the dead bodies of his own sons.[14]

The final and most significant parallel, in our view, is the scene of retribution:

"For the aid I once accorded,
You recall, I was awarded
My first wish—to be fulfilled.
Like your own, as soon as willed.
Let this maid be what I won,
This young Queen of Shamakhan."
"What?" Dadon fell back, amazed,
"What possessed you? Are you crazed?
Does some wicked demon ride you?
Have your wits dried up inside you?
What's your game, in heaven's name?
Pledge I did; but all the same
There are limits, well you knew;
And—what use is she to you?
Kindly lodge it in your head
Who I am; Why, ask instead
For my mint, a magnate's sable,
Stallion from the royal stable,
Half my tsardom if you please!"
"No, I wish for none of these!
Just you give me what I won,
This young queen of Shamakhan,"
Piped the sage in former fashion.
"No!" the Tsar spat, in a passion;
"You yourself have brought this on!
You'll have nothing! There! Be gone!
While you're in one piece! I say!
Drag the scarecrow from my way!"

(The King promises the astrologer the first beast of burden that enters the magic portal as well as its load. The beast turns out to be the mule on which the Princess is riding.)

"Behold," cried the astrologer, my promised reward." Aben Habuz smiled at what he considered a pleasantry of the ancient man; but when he found him to be in earnest, his gray beard trembled with indignation. "Son of Abu Ayub," said he sternly, "what equivocation is this? Thou knowest the meaning of my promise... Take the strongest mule in my stables, load it with the most precious things of my treasury, and it is thine..."

"What need I of wealth?" cried the astrologer, scornfully; "the princess is mine by right; thy royal word is pledged; I claim her as my own."

The wrath of the monarch got the better of his discretion. "Base son of the desert," cried he, "thou mayest be master of many arts, but know me for thy master, and presume not to juggle with thy king."

"My master, my king!" echoed the astrologer—"the monarch of a mole-hill to claim sway over him who possesses the talismans of Solomon! Farewell... reign over thy petty kingdom, and revel in thy paradise of fools...."

In Pushkin, the astrologer's refusal to accept the Tsar's favors and his demand for the Shamakhanian Queen are not motivated in any way. In Irving's legend the astrologer is a ladies' man and he refuses the rewards offered by the king because he possesses King Solomon's magic book. In drafts and even in the fair copy Pushkin calls the astrologer a Shamakhanian, that is, a fellow countryman of the Shamakhanian Queen, thus making his demand understandable.

The denouement of *The Golden Cockerel* differs significantly from its source. When Aben Habuz does not keep his promise, the magic weathercock (the bronze horseman) merely stops warning him of approaching danger. In Pushkin's tale the talisman (the golden cockerel) is an instrument of punishment and the assassin of the Tsar who had broken his oath.[15]

It would appear that Pushkin flattened the plot he borrowed from Irving, some links are missing, which accounts for the plot discrepancies and the "vagueness" that scholars have noted in the tale. Thus, for example, the "biographies" of the astrologer and the princess were not carried over into Pushkin's version, thereby creating a sense of mystery.

In contrast to Pushkin's other "folk tales," *The Golden Cockerel* lacks a traditional fairy-tale hero and miracles and transformations.

Evidently, it was not the "Harun al Rashid" style in Irving's legend that attracted Pushkin.

All plot motivations are altered in favor of making them more "naturalistic" and the satiric quality is greatly intensified.

Thus, for example, if Irving's Aben Habuz dozes to the sound of a magic lyre or simply says in the beginning: "How securely I might sleep in my palace with such sentinels...," Pushkin's Dadon is soundly asleep at the tale's beginning. Civil strife in the mountains in the legend is motivated by the talisman's influence; in *The Golden Cockerel* it has more natural causes—jealousy, etc.

All the characters are lowered in Pushkin's tale.

Dadon, like Aben Habuz, is a "retired conqueror," but the "peace-loving" King of the Moors thirsts for blood, whereas the Tsar is a lazy petty tyrant. (The Tsar's very name is taken from *The Tale of Bova Korolevich*, where Dadon is the "evil" Tsar.) In Pushkin's early poem *Bova*, Dadon is the name of the Tsar and petty tyrant whom Pushkin compares to Napoleon.

In Irving's tale the central characters, the King and the astrologer, who is also threatening, are parodied, whereas Pushkin is ironic only about the Tsar, who is a completely grotesque figure. The astrologer is mysterious and Pushkin speaks about him with tenderness: "Snowy-thatched now, like a swan." The scene of the meeting between Dadon and the Shamakhanian Queen (and the tent to which she leads him) brings to mind *The Tale of Yeruslan Lazarevich*; the similarity is even more striking in the rough draft:

> Amid the high mountain tops
> A *white, silken* tent (silk from Shamakha)
> In that tent a maiden sits
> The Queen of Shamakhan.

And in the chapbook edition of *The Tale of Yeruslan:* "And he rode into an open field towards a *white tent,* in which *sat* three beautiful maidens, daughters of Tsar Bugrigor. The world has never seen maidens as beautiful as these."

Then follows the love scene in the tent and the murder of the two sisters.

The Golden Cockerel, which Pushkin himself included in the cycle of his "folk" tales[16] (and which is usually considered in the context of Pushkin's other tales), bears the unmistakable imprint of "folk" elements.

A comparison of the rough draft and the fair copy of *The Golden Cockerel*[17] shows that during the process of rewriting the tale Pushkin lowered the lexicon, thereby bringing it closer to popular speech.[18]

The introduction of folkloric elements is motivated by the genre of the folk tale: "hosts in battle rent," "the Sorochinsk cap,"[19] the Shamakhanian "white tent," the epithet "Shamakhanian" (in folk tales it is usually "Shamakhanian silk"),[20] etc.

The traditional opening "Somewhere, in the thrice-nine kingdom" is borrowed from folklore, as is the phrase "She took him by the hand/And led him to her tent."

The trappings of the folk tale here serve to mask the political meaning.

Similarly, in the eighteenth century the genre of the "Arabian" tale often served as the code for a political lampoon or satire (Krylov's "Kaib"). Thus, Derzhavin calls the Senate, the Divan. Radishchev's *Bova,* which Pushkin imitated in his lycée poem *Bova,* is an example of the use of Russian folklore to attack the autocracy. Pushkin recalls this in his essay "Alexander Radishchev" (1833-34).

Yury Tynyanov uncovered the duality in Pushkin's semantic system: "Katenin was offended by *Mozart and Salieri* because of its semantic duality... and *Feast in Time of Plague* was written during a cholera epidemic. The semantic structure of a costume drama, presented in foreign dress, is replete with contemporary autobiographical material."[21]

The Golden Cockerel contains a number of allusions common to lampoons.[22] But the elements of "personal satire" are disguised with especial care. This is explained by the fact that Nicholas I was the object of the satire.

The quarrel between the astrologer and the Tsar has autobiographical features.

In the rough draft and even in the fair copy the allusions are absolutely transparent. In the draft:

> But with *tsars* it is bad to squabble.

The word *tsars* is then crossed out and replaced by the word *the mighty*:

> But with *the mighty* it is bad to squabble.

However, in the fair copy Pushkin reinstates the first version:

> But with *tsars* it is bad to squabble.

In the printed version the allusion is once again "encoded":

> But with *another person* it is bad to squabble.

This, in turn, called for a change in the text's "moralistic" ending. Pushkin borrowed this ending from *The Tale of the Dead Tsarevna*:

> The tale's not true, but there's a lesson for us,
> And a hint for *another person.*

In this configuration the allusion became too apparent. Therefore, in the final version the text reads:

> The tale's not true, but in it there's a hint:
> A lesson for *good fellows.* [23]

The allusion lies in the "lesson," then. The Tsar is a "good fellow."

The subject of *The Golden Cockerel* is the failure of the Tsar to keep his word.

After receiving the magic cockerel from the astrologer, the Tsar promises to fulfill his first wish:

> "Such momentous boon afforded,"
> He rejoiced, "shall be rewarded

> By a wish, to be fulfilled
> Like my own as soon as willed."

But when the time for payment comes:

> "What?" Dadon fell back, amazed.
> "What possessed you? Are you crazed?
> Does some wicked demon ride you?
> Have your wits dried up inside you?
> What's your game, in heaven's name?
> Pledge I did; but all the same
> There are limits, well you knew;..."

This is much harsher in the rough draft:

> My royal pledge
> *I am prepared to disavow*

In the rough draft the astrologer *demands* that the Tsar fulfill his promise:

> "Tsar, he said—[you promise] impertinently
> [You promised] [you swore] [to me] [promise] [you]
> [You gave me] [that] without fail
> [You] that you will fulfill your word
> [Wish] my first
> *Isn't that so? I call the whole capital to bear witness.*

The astrologer's reference to "the whole capital" (public opinion) is of interest here.

According to the original conception, the eunuch, whom Dadon orders be driven away, reproaches the Tsar:

> That's how you pay
> Said the old man.

In 1834, Pushkin knew the worth of the Tsar's word.

IV

The circumstances in which Pushkin found himself in 1834 can be characterized by the following line from *Yezersky:* "Pardoned and fettered by mercy" (Autumn 1833).

By this time it had become all too clear that the Tsar's first act of mercy—freedom from censorship—in practice led to double censorship—by the Tsar and the general censor.

After the prohibition of a whole series of works, on December 11, 1833, *The Bronze Horseman* was returned to Pushkin with the Tsar's comments, and Pushkin was forced to annul the agreement with Smirdin.

The Tsar also manifested his mercy by conferring on Pushkin the title His Majesty's Gentleman of the Chamber (Kammerjunker) on December 31, 1833.

It has been established that Pushkin died without forgiving the Tsar for being made Kammerjunker.[24]

The history of Pushkin's relations with the court after the lowest rank at court had been bestowed upon him, as well as his quarrel with the Tsar over the opening and inspection of letters to his wife, have been sufficiently illuminated in a whole series of works.

On June 25, 1834, Pushkin sent Benkendorf a letter requesting permission to resign.

The opening and inspection of Pushkin's letters to his wife (April 20-22) preceded his request to resign.

Pushkin wrote:

> I have seen three tsars: the first ordered my little cap to be taken off me and gave my nurse a scolding on my account; the second *was not gracious* to me; although the third has saddled me with being a Kammerpage close upon my old age, I have no desire for him to be replaced by a fourth. Better let well enough alone. We shall see just how our Sashka *will get along with his namesake* born to the purple: *I didn't get along with mine.* God grant that he not follow in my footsteps and *write verses* and *quarrel with tsars!* [25]

Pushkin here is undoubtedly recalling his poem "My Pedigree" (1830):

A fatal penchant for defiance
We all share: stiffnecked, as was fit,
My ancestor refused compliance
To Peter, and was hanged for it.
By this an insight may be fostered:
A potentate dislikes retort.[26]

Pushkin ties the story of his relations with the tsars to the subject of the mutual relations between the Pushkin family and the Romanov dynasty.

Pushkin's letter was conveyed to the Tsar, who felt no shame in admitting this action, and "set in motion an intrigue worthy of Vidocq and Bulgarin."

Pushkin ends the note in his diary about this matter with a very sharp attack on Nicholas: "No matter what you say, it's wise to be autocratic."

The monarch corroborated Pushkin's opinion by commissioning Benkendorf "to explain to him the senselessness of his behavior and how this all could end...."

Benkendorf "explained" and Pushkin retracted his request to resign:

A few days ago the spleen took possession of me; I submitted my resignation. But I received [...] such a dry dismissal from Benkendorf that I had to show the white feather, and I'm begging for Christ and God's sake that they not retire me. (Letter to his wife, written in the first half of July.)[27]

In his appeal to Benkendorf for permission to resign, Pushkin also requests that he not be denied access to the archives.

The fact that Pushkin in a moment of profound irritation at the Tsar nevertheless requests that he not be denied access to the archives demonstrates what great significance he attached to this and what a blow for him a refusal would be.

Beginning in the early 1830s Pushkin intended that his historical works be the basis not only for establishing his material well-being, but also his relationship with the Tsar and "high society." Neither *Eugene Onegin,* nor *Poltava,* nor *Boris Godunov* could give him the kind of social position without which life in St. Petersburg seemed intolerable.

As early as 1831 Pushkin wrote to Benkendorf:

I do not dare and do not wish to take upon myself the title of Historiographer after the unforgettable Karamzin; but I can in time fulfill my long-held wish to write the history of Peter the Great and his descendants to Tsar Peter III.

He did dare and he did wish.

Let us recall the joy with which he told his closest friends, Nashchokin and Pletnyov, that the Tsar had granted him access to the archives for writing *The History of Peter the Great.*[28]

This matter has very great significance in Pushkin's biography.

For Pushkin, the 1830s were a time of searching for a social position. On the one hand, he was attempting to become a professional man of letters, and on the other, to understand himself as a representative of the hereditary aristocracy.

The post of court historiographer was to allow him to solve these contradictions.

For Pushkin this post was inseparable from the figure of Karamzin—an advisor to the Tsar and a grandee, who attained a high position at court through his historical labors.

However, Nicholas I and his retinue did not in the least intend that Pushkin play such an important role.

In February 1834, A. N. Vulf recorded in his diary:

I found that the poet [...] was highly indignant with the Tsar, because he had dressed him in uniform, a person who had now written *the history of the Pugachev rebellion and several new Russian tales*. He says that he is going back to the opposition...[29]

This note is of great interest, since it includes information about Pushkin's intention to go back to the opposition, and also indicates that Pushkin felt insulted precisely as the author of *The History of Pugachev* and Russian tales. (Karamzin had also written tales.)

In his diary entry about his first encounter with Nicholas after the bestowal of the court rank, Pushkin mentions that he spoke with the Tsar about Pugachev (affirming himself as a historiographer[30]), but did not thank him for being made Kammerjunker (which was a clear breach of etiquette).

If we take all of the above into consideration, it becomes clear that Pushkin could interpret a categorical denial to his request for access to the archives as the gesture of a "despotic landowner" who wanted to destroy all his plans by that means.

The entire summer of 1834 passed under the cloud of his quarrel with the Tsar. Pushkin gave in, but there was still no reconciliation.[31]

On August 25, five days before the unveiling of the Alexander Column, Pushkin left Petersburg "so as not to attend the ceremony with the other Kammerjunkers."

Pushkin's departure from the capital, practically on the eve of the celebration, was without question a demonstration.

A note about this, which he made in his diary three months later, shows that Pushkin's attitude towards his situation had not changed.

While in Moscow on his journey (September 8-9), in a letter to Alexander Turgenev, Pushkin speaks with irony of his career at court: "I am grateful to Polevoi for his being kindly disposed toward the historiographer of Pugachev, the Kammerjunker, etc."[32]

On September 13, Pushkin arrived in Boldino, where he planned to write. He tells his wife about this (September 15): "I should very much like to write something or other. I don't know whether inspiration will come."[33]

But the Boldino autumn of 1834 was the least fruitful for Pushkin. He did not write anything except *The Tale of the Golden Cockerel.*

The fair copy is dated September 20.

And on September 26, A. M. Yazykov, who had visited Pushkin in Boldino, wrote: "he showed me a history of Pugachev [...], several tales in verse in the manner of Yershov, and a history of the Pushkin family."[34]

We can assume that Yazykov was the first to hear *The Golden Cockerel.*

The Golden Cockerel, which the critics greeted with silence, was first published in the April issue of *The Library for Reading* (1835).

Pushkin did not succeed in evading the censor's suspicions.

The censor Nikitenko did not allow three lines in the tale.

I cite the note Pushkin made in his diary:

The censorship did not pass the following lines in my tale about the golden cockerel:

Reign abed

and

> The tale's not true, but in it there's a hint:
> A lesson for good fellows.

The Krasovsky era has returned. Nikitenko is stupider than Birukov.

Here we see Pushkin's usual attacks against censorship (and maybe the wish to preserve these lines at least in his diary). The confrontation with the censorship did not come as a surprise to Pushkin, however.

The fair copy bears traces of preliminary "authorial" censorship. In the following excerpt

> And Dadon sends out a third
> Host, himself commander,
> *Praying to Elijah the Prophet*

the last line in the printed verson looked like this:

> Though unsure what this might profit.

One line was changed in the episode of the quarrel between the astrologer and the Tsar. In answer to the astrologer's demand, the Tsar says:

> And—what use is she to you?
> *Enough, what am I, a panderer?*

It was not possible to present that line to any censorship. The final version reads:

> Enough, do you know who I am?

Finally, in the line that serves as a key to the second level of meaning in this "folk" tale:

> But with *tsars* it is bad to squabble—

the too obvious attack is exchanged for a mild hint:

> But with *another* it costs to squabble.[35]

Likewise, in his letters to his wife (1834), Pushkin calls the Tsar "that one" (tot).

V

The episode with the Tsar's sons that Pushkin inserted into Irving's plot breaks *The Golden Cockerel* into three parts. Part I: from the beginning to the line "The noise died down and the Tsar dozed off"; Part II: to the line "[Dadon banqueted] in the royal maiden's tent"; Part III: from the line "At long last, though, forth he sallied" to the end.

We have already seen that the semantic duality in the tale's quarrel between the Tsar and the astrologer can be viewed only against the background of the events of 1834.

But the tale's first part compels us to propose something else as well.

It concerns the fact that the characterization of the Tsar emphasizes laziness, inactivity and the "desire to husband his laurels" (see "The Legend of the Arabian Astrologer"). Later these traits disappear entirely.

Pushkin never considered Nicholas I to be lazy or inactive. But he always ascribed these very traits to Alexander I: "The imperial rule: 'Don't do the job and don't run from the job'" ("An Imaginary Conversation with Emperor Alexander I" [1822], "Noel," "You and I").

And much later, in 1830:

> A ruler weak and wily,
> A baldish fop, a *foe of toil...*

And in the same work:

> I with my people, will curb everybody!
> Our tsar in his chambers said.[36]

The biography of Dadon, "the retired conqueror,"[37] fits this image perfectly.[38] It is well known that the mystically inclined Alexander associated with Masons as well as soothsayers and clairvoyants,[39] and at the end of his life dreamed of retiring to a quiet life.

Since youth he had been fearsome

....

But in old age he wished
To rest from his martial deeds
And created peace for himself...

Compare also the tenth chapter of *Eugene Onegin:* "Our Tsar slumbered" and "The Tsar forgot himself in slumber."

Pushkin may have been struck by the parallel between the character of the King in "Legend of the Arabian Astrologer"—"a retired conqueror, who languished for repose"—and Alexander I.[40]

It was undoubtedly in order to make it more difficult to decode the political meaning in *The Golden Cockerel* that traits characteristic of two reigns were merged. Nobody would think of looking for the "hale and hearty" and far-from-old Nicholas I in Dadon, an aging Tsar and a "retired conqueror."

The state of the manuscript does not in the least contradict this hypothesis.

The rough draft of the tale's beginning (to the line "Sent a runner to implore him") has not survived. The next six lines are written on the verso of the cover of the notebook (No. 2374) and the date has not been established.[41] Then follow the lines from "My golden cockerel" to "Hurled them back by sea and land." They were written down on page 15 in the same notebook with works that date from 1833 *(The Bronze Horseman)* and seven pages after the sketch "The Tsar saw before him," which according to the original plan may have been intended for *The Golden Cockerel.* But there is no doubt that the rough draft of the whole tale that begins with the line "One year, two pass peacefully" dates from the autumn of 1834.[42]

We may presume that Pushkin's last tale was not written straight off. Pushkin often left his tales unfinished *(The Tale of Ilya Muromets, How in the Warm Springtime)* or returned several times to the same subject matter *(Bova).* Part of *The Golden Cockerel,* from the beginning to the line "One year, two pass peacefully," may have been written before 1834 and it may have been conceived as a satire on Alexander I.

In the drafts the astrologer is constantly referred to as a Shamakhanian eunuch and a Shamakhanian wise man[43] and even once as an Astrakhanian.

Shamakha was annexed to Russia in 1820.

Therefore, the Shamakhanian eunuch's revenge on the Tsar and Conqueror may be connected to this event by association.

In 1834 this outline was filled in with "autobiographical material."

And so, two tsars may be reflected in the image of Dadon, one who "was not gracious" to Pushkin, and the other who "saddled [Pushkin] with being a Kammerpage in old age."

March 20, 1931-January 20, 1933
[1930s-1950s?]

Translated by Ronald Meyer

THE TALE OF
THE GOLDEN COCKEREL
&
"THE TSAR SAW BEFORE HIM..."
Commentary

T HE DRAFT MANUSCRIPT OF *The Tale of the Golden Cockerel* was first recorded by V. E. Yakushkin in his description of Pushkin's manuscripts *(Russkaya starina*, 1884, vol. XLIII, pp. 641, 644). The fair copy of the tale is kept in the Public Library of the RSFSR in Leningrad.[1]

Unlike Pushkin's other tales, *The Golden Cockerel* has a literary work as its source rather than a folk tale: Washington Irving's "Legend of the Arabian Astrologer." The collection in which this legend appears is entitled *The Alhambra, or the New Sketch Book*. It was published in Paris in June 1832. A French translation of *The Alhambra* appeared simultaneously. This translation is very close to the original and conveys the ironic tone of Irving's tales. Apparently, Pushkin used the translation and not the original. It is the French two-volume edition of *The Alhambra* that is found in the poet's library.[2]

"The Legend of the Arabian Astrologer" is a parodic, pseudo-Arabian tale, which Irving passes off as a folk legend that he has recorded. However, the most cursory acquaintance with this legend convinces one that it does not contain the characteristic features of folk poetry.

In the 1830s Pushkin was keenly interested in European folklore, in particular Spanish folklore,[3] and if he consulted *The Alhambra* because it was recommended as a collection of Spanish folk tales,[4] then he must have been disappointed.

Contemporaries knew Irving as a literary hoaxer and satirist (the author of *Salmagundi*, *The History of New York* , etc.), and critics constantly compared him with Addison.[5]

The tone and content of "Legend of the Arabian Astrologer" recall the "Oriental tales," which were the customary vehicle for political satire in the eighteenth century. This explains why Pushkin turned precisely to this source for the creation of a political lampoon—*The Tale of the Golden Cockerel*,[6] which the poet included in the list of his "folk tales."[7] Even if Pushkin did not suspect "direct satire" in "Legend of the Arabian Astrologer," then in any event, Irving's tale offered rewarding material that could be reworked into a political lampoon (the "biography" of the Moorish King Aben Habuz, a retired and peace-loving conqueror, who dreams of repose; the weathercock, magical though it is, that directs the King's actions; the uprisings in outlying districts; the aged monarch, ravaging his country to satisfy the whims of his concubine, who has incited revolution in the capital; and, finally, the motif of the Tsar not keeping his word, which was of particular interest to Pushkin).

Pushkin utilized the genre of the folk tale for political allusions, and in doing so he continues the tradition of Radishchev.[8] Radishchev's narrative poem *Bova* contains attacks on the autocracy. We know that Pushkin recognized the merits of Radishchev's *Bova*, despite its lack of "national character."[9]

Pushkin initially began to work on "Legend of the Arabian Astrologer" in 1833. The sketch "The Tsar saw before him," which dates from this period, was written in the same trochaic tetrameter as *The Golden Cockerel*. The first ten lines of this sketch incorporate a part of Irving's legend that Pushkin did not make use of in *The Golden Cockerel*. In the legend the effigies (or, as Pushkin calls them, little dolls) are magical representations of the enemy forces, which when touched by the magic wand either take flight or begin to wage internecine war and destroy each other. And then the same fate befalls the next enemy.

In Pushkin's work this motif is more complex. The second half of the sketch is a description of just such a toy fleet.

In regard to the draft of the first twenty-eight lines of *The Golden Cockerel*, whose date of composition is unknown, and which is missing from "Album 1833-35," we can only state that these lines were in final form since they were copied into the fair copy with only one correction ("they go" instead of "they throng"; the elimination of the epithet "Shamakhanian" has a special significance that will be discussed below) and without punctuation, which indicates a perfunctory transcription rather than the creative rewriting that we encounter several times in the fair copy of *The Golden Cockerel*.

The manuscript of the next six lines, located on the verso of the fly-leaf which therefore makes it difficult to date, is very close to the fair copy. The fact that the corrections were made in a different ink indicates their later provenance. It should be noted that the entire fair copy was written in this faded brown ink. We may assume that Pushkin entered the corrections in the draft during the recopying process: the word "boldly" (in connection with the line "'Tsar,' he said impertinently") indicates that in the original conception (when Pushkin still called the astrologer a Shamakhanian wise man) this character's identity was somewhat different.

Judging from the words that survive on a strip of paper at the notebook's spine ("No," "Tsar") we can assume that the part torn out between pages 5 and 6 (16 sheets) contained the draft of several lines from *The Golden Cockerel* that have not survived, as is the case with the tale's beginning.

There was undoubtedly a break in the writing of the tale after the line "He repulsed them on every side," because the manuscript on page 201 was written in a different ink than the text on the part that was torn out.

The manuscript reproduced here from the line "One year, two pass peacefully" to the end of the tale undoubtedly represents the first draft, although the condition of the manuscript is not uniform. Sometimes the poet writes a word, immediately crosses it out, once again writes it and again crosses it out (see the dialogue between Dadon and the commander). Several lines are not completed to the end (for example, "The Tsar cordially") or lack their rhyming line ("It's not misfortune that this tale is a lie"), and lines that repeat are merely indicated by a dash. Individual episodes are reworked twice (the return of Dadon, the quarrel between the Tsar and the astrologer) and even three times (the appearance of the Queen of Shamakha).

All this notwithstanding, the manuscript of the tale is very close to the final version.

Pushkin does not deviate from his original plan in the second stage of reworking individual episodes or when making the fair copy of the tale, but either introduces new details or discards material that was already written. The first page of the manuscript is an exception as regards its completeness. In comparison to the remainder of the tale's text, the verse on this first page underwent very minor reworking.

On the next page the break in continuity between the lines "The Tsar does not know where to begin" and "The troops march day and night" is filled in only in the fair copy, where the line "The Tsar does not know where to begin" is replaced by another line ("The Tsar sends out a third host") and two new lines make their appearance:

> And he leads it to the East,
> Not knowing himself, what this might profit

or:

> Praying to Elijah the Prophet,

which connects the previous episode with the Tsar's march.

The line "What is the meaning of this, he says," which is not crossed out in the manuscript, is not transferred to the fair copy. Perhaps, Pushkin had noticed that this same exclamation is encountered in Yershov's *Little Humpback Horse*,[10] which had just been published (summer, 1834). This may also explain the vacillation in the choice of landscape. The following lines were written twice:

> To the sea the Tsar leads his troops,
> What is that on the shore...

Evidently the Queen's tent was to have been situated on the seashore, but then Pushkin immediately dismisses the idea of putting the tent on the seashore and writes:

> What is that amidst the high mountains
> He sees a [White] silken tent.

The tent, the seashore, the tsar-maiden (see the analogous episode in Yershov's tale).

The order of appearance of individual motifs in the first variant is different than in the final one. In the first variant the order is: tent, maiden, sons; in the final version it is: tent, defeated host, sons, maiden. An example of how Pushkin reworks a folklore motif is the scene of Dadon's meeting with the Queen of Shamakha, of which there are three redactions:

1. He sees the [White] silken tent.
In that tent sits a maiden
[The Shamakhanian] Queen.

2. [and] [White] [silken] mysterious tent
[Opened] [and] [to] [Dadon] the maiden
The Shamakhanian Queen
[Walked out] quietly from the tent.

3. It opened and the maiden
All aglow [white] goodness
[Lambent walked out of the tent—]
[Rosy] ? [as the dawn]
Quietly greeted the Tsar.

The first redaction of this scene is fairly close to *The Tale of Yeruslan Lazarevich.*[11]

The introduction of the episode (absent in Irving's legend) of the brothers, who appear only to be killed, can be explained by the tale's satiric tendency and serves to emphasize the Tsar's depravity. Rival brothers who kill each other is a motif found in folk poetry of various nations.[12]

The steed who roams about the body of the dead hero is a motif that we find in Pushkin's early works ("The Slain Knight," *Ruslan and Lyudmila),* where the steed *is waiting* for his dead master. This last detail is not included in the final version of *The Golden Cockerel.* However, in the manuscript we read: "they are waiting for their masters."

The description of the murdered tsareviches:

The black curls were dishevelled,
The white hands lay outstretched—

was probably discarded by Pushkin because the song-like construction of these lines broke the tale's epic tone.

The scene in the tent, which came comparatively easily for Pushkin, also makes use of elements from Russian folklore. For example, the traditional fairy-tale motif:

> She took him by the hand
> And led him to her tent.

These lines were written without a single correction.

It is typical that in Pushkin's least fantastic tale the word "enchanted" appeared only in the fair copy.

The return of the Tsar recalls the Duke's return in *Angelo;* moreover in the draft this similarity is more obvious than in the printed text ("they rushed to greet the maiden"). Cf. *Angelo:* "crowds *rushed to meet* him."

In the manuscript Pushkin calls the astrologer a "Shamakhanian wise man" and a "Shamakhanian eunuch" (we find this same epithet in the tale's fair copy). This epithet was removed from the final version, since the Shamakhanian wise man's revenge on the conqueror Tsar could have been interpreted as a political allusion: Shamakha had been annexed to Russia in 1820.

We should also mention examples of Pushin's absentmindedness in connection with "Legend of the Arabian Astrologer." Irving describes the astrologer's appearance as: "His gray beard descended to his girdle," and later: "He could only perpetuate his gray hair and whiskers."

The Golden Cockerel:

> With a beard grown gray

Then Pushkin remembers that eunuchs do not have beards and the line becomes:

> All wrinkled, grown gray—

which follows Irving's description even more closely. In the final version there is neither a beard nor wrinkles ("Snowy-thatched now, like a swan").

Another instance: in Irving's legend the talisman (a bronze horseman), which has the same function as the cockerel in Pushkin's tale, was installed on the roof of the King's palace. The golden cockerel sits on a perch outside Dadon's window. However, in the draft we read:

> The cockerel flew down from his perch
> [On the roof] to the chariot

and in the fair copy it initially read:

> The cockerel on the Tsar's roof
> Stands guard...

The episode of the Tsar's quarrel with the eunuch underwent the most thorough revision. The first redaction still lacks Dadon's good-humored greeting ("'Father mine,' exclaimed Dadon, / 'Hail! How fare you? At your leisure / Come and speak; what is your pleasure?'") which contrasts strikingly with his fury, when his collocutor takes it into his head to contradict him. The eunuch immediately and "impertinently" approaches Dadon with his demand. In the next redaction this speech is lowered and simplified.

In general, an attempt to lower the lexicon and bring it closer to folk speech is typical of the revisions in the verse of *The Golden Cockerel:*

> You [wise man] old man have lost your mind

in the second revision of the episode of the quarrel looked like this:

> Or have you gone off your head?

And the line:

> Flared the Tsar—

is changed to:

> Spat the Tsar:

Pushkin did not hit upon the Tsar's answer right away. The poet either closely follows his source:

> You should have asked me
> For something I could have done

and then has Dadon absolutely refuse to honor his pledge:

> I am prepared to disavow
> My royal pledge

Then he immediately softens the refusal:

My royal pledge

(evidently, "have not forgotten") and

> I have not forgotten my pledge
> And am ready to honor it.

Then, finally, he goes back to the first variant:

> Pledge I did; but all the same
> There are limits, well you knew

In the line:

> But with Tsars it is bad to squabble

the too obvious allusion was softened:

> But with the mighty it is bad to squabble—

and, although it appears once again in the fair copy in its original form, it was completely disguised:

> But with another it costs to squabble—

The line that ended the manuscript, "It's no misfortune that this tale is a lie," was discarded by the poet. Evidently, not finding a suitable rhyme for the word "lie" (lozh'), Pushkin rejected this line altogether and exchanged it for the ending he had prepared for the draft of *The Tale of the Dead Tsarevna*. However, judging from just this one line, we can conclude that in the original conception the ending was supposed to have the same moralistic and satiric nature we find in the concluding lines of the final text:

> The tale's not true, but in it there's a hint,
> A lesson for good fellows.

Translated by Ronald Meyer

BENJAMIN CONSTANT'S *ADOLPHE* IN PUSHKIN'S WORK

I

T HE QUESTION OF THE influence of Benjamin Constant's renowned novel *Adolphe* on the work of Pushkin has already been discussed in Pushkin scholarship.[1] It is well known that Constant's romantic hero was one of the prototypes for Onegin. However, it is essential to note that Constant's novel had a significantly larger and, what is especially important to emphasize, more varied influence on the work of Pushkin than is commonly thought.

Adolphe had a special significance for Pushkin because it was linked to a number of literary problems Pushkin was working on at the end of the 1820s.

Adolphe was completed in 1807 and for a long time remained unpublished. It was not until 1815 that the first (London) edition of *Adolphe* appeared; the second (Paris) edition came out in 1816.

Constant's novel immediately captured the attention of the reading public. In 1817, Stendhal called *Adolphe* "an unusual novel." Saint-Beuve, speaking of the impression produced by *Adolphe* on contemporaries, compared the novel to Chateaubriand's *René*.[2] Sismondi, in his letter of October 14, 1816, which, according to Saint-Beuve, became an indispensable commentary on *Adolphe*, writes, among other things, the following: "In *Adolphe* the analysis of all the feelings of the human heart is so admirable, there is so much *truth* (italics mine, A. A.) in the weakness of the hero, so much intelligence of observation, vigor, and purity of style, that one reads the book with infinite pleasure. It seems to me that the pleasure this book affords me is enhanced by my recognizing its author on every page..."

As we see, the autobiographical nature of *Adolphe* on the one hand, and on the other, the truth and depth of psychological analysis in this work, which subsequently received the title "father of the psychological novel," were immediately recognized. On July 29, 1816, Byron wrote to his friend, the poet Rogers: "I have [...] also seen Ben. Constant's *Adolphe*, and his preface, denying the real people. It is a work which leaves an unpleasant impression, but very consistent with the consequences of not being in love, which is perhaps as disagreeable as any thing, except being so."[3]

Adolphe enjoyed prolonged success. In the late thirties, Gustave Planche wrote an extensive foreword to *Adolphe*; Balzac in the forties mentions *Adolphe* in a series of his novels (*Mémoires des deux jeunes mariées, Illusions perdues, Béatrix*).

Adolphe very soon became known to the Russian reader as well. As early as October 26, 1816, Vyazemsky wrote to A. I. Turgenev from Moscow: "I have sent *Adolphe* to you with the young Apostol-Muravyov."[4]

The first Russian translation of *Adolphe* appeared in 1818 under the title *Adolphe and Ellénore, or The Dangers of Amorous Ties, a True Story*. It was printed by the Orlov Province printing house.

Bearing in mind the significant ideological influence of Constant as a political writer and journalist on the leading figures of the time,[5] we may assume that Pushkin read *Adolphe* shortly after the novel's publication.

We know that Pushkin's contemporaries recognized Mme. de Staël in the heroine of *Adolphe*.[6] The widespread popularity of that name in Russia must certainly have sharpened the readers' interest in Constant's novel. In particular, Pushkin, who esteemed the works of de Staël so highly, who mentions her books *Dix années d'exile* and *D'Allemagne* in the first chapter of *Eugene Onegin*, who came to the defense of the author of *Delphine* and *Corinne* in 1825, and who in 1831 depicts Mme. de Staël in his *Roslavlyov*, must have regarded *Adolphe* with special interest.

In a letter to Karolina Sobanskaya (January-February 1830), Pushkin writes that the name of *Adolphe*'s heroine, Ellénore, reminds him of "the ardent reading of his youthful years, and the sweet phantom which fascinated him then"[7] (the Odessa period of his life).

Pushkin's interest in *Adolphe* was as extensive as that of his contemporaries.

On December 20, 1829, that is to say, before the publication of Vyazemsky's translation, Baratynsky wrote to Vyazemsky: "I am extremely curious about the translation of this worldly, metaphysical, and delicately sensitive *Adolphe* into our crude language."[8] Vyazemsky, whose foreword to his own translation of *Adolphe*[9] testifies to his ecstatic regard for Constant's novel, upon sending his translation to E. M. Khitrovo, wrote to her: "You love this novel, you will be pleased that I have dedicated it to a name that is dear to you, that is, to Pushkin";[10] and in 1832 he informed his wife: "The other day, at a ball, Mme. Zavadskaya told me that she had read my *Adolphe* three times."[11] Nikitenko's remarks in his diary regarding *Adolphe*[12] and Polevoi's translation of *Adolphe*[13] date from approximately the same time. The influence of *Adolphe* on *A Hero of Our Time*, which has been established by scholars, testifies to the impression produced by Constant's novel on Lermontov.[14] A man of another generation, I. S. Aksakov, for whom *Adolphe* was only an old French novel, in a letter from 1845 to his father, informs him of Mme. A. O. Smirnova's regard for the novel: "Without mentioning it to A.O., I borrowed from her a certain old French novel, Benjamin Constant's *Adolphe*, which she places higher than the heavens."[15]

A copy of the third edition of *Adolphe* (1824) with numerous pencilled notations is contained in Pushkin's personal library.[16] As I have succeeded in establishing, there are notes in Pushkin's own hand on pages 61 and 104, a fact that allows us to assume that he made the other notations as well.

II

PUSHKIN'S FIRST KNOWN MENTION of *Adolphe* is found in a rough draft of the first chapter of *Eugene Onegin* (stanza XXXVIII, line 9: "Like Childe Harold, gloomy, languid"), where, instead of the name Childe Harold, Pushkin wrote "Like Adolphe." And subsequently that name is met in stanza XXII of chapter 7 of *Eugene Onegin*. *Adolphe* was one of the novels which Tatyana read in Onegin's home and whose notes in the margin enabled her to guess the true character of her hero. In this way, Pushkin himself pointed to Adolphe as one of the prototypes for Onegin.[17]

In a hitherto unpublished draft of this stanza (notebook 2371, page 67), the list in which Pushkin includes *Adolphe* is extremely interesting. The transcription is as follows:

> [Although] we know that Eugene
> Long ago ceased to love reading
> [With him] however a number of works
> [Only] he [with him] only by habit carried—
> [Pages in which were reflected] [creators]
> [Staël's Corinne] [two or three] [novels]
> All of W. Scott Constant's Adolphe
> [Melmoth] [René] Constant's [Adolphe]
> All of Scott and two or three novels
> René two or three more novels
> In which the age was reflected
> And contemporary man
> Depicted [sadly] correctly enough...

Thus, it becomes clear that, according to Pushkin's original plan, the "two or three novels" of stanza XXII of *Eugene Onegin* were Maturin's *Melmoth*, Chateaubriand's *René* and *Adolphe*.[18] In the next version of these lines, Pushkin changes Staël to Byron, but the "two or three novels" are not named.

In "A Note" on the forthcoming publication of Vyazemsky's translation of *Adolphe*, Pushkin once again juxtaposes the names of Constant and Byron: "Benjamin Constant was the first to introduce that character, subsequently made famous by the genius of Lord Byron."[19] Pushkin's idea was reiterated by Vyazemsky: "Adolphe's character is a faithful imprint of his times. He is the prototype of Childe Harold and his numerous progeny."[20] The juxtaposition of Adolphe with the characters of Byron's heroes had a very important and fundamental meaning for Pushkin.

In dedicating his translation of *Adolphe* to Pushkin, Vyazemsky wrote: "Accept this translation of our favorite novel" and "We so often spoke of the excellence of this work." The fact that this "Dedication," as Vyazemsky's letters to Pletnyov make clear, was written in January 1831 does not mean that the conversations about *Adolphe* arose in connection with Vyazemsky's translation. More likely we can assume that it was precisely these conversations which prompted Vyazemsky to undertake the translation of Constant's novel.

Vyazemsky translated *Adolphe con amore,* and attached particular significance to his translation, and working on such a relatively short work for a very long time.[21]

On December 20, 1829, Baratynsky thanks Vyazemsky for the
manuscript of the translation which had been sent to him for his
examination.[22] And it was not until January 12, 1831, that
Vyazemsky asked Pletnyov to give the censor the translation of
Adolphe left in Petersburg with Zhukovsky and Delvig, promising to send the dedication ("A Letter to Pushkin") and the foreword ("A Few Words from the Translator") within a few days.[23]

On January 17, 1831, Vyazemsky sent Pushkin, from Ostafyev
to Moscow, his foreword (and perhaps his dedication as well)
with the following request: "Be so good as to read through and
reread with the most vigilant and strict attention *what I am sending to you* (italics mine, A. A.) and mark all the questionable
places. I don't want to leave my flanks open to the critics, at least
not in the foreword. Then show it to Baratynsky and return it to
me quickly... I must send it off to Petersburg, to Pletnyov, whom
I've already written to about beginning the publication of
Adolphe."

Apparently Pushkin found it necessary to make some corrections in Vyazemsky's foreword since three days later he replied:
"Leave *Adolphe* with me—within a few days I'll send you the necessary comments."[24] Therefore, we may presuppose Pushkin's
editing, if not his direct collaboration, and view the foreword as a
summary of Pushkin and Vyazemsky's conversations about
Adolphe. It is all the more likely, as has been noted, that some of
the ideas Vyazemsky expresses in the foreword repeat Pushkin's
remarks on *Adolphe.*[25]

In his foreword Vyazemsky says that in translating *Adolphe* he
had the desire to "acquaint" Russian writers with this novel.[26] Of
course, Vyazemsky knew that Russian writers could read
Constant's novel in the original and he by no means wanted to
acquaint them with Constant's novel, but to show them, by the
example of his translation, the kind of language in which the
Russian psychological novel should be written.

When we speak of the language of psychological prose, we
have in mind that language which Pushkin called "metaphysical."[27]

Pushkin believed that Vyazemsky was capable of furthering
the development of this language ("Prince Vyazemsky has his
style") and on September 1, 1823, he advised Vyazemsky to de-

vote himself to prose and "form the Russian metaphysical language." And as early as November 18, 1822, Vyazemsky wrote to A. I. Turgenev: "I am working on some prose translations from the French. First of all, it is a useful exercise for me as well."[28] Apparently prose translation by then seemed to Vyazemsky a means of enriching the Russian literary language and, in particular, of creating Russian prose, which was little cultivated and not yet very independent. Pushkin's complaints about the absence of Russian prose and the gap between prose and poetry are well known.[29]

In sending his translation to Baratynsky for his examination, Vyazemsky apparently expressed his understanding of the difficulty of translating all the nuances of *Adolphe* into Russian, because Baratynsky answered him as follows:

> I sense how difficult it is to translate the *worldly Adolphe* into a language that is not spoken in polite society, but it must be remembered that one day it will be spoken there and that expressions that now seem unrefined sooner or later will seem commonplace. It seems to me that one must not be frightened of expressions that are not current. In time they will be accepted and will enter the everyday language. Remember that those who speak Russian, speak the language of Pushkin, Zhukovsky, and yourself, the language of poets, from which it follows that it is not the public who teaches us but we who teach the public.[30]

A year before Vyazemsky's foreword was written, Pushkin, in a note about the forthcoming publication of *Adolphe*, wrote: "It will be interesting to see if the sharp and experienced pen of Prince Vyazemsky is able to conquer the difficulties of a *metaphysical language*, which is always harmonious, *worldly*, and often inspired. In this respect, the translation will be a creation in its own right and an important event in the history of our literature" (italics mine, A. A.). Here Pushkin, familiar with Vyazemsky's translation, or at least with the method of his translation,[31] expresses the same idea that Vyazemsky has stated in his foreword and Baratynsky in the letters cited. When speaking of the metaphysical language of *Adolphe*, Pushkin has in mind the creation of a language that reveals man's inner life. Pushkin likely borrowed the expression "metaphysical language" from Mme. de Staël. It is found in *Corinne*, in the chapter, *"De la littérature italienne,"* which no doubt Pushkin read carefully: *"les sentiments réfléchis exigent des expressions plus métaphysiques"* [rational thought requires a more metaphysical expression].[32]

Of course, the question arises in what ways the psychologism of *Adolphe*, which struck its readers so strongly, differs from the psychologism of novels contemporary with *Adolphe*, both the first-class ones (Staël, Chateaubriand) and the second-rate (Cottin, Krüdener, Genlis). Essentially, in *Adolphe* Constant was the first to show the duality in the human psyche,[33] the correlation of the conscious and subconscious,[34] the role of suppressed feelings,[35] and to unmask the true motives of human actions. This is why *Adolphe* subsequently received the title "father of the psychological novel," or *"le prototype du roman psychologique."* As we know, these features of *Adolphe* pointed the way for a number of novelists, one of the first of whom was Stendhal. As early as 1817, Stendhal wrote: "Dante would no doubt have understood the delicate feelings which abound in Benjamin Constant's unusual novel *Adolphe*, if such weak and miserable people as Adolphe had existed in his time; but in order to express these feelings, he would have had to enrich his language. Such as he has left it to us, it is unsuitable... for the translation of *Adolphe*."[36]

Pushkin's marginal notes in Constant's novel are extremely interesting in connection with his statement regarding *Adolphe's* metaphysical language. Next to the marked-off words (in Adolphe's letter to Ellénore): *"Je me précipite sur cette terre qui devrait s'entr'ouvrir pour m'engloutir à jamais; je pose ma tête sur la pierre froide qui devrait calmer la fièvre ardente qui me dévore,"[37]* Pushkin wrote: *"Nonsense."*

Pushkin felt the hyperbolic rhetoric of this sentence to be a breach in the "harmoniousness" of the metaphysical language, and these lamentations in the spirit of Rousseau's *New Heloise* must have rung false on the lips of a worldly seducer.

A second example is interesting as an instance of Pushkin's editing Constant's novel and relates to one of Adolphe's discourses on the duality of the human personality, of which I spoke above. In the marked-off phrase: *"et telle est la bizarrerie de notre coeur misérable que nous quittons avec un déchirement horrible ceux près de qui nous demeurions sans plaisir,"[38]* the word *"plaisir"* is crossed out and *"bonheur"* is written in the margins. This correction testifies to Pushkin's demand for exactness in nuances of meaning.

III

THE JUXTAPOSITION OF ADOLPHE with characters from eighteenth-century novels, which we find in Vyazemsky's foreword ("In the previous century, Adolphe would have simply been a madman with whom no one would have sympathized"), had already been made by Pushkin in the unfinished "A Novel in Letters" (1829), which was not published during Pushkin's lifetime, but with which Vyazemsky was probably familiar: "Reading Richardson gave me cause for reflection. What a frightful difference between the ideals of the grandmothers and their granddaughters! What do Lovelace and Adolphe have in common?"[39] Thus Pushkin mentions Adolphe's contemporaneity three times in the late twenties: in chapter 7 of *Eugene Onegin* (1828), in "A Novel in Letters" (1829), and in the note about *Adolphe* (1830). Vyazemsky repeats this assertion in the foreword to his translation.

Another parallel between Pushkin and Vyazemsky's thoughts on *Adolphe* concerns their definition of the novel's style and genre. Pushkin called the language of *Adolphe* "worldly." Compare this with what Vyazemsky says in his foreword: "This work is not only a novel of the present day *(roman du jour)* similar to the latest or drawing-room novels..."[40] As we have seen, Baratynsky also called Constant's novel "worldly."

During this period Pushkin gave a great deal of thought to the creation of a contemporary "society" novel or tale.

In "A Novel in Letters," which may be regarded as a collection of Pushkin's literary and polemical (and political) opinions that are expressed by all four correspondents, the author, through one of his heroines, says the following about the novels of the eighteenth century: "A clever man could take a ready-made plan, ready-made characters, correct the style and remove the absurdities, amplify things only hinted at—and a fine, original novel would emerge. Tell this to my ungrateful R* on my behalf... Let him embroider new patterns on an old canvas and in a little frame present us with a picture of the world and people he knows so well." We recognize here the method that Pushkin himself sometimes employed *(Roslavlyov,* "Mistress into Maid," "A Russian Pelham"). We see, then, that for Pushkin (in 1829), the problem of creating a "society" tale consisted in transforming a ready-made plot into a concrete work with defined, realistic material.

Undoubtedly, the material for Pushkin's "society" tales was drawn from his observations of the manners and customs of that society in which he lived following his return from Mikhailovskoye. There are references to the autobiographical nature of Pushkin's "society" tales of the years 1828-29[41] in Pushkin scholarship. But this, of course, does not exclude literary reminiscences.

The theme of the tale "In a Corner of the Little Square"—adultery and the fate of a woman who has openly violated the laws of society—undoubtedly points to the French tradition.[42]

In a note on the forthcoming publication of the translation of *Adolphe*, Pushkin, characterizing Constant's hero, cites stanza XXII (not yet published) of chapter 7 of his *Eugene Onegin* and associates *Adolphe* with the two or three novels

> In which the epoch is reflected
> And modern man
> Rather correctly represented
> With his immoral soul,
> Selfish and dry,
> To dreaming measurelessly given,
> With his embittered mind
> Boiling in empty action.

Pushkin made the hero of the fragment "In a Corner of the Little Square" just such a "son of his age." This becomes clear from the following parallels. In the plan of the tale: "He is satirical, absentminded." Adolphe says of himself: "Absentminded, inattentive, bored." And in another passage: "I gained the reputation of a man who is frivolous and malicious" (i.e., satirical). Further on, Pushkin characterizes Valerian Volotsky (in the draft simply called Alexei): "He did not like boredom, feared every obligation and valued above all his selfish independence." Here Pushkin also has in mind Adolphe's statement: "I compared my tranquil and *independent life* with the life of anxieties, haste, and suffering to which her passion had doomed me."[43] In addition, we should note that both these characterizations relate to one and the same situation.

In creating a contemporary hero—"a son of his age"—a man of the world, as vain and egotistical as Adolphe,[44] Pushkin was borrowing a ready-made character, explaining, lowering, and revealing him in his own way, in accordance with the characterization of Constant's hero given in chapter 7 of *Eugene Onegin*. It is not a coincidence that Vyazemsky notes such a possibility in his foreword to *Adolphe*, which, as we have seen, was edited by Pushkin: "The author has so surely marked the characteristic features of Adolphe for us from one point of view that when we apply them to different circumstances, to a different age, we can easily chart his entire fate, no matter into what scene he is cast. Consequently, it is possible (given Constant's talents) to write about several Adolphes, in various ages and costumes."

But Pushkin not only borrowed the character of Adolphe for his tale, he also placed Alexei in the same circumstances as Constant's hero. We know that at that time (and never earlier or later), most probably in connection with the personal circumstances of his own life, the problem of Adolphe keenly interested Pushkin. A monument to this interest is "When your young years," the lyric poem of 1829-30, so close in theme and tone to Adolphe, and in situation to the fragment, "In a Corner of the Little Square."

The little we know of this work allows us to affirm that Pushkin made use of the plot of the novel *Adolphe* and a number of its psychological motivations while working on this tale. The difference in the ages of the lovers is revealing. It is the same in Pushkin's tale as in Constant's novel: Volotsky is 26 years old, Zinaida, 36. Compare this with *Adolphe:* "She is older than you by 10 years. You are 26 years old." Describing Ellénore's external appearance, Constant writes: "Famous for her beauty, although no longer in her first youth."[45] In the original draft of chapter 1 of the Pushkin fragment: "Beautiful, but no longer young." Like Ellénore, Zinaida loses the social position which previously belonged to her because of her open liaison with the man she loves. This theme runs throughout Constant's entire novel; in the fragment of Pushkin's story, it is noted by a single phrase: "I have not gone out for so long that I have grown completely unfamiliar with your high society." It should be noted that the words "but I have suffered too much, I am no longer young and the opinion of society has little sway over me"—are underlined in Pushkin's copy of *Adolphe*. Ellénore asks Adolphe's permission to receive him in "a secret hideaway in the middle of the big city." Precisely the same situation that opens Pushkin's tale.

The presentation of the preceding events, as summarized in the second chapter of the Pushkin fragment,[46] is very close to the development of the action in *Adolphe:* "Count P. soon noticed my relations with Ellénore" *(Adolphe).* "X. was soon convinced of his wife's unfaithfulness" ("In a Corner of the Little Square").

But a much closer similarity is found in the description of Zinaida's rupture with her husband. Adolphe hopes that Ellénore will not break with Count P., with whom she must have a decisive confrontation; then follows the phrase which is close to Pushkin's text: "...when suddenly a woman brought me a note *(un billet)* in which Ellénore asked me to meet her in a certain street, in a certain house, on the third floor." Adolphe goes to Ellénore: "Everything is broken off, she said to me..." In Pushkin's fragment, Zinaida, too, after the confrontation with her husband, "on the same day moved to the English Embankment in Kolomna[47] and in *a short note*[48] informed Volotsky, who had expected nothing like this, of everything." Immediately after this, in both Constant's novel and Pushkin's tale, there follows the description of their dismay upon receiving this news, which is extremely important for the understanding of the characters of both heroes: "I accepted her sacrifice, thanked her for it" *(Adolphe).* "He pretended to be grateful" ("In a Corner of the Little Square"). Constant and Pushkin say almost the same thing about the feelings of their heroes: "Never had he intended to bind himself with such ties" (Pushkin); "My bonds to Ellénore," "because of the bonds that I have dragged for so long" (Constant). In Pushkin's copy of *Adolphe,* the end of the following phrase is underlined: "belief in a future that must separate us, perhaps *an unrecognized resentment of bonds that I could not dissolve, gnawed me internally."*

The situation in the first chapter of the Pushkin fragment can be explained by the following quotation from Constant's novel: "We spent monotonous evenings in silence and vexation." Compare this with the following from the fragment of Pushkin's tale: "You are silent; you don't know what to do with yourself, you leaf through books, find fault with me so as to quarrel with me..."[49]

Thus, we see that Pushkin in the fragment of "In a Corner of the Little Square" reproduces the plot of *Adolphe* (beginning with chapter 4 of Constant's novel), coloring the character of the central hero with his own attitude. Volotsky, in any case, is devoid of that "declamatory sentimentality" which, in the words of one French critic, is characteristic of Constant.

Let us not forget that for Pushkin Adolphe was a Byronic hero ("Benjamin Constant was the first to introduce that character subsequently made famous by the genius of Lord Byron"). Thus, through his exposure and satirical interpretation of Adolphe, Pushkin surpassed Byronism in his prose experiments just as he did in *Eugene Onegin*.

The satirical evaluation of the central hero's psychology in Pushkin is, of course, linked with the evaluation of his social position. It is all the more important to note that analogous satirical evaluations in Constant's novel have only secondary significance. The social significance of the satirical tendency in Pushkin's fragment ("In a Corner of the Little Square") is revealed in the argument between Zinaida and Volotsky. The theme of this argument centers on Pushkin's favorite reflections on the new aristocracy ("Aristocracy," interrupted the pale woman, "what you call aristocracy..."),[50] which are repeated almost word-for-word in two other "society" tales by Pushkin. "What is the Russian aristocracy?" a Spaniard asks Minsky ("Guests Gather at the Dacha"). "Do you know what our aristocracy is," writes Liza to her girlfriend ("A Novel in Letters"). Pushkin depicts Volotsky as "a descendant of Ryurik"[51] who demands respect from the new aristocracy.

That is why Volotsky speaks with such scorn about "the daughter of that singer." "Daughter of a singer," of course, implies not the daughter of some church singers, but a representative of the new aristocracy, so loathed by Pushkin. The line from the poem "My Pedigree" (1830)—"I did not sing in the choir with sextons"—as we know, is aimed at the Razumovskys. It is they whom Pushkin has in mind in the enumeration: "It is funny to see in the insignificant grandsons of pastry cooks, orderlies, church singers, and deserters only the arrogance of the Duke Montmorency, the first Christian baron, and Clermont-Tonnerre" ("Guests Gather at the Dacha"). The head of the house of Montmorency had the title "the first Christian baron." Compare this with the following from F. Vigel's *Notes:* "All the sons... of Cyril Gregoryevich Razumovsky were arrogant and unapproachable and considered themselves Russian Montmorencys" (vol. l, p. 303). Despite the sketchiness of the portrait, it is possible to recognize in Countess Fuflygina another representative of the new aristocracy, the lawgiver of Petersburg society, Countess M. D. Nesselrode.[52] She was Pushkin's personal enemy because of an epigram the poet had written about Nesselrode's father, Minister

Guryev. Pushkin's characterization of Countess Fuflygina is very similar to the accounts of Countess Nesselrode given by contemporaries.

Volotsky calls aristocrats "those who extend their hand to Countess Fuflygina." See the memoirs of M. A. Korff: "The salon of Countess Nesselrode... was indisputably the first in St. Petersburg; to get into such an exclusive place presented a difficult problem... but whoever established himself there found he had open admission to the entire higher circle." Fuflygina is fat. P. A. Vyazemsky wrote to A. Bulgakov about Nesselrode: "... and broadshouldered and big-bosomed and big-bellied." Fuflygina is a bribe-taker and an insolent fool. P. V. Dolgorukov later remembered Nesselrode as "a woman of limited intelligence... a bribe-taker... a scandalmonger... but distinguished by unusual energy, daring, insolence... and by virtue of this insolence she was held in speechless and humble respect by the Petersburg court circles."

The element of "malignant gossip" inherent in the genre of the society tale (see, for example, Bulwer's *Pelham)* undergoes a functional change in Pushkin's unfinished stories and acquires a sharply publicistic tendency. Thus, these stories may be viewed as illustrations of the programmatic statements Pushkin made in his articles of that period.

As for the references to the autobiographical quality of Pushkin's "society" tales, and, in particular, of the fragment "In a Corner of the Little Square," if we consider Pushkin's well-known ability to transform himself into his favorite author, we can easily allow that in the second half of the twenties Pushkin's worldly self (which he so diligently separated from his creative personality) was embodied in the worldly, bored, independence-seeking Adolphe. Compare, for example, the Pushkin fragment, "My fate is settled. I am marrying..." with *Adolphe.*[53] Therefore, if we find Adolphe in Onegin and Volotsky—that Adolphe is Pushkin. That this should have been the case was no doubt aided by the autobiographical character of *Adolphe* itself, which, like the autobiographical character of *Werther* must have suggested the idea of creating a work of an autobiographical nature. In the foreword to the third edition of his novel, Constant himself writes: "What lends a certain truth to my story is that almost everyone who has read it has spoken to me about himself as if he were a character who had been in my hero's position."

IV

THUS, WE SEE THAT in the late twenties Pushkin partially relies on *Adolphe* as he addresses the task of creating a non-Byronic contemporary hero,

The change in Pushkin's attitude toward the Byronic hero can already be seen in *Eugene Onegin.*

Pushkin scholarship has repeatedly pointed out the similarity between Onegin and Adolphe. All the convincing comparisons of Onegin and Adolphe lead to one conclusion: *Adolphe* was one of the works which gave Pushkin a skeptical and realistic position against Byron.

It should be noted that the similarity between Onegin and Adolphe grows towards the end of Pushkin's novel, and is particularly apparent in chapter 8 (1830). Now that we have a number of facts that throw light on Pushkin's attitude towards *Adolphe,* we can with greater certainty point to several more rather significant parallels between chapter 8 of *Eugene Onegin* and Constant's novel.

I will begin with variants from the rough drafts: "His wild nature overcoming." Compare this with *Adolphe*'s: *"Ce caractère qu'on dit bizarre et sauvage..."* The last line of stanza XII originally looked like this: "He wanted to occupy himself with something." Adolphe, too, dreams of activity.[54] Furthermore, in comparing chapter 8 with *Adolphe,* it is possible to find examples that are closer than any yet found. Baron T. says to Adolphe: "You are twenty-six years old. You have lived half your life without beginning anything, without accomplishing anything." In chapter 8 of *Eugene Onegin:*

> Having without a goal, without exertions,
> Lived to the age of twenty-six,
> *Irked by the inactivity of leisure...*

Later Adolphe says: "I cast a long and sad glance upon the time that had irretrievably flowed by; I remembered the hopes of youth... *my inactivity weighed upon me.*" Compare this with chapter 8: "But it is sad to think that youth/ was given us in vain..." There is also a similarity between the situation itself as presented to us in chapter 8 and the beginning of Constant's novel.

A relative of the hero, Count P., whose girlfriend Adolphe is in love with, invites him to a soirée. Prince N., Tatyana's husband, invites Onegin to a soirée.

Adolphe, wishing to see Ellénore, looks at his watch every minute; "Once more Onegin counts the hours, / once more he can't wait for the day to end."

"Finally the hour struck when Adolphe must go to the Count's."

But ten strikes...

Adolphe trembles as he approaches Ellénore.

Trembling, he goes in to the princess:

But most noteworthy of all is that in chapter 8 the worldly dandy Onegin unexpectedly becomes as bashful and shy as Adolphe when he is left alone with Ellénore:

He finds Tatyana
Alone, and for some minutes
They sit together. *From Onegin's lips*
The words come not. Ill-humored,
Awkward, he barely, barely
Replies to her.

Here Pushkin very closely follows Constant: "*tous mes discours expiraient sur mes lèvres*" (all my speeches expired on my lips).

Onegin, like Adolphe, decides against a meeting and sends a letter. For this letter Pushkin draws on a number of formulas from *Adolphe* and consults *Adolphe* for the creation of a language of amorous experience.

I know: my span is well-nigh measured;
But that my life may be prolonged
I must be certain in the morning
Of seeing you during the day...

Compare this with Constant: "*Je n'ai plus le courage de supporter un si long malheur [...] mais je dois vous voir s'il faut que je vive.*"

Adolphe, after sending his first love letter to Ellénore, fears to detect a trace of contempt for him in her smile. Compare this with Onegin's letter:

> What bitter scorn
> Your proud glance will express!

"What do I want?" exclaims Onegin. *"Qu'est-ce que j'exige?"* asks Adolphe in his meeting with Ellénore (chapter 3). In this same meeting with Ellénore, Adolphe says: "The effort by which I conquer myself in order to speak to you with a measure of calmness is evidence of a *feeling which is offensive to you*," and asks Ellénore not to punish him now that she has guessed his secret (i.e., his love). This passage is underlined in Pushkin's copy of *Adolphe*. Compare it with "Onegin's Letter":

> I foresee everything: the explanation
> Of a sad *secret* will offend you.

The expression "sweet habit" is used twice by Pushkin in declarations of love,[55] and incidentally the phrase "did not give way to sweet habit" in "Onegin's Letter" is found in the very same confrontation between Adolphe and Ellénore (*"Vous avez laissé naître et se former cette douce habitude"*).[56]

And, finally, Adolphe's letter to Ellénore (chapter 3), the second half of which is underlined in pencil in Pushkin's copy (from the words *"Tout près de vous"* to the end), contains one passage which is very close to "Onegin's Letter," written on the third of October 3, 1837.[57]

> *...lorsque j'aurais un tel besoin de me reposer de tant d'angoisses, de poser ma tête sur vos genoux, de donner un libre cours à mes larmes, il faut que je me contraigne...* (chapter 3)

> I wish to embrace your knees
> And, in a burst of sobbing, at your feet
> Pour out appeals, avowals, plaints,
> All, all I could express,
> And in the meantime with feigned coldness
> Arm speech and gaze...

These parallels demonstrate how Pushkin borrowed the psychological terminology of amorous experience in *Adolphe* for *Eugene Onegin*.

V

THE EXPERIMENTS IN GENRE that are characteristic of Push-kin's work at the end of the twenties take the most varied directions.

We may say now that Pushkin worked on the genre of his little romantic tragedies precisely at the end of the twenties. And it is quite noteworthy that we find the parallel utilization of Byron and Constant in one of these tragedies, *The Stone Guest.*

Thus, *Adolphe* was utilized by Pushkin in yet another direction of his genre quests. First, in the satirical novel *Eugene Onegin,* second, in the psychological tale "In a Corner of the Little Square," and third, in the romantic tragedy *The Stone Guest.*

The parallel between Onegin's letter ("I know: my span is well-nigh measured...") with the text of *Adolphe* has been noted above. Pushkin adapted the very same text of *Adolphe* for *The Stone Guest.* The form this adaptation takes is curious and not very usual for Pushkin. Generally, the source of Pushkin's adaptations undergoes a certain reworking and further development. Here we have an almost word-for-word translation. Pushkin inserts a quotation from *Adolphe* into the text of his tragedy. This quotation is found in the third scene of *The Stone Guest,* in Don Juan's avowal of his love. The very beginning of Don Juan's rejoinder to Doña Anna's words: "I am afraid to listen to you"

> I will be silent; only don't run away
> From one whose *sole joy* is seeing you

is quite close to *Adolphe:* "How have I deserved to be deprived of this *solitary joy*" (Adolphe is speaking of the prohibition against seeing Ellénore).[58] Later, in *The Stone Guest,* there follows a quotation from *Adolphe:*

> I do not nourish daring hopes,
> I demand nothing, but see
> You I must, as long as
> I am condemned to life.

> *Je n'espère rien, je ne demande rien, je ne veux que vous voir; mais je dois vous voir, s'il faut que je vive.*[59]

[I hope for nothing, ask for nothing, want only to see you, but it is essential that I see you, if I must live.]

The best commentary on this passage was given by Pushkin himself in "The Moor of Peter the Great" (1827): "Whatever you may say, *a love without hope or demands touches the feminine heart more truly than all the wiles of seduction.*" Compare this authorial comment in "The Moor of Peter the Great" with the following passage from the third scene of *The Stone Guest*:

> If I were a madman, I would wish
> To remain among the living, *I would have the hope*
> *Of touching your heart with a* tender *love...*

After this, it makes sense that Doña Anna, touched by a love without hope or demands, should answer:

> ...Tomorrow,
> Come to me. If you swear
> To preserve the same respect for me,[60]
> I will receive you—but in the evening—later.

Pushkin borrowed these words from chapter 2 of *Adolphe*, where, to Adolphe's demand that she receive him "tomorrow at 11 o'clock," Ellénore answers: "*Je vous recevrai demain mais je vous conjure...*" (I will receive you tomorrow, but I entreat you...). Ellénore does not finish the sentence because she is afraid of being overheard by those present, but in this context, the sentence could have no other conclusion. Pushkin finishes Constant's phrase for him.

Just as indisputable is the closeness to *Adolphe* of Don Juan's words about the secret (i.e., his love), which he has inadvertently given away:

> An accident, Doña Anna, an accident
> Carried me away, else you would *never*
> *Have known my sad secret.*

Adolphe asks Ellénore to "dismiss the memory of a moment of frenzy: do not punish me because *you know the secret,* which I should have concealed in the depths of my soul..." This phrase, as was mentioned above in connection with "Onegin's Letter," is underlined in Pushkin's copy *of Adolphe.*[61]

Like Adolphe, Don Juan begins with threats of suicide: "Oh, that I might die *now at your feet*" *(The Stone Guest)*; "I am leaving *now*... I am going to seek life's end" *(Adolphe)*.

At the beginning of scene IV, Don Juan says:

> I silently delight,
> I am immersed in dreams of being alone
> With the charming Doña Anna...

In the same third chapter of *Adolphe* we read: "The necessity of seeing her whom I loved, of delighting in her presence, ruled me exclusively." Before this, Adolphe says that in his "soul there was no longer any room for calculations or considerations and he knew himself to be truly, honestly in love" (chapter 3).

And in Adolphe's letter to Ellénore, quoted above in connection with Onegin's letter, we read: *"But if I had met you earlier, you might have been mine."* Compare this with scene IV of *The Stone Guest*: "If I had known you before..." The relationship itself of Don Juan to Doña Anna, which does not at all follow the traditions of classical Don Juans, is usually interpreted in two ways: either Don Juan is romantically in love with Doña Anna, but in that case the cynical and mildly scornful tone in which he speaks of Doña Anna in her absence lacks psychological verisimilitude; or, the inspired sincerity of his words is only a skillful game; but this interpretation, in its turn, contradicts Don Juan's words ("I am perishing—all is finished—oh, Doña Anna!"), uttered at the moment of his death, when there would be no point in pretending.

I believe that Don Juan's behavior has psychological validity if we compare Don Juan's seduction of Doña Anna with Adolphe's seduction of Ellénore. Adolphe says of himself: "Whoever were to read my heart in her absence would consider me a cold and insensitive seducer. But whoever were to see me near her would have recognized me as a novice in love, confused, and passionate."

Thus, the historical personage of Pushkin's tragedy acquires the psychological character of the worldly, contemporary seducer Adolphe,[62] the hero of the novel which Pushkin remembered in 1830 in connection with "the ardent reading of my youth" and whose heroine Pushkin compared with his correspondent.

In connection with the modernization of the character of Don Juan in *The Stone Guest*, it is interesting to note that one important historical episode of Pushkin's tragedy also has a source not historical in nature. I have in mind Don Juan's remembrances of his exile. The place of Don Juan's exile cannot be fixed with any degree of precision on the basis of Pushkin's text. The question can be clarified only by comparison with its source: Byron's *Don Juan*. In Byron, Don Juan goes to England (Canto X). The first thing he notices is the smoke blanketing London: "The sun went down, the smoke rose up." Compare this with *The Stone Guest*: "And the sky was like smoke." In Canto XII Byron calls England: "The shore of white cliffs, white necks, blue eyes." The foreign ladies in *The Stone Guest at first* pleased Don Juan: "With their blue eyes and their whiteness." As for Byron's Don Juan, "*At first* he did not think the women pretty," because "novelties please less than they impress." Compare this with *The Stone Guest*: "and even more by its novelty." In the same canto of Byron's *Don Juan*, the English girl is compared with the Andalusian girl: "She cannot step as does an Arab barb/ Or Andalusian girl from mass returning." Compare this with *The Stone Guest*:

> But the women, no I wouldn't change,
> The humblest Andalusian peasant girl
> For the foremost beauty there, it's true.

This stanza of *Don Juan* comes one stanza after the one in which Byron speaks of Russians throwing themselves headlong into the snow after a hot bath. Byron made the following notation to this passage: "Russians, as is generally known, run from a hot bath and plunge into the Neva..." Pushkin wrote about the references in Byron's poems to Russian customs in "Fragments from Letters, Thoughts and Notes": "In his poems he often speaks of Russia and of our customs" (*Northern Flowers*, 1828).

Taking all the parallels into consideration, it is difficult to regard *The Stone Guest* as a historical tragedy. Nor can it be looked upon as merely a solution to the problem of depicting universal passions. The autobiographical nature and the contemporary note of *The Stone Guest* become clear.

Thus, we see that while addressing completely different literary problems (*Eugene Onegin, The Stone Guest*, "In a Corner of the Little Square"), Pushkin turned to *Adolphe* several times, but each time in order to psychologize his work and give it that truth (verisimilitude) which readers from Sismondi to Polevoi have found in *Adolphe*. I would like to quote once again from

Vyazemsky's "Foreword" (edited, as we have noted, by Pushkin), which clarifies the view of Pushkin and his contemporaries on *Adolphe* as a work in which they recognized an authentic life: "All the drama is in the man, *all the art is in truth... There is so much truth* in all the author's observations... Women, in general, don't like Adolphe, that is, his character, and this guarantees *the truth* of his depiction... The novelist cannot follow in Plato's footsteps and improvise a republic... Whatever the relations of men and women in society, such they must be in his picture. The time of Malek-Adhel and Gustave has passed...[63] It would be difficult in such a compact sketch as *Adolphe,* with such limited and so-to-speak solitary action, to display more fully the human heart, to view it from all sides, turn it inside out and nakedly expose the cold *truth* in all its wretchedness and all its horror."

Of course, Vyazemsky is not speaking of realism in the sense of the literary school, but the mere fact that *Adolphe* was noted for its reality and its truth, that is, its verisimilitude, was contrasted to "the dreamy Arcadia of the novels" of Baroness Krüdener and novels written at almost the same time as *Adolphe* (Krüdener's *Valérie,* 1803; Cottin's *Mathilde,* 1805) testifies that for Pushkin, Constant's novel was a step towards realism.[64]

Thus, a comparison of *Adolphe* with Pushkin's writings brings one face-to-face with fundamental questions related to the problem of realism in Pushkin's work.

1936

Translated by Sharon Leiter

PUSHKIN'S *STONE GUEST*

I

A S IS WELL KNOWN, Pushkin was revered by his contemporaries in the early period of his literary career (when *The Prisoner of the Caucasus, The Fountain of Bakhchisaray,* and the early lyrics came out); his literary career developed quickly and brilliantly. And then, sometime around 1830, the readers and critics forsook Pushkin. The reason for this lies first and foremost in Pushkin himself. He had changed. Instead of *The Prisoner of the Caucasus,* he was writing The *Little House in Kolomna,* instead of *The Fountain of Bakhchisaray—The Little Tragedies,* and later *The Golden Cockerel* and *The Bronze Horseman.* His contemporaries were perplexed; his enemies and those who envied him rejoiced. His friends kept mum. Pushkin himself writes in 1830:

> There are both almanacs and journals
> Where precepts are reprised to us,
> Where nowadays they abuse me so,
> And where I would encounter such madrigals
> About myself from time to time.

In precisely what way and how did Pushkin change?

In the preface proposed for the eighth and ninth chapters of *Eugene Onegin* (1830), Pushkin polemicizes with the critics: "The age may move forward," but "poetry stays in one and the same place... Its means and ends are one and the same."

In that same year, however, in the drafts of an article about Baratynsky, Pushkin depicts the relationship between the poet and the reader in an entirely different way:

The concepts and feelings of the eighteen-year-old poet are still near and dear to everyone; young readers understand him and are delighted to recognize their own feelings and thoughts, which are clearly expressed, alive, and harmonious in his works. But as the years go by and the youthful poet reaches manhood, his talent grows, his understanding becomes greater, his feelings change. His songs are no longer the same. But the readers are the same and have only become more coldhearted and indifferent toward the poetry of life. The poet grows apart from them, and little by little withdraws entirely. He creates for himself, and if his works are still published from time to time, he encounters coldness or inattention, and he finds an echo of his sounds only in the hearts of a few admirers of poetry, who, like himself, are secluded and forgotten by the world.

It is odd that it has still not been noted anywhere that it was Baratynsky himself who suggested this idea to Pushkin in a letter in 1828, where he explains the failure of *Onegin* this way:

> I think that a poet in Russia can hope for great success only with his first immature experiments. All the young people, who find in him what are virtually their own feelings and thoughts, brilliantly expressed, are on his side. The poet develops, writes with greater deliberation and profundity, but the officers are bored by him, and the brigadiers do not accept him, because after all his poetry is not prose. Don't take these reflections as referring to yourself; they are general ones.[1]

Just how Pushkin developed Baratynsky's idea is evident from a comparison of these two citations.

Thus, it is not so much that poetry is static, as that the reader does not keep pace with the poet.

All of Pushkin's contemporaries enthusiastically recognized themselves in the hero of *The Prisoner of the Caucasus*, but who would agree to recognize himself in Eugene from *The Bronze Horseman*?

II

THE *LITTLE TRAGEDIES* CAN be numbered among those of Pushkin's mature works that not only his contemporaries, but even the poet's friends did not know.[2] There is perhaps no single work of world poetry in which such formidable moral questions are presented so sharply and complexly as Pushkin's *Little Tragedies*. The complexity is so great at times that, when combined with the breathtaking conciseness, the sense is almost obscured, which invites various interpretations (for example, the denouement of *The Stone Guest*).

I believe that Pushkin himself provides an explanation for this in his note about Musset (October 24, 1830), where he commends the author of *Contes d'Espagne et d'Italie* for the absence of moralizing and in general advises against "tacking on a moral admonition to everything." This observation in part provides a key to understanding the supposedly humorous ending of *The Little House in Kolomna* (October 9, 1830):

"Have you at least some moral admonition?"
"No... well, perhaps... I'll think, with your permission...
Here is a moral for you..."[3]

This is followed by a parody on a moral ending, clearly meant as a challenge: "Nothing more fine / Can be squeezed out of this plain tale of mine."

It is understandable that many of the standard ways of representing passions were closed to a poet who had thus posed the question about moralizing. Everything above is particularly relevant to *The Stone Guest*, which nevertheless represents an adaptation of the universal theme of retribution; and Pushkin's predecessors did not hesitate to moralize when dealing with this theme.

Pushkin takes a different path. He needs to convince the reader from the very first lines, and without resorting to explicit moralizing, that the hero must perish. The fact that *The Stone Guest* is a tragedy of retribution for Pushkin is proven by the very title he has chosen (*The Stone Guest*, not *Don Juan*). Therefore, all the dramatis personae—Laura, Leporello, Don Carlos, and Doña Anna—act only so as to prepare and hasten the death of Don Juan. The hero himself tirelessly pleads for the same:

All's for the best. Unlucky enough to kill
Don Carlos, taking refuge as a monk
Within these cloisters...[4]

But Leporello says:

That's the style.
Now let's enjoy ourselves. Forget the dead.

Pushkin scholarship has shown us how Pushkin's Don Juan resembles his predecessors. And it makes sense for us to determine now in what way he is original.

It is characteristic of Pushkin that Don Juan's wealth is referred to only once, and in passing, whereas this is an essential theme for da Ponte and Molière. Pushkin's Juan is neither da Ponte's rich man, who wants "to revel in his money," nor Molière's doleful raisonneur, who deceives his creditors. Pushkin's Juan is a Spanish grandee whom the king would not fail to recognize if he encountered him on the street. Reading *The Stone Guest* attentively, we make an unexpected discovery: Don Juan is a poet. Laura sings his verses that have been set to music; and even Juan calls himself an "Improvisor of Love Songs."

This draws him nearer to the basic Pushkin hero. Charsky, repeating one of Pushkin's favorite thoughts, says in *The Egyptian Nights*: "Our poets do not enjoy the patronage of gentlemen, our poets are themselves gentlemen...." As far as I know, no one else has thought to make his Don Juan a poet.

The situation at the tragedy's denouement is itself very close to Pushkin. In the 1820s Pushkin was tormented by the dream of a secret return from exile. That is precisely why Pushkin transferred the action from Seville (where it was set in the drafts—Seville is Don Juan's city of long standing) to Madrid: he needed the capital. Pushkin, through Don Juan, says of the king:

Send me away again.
I don't suppose I'll have my head chopped off.
I'm not accused of crime against the State.

Read "political prisoner," on whom the death penalty is customarily imposed for an unauthorized return from exile. His friends said something of the sort to Pushkin himself when he wanted to return to Petersburg from Mikhailovskoye.[5] And apropos of this,

Pushkin's Leporello, turning to his lord, exclaims: "Well, then, you should *have stayed in safety.*"

Pushkin, it is true, does not put his Don Juan into the same ridiculous and shameful situation of every other Don Juan—no amorous Elvira pursues him and no jealous Mazetto intends to beat him; he doesn't even disguise himself as a servant to seduce the housemaid (as in Mozart's opera); he is a hero to the end, but this combination of cold cruelty and childish carelessness produces an incredible impression. Hence, Pushkin's Don Juan, despite his elegance and worldly manners, is far more terrifying than his predecessors.[6]

Both heroines note this, each in her own way: Doña Anna— "You are a real demon"; Laura—"Ruffian, fiend."

If Laura perhaps is simply scolding, then the word "demon" on the lips of Doña Anna produces just the impression that Don Juan must make, in accordance with the author's conception.

In contrast to other Don Juans, who treat all women absolutely the same way, Pushkin's Juan addresses each of the three very different women with different words.

The hero of *The Stone Guest* scolds his servant in the same way as both Mozart's and Molière's Don Juans, but the buffoonish scene in the opera's finale—the gluttony of servant and master— would, for example, be absolutely impossible in Pushkin's tragedy.

Pushkin originally wanted to emphasize the circumstances surrounding Juan's proposal to meet with the Commendador's widow near his statue, but then Leporello's indignant remark: "Atop a husband's grave... he is shameless; *it will turn out badly for him!*" seemed to smack too much of moralizing to Pushkin, and he left it to the reader to guess where the meetings take place.

In neither the final text nor in the drafts of *The Stone Guest* is there even a single word of explanation for the cause of the duel between Don Juan and the Commendador. This is odd. I dare say that the reason for this unexplained omission is as follows: in all the works preceding Pushkin's (save Molière's, where, in contrast to *The Stone Guest,* the Commendador is presented as an entirely abstract figure, not linked with the action in any way), the Commendador perishes defending the honor of his daughter, Doña Anna. Pushkin made Doña Anna the Commendador's wife, not his daughter, and he himself informs us that Juan has never seen her before. The former cause falls by the wayside, but

Pushkin did not want to devise a new one that would distract the reader's attention from what was most important. He emphasizes only that the Commendador was killed in a duel

> When we we two met behind the Escorial...[7]

and not in a scandalous nocturnal fight (in which even Doña Anna takes part), which would not have been in keeping with Juan's character.[8]

If the scene of Juan's declaration to Doña Anna can be traced to Shakespeare's *Richard III*, we must remember that Richard is a consummate villain and not a professional seducer; he is motivated by political considerations, not at all from amorous ones, as he explains to the onlookers then and there.

Pushkin thereby wished to say that thoughtlessness can lead his Juan to act like a villain, although he is only a society rake.

Second, to my mind a more significant link with Shakespeare that has gone unnoticed can be found in the closing scene of the tragedy *The Stone Guest*:

> Doña Anna
> How did you dare
> Come here? If someone recognized you—death.

In the draft:

> People could recognize you.

> Juliet
> How cam'st thou hither, tell me, and wherefore?..
> And the place death, considering who thou art,
> If any of my kinsmen find thee here...
> *(Romeo and Juliet, Act II, scene 2)*

Even the scene of inviting the statue, the only one that follows tradition, reveals the real abyss between Pushkin's Don Juan and his prototypes. Pushkin has transformed the inappropriate prank of the Mozartian and Molièrian Don Juans, evoked and motivated by the fact that he read an insulting inscription on the monument, into demonic bravado.[9] Instead of the absurd and traditional invitation to dine offered to the statue, we see something unparalled:

My good Commendador, tomorrow evening
Come to your widow's house—I shall be there—[10]
And will you stand outside the door on guard?
You'll come?

That is, Juan speaks to the statue as to a lucky rival.

Pushkin retained his hero's reputation as an atheist, a reputation proceeding from *l'Ateista fulminado* (the hero of a religious drama presented in churches and monasteries).

Depraved and *godless* scoundrel named Don Juan (the monk)
Your Don Juan is a *godless* scoundrel (Don Carlos)
Don Juan is described to you as being without
   conscience, *without faith* (Don Juan himself)
I have heard you are a *godless* libertine (Doña Anna)

Accusations of atheism were a usual refrain in the young Pushkin's life.

On the other hand, Pushkin completely banished from his tragedy another feature typical of Don Juans—the wanderings. It suffices to recall Mozart's *Don Giovanni* and Leporello's celebrated aria—the catalogue of conquests (641 in Italy, 231 in Germany, 100 in France, 91 in Turkey, and in Spain, a neat 1,003). Pushkin's grandee (his exile excepted, it goes without saying) leads a completely settled metropolitan way of life in Madrid, where every "tipsy fiddler or strolling gypsywoman" would recognize him."[11]

III

PUSHKIN'S DON JUAN DOES not do or say anything that any contemporary of Pushkin's would not have done or said, aside from what is necessary to preserve the Spanish local color ("I'll take him out concealed beneath my cloak / And put him at a crossroads"). This is precisely how Dalti, the hero of Musset's *Portia*, deals with the corpse of his rival, which is found the next day *"le front sur le pavé"* ("face down on the road").

Laura's guests (obviously Madrid's golden youth—Don Juan's friends) are more like members of the Green Lamp, dining with some celebrity of that time, such as Kolosova, and discussing art, than like noble Spaniards of whatever era. But the author of *The Stone Guest* knows that this presents no danger for him. He is confident that his brief description of the night will create a brilliant and unforgettable impression that this is Spain, Madrid, the South:

> Come out upon the balcony. How clear
> The sky; the air is warm and still—the evening
> Wafts us the scent of lemon boughs and laurel;
> The moon shines bright upon the deep dark blue—

Juan sports with Laura like a Petersburg rake with an actress; he recalls Iñez, whom he has ruined, in a melancholy way; he praises the stern spirit of the Commendador, whom he has killed; and he seduces Doña Anna according to all the rules of "Adolphian" worldly strategy.[12] Then something mysterious happens that is not fully explicated. Don Juan's final exclamation, when there can be no question of pretense:

> I die—My end has come—O, Doña Anna!

convinces us that he has truly been reborn during his meeting with Doña Anna, and indeed the entire tragedy operates on the premise that at this moment he loved and was happy, but instead of salvation, from which he was but a step away, comes death. Let us note one more detail: "Leave her," says the statue. This means that Juan flings himself at Doña Anna; it means that he sees only her at this terrible moment.

Indeed, if Don Carlos had killed Don Juan, we would not have had a tragedy, but something on the order of *Les Marrons du feu,* which Pushkin so admired in 1830 for its absence of moralizing and where the Don Juanian hero *("Mais c'est du don Juan")* perishes accidentally and senselessly. Pushkin's Don Juan perishes neither accidentally nor senselessly. The Commendador's statue is a symbol of retribution, but if it had carried Don Juan away while still in the cemetery, then we would have had not so much a tragedy as a theater of horrors or *l'Ateista fulminado* of medieval mystery plays. Juan is not afraid of death. We see that he is not in the least frightened of Don Carlos's sword and does not give even a second thought to the possibility of his own death. That is why Pushkin needed the duel with Don Carlos: to show Don Juan as he really is. At the finale of the tragedy we see him in a completely different way. And it is not at all a matter of whether the statue is an otherworldly phenomenon: the nod in the scene at the cemetery is also an otherworldly phenomenon, one to which Don Juan does not pay proper attention, however. Juan is not afraid of death or punishment after death, but of the loss of happiness. Hence his last words: "O Doña Anna!" And Pushkin places him in the only situation (according to Pushkin) in which death terrifies his hero. And we suddenly recognize something we know full well. Pushkin himself provides a motivated and comprehensive explanation for the tragedy's denouement. *The Stone Guest* is dated November 4, 1830, and in mid-October, Pushkin wrote "The Shot," the autobiographical character of which no one disputes. Silvio, the hero of "The Shot," says: "What use is there for me, thought I, to deprive him of life, when he in no way values it? A wicked thought came to mind (. . .) Let's see if he'll accept death as indifferently on the eve of his wedding as he once did when he was eating cherries!" We may conclude from this that Pushkin believed death to be terrible only if there was happiness. This is exactly how Juan responds to Doña Anna's question: "And have you loved me long?"

> How long or lately
> I cannot say. But *since that love began*
> *I've learned the price of every passing moment,*
> *And what it means to speak of Happiness.*

That is, he learned the price of every passing moment when he became happy. In both "The Shot" and *The Stone Guest*, the woman whom the hero loves is present at the moment of reckoning, contrary to the Don Juan tradition. In Mozart, for example, only the buffoonish Leporello is present, in Molière—Sganarel.

The problem of happiness troubled Pushkin greatly at this time (1830). "As far as happiness is concerned, I am an atheist; I don't believe in it," he wrote to P.A. Osipova the day after finishing *The Stone Guest* (the original is in French); "The devil himself tricked me into raving about happiness as if I had been created for it"— Pushkin's letter to Pletnyov; "Ah, what a cursed trick happiness is!"—to Vyazemsky (original in French). It would be simple to cite a whole series of such quotations, and one can even say, at the risk of seeming paradoxical, that Pushkin was as afraid of happiness as others are afraid of sorrow. And inasmuch as he was always expecting trouble of all sorts, he was uneasy in the face of happiness, that is to say, in the face of the loss of happiness.

IV

BUT THAT'S NOT ALL. In addition to analogies with the auto-biographical "The Shot," we should cite quotations from Pushkin's correspondence. The first is from a letter to his future mother-in-law, N.I. Goncharova (April 5, 1830): "I pictured in my mind the errors of my early youth; they were distressing enough just taken by themselves, but calumny has intensified them even more; unfortunately, the rumors about them have been widespread" (original in French). How close this is to Don Juan's confession:

> Maybe, report is not entirely false,
> Maybe, upon a tried and weary conscience
> There lies a weight of evil. Long was I
> A model pupil of debauchery...

And: "Poor thing! She is so young, so innocent, but he is such a frivolous, such an *immoral* man" (autobiographical fragment, May 13, 1830). Here "immoral," of course, is an extenuation of "debauched." And this is just what the voice of rumor communicates.

In that same year, Pushkin addresses the very same question in a poem that was not published during his lifetime, "At moments when your graceful form...":

> Too keenly mindful in your heart
> Of past betrayal's doleful mention...
> I curse the cunning machinations
> That were my sinful youth's delight...[13]

All of Doña Anna's rejoinders are implied in this verse. Pushkin, who had just gotten married, writes to Pletnyov: "I am... happy... This state is so new for me that it seems I have been reborn"; compare with *The Stone Guest*: "My inmost being has changed." Juan says of the Commendador: "He... enjoys the bliss of *Heaven!*"; compare with Pushkin's letter to A.P. Kern: "How is it possible to be your husband? I cannot picture such a thing for myself, just as I cannot picture heaven" (original in French).

In *Eugene Onegin,* Pushkin promises that when he depicts declarations of love, he will recall:

> The language of impassioned pining
> Will I renew, and love's reply,
> The like of which in days gone by
> Came to me as I lay reclining
> At a dear beauty's feet...[14]

The similarity of these citations speaks not so much to the autobiographical quality of *The Stone Guest* as to the lyrical source of this tragedy.

V

IF PUSHKIN DID NOT publish *The Covetous Knight* for six years, afraid, as was then said, of "applications [to himself]," then we can assume the same of *The Stone Guest,* which he did not publish at all. (I shall note in passing that *The Feast at the Time of the Plague* was published in 1832, that is, almost immediately after it was written, and this is not because *The Feast* is a simple translation.) However that may be, *The Stone Guest* is the only one of *The Little Tragedies* not published in Pushkin's lifetime. It is easy to see that something that we can unearth now only with the very greatest difficulty was, in Pushkin's mind, floating right on the surface. He had invested too much of himself in *The Stone Guest* and treated it like several of his lyric poems, which remained in manuscript regardless of their quality. In his mature period, Pushkin was not at all inclined to expose "the wounds of his conscience" before the world (to which, to a certain extent, every lyric poet is condemned), and I dare say that *The Stone Guest* was not printed for the very same reason that Pushkin's contemporaries did not read until after his death the conclusion of "Remembrance," "No, no, those fierce delights I do not treasure," and "At moments when your graceful form," and not for the same reason that *The Bronze Horseman* remained in manuscript.[15]

Besides all the parallels I have cited, the lyrical source of *The Stone Guest* can be established by a connection with, on one hand, "The Shot" (the problem of happiness) and, on the other, with *The Water Sprite,* which is recounted in brief (as indeed befits a prehistory) in Juan's recollection of Iñez. Juan's rendezvous

with Iñez takes place at the cemetery of the St. Anthony
Monastery (as is clear from the draft):

> Wait: that is St. Anthony's Monastery—
> And the monastery cemetery...
> Oh, I remember everything. You used to come here...

Like the prince in *The Water Sprite*, Juan recognizes the place
and recalls a woman he had ruined. In both works she is the
daughter of a miller. And it is no accident that Juan says to his
servant: "Just go to the village, you know, that one where the
mill is." Later he calls the place the cursed *venta* (bazaar). The
final wording of these lines partially erased this similarlity, but
now that the drafts have been studied, there is no doubt that
Pushkin's tragedy begins with an obscured mention of the crime
of a hero whom fate brings to the very same place where this
crime was perpetrated and where he perpetrates a new crime.
Everything has been predetermined by this, and the shade of
poor Iñez plays a much greater role in *The Stone Guest* than has
customarily been thought.

VI

THE PRECEDING REMARKS CONCERN the Don Juan line of the
tragedy, *The Stone Guest*. But this work obviously has another line
as well—that of the Commendador. Pushkin breaks completely
with tradition here as well. In Mozart, da Ponte's Don Juan does
not want to be reminded of the Commendatore to such an extent
that when Leporello asks permission to say something, his master
answers: "All right, if you don't talk about the Commendatore."

But Pushkin's hero talks almost non-stop about the Commendador.

And what is even more important is the fact that, both in the
legend and in all its literary adaptations, the statue makes an appearance in order to appeal to Juan's conscience, so that he will
repent of his sins. This would not make sense in Pushkin's
tragedy, because Juan confesses without being coerced:

> My inmost being has changed—in love with you
> I am in love with virtue, and at last
> On trembling knees I humbly bend before it.

The Commendador arrives at the moment of the "cold, peaceful kiss" to take his wife away from Juan. All other authors depict the Commendador as a decrepit old man and an insulted father. In Pushkin, he is a jealous husband ("And I heard that the deceased was a jealous man. He kept Doña Anna under lock and key"), and it does not follow from this that he is an old man. Juan says:

> Don't torment my
> Heart, Doña Anna, with the passionate mention
> Of your spouse—

to which Doña Anna protests: "How jealous you are."

We have every right to regard the Commendador as one of the characters in the tragedy, *The Stone Guest*. He has a biography, a personality and he takes part in the action. We even know what he looks like: "he was small, thin." He had married a beauty who did not love him and was able through his love to be worthy of her favor and gratitude. Not a word of this is from the Don Juan tradition. The thought about his jealousy enters Don Juan's head (in the draft when he does not yet even know Doña Anna) from the first moment; and it is then that Leporello says of his master: "Atop a husband's grave... he is shameless; it will turn out badly for him!"

And Pushkin's Commendador is more like the "incensed jealous man" of Pushkin's youthful poem "To a Young Widow," where a dead husband appears before a widow who is unfaithful to his memory (and where the deceased is also called a happy man, as in *The Stone Guest*), than like a phantom from beyond the grave who calls on the hero to renounce his impious life.

In the seventh chapter of *Eugene Onegin* Pushkin touches on the theme of jealousy from beyond the grave in connection with Lensky's grave and Olga's unfaithfulness:

> Was the despondent bard perturbed
> By the news of the betrayal?
>
> At least, out of the grave
> There did not rise on that sad day
> His jealous shade,
> And at the late hour dear to Hymen,

No traces of sepulchral visitations
Frightened the newlywed.[16]

It is as though Pushkin were disappointed (seeking a plot where an angered and jealous shade would appear). That is why he changes the plot of Don Juan and turns the Commendador into the husband, not the father of Doña Anna.

The moving widowed fiancée, Xenia Godunova, crying over the portrait of her dead betrothed whom she has never seen in life, says: "I will be faithful to the deceased."

Tatyana's celebrated rebuff:

But I was pledged another's wife,
And will be faithful all my life.[17]

is only a pale reflection of what Xenia Godunova and Doña Anna affirm ("a widow must be faithful to the grave").

But what is even more astonishing is the fact that, in the letter cited above to N.N. Goncharova's mother (April 5, 1830), Pushkin writes: "As God is my witness, I am ready to die for her; but to die and leave her a radiant widow, free to choose a new husband for herself the next day—this thought is hell for me." And still more striking: "...should she consent to give me her hand, I would see in this merely the proof of the serene indifference of her heart" (original in French).[18] Compare *The Stone Guest:*

No,
My mother gave my hand to Don Alvaro.

And further the entire situation is the same in the letter as in the tragedy.

Thus, in the tragedy *The Stone Guest,* Pushkin is chastising his young, carefree, and sinful self—and the theme of jealousy from beyond the grave (that is, the fear of it) resounds as loudly as the theme of retribution.

A careful analysis of *The Stone Guest,* therefore, leads us to the firm conviction that behind the external borrowings of names and situations, what we have in essence is not simply a new treatment of the universal Don Juan legend, but a deeply personal and original work by Pushkin, whose principal feature is determined not by the plot of the legend, but by Pushkin's own lyrical feelings, inseparably linked with his life experience.

We have before us the dramatic embodiment of Pushkin's inner personality, an aesthetic revelation of what tormented and captivated the poet. In contrast to Byron, who (in Pushkin's view) "cast a one-sided glance at the world and human nature, then turned away from them and became absorbed in himself," Pushkin, proceeding from personal experience, creates finished and objective characters: he does not shut himself away from the world, but goes out into the world.

That is why self-avowals are so inconspicuous in his works and can be identified only through painstaking analysis. Responding "to every sound," Pushkin absorbed the experience of his entire generation in himself. Pushkin's lyrical richness allowed him to avoid the error he had observed in the dramatic works of Byron, who dispensed "a single component of his personality to each protagonist" and who thus reduced his work "to several petty and insignificant characters."

1947

Translated by Janet Tucker

PUSHKIN'S DEATH

Introduction

S TRANGELY ENOUGH, I SIDE with those Pushkin scholars who believe that the subject of Pushkin's family tragedy should not be discussed. We undoubtedly would have carried out the poet's will if we had made it a forbidden subject.

And if I, nevertheless, address this subject after what I have just said, it is because so much vulgar and malicious falsehood has been written about it, because readers so willingly believe anything at all and gratefully accept Poletika's serpentine hissing, and Trubetskoi's senile ravings and Arapova's simpering.[1] And now that we can destroy this falsehood, thanks to a good number of documents that have resurfaced, we must do so.

August 26, 1958

I

The Dutch Diplomat Baron von Heeckeren was neither a Talleyrand nor a Metternich.[2]

He was evidently incapable of anything greater, but Heeckeren could fabricate what we now designate by the elegant word "row," and, as we will see, he conducted the entire planned game flawlessly. For posterity, naturally, this sort of game has been transformed into a house of cards. One blow, and it's gone. This is because mutually contradictory documents have emerged and, in general, what was secret becomes obvious. Nevertheless, Pushkin had a dangerous and experienced enemy. And Pushkin knew that.

Contemporaries thought that d'Anthès was Heeckeren's plaything. I do not believe that. In the beginning, when he was in love with Natalya Nikolayevna, he likely deceived even him. (See his second letter, written in 1836, where he writes that having learned of Natalya Nikolayevna's love for him, he felt only respect for her. More than likely, this is his answer to Heeckeren's first warning: "Come to your senses"—or something like that.) It was he who tried to inspire Alexander Karamzin.[3] In general, d'Anthès was given an aristocratic role—he was supposed to play on his charm alone, which, thanks to his good looks, he succeeded in doing. (See the scene in Andrei Karamzin's[4] letter from abroad—d'Anthès rushes to him in the park, d'Anthès cries, etc.)

Heeckeren's next victim was N. N. Pushkina. Her role was to convey to Pushkin the failure of his politics. (This is what Pushkin considered to be an act of trust on her part and something of which he was very proud.)

We, unfortunately, know that Natalya Nikolayevna coped only too well with her assignment (see Fiquelmont's diary[5]). Heeckeren was able to accomplish this only because of Natalya Nikolayevna's distracted love for his adopted son. Sofia Karamzina[6] played an important role, as is clear from her letters to her brother. For her, d'Anthès was always right.

For the same reason the ambassador got whatever he wanted from Yekatarina Nikolayevna,[7] who readily renounced the aunt, Zagryazhskaya,[8] who had been a second mother to her, (the tone of her letter about her aunt—she calls Zagryazhskaya unbearable), and who, upon her arrival in France, immediately converted to Catholicism in secret.

All the other members of d'Anthès's *bande joyeuse*, whose existence we discovered comparatively recently, helped as much as they could. Their activities are reflected in the Karamzin family's correspondence (the absence of which so distressed Shchegolyov), and can be summed up as follows: first, they condemned Pushkin and represented him as the jealous, old husband of a beautiful woman, as a person with an unbearable temperament, and so on, and second, through their leader they certainly reported everything that took place at the Pushkins to the Dutch ambassador. It should come as no surprise that somebody warned the barons that Pushkin intended to wage war with them at Countess Razumovskaya's ball. They continued to behave this way even after Pushkin's death (Mashenka Vyazemskaya-Valuyeva).[9]

It is equally certain that Heeckeren *organized the horseguardsmen* (of course, not without d'Anthès's help) so that the d'Anthès affair became a matter of the regiment's honor. (The opinion that d'Anthès was "innocent" was so widely held that it even found its way into Tyutchev's poem, "Whether he be innocent or guilty."[10])

Immediately after Pushkin's death, the same Heeckeren (see his letter to Holland), started the rumor that Pushkin was the head of a secret revolutionary organization. This was done to frighten Nicholas I and Benckendorf,[11] which apparently was not that difficult, and consequently resulted in the secret funeral, where the gendarmes outnumbered the friends (see A. I. Turgenev's diary).[12]

However, this was not enough for Heeckeren. He still had to ensure Georges's honorable return to Europe after the collapse of his Petersburg career. He therefore continued to vouch for the honor of d'Anthès, who had not hesitated for one moment to save the good name of Mme. Pushkin and had enslaved himself forever by marrying her unattractive sister. But here is where the house of cards begins: at the same time the envoy, like a good father, is spending time with Katerina, and with a grandeur surprising to all is decorating her rooms, entertaining her, writing about her health and mood in his letters to Georges, and thus also proving himself to be a very real traitor in regard to his *belle fille,* the envoy requests that Mme. Pushkin, for whose honor Georges d'Anthès sacrificed his good life, be summoned to court (as the worst sort of adventuress) in order that she testify under oath that she seduced the fiancé and, subsequently the husband of her sister, and that he, the envoy, had averted her from the abyss into which she was heading. All this was done in terms intended to insult her, and was made known to two highly-placed ladies, with whom he, the envoy, daily shared his misgivings. Undoubtedly, one of these ladies was Countess Nesselrode, the other was "la comtesse Sophie B." of the "counterfeit note"—Countess Bobrinskaya—the wife of the master of ceremonies at the Imperial Court and Catherine II's grandson. It is not without interest that both these ladies were hostesses of two influential Petersburg salons.[13]

The letter in which this was written (March 1, 1837) is addressed to Nesselrode, but since during this period Heeckeren (according to Vyazemsky) was spending all his time at Nesselrode's, where the Countess consoled him, one has to assume that this letter belongs to that epistolary genre, where the addressee and the sender concoct the production together in order to present it to a third party. In this case that party was Nicholas I.

Perhaps it will interest some that in three years' time (December 28, 1840) the same Nesselrode wrote to Meindorf: "Heeckeren is capable of anything: he is a person without honor and conscience; in general, he has no right to respect and is intolerable in our society."

II

Neither Zhukovsky,[14] who wrote about d'Anthès to Benckendorf: "On the other hand, there was a debauchery that was both empty-headed and deliberate," nor Vyazemsky,[15] who wrote something in the same vein to Musina-Pushkina, nor, which is much more important, Pushkin himself, who called d'Anthès's behavior a *manège* [intrigue][16] (see the draft of the cartel), believed in d'Anthès's love.[17] Only Natalya Nikolayevna and the society ladies believed in it, and, surprisingly enough, this was sufficient for posterity to accept the legend in all its inviolability. This happened because it is more interesting this way. To our shame, not only did the elder Heeckeren exult over Pushkin during his lifetime, but he continues to celebrate the triumph of his diplomacy to this day. It is not surprising that Heeckeren triumphed during his lifetime; the old diplomatic fox, embroiled in intrigue, ought to have been able to conduct the entire operation successfully and even cover up his tracks, but how could Russian society fail to expose the "cotillion king," d'Anthès, tolerate the sacrifice of a great life to the vanity of a petty careerist, and for 120 years continue to repeat the suspect baron's malicious lies, transpose them into theatrical adaptations, and later into film?! The legend of d'Anthès's lasting, exalted love comes from Natalya Nikolayevna herself *(une persévérence de deux années*—two year's constancy—she writes in her letter of November 1836). Thus, Georges d'Anthès loved Natalya Nikolayevna and was true to her from the autumn of 1834? However, we now have d'Anthès's letter of January 20, 1836, in which he tells the envoy the recent news that he has fallen in love with a lady whose husband is *d'une jalousie révoltante*, disturbingly jealous. (This means that N.N. was already complaining to d'Anthès about Pushkin's jealousy.) In Shchegolyov's account everything remains a mystery. How could Pushkin, with his personality, endure his wife's two- or three-year affair and, consequently, society's gossip? Now everything has fallen into its proper place: d'Anthès fell in love in January 1836, made his declaration in February, when he received the notorious answer[18] from the lady, who was six months pregnant at the time (Pushkin's youngest daughter was born on May 23rd). We may assume that Natalya Nikolayevna did not appear in society in her last two months,[19] especially since Pushkin's mother died on Holy Saturday and they were in mourning.[20] First, Pushkin went to Mikhailovskoye to bury his mother, and then to Moscow. The poet's letters to his wife are absolutely calm (for example, "How did you drag your belly along?.."). Natalya Nikolayevna and the children moved to the expensive dacha she had rented from Dobrovolsky. Koko and Azya[21] started riding horseback with the horseguardsmen ("My respects to your riders"), i.e., d'Anthès had already made his appearance. After giving birth, Natalya Nikolayevna was ill for a month. In July she again began to go out. And only then did rumors begin to circulate (the mineral waters, horseback riding, etc.).

The elder Heeckeren returned in May after a year's absence, and only then was he able, in Pushkin's words, to bring together Pushkin's wife with his own "bastard." This information again comes from Natalya Nikolayevna and, again, it is false. D'Anthès and Natalya Nikolayevna had declared themselves to each other splendidly back in February, when the baron was traveling in Europe and he adopted d'Anthès. The phrase *"Rendez-moi mon fils"* (give me back my son)[22] does not attest to pandering, but more than likely the opposite. For that reason it is not entirely understandable how the spouse of Pushkin, a gentleman of the bedchamber, and the most beautiful woman at the Petersburg court, came to be cornered (*"dans tous les coins"*)[23] at balls and allowed the Dutch envoy to say indecent things to her. (But the fact of the matter is that in October d'Anthès was ill and Natalya Nikolayevna, of course, wanted to know how he was feeling.)

Heeckeren immediately and thoroughly understood Pushkin's line of conduct. But if, for some reason, he had not understood, it would have been explained to him immediately.

All the young people from the two homes friendly to Pushkin (the Karamzins and Vyazemskys) were for Georges—the fair-haired, witty prince of the cotillion. Natalya Nikolayevna also belonged to this group of young people. She listened calmly while Valuyev, a nineteen-year-old horseguardsman and the husband of Mashenka Vyazemskaya, asked her, "Why do you permit such a person to treat you like that?" (This was about Pushkin!)

So, Heeckeren knew what Pushkin intended to do. He wanted to show d'Anthès to be a coward and make him look ridiculous. Perhaps the contemporary reader will not fully understand how this plan threatened d'Anthès. It threatened him with the ruin of his career, because an officer of the guards, moreover a horse-guardsman, cannot publicly be shown to be a coward. He would have had to resign and would have been left with nothing. The Heeckerens could not agree to that. One had to be a hero, not a coward. And the envoy began to transform his adopted son into a hero. To this end d'Anthès had to simulate a hopeless passion at all the Petersburg balls, that is, stand against columns, sigh, cast passionate glances, pronounce specious phrases like "Let society judge me" (Merder's diary). [24]

The scandalmongers had performed their task worthily. All that remained was Pushkin. It was essential to make him aware that d'Anthès was not George Dandin, etc.,[25] but a most honorable fellow, who had not hesitated one second, but had immediately sacrificed himself for the woman he loved by marrying her unattractive sister. However, it was not so easy to inform Pushkin of this. His friends merely soothed the agitated and troubled poet or rather awkwardly tried to bring Pushkin and d'Anthès together, for which Countess Fiquelmont reproached them so bitterly (see her diary).[26]

Enemies would be careful not to bring up this subject with Pushkin, since they would risk a slap in the face or a challenge to a duel (the affair with the young Sollogub).[27] In Heeckeren's plan this mission was evidently earmarked for Natalya Nikolayevna. She alone could pass on to her husband the envoy's admonitions and stories about d'Anthès's noble conduct, which, as we know, she did, thus becoming Heeckeren's agent. And this was essential for his plan to disarm Pushkin and force him to remain silent. Heeckeren had a similar agent in Dolgorukov-*bancal* [the bandy-legged], who made the sign of the cuckold behind Pushkin's back. The duel took place when one other person appeared, one who could openly speak with Pushkin, and who evidently informed the poet that Heeckeren had won and that the version of d'Anthès's nobleness had gained the upper hand over the *tu l'as voulu, George Dandin*, etc. This person was a neighbor from Trigorskoye and an old friend of Pushkin's, Baroness Vrevskaya, who arrived in Petersburg in early 1837.[28] And this is why Natalya Nikolayevna blamed her, and not because she had known of the duel and had not taken the necessary measures. Many people knew of the duel (Vyazemsky, Perovsky...), as did, incidentally, "Pushkin's friend" Alexandrina Goncharova.[29] I should like to inform the many admirers of this lady that many years later Alexandra Nikolayevna, not without emotion, wrote in her diary that one day her *beau-frère* d'Anthès (evidently coming from Heeckeren's in Vienna) and Natalya Nikolayevna from Russia were at her estate (in Austria). And Pushkin's widow strolled for a long time on the grounds with her husband's assassin and supposedly made her peace with him.[30] Judging from Arapova's memoirs, the legend of d'Anthès's great love enjoyed currency in the Lanskoi household.[31] This could only have come from Natalya Nikolayevna.

It is completely understandable that Yekatarina Nikolayevna's wedding stirred up the rumors[32] (the sisters' relationship, Pushkin's absence at the wedding...), and that Vrevskaya was able to inform Pushkin of a whole heap of news.

And so, Vrevskaya made her fateful communication. In the eyes of society d'Anthès was a hero, etc., and if d'Anthès was a hero, then Pushkin was a laughingstock. Pushkin could not contradict this. That is how the January challenge came about.

I believe the second reason for sending the cartel is an event about which we have known for a long time, but which has been incorrectly interpreted. Nicholas I, many years later, told Korff that he had spoken with Natalya Nikolayevna about her domestic affairs practically on the eve of the duel and that Pushkin later supposedly thanked him. One has to believe that the monarch forgot something, softened something, and that this was nothing more than the usual *remontrance* (reprimand) to a gentleman of the bedchamber's wife who had occasioned gossip. If we compare this episode with what Pushkin writes in his diary about the young Suvorova (Yartseva),[33] it is clear that the Tsar's conversation with Natalya Nikolayevna was practically the last straw for Pushkin. Thus, here Nicholas I is guilty again. (Nicholas I's story ends: "His final duel was three days later...").

This means that by contemporary standards, by the etiquette of the ball and Winter Palace, the wife of the gentleman of the bedchamber, Pushkin, had conducted herself improperly.[34] And Nicholas I, of course, did not reproach Natalya Nikolayevna for the fact that d'Anthès was in love with her—however, he did not summon him and did not scold him (or the commander of the regiment) for his conduct.

D'Anthès's conduct was precisely regulated, and all the talk of his improper behavior arose after Pushkin's death, when the search for the cause of the calamity began, and searches in such instances are very primitive. (For example, the fact that d'Anthès publicly called Katerina *ma légitime* (my lawful one) does not prove anything but an attempt at colloquial speech, and does not at all hint at some "unlawful one"...).

As far as the secret that shrouds this affair is concerned—about which Vyazemsky writes twice (to Bulgakov and Musina-Pushkina on February 26, 1837)[35]—we should recall that in his letter to Mikhail Pavlovich, Vyazemsky writes that Pushkin believed the anonymous letter to be Heeckeren's caper and that he died with this conviction. (This means that Zhukovsky concealed that on his death bed Pushkin was still thinking about Heeckeren.) Is it not this belief of Pushkin's that seemed to be an insoluble mystery to Vyazemsky?

Pushkin's conviction played a major role in the pre-duel story. His meeting with Benckendorf took place because of it: upon receiving Pushkin's letter containing the phrase about the envoy being the author of the diploma, Benckendorf immediately summoned the poet to the Winter Palace.[36] There Pushkin proved his suspicion to Nicholas I. It could not be otherwise. To make such an accusation of as important a personage as the Dutch envoy and not prove it meant finding yourself in the casemate or being escorted to Nerchinsk.[37] But, we know that absolutely nothing bad happened to Pushkin after this meeting and that Nicholas I (according to Hohenlohe-Kirchberg and Smirnov) believed Heeckeren to be the author of the lampoon, because of the similarity of the handwriting.[38] Danzas said literally the same thing to Ammosov.[39] The handwriting can hardly be made out, but in any case, three of the diplomas known to us were not written by Heeckeren. However, there were at least seven other diplomas that have not survived, and there was also the text from which the correspondence was produced, and only two surnames needed to be written in. We should mention that the Heeckerens were very worried about a certain diploma of a certain format. And they were also worried about the seal, and of course with reason, and Pushkin wrote Benckendorf that he had guessed by the seal. Thus, a comparison of Pushkin's letter to Benckendorf with the diplomat's "counterfeit note" to his adopted son shows that the barons had miscalculated and that Pushkin caught them at it. And, in celebration of this Pushkin wrote the November letter. This is a document of such importance that we must dwell on it in greater detail.

Zhukovsky's Fairy Tale[40]

IN THIS FAIRY TALE, which no one has given the necessary attention, Zhukovsky allegorically relates the events of the pre-duel story. The gray wolf (d'Anthès) wants to eat the beloved ewe (N.N.), who belongs to the shepherd-marksman (Pushkin), but *he is unable to take his eyes off the other* ewes (Koko, Azya), and even smacks his lips. Now d'Anthès is called a gluttonous wolf.[41] This is how d'Anthès's wooing is portrayed later on: "But then the glutton learned that the marksman was watching him and wanted to shoot him (the challenge). And the gray wolf found this unpleasant (he cowered); and he began to make the shepherd *various proposals* (to marry K.N.), to which the shepherd agreed." Then follows the description of Pushkin's plan for revenge: "The shepherd thought, 'How can I finish off this long-tailed fancy man... *I'll gather my neighbors and we'll lasso him.'*"[42] And here is where Zhukovsky turns down the role of the pig, who is supposed to entice the wolf with its grunting, that is, lure the Heeckerens to Pushkin, where in the presence of "the neighbors"—society—the envoy's authorship will be exposed (and perhaps that of d'Anthès as well; cf. the letter to Benckendorf: "mm. les H."). Of course, that interpretation would not allow Heeckeren to remain as envoy for one more hour, nor d'Anthès as horseguardsman.

Pushkin's entire plan for the exposure of Heeckeren was unacceptable to Nicholas I, although Pushkin had convinced him that the ambassador was the author of the diploma. The Tsar evidently forbade Pushkin to send the November letter to Heeckeren and to expose him in the eyes of Petersburg society. In these drafts Pushkin writes: "Even a duel is not enough for me, no matter what the outcome be," which means that it was not enough for him to kill d'Anthès, etc. He wanted to remove the Dutch envoy from his post after shaming him in the eyes of society and both courts as the author of the anonymous letters.

In January everything was reversed: D'Anthès was a hero who had sacrificed his life to save the honor of Natalya Nikolayevna, the ambassador was under Nicholas I's protection, and Pushkin had pledged his word not to expose him. All that was left were unsubstantiated accusations—being denied entrance to the house (which, however, should not be underestimated) and a flood of obscenities that only bear witness to Pushkin's impotent rage.

The duel was fixed for November 21 (8:00 am). Instead, d'Anthès's official proposal was made and Pushkin proceeded with the realization of his revenge—the exposure of the elder Heeckeren as the author of the anonymous letters. Pushkin believed that he had sufficiently dealt with the younger by marrying him off to Koko. By this time Natalya Nikolayevna had provided her husband with sufficient material for the most unrestrained fury, and the terrifying drafts of the letters (to the elder Heeckeren) originated on this very day. Pushkin evidently wrote them almost simultaneously with his letter (at first also a draft) to Benckendorf. The letter to Heeckeren provides a commentary on the drafts of the letter to Benckendorf. Of course, he does not explain to Heeckeren how he guessed that the ambassador sent the lampoons, but merely boasts of his resourcefulness and says that they were put together carelessly. He explains to Benckendorf that he guessed that the lampoon came from a diplomat, a foreigner, etc.: (1) by the paper (the fine finish, English stock), (2) by the seal, (3) by the manner in which it was compiled. The third point can be dismissed. D'Archiac had a sealed copy of the letter—it only needed to be copied. The paper and seal could have come up in Natalya Nikolayevna's revelations, for example, if she had received some note from d'Anthès with that seal. Heeckeren had a reason for describing the seal affixed to the lampoons in his "counterfeit note" to d'Anthès. Why would an innocent person care about the kind of paper in a fool's diploma or what is depicted on the seal?

Isn't this why the Third Section required a sample of d'Anthès's handwriting? They evidently knew that the diploma was from the Dutch Embassy.[43]

If the January letter[44] is composed solely from information supplied by Natalya Nikolayevna, there is definitely the sense of yet another voice in the November letter. Not everything related to the anonymous letter was communicated by Natalya Nikolayevna. She, of course, could not know that a document that besmirched her honor was being fabricated by the Embassy. We should add that Pushkin was very proud of his information and was unwaveringly certain of its reliability. This has to be understood in the following manner: someone is present at a conversation between Heeckeren and d'Anthès, and *le coup décisif* is determined—the anonymous letter. Later this person goes to Pushkin and tells him everything, which gives him the opportunity to drag the envoy through the mud, but obviously, for entirely understandable reasons, this person wished to remain anonymous. Here one recalls Baron Byuller's story: "Lev Pushkin learned for the first time all the *insidious provocations* that led to his brother's duel from a detailed, highly entertaining story told by Count Vielgorsky at Odoyevsky's in the 1840s. It is awkward even now to print what I heard then.[45] I will say only that P. V. Dolgorukov, later known as a writer and genealogist, was named among the group of authors of the inflamatory anonymous letters" *(Russian Archive,* 1872, no. 1).[46] This has everything: the author of the anonymous letter was not one person, some sort of insidious provocations, and the name Dolgorukov.

And almost twenty years later (1860) Odoyevsky himself wrote of Dolgorukov: "This ignorant gentleman practiced only in the sphere of gossip, *the transmission of anonymous letters,* and he worked in this field with considerable success. He produced several quarrels, family disasters and, by the way, one great loss, which Russia mourns to this day."

In the light of my discovery of the unknown person, this well-known quotation takes on new significance. It means that Odoyevsky knew that some sort of *transmission of anonymous letters* had taken place.

Since Vielgorsky was one of those who received the diploma, he obviously knew from Pushkin that not all of the diplomas were written in the same hand. Until now we did not know what "insidious provocations" led Pushkin to the duel. But now we can assume Dolgorukov's double game. Was it not he who informed Pushkin and gave him the material for the November letter: the conversation between Heeckeren and d'Anthès, the anonymous letters plan, and their dispatch. It is ridiculous to think that Pushkin was fantasizing. "Messrs Heeckeren" in the letter to Benckendorf *("mes drôles"* in the November draft) shows that he knew about d'Anthès's involvement in the lampoon. This is what, in my opinion, constituted the "insidious provocations" of Dolgorukov or someone else from Heeckeren's band.

Further research confirms Dolgorukov's intimacy with d'Anthès's *bande joyeuse.* Vyazemsky writes his wife (1839) that "the bandylegged Dolgorukov is Valuyev's friend." Valuyev (Vyazemsky's son-in-law) calls himself *bancal* in his exculpatory letter to his friends before his departure abroad. D'Anthès asks him to be called as witness for the defense.

On the other hand, the same Vyazemsky rather vigorously describes the *bancal's* intimacy with Heeckeren's gang, calling the *bancal* one of the "impudent young debauchers" who surrounded the Dutch ambassador.

In 1839 Dolgorukov played a very peculiar role in the duel between Prince Lobanov-Rostovsky and Prince Lev Gagarin.[47] He proposed that the participants of this duel draw up a document about the duel, took it for safekeeping and evidently delivered it to the police, so that when the participants arrived at the place of the duel, the gendarmes were already there waiting for them.

Opponents of the version of the *bancal* as author of the lampoon point to the fact that it originated only after the Vorontsov affair (1861),[48] though Gagarin was named immediately. To this I can raise the following objection: in 1848, that is, eleven years after the dispatch of the lampoon and immediately after the French Revolution, Chaadayev[49] received a letter in Moscow signed by Louis Colardo, who was supposedly a famous French psychiatrist. He had come from Paris, which, as we know, is a city overrun with madmen of all sorts, to Moscow out of his desire to cure Chaadayev of his megalomania. A number of Chaadayev's acquaintances also received similar letters with the request that they persuade Chaadayev to accept the celebrity's services, because after he had cured him, Colardo would gain admittance to the home of that *most famous madman*, Dmitriyev-Mamonov.[50] Colardo's letter was totally insolent. Chaadayev immediately guessed that the *bancal* was the author of the letter and at once composed a very witty reply, which he evidently forgot to send.[51] I would like to call the reader's attention to the following circumstances: (1) the letter was sent to a number of people (the victim's friends); (2) Dmitriyev-Mamonov plays the same role as Naryshkin in the 1836 lampoon. One is a famous cuckold, the other a famous madman. It was written by the same hand, it was invented by the same person and that person was Prince Pyotr Vladimirovich Dolgorukov. In criminal law this is called a case of modus operandi and is irrefutable proof of the accused's guilt.

The Reasons for Sending the Diploma

EVIDENTLY THE DUTCH ENVOY, wishing to separate d'Anthès from Natalya Nikolayevna, was certain that *"le mari d'une jalousie révoltante"* [the disgracefully jealous husband] would immediately remove his wife from Petersburg after receiving such a letter, and would send her to her mother in the country (as was the case in 1834)—anywhere at all—and everything would end peacefully. That is why all the diplomas were sent to Pushkin's *friends* and not to his enemies, who naturally could not admonish the poet.

There was one exception. Sollogub's aunt—Vasilchikova. She was not a member of Pushkin's circle. She was, however, the sister of Naryshkin, who is mentioned in the diploma, and someone among the *mes drôles* could have chosen her precisely for that reason. We know that Pushkin made an attempt to keep Natalya Nikolayevna away from d'Anthès's wedding by taking her to Mikhailovskoye with him. He writes about this to Osipova, to which his neighbor answers that his beautiful wife probably will not want to leave (apparently at the height of the season) and who could think ill of this (January 1837), and even adds: *"Honi soit qui mal y pense* [Shame on him who thinks ill of this]."[52]

It seems that no one has noticed that the letter to d'Anthès, in which Pushkin retracts the challenge, has a very pointed message. It is a letter by the head of a household with a young girl in his charge, written to an individual who has dishonored her and, later, has agreed to marry her after being threatened with a duel. And nothing else. That is why the seconds did not show d'Anthès the letter. With this letter Pushkin begins his first plan of revenge, which was supposed to show d'Anthès to be a coward. The letter, of course, compromised Katerina and it is not surprising that she openly became Pushkin's enemy.

It is appropriate to note here that d'Anthès's marriage to Katerina, which seemed so ridiculous to Pushkin, suited both Heeckerens completely.

About this time rumors regarding the true nature of the relationship between the two barons had become rather persistent (see the testimony of the Dutch envoy's colleagues) and Georges definitely had to marry.[53] Given such a reputation, a brilliant career would have been difficult. It would also be the end of his career if he married the daughter of a wealthy tax-farmer.

Katerina was a lady-in-waiting to the Empress, the niece of the all-powerful Zagryazhskaya and the magnificent Stroganov. If worst came to worst, that was good enough for the barons.

But, even more important was the fact that Katerina was head over heels in love with d'Anthès and from the very first day had become a plaything in the barons' hands. She immediately converted to Catholicism after her arrival in France. She no doubt was let in on the secret, that is, she knew that Georges had to pretend to be in love with her sister (see the draft of the duel letter: *"vous avez joué à vous trois un rôle... enfin Mad. Heckern* [all three of you have played this role... finally, Mme. Heeckeren]." She was not at all jealous—they had explained everything to her. The one who was jealous was Natalya Nikolayevna, who stupidly continued to believe in d'Anthès's great passion (see Fiquelmont's diary: *disputant avec son mari sur la possibilité du changement dans le coeur à l'amour du quel elle tenait peut-être par vanité seulement* [She quarrelled with her husband about the possibility of such a change of heart, the love of somebody she cherished, perhaps, only out of vanity]."

Evidently Zhukovsky must be believed when he persuaded and reassured Pushkin (in November) that "he [Heeckeren] gave me material proof that this matter [the wedding] had been conceived much earlier." (See also Zhukovsky's fairy tale about the hunter and the wolf.)

Aunt Zagryazhskaya wrote Zhukovsky, thanking him for settling Katerina's marriage: "And so, no one will be the wiser"—hardly an appropriate way to express offering a lady-in-waiting in marriage.

Vyazemsky wrote Emilia Musina-Pushkina on February 26, 1837: "This affair is shrouded in so many mysteries, even for those of us who followed it close at hand." And so, Vyazemsky thought that he was following the affair at close range. This, however, is what he wrote to the same Emilia Musina-Pushkina on January 15th, that is, five days after Katerina's wedding. He describes the ball at the Barants on January 14th: "Madame Heeckeren looked happy, which made her ten years younger and made her look like a nun who had just taken her vows or a deceived newlywed. I cannot conceal from you that the husband also danced a lot, enjoyed himself a great deal, and that there was not a shadow of married melancholy on his face, which is so handsome and *expressive."*

That is the impression this couple made ten days before Pushkin's challenge.

Of course, this letter does not interest us because happiness made the twenty-nine-year-old Katerina look like a nineteen-year-old girl, or that she looked like a newlywed (probably a hint at her premarital attachment to d'Anthès), or for the description of d'Anthès's handsomeness and his lack of marital melancholy.... All that is an elegant gossip's banal and malicious society prattle.

What strikes us in this letter is the serene tone and Vyazemsky's evidently absolute certainty that everything was in order, that there was no need to be alarmed and, mainly, that there was no mystery (*"tant de mystère!"*). (The notes d'Anthès wrote when he was courting, the calm and happy tone that so surprised Shchegolyov, are in complete harmony with this letter.) This is the same Vyazemsky who says that Pushkin is angry with d'Anthès, because the latter had stopped courting his wife. And about this time Zhukovsky *laughed* when he learned that Andrei Karamzin was trying to figure out the *secret* of d'Anthès's marriage. After the wedding of d'Anthès and Katerina (January 10th), the best men set off for the Karamzins (see A. I. Turgenev's diary). It would have been surprising if they had not—d'Anthès considered the Karamzin home to be almost family, as we can see from Andrei Karamzin's letter.[54] I will mention in passing that the Vyazemskys sent to inquire about the duel's outcome not to the Pushkins, but to the d'Anthèses and that Vyazemsky had known about the duel for a day and had done nothing to save his friend. And in her letter to Moscow the princess simply calls d'Anthès a tile that had fallen on Pushkin's head. It is horrible that exactly a month later this same Vyazemsky will write the same Musina-Pushkina about d'Anthès's total victory: *"Celui qui après l'avoir assasiné moralement a fini par être son meurtrier de fait* [he who was his *moral assassin,* ended up becoming such in reality]."

How should these terrifying words be understood? What Vyazemsky calls moral assassination is, of course, the fact that nobody believed in d'Anthès's cowardice and that everybody was saying that he had saved N.N. through the marriage. Pushkin could not bear that. That was nothing but confirmation of the total failure of Pushkin's strategy (he was morally assassinated).

* * *

Shchegolyov is wrong when he writes that not a trace of the allegation of Heeckeren's authorship remains in the January letter. The phrase "only on this condition [...] did I not dishonor you in the eyes of your court and ours, *as* I had the right and intention" is found in the November draft in a slightly different form, but is directly related to the possibility of exposing Heeckeren as the author of the anonymous letters.

If Pushkin had ceased to believe that Heeckeren was the author of the diploma, this phrase would not have appeared in the January letter.

Now we come to Bartenev's vague and confused account of the November 21st letter, as told to him by Prince Vyazemsky: "After this (i.e., after the announcement of d'Anthès's engagement) the Tsar, having met with Pushkin somewhere, secured his pledge that if the affair were to be renewed, Pushkin would not bring it to a head without informing the Tsar beforehand.[55] Since Pushkin's relations with the Tsar were conducted through Count Benckendorf, Pushkin addressed his well-known letter before the duel to Benckendorf, in fact, intending it for the Tsar. But Pushkin decided not to send it." (In the first edition of his *Duel and Death*, Shchegolyov assumes that this letter was addressed to Nesselrode.)

Shchegolyov should have cited this extract and not the conversation with Nikolai Pavlovich. Here and only here is it said that the conversation between Nicholas I and Pushkin took place after d'Anthès's engagement and that the Tsar secured Pushkin's pledge. Pushkin broke his pledge on January 21st in the French Embassy by announcing to two witnesses, d'Archiac and Danzas, that Heeckeren was the author of the diploma. But Pushkin wrote on January 26th: "Truth is more powerful than the Tsar" (in his letter to Tol)[56] and did not conceal "his truth in his heart," as Turgenev said of him.

A Brief Summary

AND SO: SHCHEGOLYOV DOES not take into account the following circumstances: that the entire "romance" lasted one year, that Natalya Nikolayevna was pregnant until May, that she was ill until July, that the elder Heeckeren did not make his appearance until May, that the declaration took place in February 1836, that in November d'Anthès was *already* calling Natalya Nikolayevna *mijaurée* (an affected person, a foolish woman), that the plan to compromise Natalya Nikolayevna originated with the Heeckerens immediately following d'Anthès's courting, that it was proven to Nicholas I in the Winter Palace on November 23rd that Heeckeren had sent the anonymous letters (or organized their dispatch), and that Pushkin pledged his word to be silent about it, which frustrated his intention of exposing the ambassador in the eyes of Petersburg society, that evidently the Tsar had promised the poet that he would handle the matter himself, that Pushkin waited patiently all December only to have the gossip reignited by the wedding ("the rumors in the city have resumed"). Thus, it is obvious that Nicholas I had deceived him (and he had said to Vrevskaya concerning the children, "The Tsar will take care of them, he knows everything about my case"), that the marriage to Katerina suited the Heeckerens completely (which Pushkin did not know), that Katerina *était dans le jeux* [was in the know], that the duel took place because the Heeckerens' version was given more credence than Pushkin's, and Pushkin saw his wife, that is, himself, disgraced in the eyes of society. The final blow occurred when Nicholas reprimanded Pushkin's wife about her conduct. Vrevskaya's *révélations* about the Petersburg gossip coincided with this. At first Pushkin simply wanted to ruin the Heeckerens at Razumovskaya's ball, but they had been warned in advance (they had their own people in Pushkin's closest circle—all the young people). The Vyazemskys and Karamzins received d'Anthès up to the very last day. After the calamity everybody became frightened and began with all their might to stand up for Natalya Nikolayevna, who was the only person who at any moment could have stopped everything, but she was incapable of believing that d'Anthès had fallen out of love with her and that he was making fun of her. Pushkin was terribly alone during this period and his friends' behavior to a great extent was slack and lamentable. (Vyazemsky's two letters.) The conduct of both Heeckerens... He could not endure it, and simply did not know everything. And when he did find out he sent the cartel.

Translated by Ronald Meyer

ALEXANDRINA

IN JANUARY 1837, A few days after the marriage of d'Anthès and Katerina, Count Stroganov (the sponsor at the wedding) gave a formal dinner as a continuation of the wedding celebrations. After dinner the Dutch ambassador approached Pushkin and offered him an amicable settlement. Pushkin answered him coldly that he did not wish any contact between his household and M. d'Anthès. According to the customs of the day, this was an incredible scandal,[1] and something had to be done about it right away. And so Heeckeren apparently started circulating a rumor that he had been saving. It was to sound something like this: "So, you will not admit us into your house, you say? But we do not wish to enter it, knowing the outrageous things that are going on there."[2]

That was the starting point for subsequent conversations about the imaginary romance between Pushkin and Alexandra Nikolayevna Goncharova. Obviously the slanderer ought not to spread the slander himself. That would have been too naive and would have made it easier for his listeners to unravel. It was best to use someone who was close to the victim. In this case the choice apparently fell on Sofia Karamzina.

Thus, we should not be surprised that Sofia, who was obviously and constantly influenced by d'Anthès, first noticed signs of the "criminal romance" at a party that took place at the Meshcherskys on Sunday, January 24, that is, three days before the duel. From the context, we are given to understand that Alexandrina was also in love with d'Anthès and that Pushkin was jealous not because of his wife, but because of his sister-in-law.

In a letter dated January 27, 1837, we read with amazement: "On Sunday at Katrin's (E.N. Meshcherskaya—A.A.) there was a large party without dancing. In attendance were the Pushkins and the Heeckerens, who continue to act out their sentimental comedy to the delight of all society. Pushkin continues to gnash his teeth and adopt his customary tiger-like expression, Natalya lowers her eyes and blushes under the long, passionate glances of her brother-in-law. This is becoming something more than the usual immorality. Katrin directs her jealous lorgnette at both of them, and just to be certain that nobody is left without a part in the play, Alexandrina, following all the rules of the game, flirts with Pushkin, who is truly in love with her. While he may be jealous over his wife as a matter of principle, he is jealous over his sister-in-law out of true feeling. In general, all of this is terribly strange, and Uncle Vyazemsky says that he is covering his eyes and looking away from the Pushkin home."

You can smell the slander in this a mile away. If Pushkin and Alexandrina are having an affair and live in the same house, why would they make a public display of their illicit relationship? How can anyone flirt with a man who is gnashing his teeth, etc.?

"Pacha à trois queues" is the charming expression d'Anthès had used earlier to refer jokingly to the three Goncharov sisters as Pushkin's harem. And Pushkin's sister, Olga Sergeyevna, wrote to her father on the occasion of Alexandra's and Katerina's move to Pushkin's home: "Alexander introduced me to his wives— he's got three of them now." And so, after the Heeckerens took away one of the wives, there were indeed only two left. This is the fertile ground on which those whose interests it served built the legend about a romance between Pushkin and Alexandrina Goncharova. Is this not the backbone of the rumor?

Sofia Nikolayevna's account of her impressions of the Meshcherskys' party is striking for its completely new tone. Her usual tolerance and flippancy have abandoned her, for some reason, for the first time. In their place are coldness, stiffness, and a very unfeminine clarity of formulation. And all at once support comes from Prince Pyotr (Vyazemsky) (in a few hours he will be howling at the deathbed of the dying Pushkin), who supposedly covers his eyes and looks away from *the Pushkin home* (once again the home!). Instead of the personal observations characteristic of Sofia Nikolayevna's style ("lowers her eyes," "directs her lorgnette," "takes on the expression of a tiger," etc.), here we have generalizations and the repetition of received "information."

From whom, then, did Sofia Nikolayevna learn that Pushkin was "seriously in love" with Alexandrina and that he was jealous over Natalya Nikolayevna "as a matter of principle," and over Alexandrina "out of true feeling"? Let us recall that Idaliya Poletika (of whom more below), a sworn enemy of Pushkin and a friend of d'Anthès, "reminded" Trubetskoi (in Odessa, when both of them were in their seventies), that the duel was the result of Pushkin's jealousy over Alexandrina and of his fear that d'Anthès would take her away to France.[3] This monstrous nonsense, which so disturbed Shchegolyov, was undoubtedly d'Anthès's version of the events. As if she were under a spell, Sofia echoed d'Anthès without even realizing what she was doing. Soon this version of the events would be spread (with details taken from *The Decameron*)[4] by all the gentlemen of the Horse Guards[5] and hinted at by important ladies in their salons (while pursing their lips and rolling their eyes). (The phrase in Sofia's letter, "something more than the usual (?!) immorality," was perfect for this kind of situation.)

I wish to point out that with the exception of this foul incrimination, there isn't a single mention of a romance between Alexandrina and Pushkin in the Karamzins' entire correspondence. Neither Sofia in her extremely frank letters to her brother, nor her brother, Alexander Karamzin, mentions the matter in any other connection.

And had Vyazemsky really believed this version, would he have blurted out such gossip in his letters to Musina-Pushkina?

Sofia Karamzina's letter is also noteworthy because it was written on the day and at the very hour of the duel. She herself writes about this in her subsequent letter, dated January 30: "And I frivolously wrote to you about this sad drama last Wednesday, on the very day and hour when its terrible resolution was taking place." And then she describes everything that happened, but this time what she writes is not dictated by Heeckeren-d'Anthès, as it was on the previous Wednesday, but is based on Vyazemsky's or Zhukovsky's words. That is why there isn't a single word here that we haven't heard before. When the Karamzins write about Natalya Nikolayevna after Pushkin's death, none of them even mentions Alexandrina, with the exception of the one time when we are told that Natalya is very glad that her sister will travel with her.

Shchegolyov was not familiar with the Karamzins' correspondence, but having found the same material in Trubetskoi's memoirs, he exclaims: "Every word is a mistake!" Shchegolyov is right. But the important fact is that Sofia Nikolayevna and

Trubetskoi had the same source—d'Anthès. It is he who convinced Sofia Nikolayevna and Trubetskoi about the existence of
a romance between Pushkin and Alexandrina. It is his voice we
hear in Trubetskoi's memoirs. The gentlemen of the Horse
Guards were just as hypnotized by d'Anthès as were the young
people of the Karamzin-Vyazemsky circle (the *bande joyeuse*).

Shchegolyov underestimated Trubetskoi's memoir. Every
word in it is spoken not by Trubetskoi but by d'Anthès (or sometimes by Poletika, which is the same thing), and what is attributed to Danzas is spoken not by him, but by Pushkin himself.
It was from d'Anthès that Trubetskoi learned that Pushkin was
duelling because of his sister-in-law and not because of his wife.
That was to prove "poor Georges's" innocence and drag Pushkin
through the mud for having dishonored the young girl given
into his care by her mother. It was also an act of revenge for
Pushkin's November letter, which hinted at the depraved relationship between d'Anthès and Heeckeren ("your *bâtard* or the
one who is referred to as such").

Everything that Trubetskoi dictated at his summer home in
Pavlovsk is d'Anthès's version, supported by the Odessa reminiscences of Poletika. Trubetskoi had never read Pushkin or his
letters or any works about him. His simplemindedness led him
to believe the apocryphal story of the kiss, the coal, the lamp, the
candle... and the mustache. To him d'Anthès was the ideal of wit,
elegance, and savoir-faire with women, in other words—he was
as much in love with d'Anthès as the rest of the Karamzin *bande
joyeuse*.

And so, Trubetskoi's memoir is transformed from the senile
babbling that so disturbed Shchegolyov into a document of first-
rank significance: it is the only faithful record of d'Anthès's own
version of the events.

Evidently, the dissemination of this version was also entrusted
to Poletika,[6] the daughter of Stroganov, who was undoubtedly
not indifferent to d'Anthès (Katerina writes to her husband that
Idaliya wept when she learned of his departure), and a sworn
enemy of Pushkin. And Poletika remained true to her goal for the
rest of her life. She so despised Pushkin that in 1889 she called
him a rhymemonger, etc. Clearly, this was the attitude of the
whole Stroganov household to which she belonged. She maintained a good relationship with Koko [Yekaterina] and sent "un-
ladylike" information on the literary and financial aspects of the
Pushkin estate to Sultz, where d'Anthès and Katerina lived. With

malicious pleasure she wrote about the size of the posthumous edition, which, according to her, did not meet expectations, etc.

A telling correspondence can be found between Heeckeren's mention of an anonymous January letter, about which we know nothing beyond this single reference, and a story by Poletika.[7] Arapova, evidently repeating Poletika's account, claims that Lanskoi stood guard during a meeting between Natalya Nikolayevna and d'Anthès (which supposedly took place at Poletika's in January 1837). Yet at the time Lanskoi was in Rostov, according to some, according to others, he was in Voronezh. I must conclude that the meeting never took place or we would have learned of it from other sources as well.

Shchegolyov assumes that the whole story of the romance between Pushkin and Alexandrina is the invention of Arapova, the daughter of Natalya Nikolayevna and Lanskoi, intended to create a symmetry in the situation and to justify Natalya Nikolayevna's behavior. I believe that she used a story already in circulation, rather than inventing one. This version, which was invented by the Heeckerens, was cherished and fostered by Idaliya Poletika till her last breath. She never tired of drumming it into the half-witted Trubetskoi in Odessa (which he himself, fortunately, mentioned to his listeners at the summer home in Pavlovsk).[8] And it was *she* who told V.F. Vyazemskaya about Alexandrina's "confession."

Heeckeren and Poletika were people of their time and circle, and they knew very well that nothing could so besmirch and completely destroy Pushkin in the eyes of society as a rumor of this sort.[9] It is no accident that Trubetskoi writes the following about the romance between Pushkin and Alexandrina: "Nothing is written about them [the reasons for the fatal duel] in the press, perhaps because they cast aspersions on the man whose name is dear to us Russians." He still remembers, while Shchegolyov no longer remembers or understands, the indecency and monstrosity of the incrimination. Subsequently everyone retells the "legend" with tender emotion and writes verses to the poet's lady friend.

And so, having yanked at an insignificant thread (Alexandrina), we pulled out something horrible and disgusting—what would have happened if the duel of January 27 had not taken place. My work has proven that for the task of spreading any rumor the ambassador had at his disposal the whole of the regiment of the Guards (the gentlemen-officers were even prepared to repeat the

latest news from *The Decameron*),[10] at least two Petersburg salons—
Nesselrode's and Bobrinskaya's—and, as painful as it is to draw
the conclusion, the young people in two families who were
Pushkin's friends—the Vyazemskys and the Karamzins. Let us remember that even after Pushkin's death Sofia Karamzina continues
to repeat her story, worrying that something might happen to
d'Anthès.[11] And no one is concerned about the poet's own version
of the events. He was already "almost ridiculous" (the words of
Alexander Karamzin to his brother Andrei) and would soon have
become a criminal. The innocent Alexandra Nikolayevna would
have been condemned to the life of an old maid on her mother's
provincial estate and one of the Goncharov brothers would have
been obliged to kill in a duel the man who had dishonored his sister, a young girl entrusted to Pushkin by her mother. All of
Petersburg would have sympathized with the killer.

At the time this kind of relationship was considered incestuous, so it is difficult to imagine who could conceive of using as
evidence for it the words of Pushkin's father, Sergei Lvovich,
who claimed that Alexandrina was more grieved than the
widow.

Is it possible that Pushkin's father would say something that
would disgrace the name of his son who had just been killed? He
simply said (and wanted to say) that another person saw the horror of the situation and was more distressed by it than the
widow whose heartlessness shocked everyone, not only her father-in-law. Upon learning of his son's death, the old man would
not believe it for a long time. When he was finally convinced that
it was true, his words were: "I can only ask God not to deprive
me of my memory, so that I may not forget him."

We can say with certainty that there was no rumor about an
affair at the time of Pushkin's death, otherwise Alexandrina
could not have become a maid of honor in 1839.

Moreover, everyone seems to be forgetting another person
who was closely involved in the whole "matter"—that is, Natalya
Nikolayevna Pushkina.

In light of her well-known jealousy (see Pushkin's letters),
would she have stood by silently and without any reaction visible to others, while her husband carried on a scandalous affair
with her sister in her own home?

On the other hand, her jealousy over d'Anthès was visible to
all of Petersburg society. According to Sofia Karamzina, she
nearly choked when speaking of Yekaterina's wedding, did not

want to correspond with her sister, and did not even keep a portrait of her sister in the house. Yet she always saw Alexandrina as a dear, true, and trustworthy friend. If we are to believe the confabulations of Arapova, in 1852 Natalya Nikolayevna discussed with her sister the best way of informing Friesenhof, Alexandrina's fiancé, about her relationship with Pushkin.[12]

The other three proofs of this "criminal attachment" are equally ephemeral. We certainly are not obliged to believe V.F. Vyazemskaya, who was writing at the advanced age of eighty. She was obviously concerned only with absolving herself and her house of any blame (Pushkin, after all, had told her about the duel). Then there is the ridiculous matter reported by the same Arapova, who claims that after Alexandrina's premarital confession, her fiancé, Friesenhof, displayed a changed attitude towards the memory of Pushkin. And finally there is the cross or a chain that Pushkin on his deathbed supposedly requested be given to Alexandrina. That can be explained by motives of a very different nature.[13] Since Alexandrina was the only adult in the house at the time, Pushkin must have told her that he was riding off to a duel. She could not help but give him a little cross, which he left at home and ordered that it be returned to her before his death. I do not believe that we need to consider the revelations of a nurse, especially since she must have been referring to the same cross, of which the servants in the Pushkin home may have heard. The fact that Pushkin did not wish to see Azya [Alexandrina] before his death is certainly no proof of the existence of a relationship. Quite the contrary, had there been a relationship then and knowing that he was dying, he would most probably have wished to ask her forgiveness.

It seems much more likely to me that Pushkin knew that Alexandrina had been playing the same role that Yekaterina had played in the summer of 1836.

Why did Pushkin hate Yekaterina Nikolayevna Goncharova so much that he shamed her in his November letter? Most probably because, like everyone else, he knew what role she had played in the initial stage of the d'Anthès affair.[14]

Why did Pushkin categorically refuse to take leave of Alexandrina on his deathbed? Probably for the same reason. Alexandrina could not help but become a confidante and subsequently an accomplice to her younger sister. The enamored Natalya Nikolayevna needed a go-between. Closer and more trustworthy than anyone else was her sister Alexandrina who, in her diary for 18—, could write with satisfaction that Natalya had walked in the park with d'Anthès and that they had become rec-onciled. And is not her terrible note in Austria (written as a more than mature woman) a continuation of her Petersburg role? If she did not understand the indecency of her words then, what could she have understood in 1836, when, like the other mem-bers of the *bande joyeuse*, she was under the spell and *hypnotic charm* of d'Anthès?

Let us recall Zhukovsky's notes on d'Anthès's behavior to-wards Yekaterina: "In the presence of the aunt, he is tender to-wards his wife, but in the presence of Alexandrina and others who can talk about it, there is a coarseness (*des brusqueries*) in his behavior."[15] D'Anthès needed Natalya Nikolayevna to hear about his mistreatment of Katerina, which would presumably be proof of his great passion for Natalya. So Alexandrina visited the d'Anthès home and returned with tales of his near-beatings of Koko. Madame Pushkina was delighted—she was now con-vinced that he really loved her, that his was in fact a great and exalted passion (*grande et sublime passion*).

When writing about Alexandrina, those who have studied this whole issue inevitably adopt a sanctimonious, affected tone, forgetting that she was one of the fetching, wasp-waisted Gon-charov sisters whom Zhukovsky had called little lambs, at whose sight d'Anthès, a member of the *bande*, licked his chops. She constantly found herself in circles hostile to Pushkin.[16]

It appears from everything we know that Alexandrina did not stay at home, taking care of the children and household, but rather went out into society with her sisters.[17] Yet Arapova's por-trait of a modest, clever and good, but plain young girl met with great success. Nobody bothers with the fact that Arapova goes on to depict the aunt as a witch, a hysterical woman, and domestic tyrant (who forbade Natalya Nikolayevna to go riding in a car-riage with Lanskoi). The reader put his trust in her once and for all. The quotation has been engraved in stone. It is repeated to this day. There is no evidence whatsoever that Alexandrina was on Pushkin's side in the conflict. This is also true of her aunt, K.I. Zagryazhskaya.[18] Both of them sided with Natalya Nikolayevna, which is quite a different matter. As everyone knows, there is not a single good word about Pushkin in all of Arapova's memoirs.

Then, where did this suspect information originate? With Natalya Nikolayevna? But she died in 1863, when Arapova was only eighteen. Would any mother, even a hypocrite like Natalya Nikolayevna, tell her eighteen-year-old daughter about Pushkin's return from Amalia's at the break of dawn or the story of d'Anthès courting the *three* delighted Goncharov sisters?

We see here the result of Arapova's meeting with Alexandrina, which took place abroad.

According to Arapova, Pushkin was a failure who had squandered all of his inheritance, an uncouth bore, and vulgar libertine ("He was again at Amalia's"), the wicked husband of a long-suffering, tormented victim. It never occurred to Arapova to even take a look at the tender, caring, and most beautiful letters that Pushkin wrote to his wife. Her image of Pushkin was based on what she heard from her own mother, from Alexandra Nikolayevna Goncharova, and, probably, from Poletika.[19]

D'Anthès, on the other hand, is served wonderfully: his arrival, poverty, illness at a hotel, his meeting with an aristocrat who is struck by the young man's beauty and charm, their friendship... The love of the young officer of the Horse Guards—unique, exalted, life-long. Here we can also see the work of Natalya Nikolayevna, Poletika, and Aunt Azya. Let us remember that for Arapova, just as for Pushkin's children, d'Anthès was another uncle and that the tone of her writings does not differ from the biography of d'Anthès written by his grandson, Metman.

There is nothing in Alexandra Nikolayevna's later life that would support the legend of her role as "the good angel" in Pushkin's life. She preserved no memory of him. On the other hand, we can observe her continued good relationship with the d'Anthès home. We learn from the memoir of the grandson of Pushkin's murderer that Pushkin's sons, Alexander and Grigory, whom she raised, visited "Uncle Georges" at Sultz. And Arapova, who was not in the least shocked by this, reports that they listened intently to "Uncle," who told them about his Russian adventures.

Pushkin's daughters, who were also brought up by Alexandrina, corresponded with their cousins in Alsace.

In a letter that supposedly aroused even Natalya Nikolayevna's indignation, Alexandra described a dinner at the elder Heeckeren's in Vienna. She could not help but know about his role in the Pushkin affair. It was at her house that Arapova met the daughter of d'Anthès, the Countess de Vandal, and admired her bracelet—a wedding gift to Yekaterina Nikolayevna from her two sisters.

D'Anthès himself on a number of occasions had visited the Friesenhofs on their estate outside of Vienna. And, as I mentioned above, Alexandra Nikolayevna wrote with satisfaction in her diary that d'Anthès met Natalya Nikolayevna there, that they spent a whole day walking around the park and had a total reconciliation. To the very end of her life she preserved the legend of d'Anthès' *grande et sublime passion* for her sister.

1962

Translated by Uliana Gabara

Alexandrina
Drafts of the Ending

I

1. Pushkin's library and Alexandra Goncharova.
2. The portrait of "Uncle Georges" in Alexandrina's castle.
3. The cup—a present from Azya. The overcoat.

II
Conclusion

After his death there was no such thing as a cult of Pushkin in the widow's home. On the contrary, it is clear that everything associated with Pushkin was a burden for Natalya Nikolayevna. But, why did the thrifty Alexandrina not show the least bit of concern for the library or the overcoat[20] (for the childrens' sake, if nothing else)?

Recently I had the opportunity to read Alexandrina's letters to her brother Dmitri. Truth to tell, there is nothing in them except persistent pleas for money. However, it is clear from the first letter that Alexandrina went out into society with her sister Yekaterina, and from the tenth that she was undoubtedly a member of the *bande joyeuse* and therefore, like all the others, under the spell of d'Anthès. Pushkin's name is absent from these letters; there are greetings for Lanskoi. All in all, everything is as it should be.

III

In addition to the fact that Pushkin's boys, while being brought up by Alexandrina, visited d'Anthès ("Oncle Georges a tué Papa"), and that the girls corresponded with their cousins, Alexandrina did not deign to safeguard the poet's library while she lived in General Lanskoi's home. It turns out that in her letters to her brother she does not mention Pushkin even once, either living or dead, yet she does mention Lanskoi (in connection with the sale of his horse).

IV

A portrait of d'Anthès hung in the dining room of Alexandrina's castle until the beginning of the war of 1940. For me, personally, this is sufficient proof that she never loved Pushkin. Rayevsky attempts to explain the absence of Pushkin's portrait in the home of his *belle soeur* (sister-in-law) by the jealousy of the master of the house, Friesenhof. (A feeling obviously inherited by his daughter, who was, evidently, told that her mommy had committed incest.) I don't think that many would have found it more decent to hang the portraits of both—the murderer and his victim. And in any case was it necessary to hang portraits of relatives all over the place? Natalya Nikolayevna, for example, never did have a portrait of her deceased sister (who did, in fact, die so tragically),[21] because she could never forgive her victory over d'Anthès.

Undoubtedly, that portrait in the dining room was a remnant of the cult of d'Anthès, which I discussed at the beginning of my essay. It was intended to remind the mistress of the house of those "happy times" when, wherever they went, the three admiring Goncharov sisters encountered the handsome horse-guardsman (see Arapova's memoirs).

1964-1965

Translated by Uliana Gabara

PUSHKIN AND THE BANKS
OF THE NEVA

I N TITOV'S STORY "THE Solitary Hut on Vasilyevsky Island" (1829)[1] there is a strikingly detailed description of the northern tip of the island:

> Anyone who has ever had occasion to walk around all of Vasilyevsky Island on foot will undoubtedly have noticed that its different ends resemble each other very little. Its southern shore, for example, is covered by magnificent, huge brick buildings, while the northern side looks out onto Petrovsky Island and cuts deeply into the sleepy waters of the bay.[2] As you approach this end of the island, the brick structures become less frequent and are replaced by wooden huts interspersed with vacant plots, until finally all that is left are spacious gardens and on your left, a grove. After you have passed these, you come to two isolated houses and a few trees. A ditch overgrown with nettles and burdock separates the higher places from the bank that protects the island from flooding. Still further lies the meadow, which is the marshy shore itself. These sad places are deserted in summer, but even more in winter when the meadow and the sea and the wood, which casts a shadow on the shore of Petrovsky Island—when everything is buried under gray snow drifts, as if in a grave.

The author has but a few words for the southern side of Vasilyevsky Island, which he sees every day. It is the northern side, where hardly anyone ever goes, over which he practically weeps. Depressed by the dreary summer landscape, he then imagines how dismal it must be in the winter and compares it to a grave. We learn what is to the right and to the left, we feel the swampy ground underfoot. None of this is seen from the window of a coach or even a hired hack. The author is so preoccupied with the description of the northern end of the island that he does not even notice the sea. Petersburg does not exist for him. We shiver from the unexpected ringing of the clock on the Duma, for until that moment there is no Nevsky Prospect or Gostiny Dvor, no palaces and no quays on the embankments. Golodai Island has no bearing on the subject matter of the story, yet nothing in it is described in such detail.

In his book *Pushkin's Petersburg,* Boris Tomashevsky compares this description with Pushkin's treatment of the banks of the Neva in *The Bronze Horseman*:[3]

> A little island
> Lies off the coast. There now and then
> A stray belated fisherman
> Will beach his net at dusk and, silent,
> Cook his poor supper by the shore,
> Or, on his Sunday recreation
> A boating clerk might rest his oar
> By that bleak isle. There no green thing
> Will grow; and there the inundation
> Had washed up in its frolicking
> A frail old cottage. It lay stranded
> Above the tide like weathered brush,
> Until last spring a barge was landed
> To haul it off. It was all crushed
> And bare. Against the threshold pressed,
> My madman's chilly corpse was found,
> And forthwith in this very ground
> For love of God was laid to rest.

I am firmly convinced that the somewhat enigmatic fragment "When at Times a Reminiscence," written in 1830, should be read in relation to the above text.

> When at times a reminiscence
> Gnaws at my heart in silence
> And a distant suffering
> Rushes toward me like a shadow;
> When, seeing people all around,

I want to hide in the wilderness,
Having come to hate their weak voices,
Then, forgetting myself, I flee
Not to the luminous land where the sky glitters
With an inexplicable blue,
Where the sea splashes its warm wave
Against the yellowed marble,
And the laurel and dark cypress
Flourish, luxuriant in their freedom,
Where majestic Torquato sang,
Where even now in the night shadow
A distant ringing rock
Repeats the swimmers' octaves.

In my recurrent dream[4]
I rush toward the cold northern waves.
In the midst of their white-capped crowd
I see a flat island.
A dismal island—its wild shore
Is covered with winter bilberry,
Hidden by withered tundra,
Washed by the sea foam.
Here at times moors
A brave northern fisherman,
Here he spreads his net
And here he makes his home.
This is where the stormy weather
Carries my fragile bark.
.........................[5]

In this fragment everything is absolutely mysterious: the impetuous display of suffering, so unusual for Pushkin (this kind of moan is uncharacteristic of Pushkin's mature lyrics and can be compared only with "A Reminiscence," written in 1828), the readiness to sacrifice the most sacred and dearest dream of his life—Italy, or to be more precise, the dream of Italy, and the detailed description of a bit of meager northern land forgotten equally by man and God, all of this in tragic tones, out of keeping with the realistic depiction of life's fullness in "Onegin's Travels":

I feel the need for other sketches...
I like a sloping sandy track,

A wicker gate, neglected hedges,
Two rowans by a peasant shack...

....

The Flemands' piebald stock-in-trade![6]

It is worthwhile to compare the fragment "When at Times a Reminiscence" with the first chapter of *Eugene Onegin*, in which something diametrically opposite takes place. We might even suppose that the poet intended to use the same composition in reverse. In it Pushkin renounces Petersburg, its white nights etc., in favor of Italy:

Yet, 'mid nocturnal reveling
Torquato's octaves sweeter sing![7]

As commentary to his own description of the Neva and the white nights, Pushkin uses a long fragment from Gnedich's "The Fishermen," in which there appears the "Neva tundra" ("...a fresh wind blew over the Neva tundra...").[8] And the same word appears in the 1830 fragment ("Hidden by the withered tundra...").

For Pushkin Petersburg is always the North.[9] While writing poetry, he always seems to be living in some distant South. This is especially significant, since the fragment was written in Boldino (October 1830).

What happened between the first chapter of *Onegin* (1823), in which the poet was gracefully announcing his readiness to exchange Petersburg for Italy, and the tragic tone of 1830, which forced him to renounce the cherished dream?

To this very day we do not know the exact location of the graves of the five executed Decembrists. It is believed that Ryleyev's widow knew the place of their burial. It was Golodai Island, that is, the northernmost tip of Vasilyevsky Island, separated from the main part by the very narrow Smolenka River. During the reign of Nicholas there were only rumors, some more, some less reliable, which inevitably arose immediately after the execution.[10]

Pushkin was haunted by thoughts about the Decembrists, about their fate and their terrible end. From his letters we know what he thought of those who remained alive (see Pushkin's letters, his poems "The Epistle" and "In the dark recesses of the earth").[11] Now let us consider more closely his relationship with those who perished.

We find the first mention of them in the sixth chapter of *Onegin*, written immediately after Pushkin learned about the tragic events (that is, on July 26, 1826). Chapter 6 was finished on August 10, 1826. In it Ryleyev's name appears next to those of Kutuzov and Nelson. Lensky, we are told, could have been "hanged like Ryleyev."[12] Later, we see the drawings of gallows in the rough drafts of *Poltava* (1828) and in a copy of Sir Walter Scott's *Ivanhoe* that Pushkin gave as a gift to A.A. Ramensky at the Poltoratskys (together with a quotation from chapter 10 of *Onegin*) on March 8, 1829.[13] *Onegin* ends with the words: "Some are no more, dispersed the others" (1830). Pushkin did not need to recall them: he had simply never forgotten either the living or the dead.

I reject the possibility that the location of their graves was a matter of indifference to him.

We know from I.P. Liprandi's memoirs that Pushkin searched for Mazepa's grave and questioned the 135-year-old Cossack, Iskra, who "could not show him the grave nor tell him where it was to be found." Pushkin "would not give up... He kept asking whether there were other old men like him."[14] And from the text of *Poltava* we learn how sorry he was that he did not find the grave ("And the unhappy stranger would search in vain for the hetman's grave"). Pushkin wrote about Napoleon's grave on St. Helena and Kutuzov's grave in Kazan Cathedral. And in connection with the graves of the executed Kochubei and Iskra, we should recall that Pushkin repeatedly called on Nicholas I to follow the example of his great ancestor, Peter I. Any reader will remember: "In everything be like your ancestor" ("Stanzas," 1826). In Pushkin's own commentary to *Poltava* we read the following: "The decapitated bodies of Iskra and Kochubei were given to their relatives and subsequently buried in the Kiev Monastery. Above their graves there is the following inscription: '...In the year 1708, on the 15th day of July, the noble Vasily Kochubei, Judge General, and Ioann Iskra, a Colonel of Poltava, were executed at the Army Camp at Borshchagovets and Kovshevo near Bela Tserkov. Their bodies were brought to Kiev on July 17 and on that day they were buried in the sacred Pechersky Monastery, in this very place.'"

In this passage Pushkin, without a doubt, is bitterly reproaching Nicholas I, who not only did not permit the families of the executed Decembrists to have the bodies of their deceased, but even ordered that they be buried in some deserted place.

While in *Poltava*:

Yet folk remember reverently
Where in the boneyard of the just
The pious brethren bedded gently
Two suffering martyrs' holy dust.[15]

And this we find in *Poltava*, whose rough drafts are covered
with drawings of hanged men. The precise information about
the time when the bodies were returned to the families is yet another means by which Pushkin reminds the Tsar what the ac-
ceptable behavior is in such a case: "The *church* has granted them
peaceful refuge." And not only the church as such, but the center
of Orthodoxy and the most holy place in Russia, to which hun-
dreds of thousands made a pilgrimage each year from great dis-
tances. Let us keep in mind that Pushkin is speaking here about
the bodies of recently executed state criminals.

These are the words of the same poet who in two years' time
in the fragment "When at Times a Reminiscence" will again establish a cult of graves in words that are majestic and, as always
with this author, not subject to abrogation:

Two feelings are wondrously close to us,
In them our hearts find nourishment:[16]
The love of our native hearth,
The love of our ancestral graves,

Life-giving holy place!
The earth without them would be dead
Like a desert
And like an altar without a god.
                              (1830)

N.V. Izmailov, noting Pushkin's attitude towards cemeteries,
deals only with the issue of family burial plots.[17] (To his discussion we could add "Roadside Laments": "Not in the inherited
den, / Not in the midst of ancestral graves...")

All this is, of course, correct. But when Tatyana says that she is
ready to give everything

...for that gentle grassy swelling
Where cross and swaying branches grace
Poor Nanny's final resting place...[18]

and Dunya comes to visit the grave of the stationmaster, and
Maria Ivanovna, before leaving the fort, goes to bid farewell to
the graves of her parents who were buried by the church (victims
of Pugachev?!)—these are not just family graves.[19] Pushkin here
generously bestows his innermost feelings and thoughts on his
chosen heroines.

Pushkin fully shared the lofty belief of antiquity (see Sophocles,
Oedipus at Colonus) that the grave of a just man is a national treasure and a blessing from the gods.

From the same enigmatic fragment ("When at Times a
Reminiscence") we learn that Pushkin avoids conversations
dealing with a subject that is dear to him but treated disrespect-
fully by others. His use of the word "society"[20] points to the fact
that it is not a personal matter, since in social circles such personal matters were never discussed in the presence of the person
concerned. The poet is ready to flee, not to just any place, not
even to his beloved Italy, but to some taiga-covered tiny island in
the north, which exactly resembles the one where three years
later he will bury his Eugene Yezersky "for the love of God."

In the surviving stanzas of chapter 10 of *Onegin*, we read
about the Decembrist affair and there are descriptions of the participants in the movement. *Onegin* is marked by changes and
shifts from one plane to another: although irony accompanies
Lensky almost until the last hour of his life, Pushkin nonetheless
mourns him with incredible power and sorrow and returns to
him again in chapter 7. In a stanza that was ultimately not included in chapter 6 (1826), Lensky is presented as a possible participant in the uprising on Senate Square: "Or to be hanged like
Ryleyev." We can be certain that their graves were not forgotten
either.

In his memoirs Baron Rosen describes how he rode along the
shore, attempting to find the graves of his five executed friends.[21]
Pushkin's sorrowful interest in the place, which he described
three times ("Little House," 1828; the fragment "When at Times a
Reminiscence," 1830; and *The Bronze Horseman*), allows us to suppose that he, too, had searched for the unmarked graves along
the Neva shore.

That a manuscript with a lot of crossings-out can turn out to be
a stanza from *Onegin* we know from the case "To Marry—but
Whom?...," which was considered to be a separate poem until T.G.
Tsyavlovskaya (Zenger) deduced that it was, in fact, a stanza

from*Onegin*.[22] Similarly, the following lines of the fragment are, in fact, a nearly completed stanza.

In my recurrent dream	fem.
I rush toward the cold northern waves.	masc.
In the midst of their white-capped crowd	fem.
I see a flat island.	masc.
A dismal island—its wild shore	fem.
Is covered with winter bilberry,	fem.
Hidden by the withered tundra,	masc.
Washed by the sea foam.	masc.

I hope everyone will agree that the fragment is written according to all the rules of the Onegin stanza. In the last quatrain, instead of the abba rhyme scheme, there is once again the abab scheme, but we must remember that we are dealing with a working draft that has a lot of crossings-out. We do not know what Pushkin would have made of it ultimately. The opening part of the fragment is not worked out at all and in addition contains part of a completed poem from 1827 ("Who knows the land...").

In the drafts of *Poltava* Pushkin wrote above the gallows: "And I could, like a fool," and in his verses to Ushakova: "Will you sigh after me if I should be hanged?" (1827), as if he were including himself among the victims of December 14th.[23] And the nameless grave on the shore of the Neva must have seemed to him to be almost his own: This is where "the stormy weather / Carries my fragile boat."

January 23, 1963
Moscow

Translated by Uliana Gabara

Reviews & Public Addresses

ON NADEZHDA LVOVA'S POETRY

I T IS PAINFUL WHEN a poet dies, but when a young poet dies it is even more painful. You read the few lines that he has left behind with agonizing concentration, greedily scouring the still immature voice and the youthfully spare imagery for the secret of death, which is hidden from us, the living.

The book of the recently deceased poetess, Nadezhda Lvova, gives us this bitter joy.

Her poems, so clumsy and touching, do not attain that level of lucid clarity where they could be to everyone's liking, but you simply believe them, as you would believe a person in tears. Love is the major and virtually the sole theme of her book, *An Old Tale*.

But it's strange that women, who in reality are so strong and who are so sensitive to all of love's charms, know only one kind of love (torturous, painfully calculating, and hopeless) when they begin to write.

> Oh, let it be painful, agonizingly painful!
> I greet all torments with a smile of happiness.
> Obedient, I devoutly prostrate myself
> Before the hovering specter of eternal separation.

This obedience, almost a lack of will, is particularly characteristic of all of Lvova's work. Her suffering searches for an outlet in dreams, not romantic ones that she might conquer by dint of will, but acutely lyrical ones that transform every moment of her life. She is certain that she hears the "step of her dreams," that she sees the "specter of eternal separation which lightly touches her lips" and senses that "somebody is allegedly watching her with vindictive malice from the clouds."

Ad mortem is the best section of the book *An Old Tale*.

Each of the nine poems included in it seemed to me to be an incantation of death.

The first poem is particularly significant. It begins with the words:

> You, who have sung the praises of passion's secrets
>   in the abyss of time—
> Sing with me of death that brings eternal light.

And the same person who told us about her love with such bitter sadness, who recalled the meetings and separations in such a breathless voice, speaks altogether simply and confidently when she has felt the breath of death: "Now I am joyous. Now I am calm."

And there is not one extraneous word in the serene and terrifying poems in which the poet prophesies her own death:

> What use have I of caresses and kisses!
> What use have I of belated words.
> Look, look how quietly I am sleeping,
> And I cannot and do not wish
> To cast you a summons in response.

I believe that Nadezhda Lvova undermined her delicate gifts by forcing herself to write rondeaus, ghazals and sonnets. Of course, women are also capable of achieving an elevated mastery of form (for example, Karolina Pavlova),[1] but their strength lies elsewhere, it lies in their ability to express fully the most intimate and wonderfully simple things in themselves and the world around them. But anything that hinders the free development of the lyric feeling, that forces you to guess beforehand what should come only as surprise, is very dangerous for a young poet. It either encumbers his idea or seduces him with the possibility of making do without an idea altogether. These are the least successful pages in the book *An Old Tale*.

Words had not yet become Lvova's servant, but since she was a servant to words, who deeply believed in the importance of every one of them, the spirit of music hovers over her poems.

WORK IN PROGRESS

I N RECENT YEARS I have been engaged in the study of
Pushkin's works. My first study on this subject was the essay
"Pushkin's Last Tale," which was printed in 1933 in the journal *The Star*. This year my study "Benjamin Constant's *Adolphe* in
the Work of Pushkin" was published by the Academy of Sciences
in the *Annals of Pushkin Studies*.[1]

I am now working on the commentary for the third volume of
the Academy edition of Pushkin's works *(The Golden Cockerel)*.[2]
This work consumes almost all my time and has postponed the
realization of other projects.

I have devoted a lot of time to translation. Recently *The Star*
printed my translation of a long poem by the Armenian poet
Daniel Vorouzhan—"First Sin".[3] I have just completed the translation of two poems by the contemporary Armenian poet,
Charents.[4]

Apart from this, I translated into Russian all the French poetry
printed in the commentary to the first volume of the Academy
edition of Pushkin's works, in addition to Pushkin's French
poems.

I have been writing lyric poetry. I have prepared for publication my *Selected Works* (for the Soviet Writer Publishing House),
which includes not only previously published poems from all of
my books, but also poems written during the period 1930-1935.[5]

I follow Soviet poetry. Among contemporary poets I value
and esteem B. Pasternak. I recently wrote a poem that is dedicated to him. This is the final stanza of that poem:[6]

> He was rewarded with an eternal childhood,
> His penetrating eye and generosity beamed,
> And all the earth was his inheritance,
> And he shared it with all men.

Upon completion of my work on the commentary for the Academy edition of Pushkin's works, I propose to continue my research on the sources of Pushkin's work. There are a number of topics and it is difficult for me to say which I will choose.

It is possible that I will translate Shelley's tragedy *The Cenci,* which Academia intends to publish.[7]

AN ADDRESS BROADCAST
ON THE PROGRAM
"THIS IS RADIO LENINGRAD"
(September 1941)

MY DEAR FELLOW CITIZENS, mothers, wives and sisters of Leningrad. For a month now the enemy has been threatening to take our city captive and inflict serious injury on it. The city of Peter, the city of Lenin, the city of Pushkin, Dostoevsky and Blok, the city of a great culture and industry is being threatened by the enemy with death and disgrace. I, like all Leningraders, am mortally wounded by the very thought that our city, my city, could be razed. My entire life is tied to Leningrad—I became a poet in Leningrad, Leningrad gave life to my poems...

Like all of you now, I am kept alive by the single, unshakable belief that Leningrad will never become fascist. This belief is strengthened in me when I see the Leningrad women who defend Leningrad so simply and courageously and maintain its normal, human life....

Our descendants will give every mother of the Fatherland War her due, but their attention will be particularly riveted by the Leningrad woman who stood on the roof during the bombing with a boat hook and tongs in order to protect her city from fire; the Leningrad air-raid warden who aided the wounded amidst the still burning debris of the building....

No, a city that has nurtured such women cannot be conquered. We Leningraders are experiencing difficult times, but we know that our entire country and all its people are with us. We sense their anxiety for us, their love and assistance. We are grateful to them and we promise that we will always be steadfast and courageous....

A RADIO BROADCAST ON THE ANNIVERSARY OF PUSHKIN'S BIRTH
(Pushkin, June 11, 1944)

W E ARE CELEBRATING THE joyous anniversary of the birthday of our great Poet. We are celebrating it in the very place of which Pushkin himself said: "Our Fatherland is Tsarskoe Selo"—and in the year which brought the long-awaited liberation of the Poet's city. Pushkin always considered the parks in Tsarskoe Selo to be a worthy monument to Russia's military glory and writes about that in a number of his poems. The Tsarskoe Selo "protective bowers,"[1] always remained a sacred object for him. And they will be the same for us as well.

> Down the tree-rows a swarthy youngster
> Roamed the banks of the lake and pined,
> And a century now amongst us
> Have his whispering steps been enshrined.
>
> The first have spikily nested
> In needlework each low tree...
> Here his three-cornered hat once rested,
> And a dog-eared tome of Parny.[2]

NOTES IN THE MARGIN

I LEFT THE USSR at the height of the Lermontov celebrations and when I returned to my Homeland during the last days of 1964—the year of Shakespeare and Lermontov—I was greeted by a very pleasant surprise: Emma Gershtein's book, *Lermontov's Fate*, had finally come out.[1] I read this book with pencil in hand, because my interest in Lermontov borders on obsession. And I have gathered together here some of my notes, which in no way aspire to a scholarly critique, but which, I dare to hope, will reflect the feelings and thoughts of many readers of this remarkable book.

But it's not only a remarkable book, it's also a book that everybody needs. One cannot help but rejoice in facts that are so soundly proven, even when they are sad or terrifying, because they bear what our hearts thirst for, namely, the truth.

Lermontov long ago became stylized—the dagger, Tamara, a cloak, duelling.... Emma Gershtein departs from this stylized portrait and completely independently and simply tells us about the living man who quarrelled, thought, and suffered, and did not stop being a great poet because of this.

Throughout the book the author observes the principle of a critical selection of memoir material. The book is not at all a recitation of facts (even new ones), which unfortunately we meet all too often in literary scholarship. If a new figure or new material is introduced, it always supports the characterization of his role in the drama being described. (And each chapter in the book is a dramatic construct. And the entire book is without a doubt an artistic work.)

It's well known, for example, that Lermontov spent the last weeks of his life in Pyatigorsk in the company of Prince Golitsyn.[2] Another literary critic would engage in that sorry branch of science that is jokingly referred to as "Golitsyn Studies" (the Golitsyns, both the men and the ladies, were a very large family). E. Gershtein takes a different approach. Instead of telling us who is related to whom, she creates a vibrant portrait by making scrupulous use of archival documents. For example, the information about V. S. Golitsyn, who not only had a reputation as a veteran Don Juan at the court of Alexander I, but who subsequently was a first-rate officer in battle and fought with Yermolov.[3] It was he who recommended Lermontov for the Golden Saber and he was the first to describe the awful picture of Lermontov's murder. Gershtein correctly states that there are no grounds for calling the veracity of his story into question.

As a Pushkin scholar I was particularly interested in Emma Gershtein's new observations on the influence of Pushkin's verse on Lermontov's late poetry. Thus, the theme of Lensky serves as a subtext in the poems "Justification" and "Dream."[4]

E. Gershtein brilliantly marshals the evidence when she assigns new dates to "Valerik" and "The Captive Knight," grouping these masterpieces of Lermontov's genius with the cycle written just before his death.[5]

No one before Gershtein had noted that Lermontov's "Hussar" poems ("Epistle to N. I. Bukharov," certain stanzas from *The Tambov Treasurer's Wife*) date back to the manuscript of "My Pedigree" and "Yezersky," which was published in *The Contemporary* during Pushkin's lifetime.[6] Thus, the author establishes sympathy for the poet in the Lifeguard Hussar Regiment, not through the connections of family and friendship among the Hussars, but through echoes found in Lermontov's poetry.

The author is very tactful when she penetrates into the psychology of the poet's work. How unpleasant it is when, as a result of a critic's perceptive reasoning, a poet unexpectedly discovers that in such-and-such a poem he wanted to say something which he had never given a thought to. Because it does happen that a poet writes and does not himself know what has prompted him, and afterwards innumerable confirmations of the created image's closeness to life are uncovered. This is particularly true of Lermontov. This is one manifestation of his magic.

I had some reservations only about Gershtein's statement that Vyazemsky's "retreat to the free, spontaneous epistolary genre was attended... by a meagerness in his poetic creativity."[7] Who can say why a poet's creativity is prolific or meager?

I would strongly advise the readers of this book to glance at the commentary. An enormous amount of research is hidden there. The abundance of archival documents published for the first time in this book does not make it difficult to read. Nor does the complexity of the ideas. The book is "well-sprung" throughout. The reader's interest is maintained not by deliberate popularization, but by the critic's passion, the brilliance and rigor of her prose, and the comprehensiveness of her treatment of the topic.

PUSHKIN AND CHILDREN

ALTHOUGH PUSHKIN THOUGHT OF himself least of all as a "children's writer," the term that is now commonly accepted (when Pushkin was asked to write something for children, he flew into a rage...);[1] although his fairy tales were certainly not intended for children and the famous introduction to *Ruslan* was not addressed to a child's imagination either, the fates have decreed that his works be destined to serve as a bridge between Russia's great genius and children.

We have all heard innumerable times three-year-old performers recite "the learned cat" and "the weaver and the cook"[2] and have seen how the child's little pink finger points to the portrait in the child's book—and he is called "Uncle Pushkin."

Everyone knows and loves Yershov's *The Little Humpback Horse*, too.[3] However, I've never heard "Uncle Yershov."

There is not and has never been a single Russian-speaking family in which the children could remember when they first heard that name and saw that portrait. Pushkin's poetry bestows to children the Russian language in all its splendor, a language they perhaps will never hear again and will never speak, but which, nevertheless, will be with them like an eternal treasure.

During the anniversary days of 1937,[4] the appropriate commission resolved to remove the Pushkin monument, which had been erected in a darkish square in a part of the city that did not even exist in Pushkin's time, and place it on Leningrad's Pushkin Street. They dispatched a freight crane—in general, everything required in such situations. But something unprecedented took place: the children who were playing by the monument in the square raised such a howl that they were forced to telephone the commission to ask what should be done. The answer: "Let them have their monument"—and the truck left empty.

One can say with absolute certainty that at that difficult time a good half of those children had lost their fathers (and many their mothers as well), but they considered it their sacred duty to protect Pushkin.

A WORD ABOUT DANTE

Sopra candido vel cinta d'uliva
Donna m'apparve, sotto verde manto
Vestita di color di fiamma viva.[1]

I AM HAPPY THAT at today's celebration I am able to attest that my entire conscious life has passed in the radiance of this great name, that together with the name of that other great genius of mankind—Shakespeare—this name was inscribed on the banner under which my path began. And the question that I dared to ask the Muse also contains this great name—Dante.

> ...And here she was. She gazed at me and waited
> Attentively, her veil tossed overhead.
> I ask her: "Was it you then who dictated
> The script of Hell to Dante?" "I," she said.[2]

For my friends and contemporaries the greatest, unattainable teacher was always the stern Alighieri. And between two Florentine bonfires Gumilyov sees how

> The poor exiled Alighieri
> With an unhurried step descends to Hell.[3]

And Osip Mandelstam dedicated years of his life to the study of Dante's work and wrote an entire treatise, *A Conversation about Dante,*[4] and often refers to the great Florentine in his poetry:

From rough stairways, from squares,
from angular palaces
Alighieri sang the circle
of his Florence more mightily
with wearied lips.[5]

Mikhail Lozinsky[6] triumphantly carried out the heroic feat of translating *The Divine Comedy*'s immortal *terza rima* into Russian. The critics and readers in my country regarded this work highly.

I have brought together all my thoughts on art in lines graced by that same great name:

Even after his death he did not return
To his ancient Florence.
To the one who, leaving, did not look back,
To him I sing this song.
A torch, the night, the last embrace,
Beyond the threshold, the wild wail of fate.
From hell he sent her curses
And in paradise he could not forget her—
But barefoot, in a hairshirt,
With a lighted candle he did not walk
Through his Florence—his beloved,
Perfidious, base, longed for...[7]

Translated by Ronald Meyer

Letters

TO SERGEI VON SHTEIN

1.

[1906]

My dear Sergei Vladimirovich,

You, too, must forgive me; I am a thousand times more guilty in this stupid affair than you.

Your letter brought me boundless joy, and I will be very happy to return to our former relationship, especially since it is impossible to be more lonely than I am.

My cousin Shutka calls my mood "unearthly indifference," and it seems to me that, unfortunately, he is not at all indifferent to me.

All this, however, is boring nonsense which I don't even want to think about.

The only good moments are when everyone goes out to dinner to a tavern or goes to the theater, and I listen to the silence in the dark living room. I always think about the past, it's so large and bright. Everyone here is very nice to me, but I don't like them.

We are such different people. I am always silent or crying, crying or silent. Of course they find this strange, but since I have no other shortcomings, I enjoy general good will.

Since August I have been dreaming day and night of going to Tsarskoe, to Valya,[1] for Christmas, even if it's just for 3 days. As a matter of fact, I have been living for this all this time, dying from the thought that I could be there, where... well anyway, it doesn't matter.

And now Andrei[2] has explained to me that it is unthinkable for me to go, and there is such a cold emptiness in my head that I can't even cry.

My dear Shtein, if you knew how stupid and naive I am! I am even ashamed to admit it to you. I still love V. G-Kutuzov.[3] And there is nothing in my life, nothing except this feeling.

I have heart palpitations from agitation, constant torments, and tears. Since Valya's letters, I have experienced such seizures that sometimes it seems to me that I am dying.

Maybe telling you this is stupid, but I want to be open, and I have no one, and you'll understand. You are so sensitive and you know me so well.

Do you want to make me happy? If so, then send me his picture. I'll make a copy of it and immediately return it to you. Don't be afraid, I won't "pinch" it, as they say in the South.

It was good of you to write to me. I am terribly grateful to you. What are you doing and thinking, and do you see Valeria?

Yours,
Anya

P.S. I advise you to shove Tonik[4] into... Andrei told me that he's still the same. Where can I write you?

My address is: Kiev, Meringovskaya Street, building no. 7, apartment 4, A. A. Gorenko.

2.

[1906]
Kiev, Meringovskaya, 7, apt. 4

My dear Sergei Vladimirovich,

I am quite ill, but I decided to write you about a very important matter: I want to go to Petersburg for Christmas. This is impossible, first of all because there is no money, and secondly because Papa doesn't want it. You can't help me with either one of these things, but that's not the point. Write me, please, as soon as you receive this letter, whether Kutuzov will be in Petersburg for Christmas. If not, then my soul will be at peace, but if he's not going anywhere, then I will go. I fell ill from the thought that my trip might not take place (a marvelous means of achieving something), I have a fever, heart palpitations, and unbearable headaches. You have never seen me so terrible.

There is no money. My aunt nags. Cousin Demyanovsky declares his love every 5 minutes (do you recognize Dickens's style?). What should I do?

When I come, I will tell you one surprising story, only remind me, I forget everything these days.

You know, dear Sergei Vladimirovich, I haven't slept for four nights. It's horrible, such insomnia. My cousin has already left for her estate, they let the servant go, and when I fainted onto the rug yesterday, there wasn't anyone in the entire apartment. I couldn't get undressed by myself, and terrible faces seemed to appear on the wallpaper! In general, it was awful!

I have a premonition that I won't go to Petersburg after all. I want it too much.

By the way, I am able to inform you that I stopped smoking. My cousins gave a feast in my honor in celebration of this.

Sergei Vladimirovich, if only you could see how pitiful and unnecessary I am. The main thing is that nobody needs me, ever. Dying is easy. Did Andrei tell you how in Yevpatoriya I attempted to hang myself and the nail pulled out of the plaster wall? Mama cried, I was ashamed—in general it was awful.

Last summer Fyodorov[1] kissed me again, swore that he loved me, and again smelled like dinner.

Dearest, there is no light.

I am not writing poetry. Am I ashamed? Why should I be?

Answer quickly about Kutuzov.

He is everything to me.

Yours,
Annushka

P.S. Please destroy my letters. I don't even need to say, of course, that what I write to you cannot be made known to anyone.

Anya

3

December 31, 1906

Dear Sergei Vladimirovich,

A heart seizure, which continued almost uninterrupted for 6 days, prevented me from answering you immediately. Troubles flow as though from a horn of plenty: yesterday Mama telegraphed that Andrei has scarlet fever.

I spent all the holidays at the home of Aunt Vakar,[1] who can't stand me. Everyone mocked me as much as they could; Uncle knows how to shout quite as well as Papa, and if I closed my eyes, the illusion was complete. He shouted twice a day: at dinner and after evening tea. I have a cousin Sasha. He was assistant public prosecutor; now he's retired and is spending this winter in Nice. This man treated me so divinely that I was astonished, but Uncle Vakar detests him, and I was truly a martyr because of Sasha.

The words "brothel" and "streetwalker" alternated regularly in my uncle's speeches. But I was so indifferent that he finally got tired of shouting, and we spent the last evening in peaceful conversation.

In addition, I was depressed by the conversations about politics and how to cook fish. In general, it was awful!

Perhaps you would send me a picture of Kutuzov in a registered letter? I'll just make a little copy of it for a locket and send it back to you at once. I'll be eternally grateful to you.

What will he do when he finishes the university? Will he work again for the Red Cross? Why didn't you telegraph me as we agreed? I waited for a telegram day and night, I got my money and my dresses together and nearly bought a ticket.

But such is my fate obviously!

Now I am at home alone, I receive visitors, and in the interim, I write to you. This, of course, is not conducive to the orderliness of my letter—but you'll forgive me, won't you?

Write about yourself when you have the time. We haven't seen each other in so long.

I am going to have my photograph taken in a few days. Should I send you a picture?

Anya

P.S. A thousand good wishes for the New Year.

4.

[January 1907]

Dear Sergei Vladimirovich,

If you knew how mean you are being to your unfortunate *belle-soeur*! Is it really so difficult to send me a picture and a few words?

I am so tired of waiting!

Why, I have been waiting more than 5 months now.

Things are very bad with my heart, and as soon as it begins to hurt, my left arm goes completely numb. They don't write to me from home about Andrei's health, and therefore I think that he is very ill.

Perhaps you too are ill, since you are so stubbornly silent. I have finished living, without having ever begun. This is sad, but true. Where are your sisters? Most likely, in class; oh, how I envy them. I, of course, will never get to take a class, except maybe in cooking.

Seryozha! Send me a picture of G.-K. I beg you for the last time; I won't do it anymore, word of honor.

I believe that you are a good, real friend, even though you know me better than anyone else.

Ecrivez.

Anya

5.

February 2, 1907

Dear Sergei Vladimirovich,

This is the fourth letter that I have written you this week. Don't be surprised; with a stubbornness worthy of better direction, I decided to inform you about an event which must fundamentally alter my life, but this turned out to be so difficult that until this evening I couldn't bring myself to send this letter. I am going to marry my childhood friend, Nikolai Stepanovich Gumilyov. He has loved me for 3 years now, and I believe that it is my fate to be his wife. Whether or not I love him, I do not know,[1] but it seems to me that I do. Do you remember Bryusov's

> Crucified together for torment,
> My ancient enemy and my sister!
> Give me your hand! Give me your hand!
> The sword has been thrust! Hurry! It's time![2]

And I gave him my hand, but what was in my soul, only God and you, my faithful, dear Seryozha, know. Let's change the subject.

> The Inevitable ordained for everyone,
> As the highest duty—to be an executioner.[3]

Our good relationship and your letters—bright, longed-for rays—which tenderly caress my sick soul and bring me endless happiness.

Don't abandon me now, when it is especially difficult for me, although I know that my conduct can't help but astonish you.

Do you want to know why I didn't answer you at once: I was waiting for the picture of G. Kutuzov, and only after I received it did I want to announce my marriage to you. How vile, and to punish myself for such cowardice I am writing today and I am writing everything, no matter how difficult it might be for me.

You write poetry! What happiness; how I envy you. I like your poems; in general, I like your style.

The notebook of your poems is at home, and when I return, I'll send it to you, if Andrei hasn't beaten me to it. I'm not writing anything, and never will. I have murdered my soul, and my eyes are created for tears, as Iolanthe says.[4] Or do you remember Schiller's prophetic Cassandra? One facet of my soul adjoins the dark image of this prophetess, so great in her suffering. But I am far from greatness.

Don't say anything about our marriage to anyone. We still haven't decided either where or when it will take place. *It is a secret;* I haven't written even to Valya.

Write to me, Sergei Vladimirovich; I am ashamed to ask this, to take up your time, which is so dear to you, but your letters are such happiness.

Why do you call me Anna Andreyevna? Why, last year in Tsarskoe this ceremony was already out of style. With me, it's another story. But, after all, the difference in our ages and positions plays a big role.

Send me, in spite of everything, a picture of Vl. Vikt. For God's sake, there is nothing else on earth I want so much.

Yours,
Anya

P.S. Fyodorov's poems, with a few exceptions, are really weak. He has a dim and rather questionable talent. He is not a poet, but we, Seryozha, are poets. Thank you for the Sonnets; I read them with pleasure, but I must admit that I liked your notes most of all. Isn't A. Blok publishing new poems—my cousin is a great admirer of his.

Do you have anything new by N. S. Gumilyov? I have no idea what and how he is writing now, and I don't want to ask.

6.
[February 1907]

My dear Sergei Vladimirovich,

I still haven't received an answer to my letter and I am already writing again. It seems that my Kolya is planning to come to see me—I am so insanely happy. He writes me incomprehensible words, and I go to acquaintances with the letter and ask for an explanation. Every time a letter arrives from Paris, they hide it from me and deliver it with elaborate precautions. Then there is usually a fainting spell, cold compresses, and general bewilderment. This is due to my passionate character, nothing else. He loves me so much that it is positively terrifying. What do you think Papa will say when he finds out about my decision? If he is against my marriage, I will run away and marry Nikolai secretly. I cannot respect my father, I never loved him, why should I obey him? I have become wicked, capricious, and unbearable. Oh, Seryozha, how terrible to feel such a change in yourself. Don't betray me, my dear, good friend. If I live in Petersburg next year, you'll visit me often, won't you? Don't abandon me; I hate and scorn myself; I cannot bear this lie which entangles me...

I want to finish school as quickly as possible and go to live with Mama. It's stifling here! For nearly five months now I have been sleeping 4 hours a night. Mama wrote me that Andrei has recovered; I shared my happy news with him, but he (alas!) didn't believe me.

I kiss you, my dear friend.

Anya

7.

February 11, 1907

My dear Sergei Vladimirovich,

I don't know how to express the boundless gratitude which I feel toward you. May God send you the fulfillment of your most burning desire, and I will *never, never* forget what you did for me. Five months I waited for his picture; in it he's exactly the way I knew, loved, and madly feared him: elegant and so coldly indifferent, he looks at me with the tired, serene gaze of his nearsighted, light eyes. *Il est intimidant*; this can't be expressed in Russian. This very day Nanya[1] bought Blok's second collection of poetry. A great many things remind one strikingly of V. Bryusov. For example, the poem "The Unknown Woman," page 21; but it is splendid, this interlacing of the vulgar commonplace with the divine, bright vision. I influenced my cousin to subscribe to *The Scales* this year, which should be very interesting, judging from the announcement. If you knew, my dear Sergei Vladimirovich, how grateful I am to you for answering me. I am in very low spirits; I don't write to Valya and I am expecting the arrival of Nicolas at any moment. You yourself know how crazy he is, like me. But enough about him. I once lost a bet to Meshkov—my poems. That's probably why he asked you about them. I want to send him anonymously a little poem, which is dedicated to the walks we took during the summer of 1905. If you happen to know his address, tell me, please. We carouse, and Syuleri plays the chief role in our amusements. Why did you think that I would be silent after receiving the picture? Oh, no! I am too happy to be silent. I write to you and I know that he is here, with me, that I can see him—it's so absolutely marvelous. Seryozha! I can't tear my soul away from him. I am poisoned for my whole life; bitter is the poison of unrequited love! Will I be able to begin to live again? Certainly not! But Gumilyov is my Fate, and I obediently submit to it. Don't condemn me, if you can. I swear to you, by all that is holy to me, that this unhappy man will be happy with me.

I am sending you one of my recent poems. It rambles and is written without a spark of feeling. Don't judge me as a literary critic, or it will be terrible for me in advance. In your last letter you say that you have written something new. Send it; I will be terribly (a feminine word) happy to see your poems. It would be so nice if we could meet sometime. Thank you again for the picture. You don't know what you have done for me, my good Seryozha!

Anya

...I Know How to Love

I know how to love.
I know how to be submissive and tender.
I know how to gaze into one's eyes with a smile,
Beckoning, inviting, vacillating.
And my supple figure is so airy and graceful
And the fragrance of my curls caresses.
O, he who is with me is uneasy in his soul
And embraced by sweet bliss...
I know how to love. I am deceptively shy.
I am so timidly tender and always quiet,
Only my eyes speak.

They are clear and pure,
So translucently radiant,
They promise happiness.
If you believe them, they will deceive you.
They will only become bluer,
They are both tenderer and brighter
Than the pale blue gleam of a fire.
And on my lips is scarlet bliss,
My breast is whiter than mountain snow,
My voice murmurs of azure streams.
I know how to love. A kiss awaits you.

Yevpatoriya, 1906

8.

Kiev, March 13, 1907

My dear Sergei Vladimirovich,

I read your letter, and I became ashamed of my uncouthness. I obtained *The Life of Man*[1] only yesterday; I know absolutely nothing of the other works you mention. Suddenly I am seized with a desire for Petersburg, for life, for books. But I am an eternal wanderer through foreign, crude, and dirty towns: Sevastopol will be the same as Yevpatoriya and Kiev were; I lost hope long ago. I live my quickly-passing life so quietly, quietly. My sister is embroidering a rug, and I read French novels or A. Blok aloud to her. She has a special tender sort of feeling for him. She simply worships him and says that she has the other half of his soul. Write me what your circle thinks of David Aizman. They compare him with Shakespeare, and this disturbs me. Are we really to be the contemporaries of a genius? This summer our family is going to live in a summer house near Sevastopol. At the beginning of June I am going there, and would be delighted if you would come visit. We haven't seen each other in such a long time!

My poem, "On his hand are many glittering rings,"[2] was published in the second issue of *Sirius*; perhaps a short poem which I wrote when I was in Yevpatoriya will appear in the third issue. But I sent it so late that I doubt it was published.

But if it appears, write me your frank opinion of it, and also show it to one of the poets. Ignoramuses praise it—that's a bad sign. Don't be afraid to criticize my poem or convey the reactions of others, since I am not going to write anymore. It doesn't matter to me!

Everything has gone out of my soul, along with the only bright and tender feeling that illuminated it. It seems to me that you understand me well.

> ...From roses white weave me a crown.
> A crown of fragrant, snowy roses,
> You, too, in this world are alone,
> And useless life on you reposes.

I said once in a Crimean poem that "The spring air is imperiously bold."

Why did Gumilyov get involved with *Sirius?* This surprises me and puts me in an unusually jolly mood. How many misfortunes our Mikola [Gumilyov] has had to bear, and all in vain. Have you noticed that the other contributors are nearly all as famous and respected as I? I think that the Lord clouded Gumilyov's mind. It happens!

Do write me!

Annushka

P.S. When are G-Kutuzov's examinations over?

9.

[1907]

Dear Sergei Vladimirovich,

Although you stopped writing to me in the spring of this year, I have a desire to talk with you a bit anyway.

I don't know if you heard about the illness that has taken away any hope of the possibility of a happy life. My lungs are affected *(this is a secret)* and there is a possible threat of tuberculosis. It seems to me that I am going through what Inna did, and now I clearly understand her spiritual condition. Since I am preparing to leave Russia soon for a very long time, I decided to bother you with a request to send me something from Inna's things in memory of her. Aunt Masha[1] wanted to give me grandfather's bracelet which Inna had, and if you honor her request, I will be boundlessly grateful. But the matter is complicated by the fact that it is a valuable thing, and I am very much afraid that you will think that I want an ornament and not a keepsake. You haven't seen me in so long, and it could appear to you that I am resorting to chicanery. I beg of you, Sergei Vladimirovich, if such an idea occurs to you, don't send the bracelet or answer this letter; in that case, I don't want it. I hope that this won't happen, since we were once friends, and if you have changed toward me, I haven't in the least changed toward you.

Don't write Aunt Masha that I spoke to you about the bracelet. She might not understand.

Please don't talk about my illness to anyone. Not even at home, if this is possible. Andrei has been in Paris at the Sorbonne since September 5th. I am sick, melancholy, and growing thin. I had pleurisy, bronchitis, and chronic catarrh of the lungs. Now my throat is bothering me. I am terribly afraid of tuberculosis of the throat. It is worse than tuberculosis of the lungs. We are living in abject poverty. We have to wash the floors, do the laundry.

That's my life! I finished very well at the gymnasium. The doctor said that taking classes would mean my death. So, I'm not taking any—I have pity for Mama.[2]

If you could see me, you would probably say, "Ugh, what an ugly face."

Sic transit gloria mundi.

Farewell! Will we ever see each other?

Annushka

10.

[A postcard with a postmark of October 29, 1910, Kiev]

In a few days I am returning to Tsarskoe. I am reminding you of your promise to visit me. Please extend my invitation to Yekaterina Vladimirovna. We will decide on the day by telephone. I have been sick for 2 weeks.

With a handshake,
Anna Gumilyova

TO VALERY BRYUSOV

1.

[Not earlier than October 1910]
Tsarskoe Selo

Dear Valery Yakovlevich,
   I am sending you four of my poems.[1] Perhaps you will consider it possible to publish one of them.[2] I would be infinitely grateful if you would write and tell me whether I ought to continue writing poetry. Please forgive me for troubling you.

Anna Akhmatova

   My address: Tsarskoe Selo, Bulvarnaya St., the Georgiyevs' house. For Anna Andreyevna Gumilyova.

2.

October 22, 1912

Valery Yakovlevich,
   I am sending you a few of the poems[1] I wrote just the other day. I couldn't do so earlier because I had a baby and I haven't written anything all fall.[2]

Respectfully yours,
Anna Akhmatova

Tsarskoe Selo
Malaya St., 63

TO ALEXANDER BLOK

[January 6 or 7, 1914, St. Petersburg]

You know, Alexander Alexandrovich, I received your books just yesterday. You mixed up the number of my apartment and someone else has had them all this time and was reluctant to part with them. And I was longing for your poetry.

You are very kind to have inscribed so many books for me, and I am deeply and eternally grateful to you for the poem.[1] It makes me terribly happy, and that happens to me more seldom than anything in life.

I am sending you a poem I wrote for you, and I wish you happiness.[2] (But not from the poem, of course. You see, I don't know how to write as I would like.)

Anna Akhmatova
Tuchkov Lane, 17, Apartment 29

TO PAVEL SHCHEGOLYOV

April 26, 1914

Dear Pavel Eliseyevich,

I am sending you a few poems for *Day*. If you should be inclined to accept any one of them, please let me know at: Vasilyevsky Island, Tuchkov Lane, 17, Apt 29. For A. Gumilyova.

Respectfully yours,
Anna Akhmatova

TO NIKOLAI GUMILYOV

1.

July 13, 1914. Slepnyovo

Dear Kolya,

I arrived in Slepnyovo on the 10th. I found Lyovushka healthy, happy, and very affectionate. Your mother will probably write you about the weather and business. Yasinsky speaks very favorably of me in the June issue of *New Word*.[1] I try to avoid the neighbors, they're very insipid. I've written several poems which not one person has heard yet, but that, thank God, does not bother me much. Now you are *au courant* of all the Petersburg and literary news. Write me, is there any news? Jammes[2] has arrived here. As soon as I receive it in the mail, I'll send it off to you. Forgive me for unsealing Znosko's[3] letter so that the large envelope would weigh less. I received a few words from Chulkov[4] written in pencil. He's in very bad shape and I don't think we'll see him again.

Will you return to Slepnyovo? Or will you be in Petersburg from early August. Write me about all this as soon as possible. I'm sending you the drafts of my new poems[5] and am very much waiting for news. I kiss you.

Yours,
Anya

2.

July 17, 1914. Slepnyovo

Dear Kolya,

My mother forwarded your letter to me here. I've been in Slepnyovo a week today.

It's getting boring, the weather has turned bad and I foresee an early autumn. For days at a time I lie on the couch in my room, I read a bit, but write poems more often. I'm sending you one of them, which seems to have a right to exist.[1] I think that money will be very tight for us this autumn. I don't have any, and you probably don't either. You'll get a pittance from *Apollon*. And in August we'll need several hundred rubles. It would be good if we got something for *Rosary*. All this worries me a great deal. Please, don't forget that the things are pawned. If possible, redeem them and give them to somebody to hide.

Will Chukovsky read his article about Acmeism as a lecture? After all, he can do that, too. I anticipate the July issue of *Russian Thought* with a sense of foreboding. More than likely Valère will exact a horrible punishment.[2] But I think about the worst that I have already suffered and am resigned.

Kolya, write and send poems. Good luck, my dear. I kiss you.

Yours,
Anna

Lyovushka is healthy and can say everything.

TO GEORGY CHULKOV

1.

July 1914. Slepnyovo

Dear Georgy Ivanovich,

Don't be angry with me because of my silence. I'm so happy to get your letters and of course I will answer them. That you have no desire to live or die is something I understand completely.

It's quiet, boring, and a bit terrifying here. News from the outside world sounds absolutely improbable, I don't see anyone, and, in general, I am leading a quiet life. Recently I finally began to write a big piece,[1] but the quiet seems to be hindering me. And everything around me is faded, worn, and mainly, connected with a number of sad events.

I read *Satan* when I was still in Petersburg, and I think that it's your best work. Nik. Step. [Gumilyov] asked me to tell you that he also liked *Satan*. What are you writing now? Don't the mountains interfere? You're in Lausanne. All the houses there are the same color, the streets are very steep, and there are a lot of Russians.

I want you to know that I don't believe that you are old. In general, you'll never be old in the bad sense of the word.

I may go to Leysin in Switzerland for 6 weeks.[2] My brother is there to take the sun for his health. The thought of the trip makes me so happy, it's unbearable here sometimes.

Please give my regards to Nadezhda Grigoryevna.[3] How is her health, has she gotten some rest?

Don't forget me. When I have some poems I'll definitely send them to you.

Anna Akhmatova

I gave the copy of *Harvest* to Shchegolyov[4] as you requested, because I received my own copy the very same day.

2.

March 15, 1930. Leningrad

Dear Georgy Ivanovich,

Thank you for all your trouble. I am ashamed that you have to bother with my affairs. I couldn't find any of the things that I should send you. I know that my poems have been translated into English (a separate volume, translated by Duddington), German, French, Polish, Japanese, biblical (ancient Hebrew), and Ukrainian.

We are being evicted from our apartment because the building is being given to some institution.

With a kiss to Nadezhda Grigoryevna and a handshake to you.

Akhmatova

TO ANASTASIA CHEBOTARYEVSKAYA

July 16, 1915

Dear Anastasia Nikolayevna,

Just yesterday I received your letter, which was forwarded to me from Tsarskoe.

I am having a difficult summer: the newspapers don't come every day, so there's a long delay before you learn news of the war. Nikolai Stepanovich was transferred to somewhere in the south and now he writes even less often.

My health is improving very slowly, but I'm working a lot; apparently the voice of the muse can be heard more easily in the country.

It's a pleasure to send you my poem "A Prayer" for the almanac *War*.[1]

It's never been published before. I think it's better not to include my "July 1914,"[2] because the war censor doesn't like it at all. What do you think?

Please give my regards to Fyodor Kuzmich. All the best to you, I kiss you.

Yours,
Anna Akhmatova

TO FYODOR SOLOGUB

1.

July 28, 1915. Slepnyovo

It gave me great joy, dear Fyodor Kuzmich, to receive your letter. Thank you for remembering me.

I'm living with my son in the country; Nikolai Stepanovich left for the front and we haven't heard anything about him for two weeks now.

Please give my regards to Anastasia Nikolayevna.

Best wishes.

Anna Akhmatova

2.

[1923?]

Dear Fyodor Kuzmich,

In a conversation with N.L. Alyanskaya I discovered that publishing my 1922 poems in *Polar Star* would be a clear violation of my contract. I am very sorry about this situation and that I did not clarify the question of the contract earlier. With a handshake.

Yours,
A. Akhmatova

TO ANNA GUMILYOVA

1

[November 1917]

Dear Mama,

I've just received your postcard dated November 3rd. Am sending you Kolya's latest letter. Don't be angry with me for my silence, I'm having a difficult time now. Did you receive my letter? I kiss you and Lyova.[1]

Yours,
Anya

2.

[1926]

My dear Mama,

I've just now received your kind letters. Thank you for the congratulations and good wishes for my health. I tried very hard not to get sick like last year.

Thank Lyova for his letter, only he is mistaken in thinking that I was talking him out of writing poetry. I forwarded his letter to P.N.,[1] I sent it to his grandmother. I hope that you all will have a chance to rest from your girls after the holidays. How is Shurochka's[2] health?

I kiss you.

Yours,
Anya

TO VLADIMIR SHILEIKO

1.

Leningrad 20. XII. 24

Dear Volodya,

Tapa[1] is very sick, and tomorrow morning I'm taking him to the animal hospital on V[asilyevsky] I[sland]. I think that it would be difficult to send him to Moscow in the condition he is now, write me what I should do. He's very quiet and meek, but since you left he's been listless and has some kind of rash on his back.

Don't be upset, maybe everything will be all right. Thank you for the letters.

Everything here is the same, I still haven't received the salary at the Academy. Borozdin is coming by today. I kiss you.

Your sister,
Akuma[2]

2.

[1924]

Dear Volodya,

Yesterday I finally retrieved Tapa from the hospital, where he spent exactly one month. I'm sending you the bill from the hospital. I don't have any money to feed him and nurse him at home, and I can't pay for the apartment either. Please, send me your power of attorney so I can get the money from the university (Luknitsky[1] has left for the South, and the July salary hasn't been received). Everything here is the same. Good luck and give my regards to Vera Konstantinovna.[2] I await your reply.

Yours,
Akhmatova

3.

[Leningrad. January 17, 1925]

Dear Volodya,

Tapa's home, I'm still rubbing him with salve, but it won't be possible to cure him completely until spring, when it won't be dangerous to shave him. I feel very sorry for him, he's meek and touching. Write me how you are getting along and whether you are in good health. So far nobody in the building has done anything to offend me, and I'm satisfied with the apartment. My books will soon be out, I've already read the second proofs.[1]

They're predicting a flood, but Tapa and I aren't afraid.

I kiss you. Don't forget me.

Akuma

4.

May 18th, 1925
St. P[etersburg]

Dear Volodya,

Have you forgotten us? I've been home several days now—and found everything in order. Tapa was shaved yesterday and he's very embarrassed about being naked. The condition of my health is the same. Next week, when some medical conference is over, I'll go to the hospital.

How is your work going and what are your plans for this winter?

The City is suffocating after Tsarskoe.

I kiss you—God be with you.

Yours,
Anna

5.

January 30, 1927

Dear Bukan,[1]

I'm sick and in bed with something like bronchitis. Please, take care of yourself and the dog. Don't be too lazy to make a fire, eat like a human being, and stay indoors as much as possible—it's brutally cold.

How's Pliny? Manya? I kiss you.

Yours,
Akuma

6.

Sept. 1, 1927

Dear Volodya,

Thank you for the letter. Tushin has completely worn me out—I'm nursing him myself again—he's a lot of trouble. Send me your power of attorney, I need to pay the Punins[1] for his keep and I don't have any money at all.

The excerpt you sent is monstrous, but extremely expressive. I have something for you as well. Did Luknitsky write you about the plumber? They've already taken out the faucet in the hallway, there's no water in the apartment. What should be done?

Till we meet. Let me know when you're coming.

Akuma

Regards to Vera Konstantinovna.

7.

August 8, 1928

Dear Friend,

Here's the first representation of you.[1] I hope that you will permit me to make a present of it to your son.

Things with Tapa are very bad. He has cancer. The operation is today. I've been fussing over him all summer—but he's just getting worse.

He's been in the hospital a week now, and they say that they have to cut him open. The operation costs nothing, his keep is one ruble a day. I've already paid for the medicine. I don't have your power of attorney any more, when are you coming?

I feel very sorry for the dog, he understands everything.

Regards to V. K[onstantinovna],[2] kiss the little one for me.

Yours,
Akhmatova

8.

November 26, 1928

Dear Friend,

I am sending you my poems. If you have time tonight, take a look at them. I've already deleted a lot—they were very bad. Note on a separate piece of paper the ones you think don't merit publication. I'll drop by tomorrow. Forgive me for bothering you.

Yours,
Akhmatova

TO IOANNA BRYUSOVA

May 3, 1925. Tsarskoe Selo

Dear Ioanna Matveyevna,

I learned from G. A. Shengeli's letter to M. Shkapskaya that you've given permission to Gumilyov's biographer, Luknitsky, to make copies of Gumilyov's letters to V. Ya. Bryusov.[1] Since I'm involved in the project myself and know very well how important these documents are to Gumilyov's biographer, I wish to thank you for your kindness.

Respectfully yours,
A. Akhmatova

TO NIKOLAI KHARDZHIEV

1.

[Leningrad, 1932]

Dear Nikolai Ivanovich,

It is very bad that I don't know anything about you. How are you, what are you doing?

It's awful and boring here. I wanted to write you a real letter, but yesterday Ira[1] got ill and so I have my hands full.

I will be expecting news from you.

Akhmatova

2.

[Leningrad, 1932]

Dear Nikolai Ivanovich,

Thank you for your letter. If you only knew how nice it is to receive a letter from a friend. This does not happen to me often. I am glad that you are working and even want to come here. Vera Fyodorovna Rumyantseva[1] will be returning to Moscow at the end of the month and she'll bring you a letter from me. There is no news from Lyova: he has not answered any of us—I don't know what to think.[2] Everything is the same here—only worse.

I went to the Hermitage yesterday. It's a desert. The exhibit—entitled "The Period of Absolutism"—resembles a first-class bric-a-brac store somewhere in London or New York. The Menshikov galleries (which are being painted) have been decorated with a huge family crest. What a monstrosity! N.N.,[3] exhausted by the museum business, is angry and "unjust." Completely unexpectedly I have received a state subsidy, which will greatly ease my situation at home.

Can you sleep now and how are Osip and Nadya?[4]

Should there be an opportunity—please send me a letter, and don't change your mind about coming.

What are you writing about Pasternak? I'll be expecting news. Please be cheerful and, if possible, happy.

Akhmatova

3.

[Leningrad, February 1933]

Dear Nikolai Ivanovich,

I sent you a letter through your acquaintance and was waiting for an answer, but you probably did not have an opportunity to send me a letter. On the afternoon of 14th, I'm giving a lecture on *The Golden Cockerel*[1] at the old Pushkin House.

Tomorrow N.N.[2] goes to Moscow for two days to sit on a jury. I think he will call you.

I live on my last remaining bits of courage, and mainly try not to think. How is your work going?

What about your coming to Petersburg?

Please write.

Akhmatova

There is no news from Lyova.

4.

[Leningrad, summer 1933]

Dear Nikolai Ivanovich,

I received both of your letters. Thank you. I would very much like to go to Moscow in July or August. Will you be in town? Volpe[1] came to see me today and I gave him the book and the letter. The news about M. M.[2] is bad. He is begging for his bread. Of course, Nikolasha[3] wasn't arrested. That's just Moscow gossip, but he is insistently asking me for the carry-all that he gave you. This is apparently urgent. Forgive me. Thank you for *Chulkov and Levshin.*[4]

Are Pilnyak[5] and Tolstaya[6] in Moscow? I am well, as always in the summer. Greetings to V.B.[7]

Yours,
Akhmatova

What is the story with your room?

5.

[Leningrad] August 9, 1933

Dear Nikolai Ivanovich,

Vera Fyodorovna[1] will tell you about my unsuccessful attempt to go to Moscow. But I am not giving up hope. Has Lev[2] been to see you? He promised to write on the road and I am beginning to worry.

When will you take care of your health and go see a doctor? Don't distress your friends with your stubbornness.

Where has M. M. been transferred?[3]

Bonch has offered to buy my archives.[4]

Write me a few words, even if it has to go through the mail.

Akhmatova

6.

[Leningrad, 1934]

Thank you for the album.[1] It's beautiful. When will I see you next, dear Nikolai Ivanovich; somehow living has become very dull for me. I don't see anybody, and I am having trouble working. How is Moscow; ever since May my attitude towards it has changed completely.[2] Please write.

N. N. bought newspaper clippings about Futurism from the years 1913-15. There you are.

Regards.

Akhmatova

7.

[Leningrad, second half of the 1930s]

Dear Nikolai Ivanovich,

I am staying with Lidia Mikhailovna Andreyevskaya[1] (Kirochnaya 8, Apt. 69)—you've been here with Lyusya.[2] Drop in. I definitely want to say good-bye to you.

Akhm.

8.

[Tashkent] March 12, 1942

Dear Nikolai Ivanovich,

Thank you for not forgetting about me. How could you think that I was angry with you? If I have enough strength—I'll go to Alma-Ata to see you.[1] Surviving the summer here will be difficult for both of us.

I have finished the long poem you once liked.[2] There's no news from Leningrad.

Greetings to Shklovsky, Zoshchenko, and Lili Brik.[3]

Please write.

Yours,
Akhmatova

9.

[Tashkent, late April—early May 1942]

Dear Nikolai Ivanovich,

Viktor Borisovich will tell you about me and my life in Tashkent.[1]

On March 21st N. N. Punin and his family stopped in Tashkent on their way to Samarkand. He was in bad shape, he was absolutely unrecognizable. I received a letter from him recently.

Dear friend, I am having a very hard time—there is no news from Vl. Georg.[3] When will I see you—and where...

Please write. It's so hot...

Yours,
Akhmatova

10.

Tashkent, May 25, 1942

My dear friend,

I'm taking this opportunity to send you a few words.

I think about you a great deal and am worried about you.

"Don't lose your despair," as a friend of ours used to say.[1] It is getting harder and harder to talk about myself. If only we could see each other! I've been invited to Alma-Ata, but it's all so complicated. I received a postcard from Garshin yesterday. He was mentally ill and did not write to me for five months. I will be waiting for news from you.

Yours,
Akhmatova

11.

[Tashkent] July 4, 1942

My dear friend,

I was deeply touched by the letter Paustovsky's son[1] brought to me. I am grateful to you for your trust and the pure friendship which has been my comfort and joy for so many years.

Today I received a letter from N. N. Punin. He asks again for your address. And I received several telegrams from Leningrad— two from Vladimir Georgiyevich.

Please write and tell me that you are better now and that we will see each other soon. And may everything be well with you.

Yours,
Akhmatova

12.

[Tashkent] January 10, 1943

Dear Nikolai Ivanovich,

Finally, I'm home after a long stay in the hospital.[1] I am grateful to you for your concern and for remembering me. How sad that we did not see each other in Central Asia. Perhaps we will in Moscow.[2] Write me about yourself. We shouldn't lose track of each other at such a time.

Akhmatova

13.

[Tashkent] April 6, 1943

Dear Friend,

Your card was an unexpected and pleasant surprise. But what a pity that we did not see each other in Asia where a gentle, green, fresh spring began today.

I live in deathly fear about Leningrad, about Vladimir Georgiyevich. I have been ill a great deal and seriously. I have turned completely gray. I wanted to send you and Valeria Sergeyevna[1] my *A Poem without a Hero*, which has grown and acquired an "Epilogue," but I did not manage to copy it all.[2] Somehow, next time.

A telegram from Lyova. He is well and has gone on an expedition.

Please speak with Valeria Sergeyevna about the possibility of my coming to Moscow.

I doubt that I will survive a second summer in Tashkent.

From time to time I get letters from Nikolai Nikolayevich [Punin] (his address: Samarkand, Oktyabrskaya 43. V. Academy of Fine Arts).[3]

Please pass on my regards and thanks to Kruchenykh.[4]

Do you ever see the Briks?[5] And in general, how is everything? I have not seen you for so long. It's frightful to think that the leaves which were on the trees when I arrived in Tashkent had budded before the war, and now it seems that it was all in some past existence: the Marina Grove[6] and my trips to Moscow, and the farewells at the station.

Please write to me, my friend. I think of you often.

Yours,
Akhmatova

14.

[Tashkent] April 14, 1943

Dear Nikolai Ivanovich,

I am sending you *A Poem without a Hero* and a few other poems. Is it possible to forward and have all this personally delivered to Vladimir Georgiyevich Garshin (Leningrad 22, section 053). He works in the Erisman hospital and lives at Rentgen St. No. 3.

Nadyusha[1] and I are waiting for news from you. Don't forget us. Yesterday I took part in a Mayakovsky evening.[2]

Regards.

Akhmatova

15.

[Tashkent] June 2, 1943

You've completely forgotten me, Nikolai Ivanovich. Now everyone is taking off in all directions from Tashkent and I joke: "They have forgotten Firs, forgotten a man!"[1] But somehow the joke does not seem funny.

How is Moscow? How are the Briks? How is Kruchenykh the perfectionist?[2]

Any place is far from here—I wrote in one letter—yet it is impossible to leave.

I have a new, spacious, secluded, deserted house.[3] I have never lived in such a deserted house, though, as you know, ruins and waste lands are my specialty.

Did you receive my poem and the letters V.S. Poznanskaya took for you?

If it is difficult for you to write, please send a telegram. It is depressing not to hear from you for so long.

Just now it occured to me to send you a book of mine that was published here.[4] As far as I can see, its chief (and only) beauty lies in the fact that nowhere does it say where it was published. That is why it has such a cozy, roguish look. I call Zelinsky[5] my author (for heaven's sake—this is between us), and Nadya says that this is not my witticism, but Osip's. That's possible! I live above Nadya. She is now at her brother's.[6] Nadya has become very good and pure—she feels sorry for people and is infinitely gentle with me. Levka has left for the taiga; I had a telegram from him in Novosibirsk. The expedition will probably last for several months. Vladimir Georgiyevich is in Leningrad. He works from 7:30 in the morning until 11 at night without any days off. During bombing raids and shelling he gives lectures and performs dissections and in general embodies what we usually mean by the simple word "hero." Nonetheless, everyone invariably asks me: "Why can't your husband arrange something for himself?" Or: "Doesn't he deserve a vacation?" The same thing over and over again.

Let me know how you are. My address: Zhukovskaya St., 54. With a handshake.

Yours,
Akhmatova

16.
[Tashkent] June 20, 1943

Dear Nikolai Ivanovich,

Our friend (that is, Nadya's and mine), Natalya Alexandrovna Vishnevskaya,[1] will give you this letter and tell you everything about us that you wish to know.

I am ailing again—I don't have the strength to get up, yet I need and want to go to Moscow.

I sent you some letters through Poznanskaya in May, and Asya[2] took a book[3] of mine for you. You don't write because you are probably waiting for my arrival.

I have just heard the news from Rome.[4] How do you like that?

As always, I want to tell you many wonderful things, but either someone is hurrying me or I myself am in a hurry.

Still, we will see each other.
Greetings to Moscow.

Yours,
Akhmatova

The temperature here is 41 C.

17.
[Tashkent, early July 1943]

Dear Nikolai Ivanovich,
Thank you for the telegrams and for your troubles on my behalf.[1]
So far nothing is clear. As soon as something becomes clear, I'll send a telegram. Tomorrow this card will be off to you.
Greetings from Nadya.[2]

A.

18.
[Tashkent] September 27, 1943

Dear Nikolai Ivanovich,
For some reason I started worrying about you. Are you well? How are things, work, frame of mind?
Today I received a good telegram from Lyova. The expedition in which he participated is over and he is on his way back to Norilsk. My Leningrad friends write a lot and frequently. Anna Yevgenyevna Punina[1] died in Samarkand. Her death affected me greatly.
Greetings to Moscow. Please write.

Yours,
Akhmatova

Pasternak wrote me a passionate, delightful letter with a stupendous analysis of *A Poem without a Hero*.[2]
Nadya's mother died.

19.

[Tashkent] December 14, 1943

Dear Nikolai Ivanovich

As you can see, in Central Asia I have developed the ability to answer letters. I have expressed myself epigrammatically on the issue of my departure:

> "An inadequate excuse,
> You should be on your way."
> "And I almost left,
> But was stopped by scarlet fever."

I got jealous of Kruchenykh's laurels. Please give him my regards.

Thank you for your letter. It's sad that the apartment issue is still not resolved for you. Nadyusha is ill, she obviously needs to get away from here.

Until we meet.

Yours,
Akhm.

20.

[Leningrad, September 1950]

Dear Nikolai Ivanovich,

I found out where you are from Nikolai Mikhailovich[1] and I beg you to come and see me right away.

They called me today from *Ogonyok*—one line has to be changed.[2] I want your advice. I am waiting.

Akhmatova

21.

[Leningrad] October 6, 1954

Dear Nikolai Ivanovich,

I was very sorry to hear about your illness, particularly because I know from my own experience how seldom bed rest is recommended for heart patients. Usually the doctors are worried about emphysema, and don't allow you to stay in bed. Have they done an electrocardiogram? That's very important. That can be done at home so you don't have to budge. I had the same thing in 1952. And they put me in the hospital immediately. I wish you all the very best. Regards to Lidia Vasilyevna.[1]

22.

[Moscow] May 2, 1964

Dear Nikolai Ivanovich,

Please look this over. Where should your text go, how about page 6?[1]

Alexander Pavlovich Nilin is bringing the Modigliani. Otherwise, you and I would never get together. I'm infinitely grateful to him. Take a look at the drawing and return it to him. Thank you and greetings on the coming holiday!

Anna Akhmatova

Do you remember how we spent this day on the Ordynka and listened to the Easter bell?

Regards to Lidia Vasilyevna.

A.

23.

[Komarovo, 1965]

Dear Nikolai Ivanovich,

Your admirer (you saw him at my house, when Chagall's[1] daughter was here) and my collaborator on the Leopardi translation will deliver this note to you.[2] Give him what you wrote about the Modigliani drawing and he (Anatoly Naiman) will tell you about me.

I am at the hut.[3] There has been no summer at all, and I've grown completely unsociable.

It is boring to have no news of you.

Akhmatova

TO OSIP MANDELSTAM

July 12 [1935]

Dear Osip Emilyevich,

Thank you for your letter and for remembering me. I've been really sick for a month now. In the next few days I'll be going into the hospital for tests. If all ends well—I'll visit you without fail.[1]

The summer's ice cold—insomnia and weakness have worn me out completely.

Yesterday I had a call from Pasternak who turned up here on his way from Paris to Moscow.[2] It looks like I won't see him—he told me that he's dying from severe psychasthenia. What is the world coming to? Please don't get ill, dear Osip Emilyevich, and don't lose courage.

My book is being delayed for some reason.[3] Until we see each other.

With a warm handshake and a kiss to Nadyusha.[4]

Yours,
Akhmatova

TO EMMA GERSHTEIN

1.

Dec. 31, '36 [Leningrad]

Dear Emma,

I still haven't thanked you for your hospitality in the fall and your concern for my welfare.[1] Forgive me. I've been sick four months now, my heart prevents me from living and working.

They're bringing me your article on Lermontov[2] now, and I will read it on New Year's Eve.

My pension has been cancelled, which, as you can well imagine, greatly complicates my existence.[3]

I should go to Moscow, but I don't have the strength. I kiss you.

Anna

2.

[January 7, 1943. Tashkent][1]

Dear Emma,

Forgive me for not answering you right away. I know that you won't be angry. I practically died in November, but I've returned to the living now. I kiss you.

Anna

3.

[Spring 1943. Tashkent]

Dear Emma,

About two months ago Nadya[1] and I each wrote you a letter in answer to your elegant letters, but our epistolary art evidently was unlucky and had an accident somewhere in the neighborhood of Yel. Mikh. Fratkina's.[2]

Write me. How are you getting along, where is Sergei Borisovich?[3] The Osmyorkins?[4]

My Lyova writes that he's gone off on an expedition and is happy about that.[5]

He's healthy and safe.

I received my first telegram from him on March 19th.

I kiss you.

Yours,
Akhmatova

I've had typhus twice and have been in 4 hospitals.

4.

Feb. 14, 1944 [Tashkent][1]

Dear Emma,

Thank you for your kind and friendly letter. Now, as always for that matter, a friend's voice is a great comfort.

I was very sad to learn of your loss and to know that you were alone during such a difficult ordeal.[2]

I received an invitation from Moscow, and am waiting for one from Leningrad, the dispatch of which has been confirmed by telegram from the Writers' Union.[3]

We'll see each other soon.

I kiss you.

Yours,
Akhmatova

Greetings to friends.

5.

[Early June 1945. Leningrad]

Dear Emma,

Thank you once again for your letter about Lyova. It was delivered at the same time as Lyova's letter. I've been very worried for the past months, since I hadn't received a single word from him at the front.[1] I recently learned that his grandmother died in December of 1942 in Bezhetsk.[2]

I rejoice with you on our shared great happiness—victory.

Why didn't you write a single word about yourself? It's been so long since I've been in Moscow that I don't know anything about all of you. How are Nikolai Ivanovich and Yevgeny Yakovlevich?[3] Where are you working and are you working on Lermontov? I've been appointed a member of the Pushkin Commission. I was in bed for 16 days because of the flu and various complications and got up yesterday for the first time. I kiss you.

Lyova writes his address as 28807-G, and you write 28807-CH. I sent two identical postcards to those two addresses. If only he would get one of them. I live like a hermit. See few people.

Greetings and good wishes to my Moscow friends.

6.

June 15 [1945. Leningrad]

Dear Emma,

Your telegram has me concerned. What are you calling the second letter? Did you write me another letter or does this refer to the letter in which you copied out Lyova's letter dated May 28th?[1]

Right now I'm sending you a telegram: "I received your letter dated June 7th." I'm writing the 7th, but I really don't know the date—it's so smeared.

What's happened, Emma?

I wanted to answer you in detail, after I'd talked with L. Ya. Ginzburg[2] regarding your Lermontov affairs.[3] The possibility that I will soon be in Moscow is not excluded—the Ardovs have invited me to their dacha.[4]

Thank you again, dear Emma, for everything.

I'll be waiting for news.

Yours,
Akhmatova

I write Lyova often, but there's no answer yet.

7.

[Early August 1945. Leningrad]

Dear Emma,

Has Eikhenbaum written you?[1] I met him, as they say nowadays, at Ehrenburg's and brought you up in our conversation. He answered quite satisfactorily. He said that he values your work very much, that he wants to work with you, and asked whether you still live on Shchipko, etc. Of course, I wanted to write you about this right away, but I fell ill and was in bed until yesterday. Lyovushka writes fairly often. I've been offered the chance to translate several things by Baratashvili and to take part in the celebration in Tbilisi in October.[2] Then we'll see each other.

Yours,
Akhmatova

8

Sept. 26th [1952. Leningrad]

Dear Emma,

Today I'm sending Ninochka my translation of a poem by Victor Hugo ("Fragile hopes...").[1] It should be delivered as soon as possible to Goslitizdat, to Nina Ilinichna Kutsoshvili,[2] the editor of the Hugo volume. I implore you to do this, because it might get lost at the Ardovs'. This poem is going into the anniversary edition of Hugo and they're pestering me to submit it.

I would call you, but I don't trust your telephone, since I remember that they don't always get you. Call me, after sending me notification by postcard. How are your affairs and health? I feel worse in Leningrad than in Moscow, but so far I'm getting along.

The weather is unbelievable. I kiss you.

Yours,
Akhmatova

Call the office at Goslitizdat—E1-89-45—and ask when they'll pay for the Ossetians, and tell them that I'm in Leningrad.

9.

October 2nd [1954. Leningrad]

Dear Emma Grigoryevna,

I had a hard time finding your address—I can't call because I don't have a coupon. I came down with a chill on Monday—my temperature was 39.1°C. The doctor came two days in a row. The penicillin broke the fever, but I'm still very ill. I can't work because I'm weak and short of breath. Most likely it's a reaction to various disappointments. You've probably used all the bad words you know about me. I can't expect anything else. Irochka[1] is ill. Anya gets all A's. Nik. Iv.'s[2] book is already sold out. Petrov is writing about it and praises it highly.[3] Regards to him, i.e., not to Petrov, and to the dear Ignatov sisters.[4] I kiss you.

Yours,
Akhm.

10.

[September 7, 1955. Leningrad][1]

Thank you for letter feel poorly—Akhmatova.

11.

16.12. [1956. Leningrad]

Emma,

I. N. Tomashevskaya[1] visited me just yesterday and I relayed your request about Pushkin House. She promised to clarify everything soon. I'm being plagued by terrible headaches that keep me from sleeping. It's awful to think about the tragedy that has befallen your family.[2] Please convey my regards to your mother and sister. You are mistaken in your last letter. I didn't ask you for anything. I received my pension.

Akhm.

12.

[June 25, 1957][1]

Worried about your health am ill myself I kiss you—Akhmatova.

13.

Oct. 25th [1958? Leningrad]

How are you? Don't scare me. What quarrels are you talking about? Nonsense. It would be better if you'd tell me how you manage to make discoveries in the archives when you don't have any clothes or food and are practically without a roof. In my opinion you should be put on exhibit for money.

Really, all this worries me a lot.

There's nothing new here.

I kiss you.

Yours,
Akhmatova

How is Nadya?[1]

Everything here is really so bad that I don't have anything left to hope for.[2] However, Emma, you know everything.

14.

August 1, 1958. Komarovo

Emma!

It's not so easy to answer your question about my health. First, as you know, I've just turned seventy and that fact alone doesn't make one feel any better. Second, I'm carrying around four deadly illnesses, which nobody has ever promised to cure and each of them makes its presence known. To cut a long story short, my heart gives me trouble every day and I can't walk even as much as I could before the last attack. Probably this is all natural, but it's not at all pleasant to think about or, the main thing, to put into words. The last surgeon who examined me in Leningrad said that an operation was necessary but impossible because of the condition of my heart. I think that's everything. However, I live as I usually do: sit on the porch and go for walks to Plotkin's dacha, try to work. I was hard hit by M.M.'s death.[1]

I hope to talk to you by telephone about everything else in your letter (very important) when I get to my apartment in the city.

Where is Marusya and how is her health?[2] I'm not writing her because I can't write in general, and also because she can't unseal letters (that's the next stage in our shared illness),[3] but I love her and think about her constantly.

Lyova didn't receive the agreement and everything has broken down.

I kiss you.

Akhmatova

15.

January 29 [1959. Leningrad]

Dear Emma,

Roman Albertovich[1] will report to you in detail about carrying out your errand. He rose to the occasion—he phoned a hundred times and got results.

Please copy these four poems by Pant[2] in my translation and deliver them to Comrade Zimin at Foreign Literature Publishing House—by mail if nothing else. Zimin's telephone is 11-76-40. Call him today and tell him the manuscript is ready. This is very urgent.

I'm not well. You've seen this picture so often that it's not worth describing. I still hope to be in Moscow in February. Borya Ardov arrived yesterday. He says that he continues to envy your Pavlik.[3]

I see almost no one in Leningrad—I don't go out alone.

It seems that Vinogradov[4] at my request has done everything for the Sreznevskys.[5] The Academy of Sciences is making efforts on their behalf.

Write me a few words about yourself, and about Marusya.

I kiss you.

Yours,
Akhmatova

16.

[August 20, 1958. Komarovo]

Will call second time Friday evening need Vyazemsky's letters can send money kiss you—Akhmatova.[1]

TO NADEZHDA MANDELSTAM

1.

Aug. 2 [1945]

Nadyusha!

I feel so guilty before you, Edik, and Nina, that I don't where to begin.[1] I received the letters and telegraph greetings, I was delighted that you remembered me, but answered not to the point, certain that something got lost en route. I imagine how hot you must be now. And we have the violent storms that usually precede spring, with heavy rain and clouds.

Not a single word from Sofia Arkadyevna, to whom I occasionally write.

I kiss you, Ervan, and Nina. Don't forget me.

Yours,
Anna

2.

[1952][1]

Dear Nadyusha,

It was so nice to hear from you.

I've got a rough day today: tomorrow I deliver Marion.[2] I'm really sick and tired of her, and foresee a lot more bother and complications. If all goes well, I should go to the sanatorium again. In general I'm pleased with my health. When and what will I hear from you? Leningrad is a desert. I see practically no one. I seem to have gotten used to the new house, yet somehow I'm still living on the Fontanka.[3]

I don't even know your address. They're saying on the radio that it's summer in Tashkent. I remember 1944. Oh, Nadya, Nadya!

Yours,
Anna

3.

July 12, 1957

Dear Nadyusha,

I very much want to live with you in Moscow,[1] as long as I can keep my place in Leningrad.

I have a lot of work (translations) and all of it's in Moscow.

I'll be waiting for your news. Many kisses. On Sunday I'll be going to my summer place in Komarovo.

Yours,
A. Akhmatova

Krasnaya Konnitsa 4, Apt. 3

4.

Oct. 8, 1963

Nadyusha,

I'm tired of not knowing anything about you for so long. Why Pskov again? How's your health? Who's with you? Write.

Many kisses.

Yours,
Anush

5.

Dec. 27, 1963. Moscow

Nadya,

I'm sending you three short pages from "Pages from a Notebook," which I continue to work on regularly.[1] It'll probably end up being a small book.

Did we ever think that we'd live to see this day—a Day of Tears and Glory. We need to spend some time together—it's high time.

All's well with you, that is, with Osip Emilyevich. I'll call your Zhenya[2] right away.

Thank you for the letter.

Yours,
Akhmatova

TO VLADIMIR GARSHIN

October 2, 1941. Moscow

I've arrived safely in Moscow. I don't know where I will go next. Chistopol, apparently, is not a possibility. I'm well. I would very much like to hear some word of you. Greetings.

A.

TO IRINA TOMASHEVSKAYA

June 2, 1943. Tashkent

My dear friend,

Since my letters and yours have been getting lost, we've completely lost track of each other. Now Asya will tell you about my life in Tashkent. I don't even want to talk about these boring and dusty things, about the stupid and vulgar gossip, nonsense, etc.

I was seriously ill for a long time. I got better in May, but the heat is starting now and that spells ruin.

My book is small, incomplete, and strangely compiled, but it's still good that it came out.[1] Completely different people are reading it now and they read it differently.

Almost all the refugees of 1941 have left Tashkent for Russia. One thousand people are leaving with the Academy of Sciences.

The city is becoming provincial, sleepy, and alien once again.

From Leningrad I only receive letters from Vladimir Georgiyevich.[2] He asks that I remain in Tashkent until the end.

Now without the Tsyavlovskys[3] I'll never know anything about you. That's very sad.

My son Lyovushka has gone off on an expedition in the taiga—he's very pleased. All his problems ended on March 10th, but he remains assigned to Norilsk until the end of the war.

I don't know anything about Lozinsky, Lidia Yakovlevna,[4] and those few Leningraders with whom I used to meet before the war. A few days ago I encountered I. A. Orbeli[5] on the street, who for some reason had come here from Yerevan, and we greeted each other like the shades in Dante's *Purgatory.*

I have a new house with enormous poplars outside the window, some sort of enormous quietude and a small wooden staircase from which you can watch the stars nicely. This year Venus is such that one could write a poem about it. And did you receive my poem? How is Viktor Borisovich, did your son finish his studies, how is your daughter?

Greetings to Pasternak, the Osmyorkins, and all of distant, strange Moscow. From here everything is distant. I kiss you.

Yours,
Anna

TO BORIS PASTERNAK

1.

July 20 [1943]

Dear Boris Leonidovich,

Your letter was an unexpected joy for me.

It's strange that we haven't corresponded all this time, isn't it.

I congratulate you on the success of your book[1]—I would like to see it. Natalya Alexandrovna Vishnevskaya[2] will tell you about me.

She reads your poetry wonderfully, and what a voice! Goodbye.

Yours,
Akhmatova

2.

November 29, 1952

Dear Boris Leonidovich,

When I arrived in Moscow and Nina[1] told me that you were in the hospital, it seemed that the radiant boundary of my Moscow existence had been sealed off. Moreover, everything: the streets, meetings, and people became less interesting and were covered in a fog. This is not enchantment!

My dear friend, in the summer of '51 I made the same long hospital journey and know how boring and difficult it is.[2] But Lozinsky is right when he says that a hospital has a charm of its own. I hope that your hospital confinement will end with the coming of '52 and that once again everything will be as it had been before: the snowy Moscow outskirts, and music, and work, and friends.

Everybody asks about you, and is waiting for you. Nemchinova admires your Shakespeare, which, as of course you know, Goslitizdat will reprint. And I hear from all quarters: Pasternak is reading Chekhov.

Take care of yourself, Boris Leonidovich—I hope to see you soon. This letter, which I have been writing you in my head since the first day of my arrival in Moscow, has become so short. You—a master of epistolary style—should not censure me, after all, I never write anybody.

Yours,
Anna Akhmatova

The letter is typed so as not to cause you trouble with the deciphering of my scrawl.

TO VERA SUTUGINA

1.

August 2, 1945. Leningrad

Dear Vera Alexandrovna,
Your card with the picture of our house embarrassed me. Please believe me that I was very moved by the fact that you thought of me and by the kindness of Krachkovsky who delivered the letter himself. In Tashkent I fairly frequently saw Al. N. Tikhonov, who had begun writing unusually interesting memoirs.[1] I am living completely alone, still in the same room. There's an orchard outside my window and the gentle Leningrad sky. I kiss you.

Yours,
Akhmatova

2.

August 29, 1965. Komarovo

Dear Viva!
It is certainly very sad that we see each other so seldom. It happens mostly because both of us frequently don't feel well.
I will definitely call you when I'm in town. And you must call me too. I swear not to demand memoirs from you again.

My new book, *The Flight of Time*, should come out in the next few days. I'll save you a copy. I kiss you.

Yours,
Akhmatova

TO LEV GUMILYOV

1.

July 1 [1953]

My dear son, Lyovushka, again I haven't written to you for a long time and I don't even have the usual excuse—work.

I'm resting now after the sanatorium, where it was very nice and cool and I had a private room and generally good treatment.

But I've become unsociable and find such large company a bit difficult. It occurred to me that I should send you cigarettes and not *papirosy*—it doesn't make sense to send you holders for *papirosy*. Just like you, I find it hard to picture my life in Leningrad without the House on the Fontanka. However, the Neva flows, the Hermitage still occupies its place, the white nights wander the streets and gaze into the windows. At least that's how it seems to me in Moscow, which now also is a beauty in its own way: the fountains gush, the scent of the lime trees permeates even the buses, the poppies are blooming, and the delicate central Russian sky above.

On July 29th I was at A. A. Osmyorkin's funeral.[1] He died with brush in hand, like a real artist. I'm writing at the post office—it seems that this is the only place where I'm visited by the epistolary muse.

I'll write you a real letter from Leningrad, my dear little octopus, Lyovushka. I won't be there long, because I've been invited to the dacha outside of Kolomna, where I vacationed last year. Take care of yourself—don't drink tea that is too strong. Well, it seems the rain is coming to an end, and this letter is coming to an end. I can go home. In July I'll send you by mail 200 rubles and of course a package.

I embrace you tightly.

Mama

2.

September 20, '54

Just today, my dear Lyovushka, I sent you two postcards. I went to get my pension myself on Gorokhovaya—remember? The day is bright—the sky is summery. I still haven't sent you your birthday package, but all the provisions have been purchased.[1]

I ran into the Huns again in the Chinese anthology that I'm still reading. Now it's the first century A.D. Two Chinese (Generals S and W) and Li Ling were captured by the Huns and spent 19 years in captivity. Then one (Sa Wu) returns to his homeland, and the other sings a song, which is translated into English and without rhyme.* Did I write you that I saw a Peking edition of Tsu Yuan (1954) in English? Translated by a Chinese.

I kiss you.

Mama

* This is my prose translation for you:

> I have traveled 10 thousand li
> Through the sands of the desert,
> Serving my lord,
> In order to defeat the *hordes of Huns*

and so on. Do you receive my excerpts from the anthology and the word-for-word translations? Maybe they're of no interest to you?

3.

[1956]

Dear Lev,

My editor[1] called the next day and apologized that he is unable to see me, since he has a meeting at the Union.

He has already sent the book to the publisher. I didn't feel comfortable initiating a complicated conversation on the telephone. He was so cordial and sympathetic, and, of course, he won't refuse to see me when I ask him. I'm waiting to finalize the contract. After that I will go home right away. I'm very tired and miss it. I kiss you and Tanya. Greetings to Ira, Anya, R.A.

Mama

TO ALEKSIS RANNIT

1.

Dear Mr. Rannit!

Thank you for the poems (it's a pity that you sent only the translation)[1] and the kind letter.

It's difficult to understand why somebody found it necessary to disturb my ashes and communicate absurd legends that I was in Paris in 1938.[2] I have not been in the West since 1912, and in 1938 did not travel further than Moscow.

I'm absolutely certain that your work will be interesting and necessary, but I'm a bit concerned about the biographical part. In any case, I am letting you know in advance that it's not possible to make use of the writings of Georgy Ivanov and L. Strakhov-sky.[3] They do not contain a single word of truth.

Forgive me for not answering you right away—I am still very weak after my illness and am now living out of town.

Anna Akhmatova
February 18, 1962
Komarovo

2.

Dear Mr. Rannit!

I am writing you today just so that you know that your letter of March 8th has been received.

Permit me in turn to ask you a few questions: why do my poems seem blue to you, when for half a century everybody thought that they were white?[1] Why didn't you send me the original of your poem?—I read English freely.

Did you see my "A Word about Pushkin" in *The Literary Gazette* during the anniversary celebration?

I was pleased to learn that you are of the same opinion as I regarding Georgy Ivanov and Strakhovsky. And therefore, when I read your work, I will not have to endure the experience that is described in the last chapter of Kafka's *Metamorphosis*, when the hero is led through a brightly lit and perfectly congenial Prague, only to be murdered in a dark shed.

Everything you write about my poetry is very kind. But once and for all, I'm not inclined to believe praise. On the other hand, I blindly believe any maligning whatsoever.

I'm sending you a list of poems that have been printed in various publications since the 1961 book and several answers to your questionnaire.

I wish you success.

Anna Akhmatova
May 24, 1962
Moscow

Enclosure to Akhmatova's letter to Aleksis Rannit (May 24, 1962)[2]

So as not to hold you up, I'm sending you a few answers to your questions.

2. I wrote my first poem when I was 11 years old. I've been publishing since spring 1911. For example: *Apollon*, no. 4, 1911.

3. Nobody at home encouraged my first efforts, rather they were at a loss as to why I needed this.

4. Pushkin (both the first and the second).

5. Teacher—Annensky.

8. I never used any textbooks—I listened to discussions about poetry in the Poets' Guild in 1911-1914.

Among the people you list, the late Boris Viktorovich Tomashevsky was my teacher in the study of Pushkin, and Georgy Arkadyevich Shengeli, with whom I was friends and often met, would sometimes ask me to pronounce some line of mine for his research.

9. I do not know how long the process of creating a poem takes, about all this see my poem (p. 287) "One, like an anxious thunderbolt."[3]

10. It is not for me to judge whether I have contributed something to Russian poetry.

Akhm.

3.

Dear Mr. Rannit!

It seems impossible for me to get to Leningrad, I'm still in Moscow and do not know whether a letter from you is waiting for me at home. Now I am answering your last letter, dated January 2nd.

After I'd read your questions, I thought for a bit, paraphrasing Chekhov's old woman: "It's been a long time, sinner that I am, since I've filled out a questionnaire." I'll answer briefly.

Among artists I liked the Spanish more than anybody, in particular El Greco. In general, in my youth I liked the water and architecture, and now—the earth and music.

In 1921 I wrote the ballet libretto to Blok's *Snow Mask.* I was not pleased with my portraits (except maybe the Tyshler).[1] Perhaps another time I will write more.

I wish you success.

Akhmatova
February 20, 1963

TO KORNEI CHUKOVSKY

Dear Kornei Ivanovich!

The need to write you grows daily (I haven't written letters for 30 years now) to tell you what an enormous and wonderful task you have performed by creating that which you chose to call "Reading Akhmatova."[1] You have written lucidly, gracefully, simply and irrefutably about my work and my *Triptych,* which you remember from Tashkent.

The most dissimilar people have read your work, and it has been a long time since I've seen that any article was so liked, that it stimulated such excitement and approval, and I am just left to wonder at how much you guessed correctly.

You have said the most essential and main thing about the poem.

Thank you.

Anna Akhmatova
November 6, 1962
Moscow

TO SEMYON WEINBERG

1.

Dear Mr.Weinberg,
Everyone to whom I have shown your translations has found them to be excellent. I myself have done this kind of work and I know what it entails.

You have succeeded in preserving everything, practically down to my breath; the treatment of words is careful, the meaning is preserved completely. My poems have not come out so well in any other language. If you have any other translations of my poems, please send them to me.

I thank you.

Anna Akhmatova
December 22, 1962
Moscow

2.

Forgive me, dear Doctor, for my interminable silence. I have so many reasons for it that I cannot even attempt enumerating them.

I was glad to receive your translations. I like them.

Best wishes,
Anna Akhmatova

January 17, 1965
Leningrad

TO GEORGES NIVAT

Dear Mr. Nivat!

In the near future I hope to send you a detailed and persuasive letter regarding your translation of S. K. Makovsky's sketch.

This sketch contains numerous errors which must be attributed to the writer's age and his poor sources.

Everything that you've done is wonderful. The translations of the poems are careful and accurate.

I thank you.

Anna Akhmatova
June 7, 1963
Moscow

TO VIKTOR GORENKO

1.

Dear Viktor,

I feel terribly guilty. I received your photograph, for which I thank you, and the wonderful nylon stockings. But my constant travels from Moscow to Leningrad and from Leningrad to Moscow, and especially my serious heart problems and lengthy hospital stays (I've already had three attacks), have disturbed the normal course of my life. There's really nothing I can tell you about myself. I'm translating a little, at the moment from Romanian, and am working on Pushkin.

Once again, thank you for not forgetting your sister.

Yours,
Anya

I'll spend the whole summer at the dacha in Komarovo with Hannah. I kiss you.

June 7, 1963
Moscow

2.

Dear Viktor,

I was so happy to receive your kind letter. Thank you for your offer to send packages, dear brother, but that's unnecessary. I'm on such a strict diet that it's useless to send me anything edible. As for clothing, I don't need it: whatever I have will probably be enough until the end.

I can't pass on your regards to Lyova—he hasn't been to see me for two years, but I hear that he's defended his doctoral dissertation and is doing research.

If a collection of my poems should be published, I will, of course, send it to you with pleasure and will certainly inscribe it. The collection published in 1961 was bought up in a few minutes by some maniacs; I don't even have a copy myself.

Stay well.

I kiss you.

> Your sister,
> *Anna*
> July 20, 1963

3.

Dear Viktor,

I'm sending you my most recent photograph. Many consider it to be the best. It occurred to me that I *can* fulfill your request to send you a collection of my poetry with an inscription.

I'm enclosing the inscription in this envelope; buy a book of my poetry and glue this inscription onto the title page.

Stay well.

> Yours,
> *Anna*
> September 15, 1963

4.

December 1, 1964. Moscow

Dear Viktor,

It so happened that I lost your address and didn't answer or thank you right away for your wonderful present of the black kimono. It gives me special pleasure to wear it. Today I'm leaving for Rome and Sicily, where I'm to be awarded a prize for poetry. I have a travel permit for 10 days only. I'm of course very anxious about whether my health will hold out. I'm sending you my latest photograph—it's better than all the others. Give my regards to your wife. I kiss you.

Always yours,
Anya

5.

WESTERN UNION. TELEGRAM.
Victor Gorenko care Lis Olheunky (TA3-5642 Apt)
3299 Radio Drive Bronx N.Y.

Staying one week Hotel President Russell Square London can cable or call me terminus 8844

Sister Anna

6.

Dear Viktor!

Today I was given three photographs of myself when young (good ones). I want you to have them and I'm sending them to you.

The summer passed indifferently; because of the bad weather I hardly walked and have become somewhat weak.

When I return to town, I'll write in greater detail.

Don't forget your sister. The main thing is, stay healthy. Greetings to my dear *belle-soeur*.

Yours,
Anya
Aug. 18, 1965

TO FYODOR MALOV

Lomonosov Prospect 19, Apt. 48

Moscow [1964]

Dear Fyodor Ivanovich,

I want to say a few words regarding my cycle "Midnight Poems."[1] In all there are seven poems, dedication and the fragment "So that the stranger from a distant century."[2] You took note of this cycle from just two poems. I would like you to read the entire cycle (*Day of Poetry*, Moscow, 1964). The book should come out in November or December of this year. Maybe then you will deign to tear yourself away from your agricultural concerns and spare a few minutes for a letter to me.

If for some reason "Midnight Poems" are not included in the almanac, I think that I can send you the entire cycle.[3]

Akhmatova

TO JOSEPH BRODSKY

1.

Oct. 20, 1964

Joseph,

In the course of the endless discussions I have with you day and night, you ought to know everything that has taken place or has not taken place.

This did:

> And here is fame's
> High threshold,
> But a sly voice
> Admonishes,[1] etc.

This did not:

> It is shining—this is Judgment Day,[2] etc.

Promise me one thing—that you will stay perfectly healthy, there's nothing on earth worse than hot-water bottles, shots, and high blood pressure, and the worst thing about all this is that it's irreversible. And if you are healthy, golden paths, happiness, and that divine communion with nature, which so captivates all those who read your poetry, may await you.

Anna

2.

Joseph,
    Candles from Syracuse. In turn I am sending you a most ancient flame, practically stolen from Prometheus.
    I'm in Komarovo in the Writers' House. Anya[1] and company are in the hut. I went there today and recalled our last autumn—the music, the well, and your verse cycle.
    And again the salutary words surfaced: "The main thing is the greatness of the conception."
    The sky already turns rosy in the evening, even though we still have a large chunk of winter ahead of us.
    I want to share with you my new misfortune. I'm dying of black envy. Read the 12th issue of *For[eign] Lit[erature]*—Léon Philippe's "Inquiry"... I envy every word, every intonation. Not bad for an old fellow! And what a translator! I've never seen the like. Sympathize with me a bit.
    The poem on Eliot's death[2] is perhaps not inferior, but I don't experience envy. On the contrary, the idea that it exists makes me happy.
    I just received your telegram. Thank you. It seems that I've been writing this letter for a long time.

Anna
February 15, 1965
Komarovo

3.

Dear Joseph!

Since the number of my letters to you that have gone unsent has reached three digits, I've decided to write you a real one, i.e., a real, existing one (in an enveleope, with a stamp, with the address), and I've become a bit embarrassed.

Today is St. Peter's Day—the very heart of summer.[1] Everything shines and gleams from within. I recall so many different St. Peter's Days.

I'm at the hut. The well creaks, the ravens caw. I'm listening to the Purcell *(Dido and Aeneas)* that was brought on your recommendation. It is so powerful that it's impossible to talk about.

It turns out that we departed England one day after the disastrous storm the newspapers reported. When I learned about this, I understood why the north of France looked so terrifying from the window of the train. And I thought: "The sky must look like that when there's a decisive battle" (of course, it turned out to be the anniversary of Waterloo, which I was told in Paris). Black, wild clouds rushed at one another, the ground was entirely flooded by storming, turbid water: rivulets, streams, and lakes overflowed their banks. Wooden crosses stuck out of the water— there are a great number of cemeteries and graves there from the last war. Then there was Paris, burning hot and unrecognizable. Then the return trip, when all I wanted was to get to Komarovo as quickly as possible; then Moscow and everybody on the platform with flowers, everything was like the best dream possible.

Have the mosquitoes let up? They're already gone here. Tolya[2] and I are finishing the Leopardi translation, while lines wander about somewhere in the distance, calling to one another, and nobody will go with me to where the Rastrelli wonder shines—the Smolny Cathedral.[3]

Your words from last year are still in force: "The main thing is the greatness of the conception."

Thank you for the telegram—the classical style works well for you, both in the epistolary genre and in your drawings; I always recall Picasso's illustrations to *The Metamorphosis* when I see them.

I'm reading Kafka's journals.
Write me.

Akhmatova

P.S. I think you would have enjoyed my meeting with Garri.[4] His wife is charming.

And here is a quatrain that I had completely forgotten and lost, which turned up in my papers.

> Your crazed eyes
> And icy speeches,
> And the declaration of love
> Before the first encounter.

Maybe this is from "Prologue"?

A Note on the Translations

Edith Stevens translated the letters to von Shtein. Uliana Gabara translated the letters to Bryusov, Shchegolyov, Chebotaryevskaya, Sologub, Bryusova, O. Mandelstam, N. Mandelstam, Khardzhiev, Weinberg, Nivat, Gorenko, Gumilyova, Chulkov, Garshin and Sutugina. The remainder were translated by Ronald Meyer.

Afterword

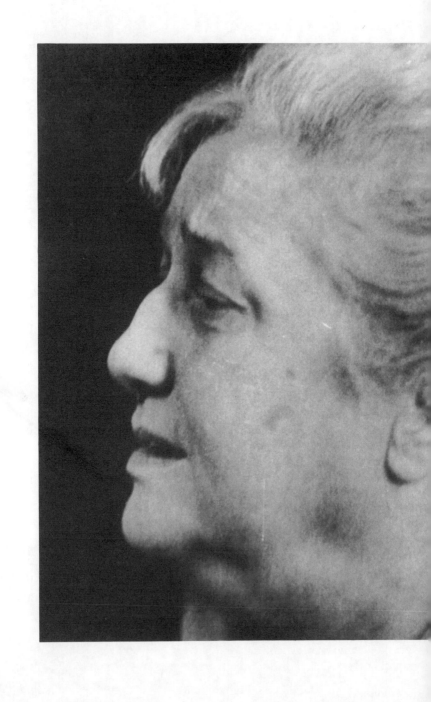

AKHMATOVA'S PROSE

Emma Gershtein

ANNA AKHMATOVA'S FIRST, AND for many years only, prose work appeared just before the publication of *Rosary*. Her review of Nadezhda Lvova's collection of poems, entitled *An Old Tale*, was printed in the January 1914 issue of *Russian Thought*.[1] Imbued with compassion for the young poetess who had chosen to end her life, this review combined a professional critique of the strengths and weaknesses of Nadezhda Lvova's talent with interesting reflections on the distinguishing traits of women's lyric poetry. The twenty-four-year-old Akhmatova wrote like "an authority." Nothing anticipated Akhmatova's subsequent admission, "I don't know how to write prose"—a statement she made to Kornei Chukovsky when he visited her in late 1921. He found Akhmatova at work on a libretto for the composer Artur Lourié's ballet *The Snow Mask*, based on Blok.[2] Akhmatova asked her visitor to listen to two scenes, paying especially critical attention to the style. But Chukovsky made no attempt to assess the scenic and literary merits of the libretto. Akhmatova's work seemed "valuable" to him as a "wonderfully sensitive commentary on *The Snow Mask*."[3] Thus, Akhmatova made her presence as a literary critic known at the outset of her poetic career.

Lourié's score for *The Snow Mask* was published, but Akhmatova's libretto has not survived. However, her work on Blok's lyric cycle had made a considerable impression on her creative consciousness. One of the early versions of *A Poem without a Hero* contained the words: "In my dreams I seemed to be the one writing the libretto for Artur. And there was no getting rid of the music." Akhmatova's affinity for the genre of criticism moved in new directions. In a later autobiographical note she recorded: "1924. The beginning of my Pushkin studies in the Marble Palace (André Chénier).[4] Grigory Gukovsky. Conversations with him about Pushkin."[5] She is referring to the well-known scholar who had just then graduated from the university, but had already embarked on a brilliant scholarly career, and was seemingly discovering eighteenth-century Russian literature anew. In his diary of 1925-27, the young poet and prosaist Pavel Luknitsky gives a detailed account of Akhmatova's systematic and enthusiastic study of André Chénier's poetry.[6]

Reading the eighteenth-century French poet alongside Pushkin's poetry led Akhmatova to extremely interesting parallels and discoveries. These were extended by a steadily widening circle of reading, which embraced the eighteenth-century French poets, the German Romantics, and classical writers. Her fruitful observations on how the traditions of European poetry are refracted in Pushkin's work could not have been made had she not read the works in the original. Akhmatova knew French from childhood and had a secondary-school level grasp of German. Yet in her short autobiographical account of how she studied the architecture of old Petersburg and Pushkin's works, Akhmatova forgot to mention that during that time she learned to read English fluently. Hence her knowledge of Shakespeare, which served as the source of many of her creative finds, while her close familiarity with the works, correspondence, and biography of Byron enabled her to speak of him as an interested party who was Pushkin's contemporary.

As we know, the 1920s were a crucial period in Akhmatova's literary biography. She was cut off from the general reader, who was looking for new themes in contemporary poetry after the October Revolution. Akhmatova's poetry rarely appeared in the press. Of course, she did not stop writing, but there were too few poems at the time to have comprised another new volume. Yet, as we can see, during this difficult period the poet was neither morally devastated nor idle. The number of notes in the margins of the books she read kept increasing, and each of them could have served as a topic for an independent scholarly presentation. One list of these notes by topic contained twenty-five headings. On November 24, 1945, Akhmatova reported in *The Literary Gazette*: "Right now I'm collecting and arranging my notes on Pushkin (1926-1936); there are twenty-five of them in all, and they're very diverse in content. Among them are notes on Pushkin's self-quotation and observations on Pushkin's literary style and the colorful epithet in Pushkin. Put together, these notes will comprise a book about Pushkin."

This book never materialized, nor has the manuscript been found, but in 1959, when Akhmatova was drawing up a new outline for a collection of her articles on Pushkin, she included the marginalia as one of its sections. It was then that she compiled a new list of contents for these notes. By then they no longer numbered twenty-five, but fifty. This synopsis was published posthumously in a scholarly edition with a commentary by the editors.[7]

Akhmatova's notes contain references to two other works, "Pushkin and Mickiewicz" and "Pushkin and Dostoevsky," the manuscripts of which have been lost. Nor have Akhmatova's materials for her research on *Mozart and Salieri* been found.

The article entitled "Pushkin's Last Tale" included in the present volume grew out of Akhmatova's discovery of a literary source for *The Tale of the Golden Cockerel*: the prose tale "The Legend of the Arabian Astrologer" by the American writer Washington Irving. Pertinent here is Akhmatova's new reading of Pushkin's fragment "The Tsar saw before him," which had previously eluded Pushkin scholars. The fragment proved to be a verse translation of one of the episodes from Irving's "Legend." Akhmatova's discovery is now included in all commentaries to editions of Pushkin's works. The strength of Akhmatova's study lies in its identification of polemical topical elements in *The Tale of the Golden Cockerel*, which articulate Pushkin's political stance. This article, published in 1933 in a "thick" journal, was Akhmatova's first as a literary critic, and remains a vital part of Pushkin studies to this day, serving as a stimulus to pursue Akhmatova's observations further and to examine them in greater depth, or as a worthwhile subject for scholarly polemics. Specifically, recent scholars have cited new sources without repudiating the connections between Pushkin's tale and Irving's story.

As regards the article "Benjamin Constant's *Adolphe* in Pushkin's Works," leading contemporary scholars concur that it is a model of first-class Soviet scholarship on Pushkin. We must admit, however, that there is nothing reminiscent of a poet's prose in its stylistic features. This is a piece of purely workmanlike analytical prose, devoid of all figurative elements and affect.

There is no trace of the metaphorical bent that surfaced so frequently in Akhmatova's everyday speech. But to make up for that, her very method of adducing evidence and her logically impeccable argumentation bring to mind Osip Mandelstam's characterization of Akhmatova's research strategy: "It's an out–and–out chess game."

Akhmatova's article on *Adolphe* and Pushkin is the one Pushkin specialists refer to most frequently in their research, for the most part agreeing with Akhmatova's ideas and her deciphering of the great poet's cryptography.

The third scholarly article Akhmatova published during her lifetime, "Pushkin's *Stone Guest*," was written in a freer manner. There was more than a ten-year break between this article and the preceding one—a time of tragic suffering and hard blows dealt by fate. But during this period her poetic gift had revived. Even before the war she had written such major poems as "The Basement of Memory," "When they inter an epoch," "Shakespeare's 24th Play," the narrative poem *The Way of All the Earth*, and had started *A Poem without a Hero*... Surveying the course of her development, Akhmatova wrote: "My writing has changed and my voice sounds different [...] There can be no return to my former manner. It's not for me to judge what's better and what's worse. 1940 was the apogee. The poems kept coming without interruption, rushing and breathless, stepping on each other's heels." Among these poems there were lamentations, which poured from her heart of their own accord during the years of misery. They were subsequently unified into a separate cycle: *Requiem*.[8]

This new artistic experience affected the development of Akhmatova's scholarly thought. The problematics in her work on Pushkin changed. "For a long time I've been drawn to the idea of looking deeper into Pushkin's creative laboratory," she announced as early as 1957. "I've already completed one such study about *The Stone Guest*."[9]

The article was published in 1958, although it had been written in 1947. While she was preparing it for publication, Akhmatova added a number of extended insertions, and its appearance in print evidently served as an impetus for new reflections and observations.

In her work on *Adolphe* Akhmatova had already linked Pushkin's interest in this novel with his search for various solutions to genre: "While trying to solve completely different literary problems (*Eugene Onegin, The Stone Guest,* 'On the Corner of a Small Square'), Pushkin turned several times to *Adolphe,* but each time in order to psychologize his works." This illustrates the type of research Akhmatova favored, in particular in her work on *The Stone Guest:* "We have before us the dramatic incarnation of the poet's inner personality," we read at the end of this article. That is a very bold conclusion because, as everyone knows, the action of Pushkin's romantic tragedy is set in Spain, and the fantastic plot has nothing in common with the facts of the poet's biography.

Similarly, this illuminates the method Akhmatova used as she proceeded with her analysis of the most diverse Pushkin works. She brings out unexpected inner personal themes even in Pushkin's highly plot-oriented pieces. The invocation of fate proves to be just such a central theme in *The Tales of Belkin.* Two prose fragments and "The Commander," that is, works completely different in genre, are united, in her opinion, by a single theme: the problem of suicide. In the "demonic" tale passed on by Titov from Pushkin's words, it is jealousy. In the draft of the poem "When recollections alone" Akhmatova divines Pushkin's persistent preoccupation with the graves of the five executed Decembrists.

Akhmatova's notes on Pushkin expanded into a kind of musical suite about the psychology of the poet's creative process.

And parallel to this appeared another suite in Akhmatova's manuscripts—a series of fragmented notes about the psychology of her own creative process. These problems interested Akhmatova a great deal in the final decade of her life (1957-66). We shall return later to her intimate revelations—the revelations of a poet about the inception of her poems. But first it is necessary to address another sphere of Akhmatova's interests. We shall consider here two of her works that elicited considerable commentary in our press, commentary that frequently turned into outright censure. The articles in question are "Pushkin's Death" and "Alexandrina," which demonstrate Akhmatova's powers as pamphleteer and polemicist. They inevitably recall an improvisation that Mandelstam either wrote or recited in 1934, when Akhmatova was a guest at his home in Moscow:

> Bees get accustomed to beekeepers,
> Such is the nature of the bee,
> Yet I've kept count of Akhmatova's stings
> For years now twenty-three.

Akhmatova's irate philippics against Natalya Nikolayevna Pushkina and Alexandrina Goncharova also bring to mind the ecstatic lines the young Marina Tsvetaeva addressed to Akhmatova: "Hook-nosed / She, whose deadly ire...."[10]

Akhmatova's "A Word about Pushkin" is another acerbic piece written with great publicistic verve. With devastating sarcasm she confronts the whole stately world of imperial Petersburg, which had hindered the great poet in his work and life.

These articles illuminate Akhmatova's own image, foreshortening it in a special way that adds to our sense of her personality. In essence, Akhmatova formulated an artistic conception of Pushkin's tragedy based on her study of all the circumstances surrounding the catastrophe. All its participants are subject to criticism, insofar as their actions and all aspects of their behavior played an important role in the development of events. How is it possible to refuse to delve into the minds of the dramatis personae? Yet, for some reason many readers and, alas, writers, impose a taboo on discussing the image of Pushkin's wife. Natalya Nikolayevna has become the object of a bona fide cult that verges on the unnatural.[11] Perhaps the impassioned accusations Akhmatova hurls at Natalya Pushkina will sober up somewhat the fanatical admirers of the poet's wife. Akhmatova's interpretation of the events is a subject for discussion by specialists, and we shall not dwell on it here. I merely wish to point out that one of her deductions has been corroborated—regarding the people who started the rumors about Pushkin's illicit relationship with Alexandrina Goncharova. Akhmatova was convinced that the elder Heeckeren, Pushkin's worst enemy, had started circulating this rumor. Explicit confirmation of this can be found in the documents of the military inquest into d'Anthès's duel with Pushkin. These materials show clearly that the court noted the difference between d'Anthès's "expressions," which "could have provoked Pushkin's sensitivity as a husband," and Heeckeren's actions, which offended "not only Pushkin's, but also his wife's" honor. "A Note on Foreigners' Involvement in the Duel" mentions the Dutch ambassador's participation in the affair prior to the duel: "Moreover, from the testimony of the defendant... Danzas, which is based on Pushkin's words, it is evident that Baron Heeckeren planted in the public mind a bad opinion of Pushkin's and his wife's behavior."[12] This is but one example of Akhmatova's insight in her work on Pushkin's duel and death (see the commentary to her book *About Pushkin*).[13]

The genre of memoirs played a major role in Akhmatova's work during her final years. Several redactions of her extensive outline for a book entitled *My Half Century* have been preserved. But large-scale narrative was probably incompatible with Akhmatova's creative manner. Had the idea for this book been realized, it would evidently have been broken down into a series of novellas. Akhmatova articulated her guiding principle very precisely: "The human memory is so constructed that it works like a projector, illuminating individual moments, while leaving the rest in impenetrable darkness. One can and should forget some things, even with a superb memory." Akhmatova described her meetings with Amedeo Modigliani in Paris in just such a manner; she ignores the inessential, but freely makes use of individual episodes and impressions. The result is a finished portrait of the young artist, when he was still awaiting recognition. Her memoir of Blok[14] is admittedly limited by the narrowness of the task the author sets herself: to recount only the few meetings with her elder contemporary. Akhmatova does not attempt to create a literary portrait of the poet. But the absence of a detailed portrait in the sketch is compensated for by the almost aphoristic mode of characterization found in Akhmatova's notes: "I consider Blok not only the greatest European poet of the first quarter of the twentieth century (I bitterly mourned his premature death), but a man and an epoch in one, that is, the most characteristic representative of his time."

The sketch of Mikhail Lozinsky reflects a profound grasp of the significance of the noble literary calling to which this eminent master of translation dedicated himself. The emotionally charged portrait of a friend and comrade-in-arms casts a new light on the lines Akhmatova addressed to him:

> ...A lofty freedom of the soul,
> Which is called friendship...

This brings to mind her observations about the reciprocal interaction of two different types of literary creation: "From poetry can arise the prose we need, which will give us back the poetry renewed."

In 1957 Akhmatova began writing her reminiscences about another comrade-in-arms and friend, the poet Osip Mandelstam.[15] The title of Akhmatova's work—"Pages from a Diary"—points to the author's original intention to produce an artistic essay in a small genre. But these reminiscences gradually expanded; Akhmatova kept returning to them in the course of subsequent years, adding stories about various periods in their friendship, about important events in Mandelstam's life, and about his death. Unfortunately, she did not organize these numerous additions into a unified whole, and the work remained unfinished.

Among Akhmatova's unfinished prose memoirs, the fragments of her autobiography must be singled out. In her preparations for this work, she made several general observations about the genre of reminiscences and expressed her original view on "such an important and profound period as childhood in the life of every person." The description of her own childhood is marked by the subtle nuances in her perception of reality that are characteristic of Akhmatova's entire output. As always, smell, color, and sound play an important role in her reminiscences. Her attempt to describe morals and manners is of special interest: for instance, her descriptions of Petersburg, Tsarskoe Selo, and Pavlovsk of the 1890s and 1900s, which reveal her keen eye. While recounting her adolescence spent in these places, Akhmatova does not forget the literary influences that affected the formation of her personality. It is interesting that her favorite works include those which she esteemed in her maturity. The first novel that kept her awake all night was Dostoevsky's *The Brothers Karamazov*. And Akhmatova always spoke of Knut Hamsun's *Mysteries*[16] as the great Norwegian writer's best novel. *Victoria*, the love poem that Boris Pasternak had singled out so distinctly, appealed to her less than *Pan*,[17] which is not surprising. The motifs of this romance are close to Akhmatova's early love lyrics, to the small dramatic novellas about love as a struggle, about contests between strong characters who resemble Lt. Glahn, the hero of *Pan* (just recall such poems as "A dark veil, underneath she twisting/Her hands..."or "And when we had cursed each other...."[18]

But let us return to Akhmatova's revelations about the inception of her poems, to what we earlier called a suite about the psychology of her own creative process.

As we saw earlier, while meditating on the rough draft of Pushkin's poem "Remembrance," Akhmatova noted: "This is that *first layer* which poets virtually hide from themselves (more on that elsewhere)." A line leads from here to her diary entries about her own poems, which seemed to "be generated spontaneously of their own accord." Akhmatova continues:

> In some [poems] the author is doomed to hear the voice of a violin that once helped him compose, and in others the rumble of a traincar that prevented him from writing them. Poems can be associated with the scent of perfumes and flowers. The wildrose in the cycle *Wildrose Blooming*[19] really did emit the intoxicating fragrance at some moment that is connected with this cycle. This, however, applies not just to my own poems. In Pushkin I hear the waterfalls of Tsarskoe Selo ("these living waters"), the end of which I myself witnessed.[20]

One can see a direct connection between the words about the hidden "first layer" in Pushkin's poem and the creative history of Akhmatova's narrative poem *The Way of All the Earth*, which she recounted in the "Letter to **"[21]:

> In the first half of March 1940, totally unconnected lines started to appear in the margins of my drafts. This is especially true of the draft of the poem "A Vision" [...]. The sense of these lines seemed vague to me then [...], even strange. For quite some time there was no promise of their being transformed into something united and they seemed to be the usual stray lines, until their time came and they took their place in the forge and came out as you see them here.

Akhmatova constantly draws a similar sharp distinction between initial inspiration and the conscious work of an exacting master. Hence her diary entry for December 24, 1959, mentions the poem "Michal"[22] as something that as yet "is not yielding, that is, something that seems secondary to me."[23] And the early narrative poem *At the Edge of the Sea*, according to the author, came into existence under the unconscious influence of the rhythm and images of Blok's poem "Venice," although Akhmatova "heard" something completely different in theme and plot and it is somewhat distant in poetic meter: "Bays cut into the low-lying shore./ All the sails were fleeing out to sea."[24]

It was no accident that the narrative poem *The Way of All the Earth* was originally titled "Visions" or "Nocturnal Visions." Akhmatova's poetry often was born out of her creative dreams. Two diary entries reveal the actual substratum of her creative process, although they deal not with poetry, but with nature. In the draft cited above (December 24, 1959), speaking about winter's presentiment of spring, Akhmatova continues: "So much that is wonderful and joyous is connected with this, that I'm afraid of spoiling it by telling anyone about it." Such sensations were a reality for her no different from the houses and alleys of the Tsarskoe Selo of her childhood or the smells and sounds of Pavlovsk Station. "I also think," continues Akhmatova, "that I'm somehow connected with my Korean rose, with the demonic hydrangea, and the silent, dark life of roots. Are they cold right now? Have they got enough snow? Is the moon watching them? All these things are of vital concern to me, and I don't even forget them when I'm asleep." "And the underwater movement of the creatures of the deep,/And the stirring of the valley's vine..."—one involuntarily recalls the great lines from Pushkin's "The Prophet."[25] But Akhmatova did not venture to call these dreams lofty inspiration. In the little story "Birches" she compares one of these dreams to a spell. A birch grove outside of Moscow that had stunned her in the autumn still disturbed the poet's imagination on the very brink of spring, evoking the most remote associations. Here we have the ancient altar of Pergamum, with its eloquent depiction of the gods' battle with the Titans,[26] and the even more ancient Druids, with their religious worship of the faces of nature and sacrificial rites enacted in the depths of the forests. Akhmatova's exclamation at the end of the story "Birches" is characteristic of an artist: "...I don't want this to be a dream. I need them *real.*" That is why Akhmatova, riding along the Uspensky highway in the spring, exclaimed when she saw the same birch grove: "So it does exist? It exists? And I kept thinking it was a dream."[27]

Akhmatova remembered some of her creative dreams for years, as in June 1958, when she noted of *A Poem without a Hero:* "During the night in my sleep I saw (or heard) my narrative poem as a tragic ballet. That's the second time; the first time was in 1944. I remember everything: the music, and the sets, and the costumes, and the large clock (to the right), which chimed midnight of the New Year."

That brings us to a special phenomenon in Akhmatova's life as a poet—her ceaseless work on *A Poem without a Hero.*[28] As we know, over the course of twenty-two years Akhmatova returned periodically to this work, adding to it and revising it, each time noting the date of its completion, but nonetheless returning again and again to what appeared to be a completed work. *A Poem without a Hero* became Akhmatova's constant companion in her last years. This process is reflected in the unfinished libretto of the ballet based on motifs from *A Poem without a Hero* and in the magnificent *Prose about the Poem*. It is difficult to view these notes as a commentary to the *Poem without a Hero* that we know. In her attempts to reveal its subtext, the author seems to be tracing the contours of some new large-scale work. Akhmatova constantly felt the presence of some second, unborn narrative poem. Perhaps that's what she was talking about in the enigmatic verse fragment "An Unprecedented Evil Has Befallen":

> One has both consciousness and memory,
> And the endurance of better times,
> Another—an inextinguishable flame,
> Another is two bright eyes
> And a cloudlike wing.

The poet's intimate revelations about her relations with the Muse will long serve as something for the sensitive reader to ponder and as a subject of discussion for literary historians.

Translated by Helena Goscilo

Notes

NOTES

The majority of the texts translated in this volume can be found in the following edition: Anna Akhmatova, *Sochineniia v dvukh tomakh,* vol. 2 (Moscow, 1986). Other sources are detailed in the notes to the individual works. The bibliography lists the various editions consulted.

References to English translations of Akhmatova's poetry, unless noted otherwise, are to the following editions:

The Complete Poems of Anna Akhmatova, bilingual edition, translated by Judith Hemschemeyer, edited by Roberta Reeder, 2 vols. (Somerville, MA., 1990), abbreviated here as *Complete Poems.*

Anna Akhmatova, *Selected Poems,* edited by Walter Arndt (Ann Arbor, 1976), abbreviated as *Selected Poems.*

The editor gratefully acknowledges the work of the commentators on Akhmatova's prose used in the compilation of the notes below.

Preface

1. Quoted in L. A. Mandrykina, "Nenapisannaia kniga. Listki iz dnevnika A. A. Akhmatovoi," *Knigi. Arkhivy. Avtografy. Obzory, soobshcheniia, publikatsii* (Moscow, 1973), p. 64. Unless otherwise noted, translations from the Russian of secondary sources are mine–R. M.

2. Nadezhda Mandelstam, *Hope Abandoned,* trans. Max Hayward (New York, 1974), p. 454.

3. Lidia Chukovskaia, *Zapiski ob Anne Akhmatovoi,* vol. 2 (Paris, 1980), p. 397.

Biographical Sketch

Unless otherwise noted, translations of Akhmatova's poetry in this sketch are from the volume *Selected Poems.*

1. Ariadna Tyrkova-Vil'iams, *Teni minuvshego,* quoted in A. Akhmatova, *Desiatye gody,* ed. R. D. Timenchik (Moscow, 1989), p. 30.

2. Lidia Ginzburg, *Chelovek za pis'mennym stolom* (Leningrad, 1989), p. 46.

3. Ibid., p. 46.

4. Ibid., p. 331.

350   Anna Akhmatova

5. Emma Gershtein, "V Zamoskvorech'e," *Literaturnoe obozrenie*, no. 7 (1985), p. 105.

6. Joseph Brodsky, "The Keening Muse," in his *Less Than One. Selected Essays* (New York, 1986), p. 35.

7. Nadezhda Mandelstam, pp. 38-39.

8. E. I. Liamkina, "Vdokhnovenie, masterstvo, trud (Zapisnye knizhki A. A. Akhmatovoi)," *Vstrechi s proshlym*, 2d ed. (Moscow, 1980), p. 412.

9. Nikolai Gumilyov, "Acmeism and the Legacy of Symbolism," in his *On Russian Poetry*, trans. David Lapeza (Ann Arbor, 1977), p. 23.

10. Nadezhda Mandelstam, pp. 38-41.

11. Ibid., p. 47.

12. Quoted in Roberta Reeder, "Mirrors and Masks: The Life and Poetic Works of Anna Akhmatova," in *Complete Poems*, p. 60. The translation has been slightly emended.

13. V. M. Zhirmunskii, *Tvorchestvo Anny Akhmatovoi* (Leningrad, 1973), rpt. in *Anna Akhmatova. Tri knigi* (Ann Arbor, 1990), p. 320.

14. Anna Nikolayevna Gumilyova (née Engelgardt, 1895-1942), Gumilyov's second wife.

15. P. N. Luknitskii, *Acumiana. Vstrechi s Annoi Akhmatovoi*, vol. 1, 1924-25 (Paris, 1991), pp. 179-80.

16. N. V. Nedobrovo, "Anna Akhmatova," trans. Alan Myers, *Russian Literature Triquarterly*, no. 9 (1974), pp. 221-36.

17. Anna Akhmatova, *Complete Poems* (Somerville, MA., 1990), vol. 1, p. 401.

18. See G. P. Struve, "Anna Akhmatova i Boris Anrep," in A. Akhmatova, *Sochineniia* (Paris, 1983), vol. 3, pp. 428-65.

19. Pavel Luknitskii, p. 158.

20. Ibid., p. 144.

21. Ibid., p. 145.

22. Anatoly Naiman, *Remembering Anna Akhmatova*, trans. Wendy Rosslyn (London, 1991), p. 72.

23. Pavel Luknitskii, p. 44.

24. V. M. Zhirmunskii, p. 464.

25. Lidia Chukovskaia, vol. 2, p. 434.

26. Nadezhda Mandelstam, p. 456.

27. Ibid., p. 456.

28. Eikhenbaum's *Anna Akhmatova. Opyt analiza*, Vinogradov's *O poezii Anny Akhmatovoi (Stilisticheskie nabroski)*, and Zhirmunsky's *Tvorchestvo Anny Akhmatovoi* are reprinted in *Anna Akhmatova. Tri knigi* (Ann Arbor, 1990).

29. Lidia Ginzburg, p. 145. The humming refers to Akhmatova's method of poetic composition.

30. Nadezhda Mandelstam, p. 221.

31. Lidia Ginzburg, p. 86.

32. G. P. Makogonenko, "Iz tret'ei epokhi vospominanii," in *Ob Anne Akhmatovoi. Stikhi. Esse. Vospominaniia. Pis'ma* (Leningrad, 1990), p. 263.

33. See O. I. Rybakova, "Grustnaia pravda," in *Ob Anne Akhmatovoi*, pp. 224-30.

34. *The Central Committee Resolution and Zhdanov's Speech on the Journals "Zvezda" and "Leningrad,"* trans. Felicity Ashbee and Irina Tidmarsh (Royal Oak, MI., 1978), pp. 52-53. I have made minor adjustments to the translation.

35. Lidia Chukovskaia, vol. 2, p. 472.

36. See Isaiah Berlin, "Anna Akhmatova: A Memoir," in *Complete Poems,* vol. 2, pp. 24-45.

37. Anatoly Naiman, p. 18. The translation has been slightly edited for this volume.

38. Ibid., p. 30.

PAGES FROM A DIARY

Pages from a Diary

1. Akhmatova is mistaken about T. S. Eliot's year of birth. The author of *The Waste Land* was born in 1888.

2. Anna Yegorovna Stogova (née Motovilova, 1817-63), Akhmatova's maternal grandmother. According to family legend, the Akhmatovs were descendants of the Tartar Khan Akhmat (d. 1481).

3. Anna Bunina (1774-1829), the first woman poet of note in Russia, was a distant relative of Akhmatova's grandfather, E. I. Stogov (1797-1880). See Barbara Heldt's *Terrible Perfection: Women in Russian Literature* (Bloomington, IN, 1987) for a brief survey of Bunina's career.

4. Marfa Boretskaya, widow of a famous burgomaster (*posadnik*), and her sons led a revolt against Tsar Ivan III in the fifteenth century. Boretskaya and her grandson were deported to Muscovite territory after the unsuccessful revolt.

5. Nikolai Karamzin (1766-1826), author of the tale "Marfa, The Burgomaster's Wife" and *History of the Russian State.*

6. Slepnyovo—the estate belonging to Akhmatova's mother-in-law, Anna Gumilyova (1854-1942).

7. Count Alexei Vronsky, from Leo Tolstoy's *Anna Karenina.*

8. The reference is to Alexander Pushkin's prose tale "The Queen of Spades" (1833). The Countess's funeral is described in chapter 5.

9. The Russian text of this short paragraph can be found in Anna Akhmatova, "Avtobiograficheskaia proza," *Literaturnoe obozrenie,* no. 5 (1989), p. 11.

10. Iya Gorenko (1894-1922) died of tuberculosis in Sevastopol.

11. In the sketch "Shukhardina's House" Akhmatova names the landlady Yevdokia and not Yelizaveta.

12. Nastasya Filippovna, the heroine of Fyodor Dostoevsky's *The Idiot* (1868).

13. Gumilyov's poem "From the Serpent's Lair."

14. Idaliya Poletika was one of Alexander Pushkin's bitterest enemies in society. See Akhmatova's essay, "Pushkin's Death."

15. This excerpt and the following were written by Akhmatova to be inserted in the memoirs of her lifelong friend, Valeria Sreznevskaya (1888-1964), which accounts for the third-person narration. Sreznevskaya undertook her memoirs at Akhmatova's insistence, but Akhmatova was not happy with the results. Sreznevskaya's reminiscences were published under the title "Daphnis and Chloe" in *Ob Anne Akhmatovoi* (Leningrad, 1990), pp. 15-25.

16. See *Selected Poems,* p. 11, for an English translation of "Song of the Last Encounter" (1911), published in Akhmatova's first book, *Evening.*

17. A quotation from Pushkin's *Eugene Onegin* (chapter 2, stanza ii).

18. *Northern Flowers* (1825-32), an elegant literary almanac founded by Baron Anton Delvig, published Pushkin, Gogol, and most of the great writers of the Golden Age.

352   Anna Akhmatova

19. Osip Senkovsky (1800-58) published his own fiction under the pen name Baron Brambeus in his journal *Library for Reading*.

20. Maria and Olga Kuzmin-Karavayeva, neighbors of the Gumilyovs in Slepnyovo.

21. Natan Altman (1889-1970) painted one of the best-known portraits of Akhmatova, which now is part of the collection of the Russian Museum in St. Petersburg. Akhmatova often stated that she was not fond of Altman's highly stylized representation.

22. The Russian actress Vera Komissarzhevskaya (1864-1910), famed for her portrayal of Nina Zarechnaya in Chekhov's *Uncle Vanya* and Nora in Ibsen's *Doll House*, founded her theater in 1904.

23. Alexander Blok (1880-1921), foremost poet of Russian Symbolism, is the subject of a separate memoir by Akhmatova, included in the present volume. In that memoir Akhmatova writes about Blok's *Notebooks* as a reliable source for dating events.

24. The composer Igor Stravinsky (1882-1971), prima ballerina Anna Pavlova (1881-1931), operatic bass Fyodor Chaliapin (1873-1938), actor and director Ivan Rostovtsev (1873-1947), composer and pianist Alexander Scriabin (1872-1915), producer and director Vsevolod Meyerhold (1874-1940), ballet impresario Serge Diaghilev (1872-1929). In this fragment devoted to the 1910s, a subject to which she will return, Akhmatova is reacting against the tendency to consider the twenties in Russia as a decade of the flowering of the arts and to ignore the achievements of the preceding decade.

25. Igor Severyanin (pseud. of Igor Lotaryov, 1887-1941) attempted to widen the parameters of Russian poetry by introducing "unpoetic" subject matter. Akhmatova speaks of him only with condescension in her prose.

26. The Congress of Vienna (1814-15) was convened after Napoleon's downfall. Though Akhmatova goes on to note that "dates on the calendar have absolutely no meaning," she has chosen to set the beginnings of the two centuries 100 years apart by her allusion to the Congress of Vienna. The notion that the twentieth century begins in 1914 is central to Akhmatova's *A Poem without a Hero*.

27. Serge Diaghilev's journal *The World of Art* (1898-1904).

28. Lev Uspensky's (1900-78) "From the Notes of an Old Petersburger" (*The Star*, no. 6, 1957).

29. This fragment was conceived as an introduction to the short narrative poem *The Way of All the Earth* (1940, *Complete Poems*, vol. 2, pp. 375-83), which in Akhmatova's draft also carries the title "The Kitezh Woman." Akhmatova considered this long poem to mark a new departure in her verse. The poem was published without the prose introduction, but this experiment of prefacing a verse narrative with a short prose foreword is realized in *A Poem without a Hero*.

30. According to V. M. Zhirmunsky, one of the preliminary titles of *The Way of All the Earth* was "Visions" or "Nocturnal Visions," although Akhmatova here uses the singular form, "Vision." See V. M. Zhirmunskii, *Tvorchestvo Anny Akhmatovoi* (Leningrad, 1973; rpt. Ann Arbor, 1990), p. 419.

31. "The Kitezh Woman" is one of the working titles for *The Way of All the Earth*. The poet Nikolai Klyuyev nicknamed Akhmatova "the woman from Kitezh." According to legend, the city of Kitezh was saved from the Tatar invasion by prayer. Akhmatova had a high regard for Rimsky-Korsakov's opera *The Tale of the Invisible City of Kitezh and the Maiden Fevronya*.

32. "Dostoevsky's Russia" ultimately took its place as the "First Elegy" in the cycle of *Northern Elegies,* where it is titled "Prehistory" and is dated 1940 Leningrad—1943 Tashkent *(Complete Poems,* vol. 2, pp. 340-45).

33. Akhmatova's reconstruction of the poem "Fifteen-year-old Hands" was published as "From the Cycle *Youth*" *(Complete Poems,* vol. 2, pp. 120-23).

34. The opening line of Akhmatova's sketch "Shukhardina's House."

35. August 14, 1946: the date of the Central Committee's Resolution condemning Akhmatova and Zoshchenko.

36. The last two lines from the opening quatrain of Akhmatova's "Let whoever wants to, relax in the south" *(Complete Poems,* vol. 2, pp. 252-53).

37. This fragment appears in *Sochineniia* (1986) in censored form. The text translated here was first published in Akhmatova, *Stranitsy prozy* (Moscow, 1989) and reprinted in the Paris weekly *Russkaya mysl'* (Russian Thought) in the January 19, 1990 issue.

38. Lev Gumilyov was arrested for a third time on November 6, 1949, and not released until 1956.

39. Akhmatova lived with her family in Gungerburg (present-day Ust-Narva), located on the Bay of Finland, during the summer of 1894.

40. The 1906 strike in Odessa.

41. Alphonse Daudet (1840-97), best known for his *Lettres de mon moulin* (1869), sketches of life in Provence. The bulk of his writings render Parisian life in a broadly naturalistic style.

42. Autobiographical prose narratives by Boris Pasternak *(Safe Conduct,* 1931) and Osip Mandelstam *(The Noise of Time,* 1925).

43. The physiological sketch, derived from the French *physiologie,* enjoyed widespread popularity in Russian literature of the 1840s. The Russian practitioners of the genre attempted a "realistic" portrayal of life, particularly of the urban lower classes, by introducing elements that had formerly been viewed as being outside of literature. See, for example, the almanac *The Physiology of Petersburg.*

44. Lines from the second stanza of Akhmatova's "Let whoever wants to, relax in the south" *(Complete Poems,* vol. 2, pp. 252-53).

45. Compare Akhmatova's poem "The Muse" (1924): "I ask her [the muse]: 'Was it you then who dictated / The script of Hell to Dante?' 'I,' she said" *(Selected Poems,* p. 87).

46. Akhmatova's "On a White Night" (1911).

47. "I came to take your place, sister" *(Complete Poems,* vol. 1, pp. 350-53).

48. A quotation from Pushkin's unfinished poem, written on the occasion of the 1836 anniversary of the Tsarskoe Selo Lycée ("Byla pora: nash prazdnik molodoi").

49. Akhmatova's "Michal" (1959-61, *Complete Poems,* vol. 1, pp. 568-71) opens with an epigraph from I Samuel 18: "And Saul's daughter Michal loved David... And Saul said, I will give him her, that she may be a snare to him."

50. Vyacheslav Ivanov (1866-1949), Russian Symbolist theorist and poet. Ivanov's home in Petersburg—The Tower—was one of the major literary salons. Akhmatova read the poem "They came and said: 'Your brother has died'" (1910). Ivanov, Akhmatova records, "made a sour face and said, 'What lush romanticism,' which was a highly dubious compliment then."

51. Irina Punina, Nikolai Punin's daughter from his first marriage to Anna Arens.

52. The Pergamum altar to Zeus, erected in 180 B.C., depicts the battle between the gods and the giants.

53. D. Di Sarra's introduction to a collection of Akhmatova's poetry in Italian translation (Firenze, 1951).

54. Mikhail Kuzmin (1875-1936), poet, prose writer, dramatist, and author of the preface to Akhmatova's *Evening*.

55. Sergei Gorodetsky (1884-1967), fellow Acmeist poet, made a much heralded debut with his book *Spring Corn* (1907), but his subsequent collections never made good the promise of that debut. Françoise Sagan (b. 1935) published her first novel at the age of nineteen.

56. The publisher S. M. Alyansky (1891-1974) headed Alkonost Publishers in the 1920s.

57. G. Lelevich's 1923 article "Anna Akhmatova (Cursory Remarks)" and V. Pertsov's "Literary Watersheds" (1925).

58. "A Sketch" appears in *Sochineniia* (1986) in censored form. The present translation is from the text published in *Russkaya mysl'* (January 19, 1990), which is a reprint from *Stranitsy prozy*.

59. Peter the Great's little log house, built in 1703, was the first structure erected in his newly-founded city.

60. Alexei, son of Peter the Great, was one of the first of a long and distinguished list of political prisoners to be incarcerated in the Peter-and-Paul Fortress.

61. Akhmatova lived in the Marble Palace with her second husband, the Assyriologist Vladimir Shileiko (1891-1930). Thirty-two varieties of marble were used in the construction of the Marble Palace, which later housed the Leningrad Branch of the Central Lenin Museum.

62. Akhmatova was a habitué of The Stray Dog, a cabaret and literary salon. See her 1913 poem "Cabaret artistique" ("We are all carousers and loose women here," *Complete Poems*, vol. 1, pp. 304-7); see also Michael Green's article on The Stray Dog's founder, Boris Pronin—"Boris Pronin, Meyerhold and Cabaret: Some Connections and Reflections," in *Russian Theatre in the Age of Modernism*, ed. Robert Russell and Andrew Barratt (New York, 1990), pp. 66-86.

Akhmatova's Note to The Stray Dog: The Formalist critic and Pushkin scholar Boris Tomashevsky (1890-1957) and his wife Irina were close friends of Akhmatova. Zoya Tomashevskaya writes of her parents' relationship with Akhmatova in "Ia—kak peterburgskaia tumba," *Ob Anne Akhmatovoi* (Leningrad, 1990), pp. 417-38.

63. The poet Vladimir Mayakovsky committed suicide on April 14, 1930. The quotation "sculpture of a horses's head" is from Mayakovsky's *Man*, and refers to an actual building on Zhukovsky Street.

64. Raskolnikov, the protagonist in Dostoevsky's *Crime and Punishment*, murders the old pawnbroker in the novel's opening pages.

65. The House on the Fontanka (Fontanny dom), Akhmatova's residence from 1926 to 1941 and 1944 to 1952. Built in the mid-eighteenth century for P. Sheremetiev, the house provides motto—Deus conservat omnia—and setting for *A Poem without a Hero*. The Akhmatova Museum in the House on the Fontanka opened its doors in 1989.

66. See Akhmatova's 1917 poem "In this church I heard the Canon / of Andrei Kritsky..." (*Complete Poems*, vol. 2, pp. 554-55).

67. Paul I, son of Catherine the Great, was murdered in the Mikhailovsky Palace in 1801.

68. Fyodor Dostoevsky endured mock execution in 1849 on Semyonov Square for his affiliation with the Petrashevsky Circle. Dostoevsky's sentence was commuted to Siberian exile.

69. Lines from Akhmatova's "I hid my heart from you" (1936, *Complete Poems*, vol. 2, pp. 82-85).

70. The last quatrain from Akhmatova's "With the rabble in a ditch" (1946, *Complete Poems*, vol. 2, pp. 626-27).

71. Kresty Prison, political prison in Leningrad, named for its cross *(krest)* formation.

72. A quotation from *Requiem* (Poem IV).

73. Akhmatova refers to the Leningrad flood of 1924.

74. A quotation from chapter 2 of *A Poem without a Hero*.

75. Nikolai Gumilyov was arrested on August 3, 1921.

Yury Annenkov (1889-1974) sketched many of the leading cultural figures of the day. See his *Portraits* (1922), which reproduces his 1921 drawing of Akhmatova.

76. See Akhmatova's tribute to the poet and translator Mikhail Lozinsky, printed in the present volume.

77. Akhmatova recalls her visit to the artist Natan Altman and how she walked on the ledge outside his seventh-floor room in *Epic Motifs* (*Complete Poems*, vol. 2, pp. 326-35).

Briefly about Myself

"Briefly about Myself" first published in 1966, is the only autobiographical statement Akhmatova herself prepared for publication. Though written in 1965, Akhmatova must still practice self-censorship and therefore does not mention the Central Committee's Resolution (1946) or the execution of her ex-husband, Nikolai Gumilyov.

1. Andrei Gorenko (1848-1915), Ahkmatova's father, had been asked to resign his commission as a result of his ties with the People's Will Party.

2. The image of Tsarskoe Selo (and Pushkin, its most illustrious resident) runs throughout Akhmatova's poetry, from the early "In Tsarskoe Selo" (1911, *Selected Poems*, pp. 7-9) to this 1961 poem "A Tsarskoe Selo Ode"(*Complete Poems*, vol. 2, pp. 310-13).

3. Akhmatova's sister Inna (1883-1906) and brother Andrei (1886-1920).

4. Alexander Pushkin (1799-1837) and Mikhail Lermontov (1814-41), Russia's two poetic geniuses of the early nineteenth century, would seem to offer more suitable material for a child than the odes of Gavriil Derzhavin (1743-1816), the great poet of the eighteenth century. Nikolai Nekrasov (1821-78) portrays "realistic" peasant life in his *Red-Nosed Frost* (1863).

5. Inna Erazmovna (née Stogova, 1852-1930), Akhmatova's mother.

6. Akhmatova divorced the Acmeist poet and theoretician Nikolai Gumilyov (1886-1921) in 1918. In 1921 Gumilyov was arrested on the false charge of conspiracy and shot. His literary rehabilitation did not take place in the USSR until 1986. Akhmatova writes of Gumilyov and his role in the Acmeist movement in her autobiographical prose fragments.

7. The American inventor, Thomas Alva Edison (1847-1931).

8. Both Akhmatova and Gumilyov considered the poet Innokenty Annensky (1856-1909) to be their mentor. Annensky's *The Cypress Chest* appeared in 1910. The entire volume has been translated by R. H. Morrison (Ann Arbor, 1982).

9. The Poets' Guild, founded in 1911 by Nikolai Gumilyov and Sergei Gorodetsky, was conceived as an opposition to Symbolism, and Vyacheslav Ivanov's Academy of Verse, in particular. The poets Osip Mandelstam (1891-1938), Mikhail Zenkevich (1891-1973), and Vladimir Narbut (1888-1944?) were members of the first Poets' Guild.

10. The notion that 1914 marked the beginning of the "real twentieth century" is fundamental to Akhmatova's *A Poem without a Hero.*

11. Mikhail Zoshchenko (1895-1958), best known for his brilliant short stories, was always highly regarded by Akhmatova. Andrei Zhdanov named both Akhmatova and Zoshchenko in his infamous attack on the Leningrad monthly *The Star.*

12. Lev Gumilyov (b. 1912) was arrested on November 6, 1949 and not released until 1956. This was his third arrest (earlier ones occurred in 1935 and 1938).

13. *A Poem without a Hero,* begun in 1940, is generally considered Akhmatova's masterpiece. Akhmatova here dates the completion of the poem in 1962, but she continued to return to this work until her death.

14. Akhmatova was awarded the Taormina Prize for Poetry in Italy in 1964.

15. In 1965 Akhmatova received an honorary doctorate from Oxford University. She stopped in Paris on her return home.

16. Akhmatova was incensed by foreign critics' conjectures that she had stopped writing poetry, when the fact was that she could not be published, particularly after the 1946 Resolution by the Central Committee, which was not rescinded until 1988.

Reviewing the Past

First published by R. D. Timenchik in Anna Akhmatova, "Avtobiograficheskaia proza," *Literaturnoe obozrenie,* no. 5 (1989), pp. 5-6. The notes to this and the following sections taken from Timenchik's publication draw heavily on his extensive commentary.

1. Georgy Alexandrov (1908-61), editor of the newspaper *Culture and Life.*

On the Occasion of the Fiftieth Anniversary of My Literary Career

First published by R. D. Timenchik in "Avtobiograficheskaia proza," p. 6.

1. Viktor Burenin (1841-1926), an opponent of modern poetry, quoted three Akhmatova poems that had appeared in *Apollon* and accompanied each with a parody *(New Time,* April 29, 1911).

2. Ivan Bunin (1870-1953), the future Nobel laureate, published his Akhmatova parody, "The Poetess," in an Odessa journal in 1918.

3. Valery Bryusov (1873-1924), Russian Symbolist poet, prose writer and critic. Marina Tsvetaeva gives her account of Bryusov's role in The Evening of

Poetesses (1920) in her "Hero of Labor (Notes about Valery Bryusov)," where she describes Bryusov's introductory remarks: "Woman. Love. Passion. From time immemorial woman has been able to sing only of love and passion.... The best example of this one-sidedness in women's literature is the well-known poetess... Akhmatova" (M. Tsvetaeva, "Geroi truda," *Izbrannaia proza v dvukh tomakh* [New York, 1979], vol. 1, pp. 202-3).

4. Adalis (pseudonym of Adelina Efron, 1900-69) participated in The Evening of Poetesses.

5. Kornei Chukovsky's article "Akhmatova and Mayakovsky" (1921).

6. D. N. Zhuravlev, *Zhizn'. Iskusstvo. Vstrechi* (Moscow, 1985), p. 324.

7. The prose writers Boris Pilnyak and Yevgeny Zamyatin were severely attacked in the press for publishing their works abroad. The two works in question, Pilnyak's "Mahogany" and Zamyatin's *We*, are both included in *Russian Literature of the Twenties*, ed. C. Proffer, et al. (Ann Arbor, 1987); see also Zamyatin's letter to Stalin (June 1931) printed in the same anthology.

8. *Willow* is a section title in *From Six Books*.

9. Ivan Sergiyevsky (1905-54), literary critic.

10. Alexander Fadeyev (1901-56), best known for his novel *The Rout*, held influential positions in the literary bureaucracy (he headed the Writers' Union from 1946 to 1954) and criticized Akhmatova in the spirit of Zhdanov.

11. Alexander Yegolin died on May 6, 1959. During the 1940s Yegolin worked in the Central Committee.

12. The only review of *Poems* (1958) was written by Lev Ozerov and printed in *Literaturnaia gazeta* (June 23, 1959), a month after Akhmatova wrote this sketch.

13. A quotation from Pushkin's *Eugene Onegin*, chapter 10.

14. Renato Poggioli, *Il fiore del verso russo* (Torino, 1949) and Akhmatova, *Poésies*, trad. S. Lafitte (Paris, 1959).

15. See Akhmatova's "Reminiscences of Alexander Blok" in this volume.

16. Leonid Strakhovsky's pseudonym was Leonid Chatsky, not Shatsky. Strakhovsky is the author of *Craftsmen of the Word. Three Poets of Modern Russia. Gumilyov. Akhmatova. Mandelstam* (Cambridge, 1949).

17. The poet Georgy Ivanov (1894-1958), member of Gumilyov's Poets' Guild, emigrated to Paris in 1922 with his wife, poetess Irina Odoyevtseva (1901-90). Ivanov and his book of memoirs *Petersburg Winters* (1928) are dealt with severely and in more detail in Akhmatova's "On the History of Acmeism."

18. William E. Harkins, *Dictionary of Russian Literature* (New York, 1956).

19. Seghers, a publishing house in Paris.

20. Natalya Kind and Ivan Rozhansky.

21. Robert Payne, *Les trois mondes de Boris Pasternak* (Paris, 1963), p. 91, a translation of his *The Three Worlds of Boris Pasternak* (1961).

22. This note and the following appear in V. A. Chernykh's publication of Akhmatova, "Iz dnevnikovykh zapisei," *Literaturnoe obozrenie*, no. 5 (1989), p. 14.

23. N. Osinsky and A. Kollontai, prominent Bolsheviks, published positive remarks regarding Akhmatova's work.

Random Notes

Published by R. D. Timenchik in "Avtobiograficheskaia proza," pp. 6-7.

1. Georgy Chulkov (1879-1939) proposed to reconcile personal freedom and a communal way of life in his *On Mystical Anarchism* (1906).
2. Blok describes this gathering in his diary for October 20, 1911.
3. See Alexander Blok's 1910 essay "On the Contemporary State of Russian Symbolism," *Sobranie sochinenii v vos'mi tomakh* (Moscow, 1962), vol. 5, pp. 425-36.
4. Nikolai Gumilyov's *Foreign Skies* appeared in 1912.
5. Alexander Blok, *Sobranie sochinenii*, vol. 7, p. 140.
6. The poem "Terror, fingering things in the dark" (*Complete Poems*, vol. 2, pp. 584-85).
7. *Selected Poems*, pp. 75-76.
8. Akhmatova moved into the Marble Palace to live with Vladimir Shileiko in 1918. Their room had a view of the Field of Mars.

On the History of Acmeism

Published by R. D. Timenchik in "Avtobiograficheskaia proza," pp. 7-8.

1. Viktor Zhirmunsky's well-known essay "Symbolism's Successors" is translated by Stanley Rabinowitz in his *The Noise of Change: Russian Literature and the Critics* (Ann Arbor, 1986), pp. 218-47.
2. Gleb Struve's introduction to Gumilev, *Sobranie sochinenii*, vol. 1 (Washington, D.C., 1962).
3. It is unclear whose letter Akhmatova has in mind.
4. Bryusov's article "New Trends in Russian Poetry. Acmeism" appeared in *Russian Thought* (1913).
5. Andrei Bely (1880-1934), Symbolist poet and author of *Petersburg*, one of the great novels of the twentieth century, wrote four volumes of "memoirs" that are not factually reliable. The incident Akhmatova refers to is from *The Beginning of the Century* (1933).
6. Bely's collection of essays, *Symbolism* (1910).
7. For Gorodetsky's letters to Gumilyov and the latter's reply, see *Izvestiia AN SSSR, seriia lit. i iaz.*, no. 1 (1987), pp. 70-71. E. G. Gershtein provides the most balanced account of Sergei Rudakov and the fate of the archive in her *Novoe o Mandel'shtame* (Paris, 1986).
8. The second Poets' Guild met during the period 1916-17; the third guild was founded in 1917.
9. Osip Mandelstam, "The Morning of Acmeism," *Complete Critical Prose and Letters*, ed. Jane Gary Harris (Ann Arbor, 1979), pp. 61-65.
10. A. Blok, "Svirel' zapela na mostu," *Sobranie sochinenii*, vol. 3, p. 158.
11. The peasant poet Nikolai Klyuyev (1884-1937) published his first collection, *The Chimes of the Pines*, in 1912, accompanied by Valery Bryusov's preface. Gumilyov's review of that collection begins: "This winter brought poetry lovers an unexpected and precious gift..." (Gumilev, *On Russian Poetry*, trans. David Lapeza [Ann Arbor, 1977], p. 100).
12. The journalist Ivan Radetsky.
13. Akhmatova's reading, given in the fall of 1921.

14. The early poem, "The Song of the Last Encounter," opens:

> How past mending my heart was frozen,
> Yet the tread of my feet was light.
> For my left I found I had chosen,
> The glove that belonged on the right.
> *(Selected Poems, p. 11)*

15. Lines from Akhmatova's "All is looted, betrayed, past retrieving" *(Selected Poems,* p. 69).

16. An excerpt from Alexander Surkov's Afterword reads: "Raised in the rarified atmosphere of a family from the gentry class, and connected by a thousand threads to the gentry culture that was ruthlessly destroyed by the Revolution, Akhmatova was unable to understand the new Russia that was coming into being during those early years" (Afterword to Akhmatova, *Stikhotvoreniia* [Moscow, 1961], p. 298).

17. Evidently a slip of the pen—it should probably read 1922.

18. V. V. Vinogradov, *O poezii Anny Akhmatovoi. Stilisticheskie nabroski* (Leningrad, 1925); B. Eikhenbaum, *Anna Akhmatova. Opyt analiza* (Leningrad, 1923); both studies are reprinted in *Anna Akhmatova. Tri knigi* (Ann Arbor, 1990).

19. "Fragments from *The Russian Trianon*" *(Selected Poems,* p. 118, *Complete Poems,* vol. 2, pp. 334-37).

20. Sergei Makovsky (1877-1962), poet and editor of *Apollon,* emigrated to Paris in the 1920s. Author of two volumes of memoirs: *Portrety sovremennikov* (1955) and *Na Parnase serebrianogo veka* (1962).

21. Vera Nevedomskaya, a neighbor of the Gumilyovs in Slepnyovo. Dmitry Kardovsky (1822-1943), artist and teacher.

22. Nikolai Gumilyov dedicated his *Quiver* to Tatyana Adamovich, sister of the poet Georgy Adamovich.

23. The literary critic Roman Samarin (1911-74) and the poet Georgy Shengeli (1894-1956).

24. In the drafts of her Pushkin essay, "Alexandrina," Akhmatova considers prefacing the work with the following epigraph:

> *From a conversation overheard:*
> *First:* "What a resemblance there is between slander and truth."
> *Second:* "Yes, the only thing that doesn't resemble truth is truth itself."

(Quoted in Lidia Chukovskaia, *Zapiski ob Anne Akhmatovoi* [Paris, 1980], vol. 2, p. 389.)

25. Sergei Shtein (1882-1955) and Akhmatova's sister Inna Gorenko (1885-1906) were wed in 1904.

26. Akhmatova refers to the manuscript of Alexei Orlov, son of a teacher in Tsarskoe Selo, which uncovers factual errors in Rozhdestvensky's *Pages from a Life.*

27. E. Gollerbakh (1895-1942), art historian and author of *The City of Muses.*

28. The poet Nikolai Otsup (1894-1958), born in Tsarskoe Selo, emigrated in 1922. Ostup defended his dissertation on Gumilyov. His *Literary Sketches* (1961) also contains an essay on Gumilyov.

29. Valery Bryusov's infamous one-line poem.

30. *Let's Be Like the Sun* is the title of Konstantin Balmont's (1867-1942) best-known collection of verse (1903).

31. Nikolai Gumilev, *Selected Works* (Paris, 1959).

Nikolai Gumilyov and Acmeism

This piece and the remainder of the autobiographical sketches that are translated in this volume were culled from Akhmatova's notebooks by V. A. Chernykh—"Iz dnevnikovykh zapisei," *Literaturnoe obozrenie*, no. 5 (1989), pp. 11-17. Akhmatova's archive holds twenty-one notebooks or journals for the period 1956-66, but only a fraction of these has been published. The commentary to the translation draws heavily on Chernykh's notes, which I gratefully acknowledge.

1. *Complete Poems*, vol. 1, pp. 282-83.

2. There is a break in the text.

3. N. Gumilyov: "Akhmatova has caught almost the entire range of female experience and every contemporary poetess must pass through her work in order to find herself" (review of *Arion*, published in *The Life of Art*, 1918).

4. N. Gumilyov: "An immeasurable gulf separates him [Ivanov] from the poets of line and color, Pushkin or Bryusov, Lermontov or Blok. Their poetry is a lake which reflects the sky, the poetry of Vyacheslav Ivanov is the sky reflected in a lake" (Gumilev, *On Russian Poetry*, p. 89).

1910

1. V. Pyast, *Meetings* (Moscow, 1929).

2. *Complete Poems*, vol. 1, pp. 280-81; vol. 2, pp. 496-97.

3. Zinaida Gippius (or Hippius, 1869-1945), poet and by several accounts a thoroughly unpleasant woman.

4. The translator Alexandra Chebotaryevskaya (1869-1925).

5. Nikolai Berdyayev (1874-1948), religious philosopher.

6. Maria Zamyatina (1865-1919), Ivanov's housekeeper and secretary.

7. Ivanov married his stepdaughter Vera (1890-1920) after the death of his wife in 1907.

8. Mikhail Kuzmin, at first a frequent visitor to Ivanov's Tower, became for all practical purposes a member of the family. One of the versions of their eventual rift is that Ivanov's stepdaughter Vera was pregnant (with Ivanov's child) and that Ivanov asked Kuzmin to marry her to avoid scandal. The homosexual Kuzmin refused. See John E. Malmstad's "Mixail Kuzmin. A Chronicle of His Life and Times," in M. A. Kuzmin, *Sobranie stikhov* (Munich, 1977), vol. 3. Kuzmin's "Pokoinitsa v dome" was first published in *Russkaia mysl'* (1913) and is available in his *Proza*, ed. Vladimir Markov and Friedrich Scholz (Berkeley, 1985), vol. 4, pp. 5-110.

Clearing up a Misunderstanding

1. The American Slavist Sam Driver, author of a dissertation on Akhmatova, "The Poetry of Anna Akhmatova" (Columbia University, 1967) and *Anna Akhmatova* (New York, 1972).

Rosary

1. N. V. Nedobrovo's article "Anna Akhmatova," *Russian Thought*, no. 7 (1915), pp. 50-68; rpt. Akhmatova, *Sochineniia* (Paris, 1983), vol. 3, pp. 473-95. Akhmatova always considered Nedobrovo's essay to be one of the best studies of her poetry.
2. S. Bobrov's article was published in *Sovremennik* (1914); D. Talnikov, "A. Akhmatova. *Chetki,*" *Sovremennyi mir*, no. 10 (1914), pp. 208-11.
3. *Complete Poems*, vol. 1, pp. 304-7. The poem originally appeared under the title "Cabaret artistique."
4. Akhmatova, *Stikhi* (Berlin: Efron, 1922).
5. Dmitry Maximov (1904-87), eminent Blok scholar.
6. B. Mathesius. Afterword to A. Achmatova's *Bilé hejno* (Prague, 1947).
7. Fyodor Sologub (1863-1927), author of *The Petty Demon*.
8. The prose writer and critic Dmitry Merezhkovsky and his wife Zinaida Gippius.
9. The January 1913 issue of *Apollon* carried two Acmeist manifestoes: (1) N. Gumilyov, "Acmeism and the Precepts of Symbolism"; (2) S. Gorodetsky, "Some Currents in Contemporary Russian Poetry."
10. *The Hyperborean* carried the following notice: "The editors believe it is essential to announce that *The Hyperborean* is not an organ of the Poets' Guild, nor is it a journal of the Acmeist poets" (*Giperborei*, no. 5).
11. B. Lavrenev, "Zamerzaiushchii Parnas," *Zhatva*, no. 4 (1913); A. Red'ko, "U podnozhiia afrikanskogo idola," *Russkoe bogatstvo*, no. 6-7 (1913); A. Blok, "Bez bozhestva, bes vdokhnoven'ia," *Sobranie sochinenii*, vol. 6.
12. V. F. Khodasevich, "Anna Akhmatova. *Chetki,*" *Sobranie sochinenii*, ed. Robert Hughes and John Malmstad (Ann Arbor, 1990), vol. 2, p. 144.
13. Leonid Kanegisser (1898-1918), poet and reviewer of *Rosary* (*Severnye zapiski*, May 1914).
14. German Lopatin (1845-1918), a member of the People's Will, had been imprisoned from 1884 to 1905.
15. Fyodor Stepun (1884-1965), philosopher and cultural historian.

White Flock

1. Akhmatova, *Izbrannye stikhotvoreniia* (New York, 1952).
2. Akhmatova, *Stikhotvoreniia. 1909-1960* (Moscow, 1961).
3. "I have a certain smile" from *Rosary* (*Complete Poems*, vol. 1, pp. 316-17).

Anno Domini

1. "New Year's Ballad" (1923, *Complete Poems*, vol. 1, pp. 616-617).
2. "Lot's Wife" (1924, *Selected Poems*, pp. 81-82).

On *Petersburg Winters*

1. *Selected Poems*, p. 69.
2. Angelo Maria Ripellino, Introduction to *Poesia russa del Novecento* (Parma, 1954).
3. G. Chulkov, *Nashi sputniki* (Moscow, 1922).
4. Yu. Aikhenval'd, *Poety i poetessy* (Moscow, 1922).
5. Boris Pasternak's "To Anna Akhmatova" appeared in *Krasnaia nov'* (1929).
6. E. Lo Gatto, *Storia della letteratura russa contemporanea* (Milan, 1958).
7. See Zoya Tomashevskaya, "Ia kak peterburgskaia tumba," *Ob Anne Akhmatovoi* (Leningrad, 1990), pp. 417-38.

Pseudo-Memoirs

1. Akhmatova lived on Krasnaya Konnitsa (no. 4, apt. 3) from 1952 to 1961.
2. Nikolai Punin's granddaughter, Anna Kaminskaya.
3. "Seaside Sonnet," which originally was published as "Summer Sonnet," and "Music," were the first poems that appeared after a lengthy break (*Literatura i zhizn'*, April 5, 1959; *Complete Poems*, vol. 2, pp. 278-81).

Excerpts from the Last Diary Entries

1. Akhmatova had been hospitalized since November 1965.
2. Irina Punina.
3. The poet Maria Petrovykh (1908-79).
4. Anatoly Naiman, poet and author of a memoir about Akhmatova: *Rasskazy o Anne Akhmatovoi* (Moscow, 1989). Published in English as: *Remembering Anna Akhmatova*, trans. Wendy Rosslyn (London, 1991).
5. This is one of several surviving plans for Akhmatova's book of prose. L. A. Mandrykina discusses Akhmatova's various plans in her "Nenapisannaia kniga. Listki iz dnevnika... A. A. Akhmatovoi," *Knigi. Arkhivy. Avtografy...* (Moscow, 1973), pp. 57-76.

The plan translated here divides the book into verses addressed to specific individuals (Sreznevskaya, Pasternak, Bulgakov, Tsvetaeva, and Annensky) and prose reminiscences.

6. The British scholar Amanda Haight (1939-89) wrote her doctoral dissertation on Akhmatova, which laid the ground for her *Anna Akhmatova: A Poetic Pilgrimage* (New York & London, 1976).
7. Yulia Zhivova, editor at Goslitizdat.
8. Akhmatova was hospitalized in Leningrad from October 1961 to January 1962.
9. "Native Land" carries the date and place of composition: "1961. Leningrad. The Hospital in the Harbor." (*Complete Poems*, vol. 2, pp. 312-15.)

10. On orders from Peter the Great, the diplomat Pyotr Tolstoy (1645-1729) secured the return of the Tsarevich from Italy to Russia in January 1718. The Tsarevich was sentenced to death in June of that same year.

11. A quotation from Alexander Pushkin's "Dorozhnye zhaloby."

12. Tsar Alexei Mikhailovich reigned from 1645 to 1676.

13. Anna Kaminskaya.

14. The art critic, Tatyana Aizenman.

15. Dmitry Shostakovich.

16. Akhmatova's television appearance with her reminiscences of Lozinsky and Blok were broadcast in 1965.

17. Akhmatova is probably referring to Anatoly Naiman, who has a poem titled "Disappearance."

18. The poet and translator Semyon Lipkin (b. 1911), was always singled out by Akhmatova as one of the promising poets of the younger generation (L. Chukovskaia, *Zapiski ob Anne Akhmatovoi*, vol. 2, pp. 587-88).

19. Yevgeny Yevtushenko (b. 1933), one of the most popular poets of the 1960s, often criticized for the theatricality of his verse, which some believe masks the poetry's intrinsic barrenness.

20. The idiosyncratic and experimental prose writer Alexei Remizov (1877-1957).

21. B. Yakovlev's notes on Lenin's last letters were published in the same issue of *Youth* as Yevtushenko's poems. Lenin wrote that Stalin should be removed from power. Zinoviev and Kamenev were executed for treason in 1936.

22. February 16th was Akhmatova's nameday; her patron saint was the prophetess Anna (see Luke 2).

23. Mikhail Ivanovich Budyko (b. 1920), member of the Academy of Sciences, became acquainted with Akhmatova in 1962. His fifteen meetings with Akhmatova form the basis of Budyko's "Rasskazy Akhmatovoi," *Ob Anne Akhmatovoi*, pp. 461-506.

24. The opera by Modest Mussorgsky (1839-91).

25. The poet Arseny Tarkovsky. Akhmatova wrote a favorable review of Tarkovsky's poetry.

26. The translator, Nika Glen.

27. Alain Robbe-Grillet's screenplay.

28. Fragments survive from "Prologue," the second act of Akhmatova's play *Enuma Elish (Complete Poems*, vol. 2, pp. 384-93).

29. A Lenten prayer.

30. Nina Olshevskaya.

31. Akhmatova's inexact rendering of Robbe-Grillet's title.

32. The Dead Sea Scrolls found at Qumran.

33. Theodor Mommsen (1817-1903), German historian and author of *History of Rome,* was awarded the Nobel Prize for Literature in 1902.

MY HALF CENTURY

Alexander Blok

In her memoir of Alexander Blok (1880-1921), Akhmatova limits her sketch to recording her infrequent meetings with the most celebrated poet of the preceding generation. Akhmatova's memoir was written for a Leningrad television broadcast that aired on October 12, 1965. Two studies that provide a good introduction to Blok's life and work are Konstantin Mochulsky, *Aleksandr Blok*, trans. Doris V. Johnson (Detroit, 1983) and Avril Pyman, *The Life of Alexander Blok* (New York, 1979-80), 2 vols. V. N. Toporov addresses the problem of the Blok-Akhmatova verse "dialogue" in his *Akhmatova i Blok. K probleme postroeniia poeticheskogo dialoga: "blokovskii" tekst Akhmatovoi* (Berkeley, 1981).

1. Emile Verhaeren (1855-1916), Belgian poet, dramatist and critic.

2. The Bestuzhev Institute for Women was founded in 1878 by Konstantin Bestuzhev-Ryumin.

3. Ariadna Tyrkova (pseud. of A. Vergezhsky, 1869-1962), writer and social activist.

4. The society was founded in 1909 by Vyacheslav Ivanov, Innokenty Annensky and Sergei Makovsky. The meetings were held in the editorial offices of *Apollon*.

5. Akhmatova's 1913 poem "We are all carousers here..." (*Complete Poems*, vol. 1, pp. 305-7).

6. A line from the poem mentioned above in note 5.

7. A quotation from Blok's "The Unknown Lady" (1906).

8. Akhmatova visited Blok on December 15, 1913.

9. Akhmatova showed the television audience a copy of Blok's *Verses on a Beautiful Lady* (1904).

10. Blok's "To Anna Akhmatova" is dated December 10, 1913. The following translation by Barbara Heldt was published in *The Silver Age of Russian Culture*, edited by Carl & Ellendea Proffer (Ann Arbor, 1975), p. 88:

> "Beauty is frightening," they will tell you—
> Lazily you will arrange
> A Spanish shawl on your shoulders,
> A red rose in your hair.
>
> "Beauty is simple," they will tell you—
> Clumsily with a motley shawl
> You will cover a child up,
> A red rose on the floor.
>
> But, distractedly heeding
> All the words sounding around you,
> Sadly lost in thought
> You will say about yourself:
>
> "I am neither frightening nor simple;
> I am not so frightening, that I would simply
> Kill; I am not so simple
> That I do not know how frightening life is."

11. A reference to Lyubov Delmas, whom Blok first saw performing the lead in Bizet's *Carmen* in October 1913. Delmas inspired Blok's *Carmen* cycle, as well as a number of other poems during the period 1914-20.

12. The poet Benedikt Lifshits (1887-1939).

13. A. Blok, *Zapisnye knizhki* (Moscow, 1965), p. 234.

14. Blok's entry for December 13, 1914. Ibid., p. 250.

15. The last piece from Akhmatova's "Three Poems," a cycle dedicated to Blok. The poem Akhmatova cites here has two obvious references to Blok's poetry. The first line alludes to one of Blok's best-known poems—"Night, the street, the street lamp, the drugstore" (1912)—and the reference "To Pushkin House" recalls Blok's 1921 poem of the same title.

Mikhail Lozinsky

Mikhail Lozinsky (1886-1955), a founding member of the Poets' Guild, is regarded as one of the foremost translators of the Soviet period. Akhmatova's tribute to Lozinsky was broadcast on Leningrad television in May 1965 during a program devoted to his memory.

1. Lozinsky's translation of Dante's work was awarded a State Prize in 1946.

2. Lozinsky translated Cervantes and Lope de Vega's *La viuda valenciana* (The Widow of Valencia), to which Akhmatova makes reference below.

3. The early Romantic poet Vasily Zhukovsky (1783-1852) introduced new tendencies in European literature through his adaptations of Thomas Gray, Byron, and many others. Zhukovsky's major work was his translation of *The Odyssey*.

4. The poem dedicated to Lozinsky opens Akhmatova's *Reed* and carries the title "Inscription on a Book."

Amedeo Modigliani

Amedeo Modigliani (1884-1920), Italian painter, sculptor, and leading figure among the French artists of the Left Bank. Between 1910 and 1914 he almost abandoned painting in favor of sculpture. A prolific sketcher, his drawings attracted the attention of Brancusi who encouraged him to sculpt heads in stone. Their elongated form and simple lines reflected the influence of African art, and when financial difficulties forced him to resume painting, these features became the distinctive trademark of his portraits. He is best remembered for his nudes and portraits of women, which are depicted with remarkable sympathy and personal effect. His untimely death was hastened by his addiction to drugs and alcohol, in spite of the loving care of his wife Jeanne Hebuterne.

Modigliani's portrait of Akhmatova was always accorded pride of place in her several residences.

1. Beatrice Hastings, an Englishwoman and poetess, lived with Modigliani from 1914 to 1916 and posed for several paintings. Her expression *perle et pourceau* was quoted in a monograph by Jacques Lipchitz, *Amedeo Modigliani* (Paris, 1954).

2. A reference to Isaiah Berlin, who visited Akhmatova in November 1945 while serving in the British diplomatic service in Moscow.

3. *Apollon*, a prestigious Russian monthly journal of the arts published from 1909-17 in Petersburg.

4. *The World of Art* (1898-1904), a leading art journal published in Petersburg and devoted to the promotion of modernism in Russian intellectual circles.

5. Alexander Tyshler (b. 1898), prominent Soviet stage designer and artist who met Akhmatova and made a series of drawings of her in Tashkent in 1943.

6. Alexandra Ekster (1882-1949), artist and theater designer noted for her structurally innovative cubist sets and colorful costumes. She emigrated to Paris in the 1920s.

7. Akhmatova met the artist Boris Anrep, with whom she had a love affair, in 1916. A significant portion of her collection *White Flock* is dedicated to him. After 1917 she heard of him only two or three times and did not see him again until 1965.

8. Natan Altman's painting of Akhmatova was reproduced in *Apollon* in 1916.

9. Akhmatova and Nikolai Gumilyov officially separated in 1918.

10. *Les chants de Maldoror* (1868, reprinted in 1890), by the French poet Isidore Ducasse (1846-70) who wrote under the pseudonym Comte de Lautréamont. It is a book of prose fragments depicting in hallucinatory fashion the impressions of Maldoror, a demonic figure who hates both God and mankind. The book is filled with vivid imagery and nightmarish episodes that are, at times, erotic and malicious. Because of these qualities Lautréamont was proclaimed a precursor of the Surrealists.

11. The acronym of the New Economic Policy instigated by Lenin in 1921.

12. Alexander Tikhonov (1880-1956), writer and journalist who collaborated with Gorky in organizing and publishing proletarian writers. After the Revolution he became a prominent editor and publisher.

13. *From Montmartre to the Latin Quarter* by Francis Carco (1886-1958). Carco wrote verses and novels of bohemian life in Montmartre.

14. *Montparnasse 19* (1958, director Jacques Baker). The scenario by Max Ophuls and Henri Janson was based on Michel Georges-Michel's novel *Montparnassiens*. Modigliani was played by Gérard Philippe. This is the "popular novel" that Akhmatova mentions.

Mandelstam

Although Akhmatova attached particular importance to her memoir of Mandelstam, there is no definitive text of this work. Early publications of the memoir include the variant published in *Vozdushnye puti* (New York), no. 4 (1965), pp. 23-45, and *Sochineniia*, vol. 2 (Paris, 1968). The text translated here is from the edition compiled by Vitaly Vilenkin, a friend of Akhmatova's and the author of a book on her life and works, *V sto pervom zerkale* (Moscow, 1987). Other recent reconstructions include L. A. Mandrykina's text, published in *Zvezda*, no. 6 (1989), pp. 20-34, commentary by L. A. Il'iunina and Ts. T. Snegovskaia, pp. 34-38; and *Sochineniia*, edited by M. M. Kralin (vol. 2, Moscow, 1990), pp. 151-74.

Vilenkin's edition of "Osip Mandelstam" appeared in *Vosprosy literatury*, no. 2 (1989), pp. 178-217. The introduction and commentary below are by Vilenkin unless otherwise noted. They have been abridged and adapted for the purposes of this volume. I have also benefitted from the commentary done by Il'iunina, Snegovskaia, and Kralin. [Ed.]

Anna Akhmatova's memoir of Osip Mandelstam is part of a book conceived in 1957 or perhaps earlier. Judging from sketches of an outline that survive in her archives, it was to have included much of what she wrote in prose about herself, her contemporaries, her city, Tsarskoe Selo, the fate of her books, Acmeism, and lyric poetry. Under the rubric "Marginalia" she planned to include ideas, riddles, discoveries, and polemical comments that had arisen over the course of many years from her study of the works of Shakespeare, Dostoevsky, Leo Tolstoy, Pushkin, and Gogol. The drafts of the outlines for the book deal both with finished pieces and works-in-progress, as well as unformulated ideas. These short outlines and individual notes that pertain to them show clearly the free compositional structure and the intentional fragmentary quality of even the more extended and developed autobiographical and memoir sections. ("Any attempt to write connected memoirs is a falsification. No human memory is constructed to remember everything in order." And again: "It doesn't matter at all where you begin—the middle, the end, or the beginning.") The outlines attest that this book was to be written in the first person in order to bring the reader into direct contact with the author's personality, without any mediating agent. The term "novella" here and there in her notes is somewhat arbitrary and does not designate the genre of the work, but rather Akhmatova's desire to be free of such terms as article, essay, etc. The subtitle of the first section, "Pro Domo Mea," in essence refers to the entire book.

Akhmatova records the date in the first surviving draft of the outline: 1957, Komarovo. The chapter about Mandelstam follows her autobiography and is included in the section "People's Fates." In the last known outline, entitled "Prose" (in my opinion, Mandrykina dates it correctly: 1962-63), this chapter precedes the autobiography. The years 1957-63 are precisely the period during which Akhmatova's memoir of Mandelstam was written and revised.

It is clear that Akhmatova conceived this chapter and wrote it as part of the book about herself (one of the drafts is entitled "Chapter" with a question mark), her life and literary fortunes, and several fates typical of her generation, primarily of artists in the broad sense of the word. She reserved the right to digress freely into totally different areas of thought, testimony, characterization, and evaluation (the so-called "Marginalia" are comprised of facts, literary discoveries, polemics, etc.). It is very important to keep in mind that Akhmatova did not write her memoir of Mandelstam as an independent biographical essay or memoir, but precisely as a "chapter" closely connected with the story of her own life and in the context of artists' fates—hers and those of her generation. This defines both the essence and the unusual tone, as well as the "extra-generic" nature of what she wrote about the man who was both her friend and a poet. In particular, it sheds light on the essential quality of a number of digressions that by no means can be termed lyrical. I do not think it accidental that the author included them here in the salmagundi entitled "Pages from a Diary." (Akhmatova apparently never kept a regular diary.) This is emphasized both by the final title that she chose and by the opening that begins mid-sentence, as well as by the date at the upper right hand corner (July 28, 1957)—a date that makes no sense from the diaristic point of view for such a substantial manuscript, which she actually worked on during the course of several years. Moreover, the designation "Pages from a Diary" appears more and more frequently in the manuscripts of

Akhmatova's later years and is always somewhat enigmatic: more than once it provides a refuge or a "cover" for something she wanted to say that was very important, complex, or especially cherished, "so that all this remains," as she would sometimes say about these pages.

There is no final draft of Akhmatova's memoir of Mandelstam in the Saltykov-Shchedrin State Public Library (St. Petersburg). According to the information we have, there is none in TsGALI SSSR (Moscow). We may assume that a definitive manuscript never existed. [Vilenkin here discusses textological matters of interest only to specialists.—Ed.]

V. Vilenkin

1. In April 1957 Akhmatova was informed that she had been appointed to the commission to oversee Mandelstam's literary estate, which undoubtedly prompted her to return to her memoir of Mandelstam. [Il'iunina]

2. Akhmatova's friend, the poet and translator Mikhail Lozinsky (1886-1955). See her memoir of Lozinsky in the present volume. [Ed.]

3. Mandelstam's autobiographical book of prose *The Noise of Time* (1925) opens with impressions from the 1890s. The work is ably translated by Clarence Brown in *The Prose of Osip Mandelstam*, 2d. ed. (Princeton, 1967). [Ed.]

4. See Mandelstam's eloquent tribute, "Conversation about Dante," not published in the USSR until 1967. The work is translated in Mandelstam's *Complete Critical Prose and Letters*, edited by Jane Gary Harris (Ann Arbor, 1979), pp. 397-442. [Ed.]

5. Nadezhda Mandelstam (née Khazin, 1901-80), author of *Hope Against Hope* and *Hope Abandoned*, essential reading on Mandelstam's life and works and twentieth-century Russian literature in general. [Ed.]

6. In one of the drafts, Akhmatova writes: "O. E. [Mandelstam] was unfair about Blok. He always criticized him for his 'prettiness' [krasivost']."

7. Akhmatova's note: "Time proved him right. (See Pasternak's 'Autobiography,' where he writes that at one time he did not adequately appreciate four poets: Gumilyov, Bagritsky, Khlebnikov, and Mandelstam.)"

8. This sentence is continued in one of the drafts: "'I am anti-Tsvetaeva,' perhaps because he did not know the émigré Tsvetaeva."

9. It's worth recalling, for example, the ending of Mandelstam's "Stanzas" (1935), here rendered by Clarence Brown and W. S. Merwin in their translation of Mandelstam's *Selected Poems* (New York, 1974), p. 80:

When my string's tuned tight as Igor's Song,
when I get my breath back, you can hear
in my voice the earth, my last weapon,
the dry dampness of black earth.

10. Several lines from Akhmatova's drafts may be inserted here:

(A.) "Mandelstam was rather deaf to praise, but every cavil upset him very much."

(B.) "In my presence he called his poem about a remnant of a Scottish blanket a key to his work" (the 1931 poem "Midnight in Moscow. The Buddhist summer is luxurious").

(C.) "Mandelstam used to say, 'I am a meaning person [smyslovik].'"

(D.) "He used to say, 'I don't have rhymes—Aseyev does.'"

(E.) "All three of us (Pasternak, Mandelstam, and myself) had long periods when we didn't write poetry. Boris had one between *Second Birth* and the nine poems from *On Early Trains*, which he read to me in June 1941. Mandelstam had it between 'Music at the Train Station' and.... And I had one between 1924 and 1936 ('To the Artist' and the 1936 cycle, maybe 'The Poet'). And God only knows what it means."

Akhmatova is mistaken in her attribution of Mandelstam's period of temporary "silence." There was no prolonged break in his writing after "Music at the Train Station."

11. R. D. Timenchik has established that the two lines Akhmatova quotes from memory (there are mistakes) belong to the minor poet Tikhon Churilin ("November," published in 1916). [Ed.]

12. This episode is developed in the draft manuscript: "Mandelstam told me that he had been at Annensky's and that the latter (strange as it may seem) advised him to take up translation. Osip couldn't help himself and said that he had translated a poem...." After which Akhmatova cites the same line and the translation.

13. The room Nikolai Gumilyov (1886-1921) rented on Tuchkov Lane. Tsarskoe Selo was the permanent residence of Gumilyov and Akhmatova (Malaya Street, no. 63).

14. Vyacheslav Ivanov (1866-1949) reigned supreme at his literary salon, nicknamed The Tower. [Ed.]

15. The historical novelist Count Alexei Tolstoy (1883-1945), best known for his epic *The Road to Calvary*. [Ed.]

16. Akhmatova is referring to the green cover of Mandelstam's collection *Stone* (St. Petersburg, 1913).

17. One draft reads: "...S. Makovsky published us virtually at the same time in *Apollon*. Makovsky said to me: 'He's more daring than you.' That was our beginning (1911)."

18. The unreliability of anything penned by the poet Georgy Ivanov (1894-1958) is a constant motif in Akhmatova's autobiographical prose. Here she is referring to Ivanov's "The Poets," published in Paris in 1956. [Ed.]

19. Georgy Ivanov writes that Akhmatova's friend, the poet and critic Nikolai Nedobrovo, was "an infrequent guest at the Tuchkov apartment." [Ed.]

20. In his memoirs, Vladimir Pyast (1886-1940) confidently attributes this epigram on Mikhail Lozinsky to Mandelstam and quotes the text:

Leonid's son was sparing, bidding his guest farewell.
Rarely did he thrust a fifty-kopeck piece or ruble into his hand;
If the guest were modest and requested a mere thirty kopecks,
Leonid's son, triumphant, handed it right over...

"I've probably forgotten how the final pentameter went exactly," Pyast adds parenthetically (*Vstrechi*, Moscow, 1921, p. 21).

21. Vladimir Shileiko (1891-1930), Orientalist, poet, translator, and Akhmatova's second husband. [Ed.]

22. The poet and translator Mikhail Zenkevich (1891-1969) was a member of the original Poets' Guild. [Ed.]

23. Irina Odoyevtseva explains the origin of Goldtooth very simply in her memoir *On the Banks of the Neva*: "O.E. had a gold cap on a front tooth, which was a source of friendly jokes."

In his *Meetings*, V. Pyast attributes the epigram to Lozinsky and cites the complete text, though he omits his own surname:

> He won't give a copper for his life,
> He who saw gathering at the club
> Icy Blok and ugly [Pyast]
> And Goldtooth, the terror of his friends.

The Poets' Club in question opened in 1921 in the Muruzi house on Liteiny Prospect.

In Zhukovsky's translation of Schiller's "Chalice," we find the following line: "And the terror of the seas—Onetooth."

24. Aneta's husband: Nikolai Gumilyov.

25. The Acmeist poet Vladimir Narbut (1888-1938) is dubbed the "wolf" for his eponymous poem. [Kralin.]

26. Maria Moravskaya (1889-1947)—member of the Poets' Guild. [Kralin.]

27. The poet and literary critic, V. V. Gippius (1876-1941). [Ed.]

28. Lozinsky was the organizing force behind the Acmeist journal *The Hyperborean*. [Ed.]

29. A reference to Gumilyov's early collection, *Pearls* (1910).

30. The Gumilyovs' son, Lev (b. 1912). [Ed.]

31. Irina Odoyevtseva recalls this line somewhat differently in Gumilyov's rendition: "The fur on her muff was worn" (*On the Banks of the Neva*).

32. Ten letters by Mandelstam to Vyacheslav Ivanov, dated 1909-11, were published by A. Morozov in *Zapiski Otdela rukopisei GPB im. V. I. Lenina*, vyp. 34 (Moscow, 1973).

33. Vyacheslav Ivanov's 1909 course on versification was subsequently called the ProAcademy by the young poets of the time. That same autumn the Academy of Verse, also known as the Poetic Academy, came into being at Ivanov's Tower.

34. The following lines from Akhmatova's working copy may go here: "But he was the author of enigmatic, short and absolutely unique poems, which our entire generation carried in their hearts their whole lives through—through everything."

35. Eugenia Gertsyk (1879-1944), translator and friend of Vyacheslav Ivanov. [Il'iunina.]

36. In his commentary to Mandelstam's letters to Ivanov, A. Morozov writes: "Despite the group split and heated polemics in the press, the attitude of the 'younger poets' towards the 'maîtres' of Symbolism, although more distant than earlier, remained respectful. Mandelstam's attitude—for him these maîtres were primarily Vyacheslav Ivanov and Fyodor Sologub—can be seen in two inscriptions written in his first collection, *Stone* (1913), the year of the Acmeist manifestoes: 'To Vyacheslav Ivanov with joyful admiration. The Author. May 13, 1913; To Vyacheslav Ivanov with profound gratitude and genuine fondness. The Author. October 2, 1913. Petersburg.'"

37. Evidently, an allusion to the Society of Friends of Gafiz, which met "on their sofas" at Ivanov's (see N.A. Bogomolov, "Epizod iz peterburgskoi kul'turnoi zhizni 1906-1907 godov," *Blokovskii sbornik*, vol. 8 [Tartu, 1988]) or a reference to the lavish editorial offices at *Apollon*. [Il'iunina.]

38. The Symbolist poet and prose writer, Fyodor Sologub (1863-1927) was famed for his extremely correct, sometimes pompous, demeanor. [Ed.]

39. Nikolai Khardzhiev (b. 1903), art critic and longtime friend of the Mandelstams and Akhmatova. See Akhmatova's letters to Khardzhiev. [Ed.]

40. Mandelstam's poem "Kak chernyi angel na snegu" (1910) was first published in New York in 1963 (*Vozdushnye puti*, no. 3). [Ed.]

41. Akhmatova's poem from *White Flock*, "How can you bear to look at the Neva?" (1914, *Complete Poems*, vol. 1, pp. 398-99). In the final version (*Flight of Time*, 1965) the last line reads: "Like roses, they flower in the snow."

42. Mandelstam has two poems titled "The Egyptian": "Ia izbezhal surovoi leni" (1913) and "Ia vystroil sebe blagopoluch'ia dom" (1914). [Il'iunina.]

43. Among the few scarce notes about Nikolai Gumilyov's meetings with Mandelstam that survive in Ahkmatova's rough drafts is the following: "In the years of the Guild, we (Kolya and I) dropped in on Osip or went to pick him up. At the time he was living on Vasilyevsky Island, where he was renting a room from an officer who was a military instructor. He pointed out the window to where the cadets were playing soccer (a novelty then) and recited his poem 'Soccer': 'And in the courtyard of the military school....' Later it was published somewhere."

In 1913 Mandelstam wrote the poem "Soccer" (published in 1914 in *The New Satyricon*) and "Another Poem about Soccer," which was not published until 1973 (*Stikhotvoreniia*, Biblioteka poeta, pp. 219-20). Akhmatova recalls the second poem and quotes a line from the first stanza:

> The heavy morning frost was dispersed,
> Day came barefooted;
> And the boys are playing soccer
> In the courtyard of the new military school.

44. Salomea Andronikova Halpern (1888-1982), famed Petersburg beauty and addressee of Mandelstam's poem "Solominka."
Akhmatova's note: "Compare my line 'Do I not await the hour of death?' with the line 'And what does a woman alone know about the hour of death?'"

45. Mandelstam addressed a cycle of poems to Olga Arbenina (1901-80), actress and artist. [Ed.]

46. Yury Yurkin (1895-1938), poet. [Ed.]

47. English translation in *Selected Poems*, p. 32. [Ed.]

48. The 1931 poem "I saw the world of power through a child's eyes" (*Selected Poems*, pp. 58-59).

49. Akhmatova is recalling two poems, written a decade apart: "In a cold Stockholm bed" is a line from the 1935 poem "Can a dead woman be praised?"; the second poem dates from 1925: "Life fell like summer lightning." Of the first poem, Akhmatova once remarked: "It's a marvelous poem, isn't it?"

50. Maria Petrovykh (1907-79), poet, translator, and close friend of Akhmatova. [Ed.]

51. *Selected Poems*, pp. 73-74.

52. Vera de Bousset, actress at the Kamerny Theater, emigrated with the artist Sergei Sudeikin. The phrase Akhmatova recalls here is the ending of the first stanza of "The thread of gold cordial flowed from the bottle" (1917, *Selected Poems*, pp. 18-19).

53. Natalya Shtempel (b. 1910), Voronezh schoolteacher and intimate friend of Mandelstam. [Ed.]

54. Anna Radlova (1891-1949), poet and translator.

372   Anna Akhmatova

55. Akhmatova's note: "An allusion to Valerian Chudovsky [philologist and literary critic], Radlova's faithful knight (he died in the 1930s)."

56. See Mandelstam's early essays "François Villon" and "Pyotr Chaadayev," both translated in *The Complete Critical Prose and Letters*. [Ed.]

57. Hylea: the name adopted by a group of Futurists (later known as Cubo-Futurists), whose members included D. and N. Burlyuk, V. Kamensky, A. Kruchonykh, B. Lifshits, V. Mayakovsky and V. Khlebnikov.

There is another line in one of the drafts: "Ask Z[enkevich] about how he and Osip gave readings with the Cubo-Futurists."

58. Sergei Gorodetsky (1884-1967), one of the founders of Acmeism.

59. Mandelstam's poem "Akhmatova" opens with the line "Half-turned, o sadness."

60. The founder of The Stray Dog, Boris Pronin (1875-1946). [Ed.]

61. Valeria Sreznevskaya (1888-1964), Akhmatova's friend from their days together at school in Tsarskoe Selo. Her memoirs are printed in *Ob Anne Akhmatovoi* (Leningrad, 1990). [Ed.]

62. In one copy of the manuscript there are two and one-half lines of ellipses—evidently some names are still missing from the list. To the right of this, at Akhmatova's dictation, are listed the following poets, who most likely attended Guild meetings: N. Radimov, V. Yunger, N. Burlyuk, V. Khlebnikov.

In another copy, Radimov's name is inserted after Lozinsky's. To the right a vertical line separates members of the Guild from poets who simply attended meetings: V. Yunger, Makridin, N. Burlyuk, V. Khlebnikov, Count Komarovsky (added in pencil).

63. Mandelstam's poem "A hush that evening in the organ forest" (1917, *Selected Poems*, p. 20). Akhmatova cites the beginning of the second line.

64. Akhmatova is citing from memory Mandelstam's 1917 poem "I did not seek in blossoming moments." The poem has also been published under the title "To Cassandra" (Mandelstam, *Sobranie sochinenii*, vol. 1 [Washington, D.C., 1967]).

65. Akhmatova drew a personal connection with two other Mandelstam poems of this period. They are both designated in the first drafts of her memoir, but by lines within the poems, rather than first lines: "That's the swallow my daughter" (i.e., the poem "The clock-cricket singing," *Selected Poems*, p. 21) and maybe "He will refuse to attempt it" (from the poem "When on the squares and in the quiet of a cell"). Both are later deleted in one copy of the draft, but remain in another.

66. Akhmatova continues this sentence in one of the drafts: "...and he unexpectedly got very offended and stopped visiting Botkinskaya Street altogether."

67. In 1918-19, Akhmatova lived with her second husband Vladimir Shileiko at 3 Zachatyevsky Lane in Moscow.

68. Translated by Kristin A. DeKuiper in Anna Akhmatova, "Mandelstam," *Russian Literature Triquarterly*, no. 9 (Spring 1974), p. 246.

69. Mandelstam's letters to his wife are translated in *The Complete Critical Prose and Letters*. [Ed.]

70. Mandelstam's poem "Life fell like summer lightning" (1925).

71. See Mandelstam's 1920 poem "Heaviness and tenderness—sisters: the same features" (*Selected Poems*, p. 24).

72. Lines from Mandelstam's poem "I did not seek in blossoming moments," which is dedicated to Akhmatova.

73. In the first edition of *Stone* and subsequent reprintings the poem "Tsarskoe Selo" began with the stanza:

> Let's go to Tsarskoe Selo!
> Free, fickle and drunken
> Uhlans smile there,
> Mounting a firm saddle...
> Let's go to Tsarskoe Selo!

In the Poets' Library edition of Mandelstam, N. Khardzhiev prints a different version of the beginning, using an authorized copy of 1927 (perhaps influenced by conversations with Akhmatova):

> Let's go to Tsarskoe Selo!
> There the tradeswomen smile,
> As Hussars after revelries
> Mount a firm saddle...
> Let's go to Tsarskoe Selo!

The stanza became "more correct," but seems to have lost its poetic expressiveness and elasticity.

74. Pavel Luknitsky (1900-73), poet, prosaist, and friend of Akhmatova and the Mandelstams. [Ed.]

75. One of the drafts contains the following: "In March 1921, I was standing in line 'to register' at the House of Scholars, and Nikolai Gumilyov turned up in the next line. I rarely saw him then. Finding himself next to me, he started talking about Mandelstam's poetry and was especially enthusiastic about the poem about Troy ('I could not keep your hands in my own'). He always had a very high opinion of Mandelstam's poetry."

76. Lines from Mandelstam's "The day was five-headed" (1935), trans. by Bernard Meares, Osip Mandelstam, *50 Poems* (New York, 1977).

77. "Grigory Gukovsky [1902-50] also visited the Mandelstams in Moscow." [Akhmatova's note.]

78. "The Leningrad literary critics Lidia Ginzburg and Boris Bukhshtab were always loyal to Mandelstam and are both experts on his poetry. In this connection we should also recall Caesar Volpe, who published *Journey to Armenia* in *The Star* (1933)." [Akhmatova's note.]

Volpe published *Journey to Armenia*, despite the censor's prohibition, and was relieved of his editorial duties at *The Star*.

79. "The meetings and conversations with Bely in Koktebel had a profound effect on him (when?). He telephoned me in Leningrad and told me about Bely's death: 'I was just a pallbearer at Andrei Bely's funeral.'" [Akhmatova's note.]

See Mandelstam's poem on Bely's death: "Blue eyes, and the bone of the forehead glowing" (1934, *Selected Poems*, p. 71).

80. "His position in Moscow was always complex, unclear, and tormenting. (This is a large topic.)" [Akhmatova's note]

81. Isaak Babel (1894-1941), master prose stylist, best known for his *Red Cavalry*; Mikhail Zoshchenko (1895-1958), arguably Russia's comic genius of the twentieth century; the novelist and playwright Leonid Leonov (b. 1899), whose major works in the 1920s include *The Thief* and *The Badgers*. [Ed.]

82. Konstantin Fedin (1892-1977) began his career with the ambitious novel *Cities and Years* (1924), which draws on the problem of the Russian intelligentsia, history and society. *The Rape of Europe* was written in the mid-thirties, by which time Socialist Realism had become doctrine. [Ed.]

83. Akhmatova continues this sentence in one copy of the manuscript: "...after their last Crimean summer ('And we'll pour your azure and our Black Sea together'—'Ariosto' [*Selected Poems*, pp. 66-67]) he needed the South and the sea almost as much as he needed Nadya ('Oh, give me an inch, a needle's eyeful of blue sea!..')."

84. One manuscript reads: "Osip was all afire with Dante—he had just learned Italian—and he was reading *The Divine Comedy* day and night."

85. The lines from Dante's *The Purgatorio* are from John Ciardi's translation of *The Divine Comedy* (New York, 1977), p. 368.

86. One draft reads: "Afterwards we often read Dante together." The notation below reads: "1962, Christmas, The Harbor, last day in the hospital."

87. "I saw with my own eyes Klyuyev's declaration at Varvara Klychkova's (sent from the camps, petitioning for amnesty): 'I, sentenced for my poem, "The Blasphemers of Art," and for some mad lines in my drafts....' (I took two lines as an epigraph for my 'Tails.')"

In another draft Akhmatova recalls Klyuyev (1887-1937) in another connection and then cites, apparently, another of his requests for amnesty: "At one of the Acmeist public readings (1910s) a bearded man named Radetsky was raving mad. He shook his fist and shouted, 'These Adams and that skinny Eve!' (about me). At the same meeting N. Klyuyev disowned us. N.S. [Gumilyov] was shocked and questioned Klyuyev in my presence about his action. 'A fish seeks the deepest place, a man the best place,' he answered. Nevertheless, Klyuyev is a real and very important poet. Klychkova showed me his 'Petition for Amnesty': 'I, sentenced for reading my poem "The Burning Place" and for mad lines in several of my rough drafts....' Osip quoted me two lines from Klyuyev: 'A jasmine bush / Where Dante walked and the air was empty.'"

Klyuyev's poem "I am angry at you and berate you sadly" is addressed to Akhmatova:

> Akhmatova is a jasmine bush,
> Scorched by gray asphalt,
> Has she lost the path to the caves,
> Where Dante walked and the air was thick,
> And the nymph spun crystal flax?
>
> (*Den' poezii*, Moscow, 1981, p. 189)

88. Akhmatova chooses incidents and details from *The Noise of Time*. For example: the Jewish teacher who gave his lesson without taking his cap off in the chapter "The Bookcase"; and "Why, alongside her [Komissarzhevskaya], did Savina seem to be an expiring *grande dame*, exhausted by a shopping trip?" (*Selected Prose*, p. 124). [Ed.]

89. What Akhmatova intended to quote has not been established.

90. *Fourth Prose* is available in English in *The Complete Critical Prose and Letters*. [Ed.]

91. The satire against Stalin that was the cause of Mandelstam's first arrest. (See *Selected Poems*, pp. 69-70.) [Ed.]

92. One draft reads: "One must acquaint words with each other (O.E.'s term), that is, put together those words which never stood side by side before."

93. The poem was written in 1937.

94. Akhmatova's poem "It was dawn when they took you. I followed" from *Requiem*. The entire *Requiem* cycle is translated by Robin Kemball in Akhmatova, *Selected Poems*, ed. Walter Arndt (Ann Arbor, 1976). [Ed.]

95. There are several passages related to this day in the diary of Mikhail Bulgakov's widow, Yelena Sergeyevna (1893-1970):

April 6, 1935. Akhmatova dined here. She came to petition on behalf of an acquaintance who had been exiled from Leningrad.

April 13, 1935: Misha [Mikhail Bulgakov] went to see Akhmatova this afternoon. She is staying at the Mandelstams. [The Bulgakovs lived in the same building on Nashchokin Lane.] They want to publish Akhmatova's book, but only selectively. [It was not published.] Mandelstam's wife recalled seeing Misha walking with a sack on his shoulders in Batum fourteen years ago. That was when he was so poor that he was selling a kerosene stove at the bazaar.

October 30, 1935: Today there was a ring at the door. I go out and there's Akhmatova with such a terrible face and so emaciated that I didn't recognize her. Neither did Misha. It turned out that they arrested her husband (Punin) and son (Gumilyov) the same night. She had come to deliver a letter to Iosif Vissarionovich [Stalin]. She was mumbling to herself, obviously in a state of nervous collapse.

November 4, 1935: Akhmatova—with a telegram. Punin and Gumilyov wired that they were in good health. That means that they've been released. I'm happy for Akhmatova. (V. Vilenkin Archive.)

96. Akhmatova, *Complete Poetry*, vol. 2, pp. 572-73.

97. Alexei Remizov's humorous Order of the Great Free Monkey Chamber, "a secret society of writers, artists, musicians, and other people in the arts." Each member was issued an ornately stylized charter, drawn by Remizov in his own hand.

98. Akhmatova is in error—the Danko work is dated 1923.

99. Semyon Kirsanov (1906-72), poet. [Ed.]

100. *Selected Poems*, p. 60.

101. Akhmatova's note: "Everything about this phone call requires the utmost scrutiny. Both widows, Nadya and Zina [Pasternak], have written about it and there is endless folklore on the subject. A certain Trioleshka has even dared to write that Pasternak did Osip in. (That was during the Pasternak Days [i.e., during the campaign waged against Pasternak when he accepted the Nobel Prize]— the article in the paper *Les lettres françaises*). Nadya and I thought that Pasternak earned a B+ for his handling of the affair.

"X. has even more shocking information about Mandelstam in his book about Pasternak. His description of the situation and the history of the phone conversation with Stalin is monstrous. All this smacks of information from Zinaida Pasternak, who hated the Mandelstams with a passion and thought that they had compromised her 'loyal husband.'"

102. Ahkmatova is in error. Gorodetsky's speech was printed in *The Literary Gazette* on March 27, 1936. [Il'iunina.]

103. One draft reads: "Koktebel is a hot bed of slander and gossip. The role of the Briks' salon where Mandelstam and I were called internal émigrés. (Gorodetsky in May 1934.)"

And in the same draft: "Mandelstam always said that Georgy Ivanov had a petty and malicious mind and that Gorodetsky substituted vitality for intelligence (1933). The stream of slander that this monster has spewed out about his two dead colleagues (Gumilyov and Mandelstam) is unequalled (Tashkent, the evacuation)."

104. Robert Payne, author of *The Three Worlds of Boris Pasternak* (1962).

105. Serafima Narbut, wife of the poet, was arrested in 1936 and died in a labor camp in 1938. [Kralin.]

Nina Olshevskaya, at the time an actress at the Moscow Art Theater, and a close friend of Akhmatova. [Ed.]

Emma Gershtein (b. 1903), literary critic and friend to the Mandelstams and Akhmatova. See Akhmatova's letters to Gershtein. [Ed.]

106. Quotation from Mandelstam's "Our lives no longer feel ground under them."

107. See Mandelstam's poem "The day was five-headed..." (1935).

108. Demyan Bedny (1883-1945), poet and satirist, who placed his talents at the disposal of the Communist Party.

109. A line from the final poem in "Stanzas" (1935, *Selected Poems*, p. 80).

110. Mandelstam's "A Letter about Russian Poetry" was published in Rostov, not Kharkov. The following is an excerpt from *Complete Critical Prose and Letters*: "Akhmatova introduced all the enormous complexity and wealth of the nineteenth century novel into the Russian lyric. If not for Tolstoy's *Anna Karenina*, Turgenev's *Nest of Gentlefolk*, all of Dostoevsky and even some Leskov, there would be no Akhmatova. Akhmatova's genesis lies entirely in the realm of Russian prose, not in poetry. She developed the poignant and unique poetic form with a backward glance at psychological prose" (p. 158). [Ed.]

111. In Akhmatova's manuscript entitled "Rudakov," she characterizes the man in greater detail and the tone is much harsher, since she does not allow for any psychological illness. Not only Mandelstam, but also Anna Akhmatova befriended Sergei Rudakov, a young philologist and poet, exiled to Voronezh. It is to *his* memory that she dedicated the poem "To the Memory of a Friend" (1945). Emma Gershtein is probably more objective in her treatment of Rudakov's relationship with Mandelstam (*Novoe o Mandel'shtame* [Paris, 1986]).

112. "Concert at the Railway Station" is dated 1921 (*Selected Poems*, p. 39). Akhmatova is inexact in naming the title.

113. The "Armenia" cycle was printed in 1931, not 1930. [Il'iunina.]

114. Akhmatova's note: "[Shatsky-Strakhovsky] writes that he saw [Gumilyov] for the last time in the Summer Garden in April 1918. That is impossible. N.S. [Gumilyov] did in fact return to Petersburg in April 1918 after a year's absence. But then, when and in which verse studio did Strakhovsky study under Gumilyov? The studios didn't start until after April 1918. Thus, the whole *apprenticeship* of which he is so proud falls by the wayside. His recollections of the studio classes are evidently borrowed from the real participants (Otsup, Odoyevtseva), perhaps when they were already in emigration. The most amusing thing of all is that the well-known venerable Harvard University published this under its imprint.

"Swift warned us long ago that there are people who know *exactly* what the king said privately to his prime minister. Strakhovsky belongs to this group. He knows what N.S. said to the prosecutor at interrogations. (We do not know what Pilnyak and Babel said at their interrogations.)

"The unwarranted familiarity, lack of ceremony and lies of Homeric proportions in this book can only be compared to Georgy Ivanov's shameless memoir, *Petersburg Winters*, where he has Blok going to *Saratov* (instead of Shakhmatovo), and Komarovsky for some reason is turned into a redhead. [...] Strakhovsky is

forever respectfully quoting Georgy Ivanov as an expert on the period. I realize
that what I am writing now is practically useless...."

115. Arseny Tarkovsky and Semyon Lipkin were always highly regarded by
Akhmatova as promising poets of the younger generation. The scene Akhmatova
describes above, where Mandelstam is shouting at the unpublished poet as he
runs down the stairs, most likely came from Lipkin, who recounts the event in
his memoir of Mandelstam. [Ed.]

116. Artur Lourié (1892-1967), composer and musicologist, and Akhmatova's
friend of many years.

117. Vilenkin points out that Mandelstam's anger was feigned and that he
probably relished the sound play of MKHAT (Moscow Art Theater) and
Akhmatova.

118. One draft reads: "A second no less remarkable quality of Mandelstam's
poetry is its almost Pushkinian universality."

119. *Selected Poems*, p. 88.

120. Ibid., p. 100.

121. Akhmatova's note: "The Mandelstams didn't have any money."

122. One draft reads: "The Yezhov Terror."

123. Emma Gershtein's short note to Akhmatova has been quoted many
times; Lena refers to Yelena Galperina-Osmyorkina (1903-87), wife of the artist.

One draft reads: "Just when I had finished writing this Ira [Irina Punina] arrived from the city and brought a letter from Nadya. It ends: '...and Osya, thank
God, died.'"

124. The letter was sent from a transit camp near Vladivostok.

Innokenty Annensky

1. From Annensky's poem "Kolokol'chiki." It should read "Lidu didu ladili"
(They prepared Lida for an old man). In the poem the bells tell the tale of a wedding to a traveler.

2. A type of verse from Russian folklore; the number of syllables and accentu-
ation are free, as is the rhyme scheme.

3. Alexander Blok's letter to Annensky (March 12, 1906). *Quiet Songs* was
Annensky's first book of poems.

4. Translation by R. H. Morrison in Innokenty Annensky, *The Cypress Chest*
(Ann Arbor, 1982).

5. A transliteration of these lines shows the half-zaum (trans-sense) character
of the poem:

> Kolokoly-balaboly,
> Kolokoly-balaboly,
> Nakololi, namololi,
> Dale bole, dale bole...
> Nakololi, namololi,
> Kolokoly-balaboly.
> Lopotun'i naletali,
> Bolmotaly naviazali,
> Lopotali—khlopotali,
> Lopotali, bolmotali,
> Lopotaly polomali.

Nikolai Gumilyov

Akhmatova was prompted to undertake her sketch of the life and works of Nikolai Gumilyov (1886-1921) by the appearance in the West of the first volume of Gumilyov's *Collected Works* (Sobranie sochinenii, 4 vols., Washington, D.C., 1962-68), edited by Gleb Struve and Boris Filippov. The outlines and rough drafts translated here represent Akhmatova's critical response to that volume, in particular Gleb Struve's Introduction. Akhmatova strongly objected to Struve's trivialization of her role in Gumilyov's biography and his use of unreliable sources, especially the memoirs of emigrés. Akhmatova, therefore, centers her sketch around the poems dedicated to her explicitly, as well as those poems which in her opinion speak about her. Unfortunately, Akhmatova did not complete her piece on Gumilyov.

As Akhmatova writes, in the mid-1920s she was instrumental in assembling Gumilyov's archive. Her primary assistant in this project was Pavel Luknitsky (1902-73), who collected Gumilyov's books and manuscripts, and interviewed his family, colleagues, and friends. Luknitsky's diaries of this period and his collection of Gumilyov materials are fundamental sources for the study of Gumilyov (see, for example, Pavel Luknitskii, *Vstrechi s Annoi Akhmatovoi, tom I, 1924-25* [Paris, 1991] and V. K. Luknitskaia, "Materialy k biografii N. Gumileva," in Nikolai Gumilev, *Stikhi. Poemy* [Tbilisi, 1988], pp. 15-73). According to Luknitsky, Akhmatova planned to write at least two essays on Gumilyov's poetry that would assess the influence of Annensky, Baudelaire and other poets. These projects were evidently not realized.

This translation is based on the text as published by K. N. Suvorova and V. A. Chernykh: "Samyi neprochitannyi poet. Zametki Anny Akhmatovoi o Nikolae Gumileve," *Novyi mir*, no. 5 (1990), pp. 219-23. A fuller version is promised for the Akhmatova volume of *Literaturnoe nasledstvo*.

All references to Gumilyov's works, unless otherwise noted, are from the Biblioteka poeta edition of his verse: Nikolai Gumilev, *Stikhotvoreniia i poemy*, ed. M. D. El'zon (Leningrad, 1988), everywhere abbreviated below as *BP*.

1. Gumilyov's two acrostics, dedicated to Akhmatova, "Addis Ababa, city of roses" and "Acrostic" (*BP*, pp. 389, 395).

2. A reference to Gumilyov's "Adam's Dream" (*BP*, p. 156). In "Adam's Dream" the contradictory image of Eve encompasses both infernal woman and compassionate saintliness, which is most obviously expressed in the lines: "There's Eve—a fornicatress, prattling incoherently, / There's Eve—a saint whose eyes mirror her sorrow."

3. The autograph of Gumilyov's "Rusalka" (1904), bearing the dedication "To A. A. Gorenko," is in the collection of Yury Oksman in the Central Government Archive of Literature (TsGALI) in Moscow. The Russian text is printed in Gumilev, *Stikhi. Poemy* (Tbilisi, 1988), pp. 95-96.

4. Vsevolod Rozhdestvensky (1895-1977) and Nikolai Otsup (1894-1958), both minor poets, were born in Tsarskoe Selo and participated in the Poets' Guild. Otsup emigrated in 1922 and became a prominent writer in Russian Paris. In 1951 he defended his doctoral thesis on Gumilyov.

5. "Ezbekieyeh" (the title refers to a garden in Cairo) is addressed to Akhmatova, as is "Memory," which opens Gumilyov's book *Pillar of Fire* (1921, *BP*, pp. 271, 309).

6. A quotation from Gumilyov's "Beatrice" (*BP*, pp. 47-48).

7. A play on the title of Maximilian Voloshin's *Deaf-and-Dumb Demons* (1919).

8. Charles-Marie-René Leconte de Lisle (1818-94), poet and leader of the French Parnassians.

9. Akhmatova details the conflict between Gumilyov and Ivanov and Bryusov in her autobiographical prose.

10. Gumilyov's poem "Do you remember the giants' palace..." (*BP*, p. 139), according to Akhmatova, was addressed to her.

11. Kolya—the diminutive form of Nikolai.

12. "The Lakes" (*BP*, p. 137) was also addressed to Akhmatova.

13. This quotation and the following are from Gumilyov's early books *The Path of the Conquistadors* (1905) and *Romantic Flowers* (1908).

14. "Anna Comnenus" (*BP*, p. 385). Anna Comnenus (1083-ca. 1148) was the daughter of the Byzantine emperor.

15. "Ballad" (*BP*, pp. 175-76). According to Akhmatova, this poem was presented to her as a wedding present.

16. "She" (*BP*, p. 167). The line Akhmatova quotes differs from the text as printed in the Biblioteka poeta edition. Akhmatova writes: "to study the radiant pain" *(uchit'sia svetloi boli)*, whereas the adjective in the volume of Gumilyov's works is *sladkoi* (sweet).

17. Gumilyov dedicated the second part of *Foreign Skies* (1912) to Akhmatova. These three poems are all from that part and, according to Akhmatova, all refer to her specifically. Akhmatova is inexact in her naming of two of the poems, which probably indicates that she was writing from memory, although it is possible that she is citing variant titles that have not survived in Gumilyov's manuscripts. "The Tightrope Walker" refers to Gumilyov's poem "The Animal Tamer" (*BP*, p. 176), which opens with an epigraph from Akhmatova's "At the new moon he abandoned me" (*Complete Poems*, vol. 1, pp. 284-85). In the Akhmatova poem the female tightrope walker is abandoned by her lover; in Gumilyov's poem the tightrope walker holds the animal tamer's fate in her hands.

Akhmatova later devotes a separate section to Gumilyov's "Margarita" (*BP*, pp. 178-79).

"The [Female] Poisoner" refers to Gumilyov's "The Poisoned One" (*BP*, p. 177), which closes with the lines: "And it's sweet for me to know—don't cry, my dear / That you have poisoned me."

18. See Akhmatova's "Mikhail Lozinsky."

Mikhail Zenkevich's (1891-1973) first collection of verse, *Wild Porphyry* (1912), was published by the Poets' Guild.

19. A. A. Gumilyova, the wife of Gumilyov's brother Dmitry (Mitya).

20. "The Joys of Earthly Love," a cycle of three prose novellas, was published in the Symbolist journal *The Scales* (1908); reprinted in N. Gumilev, *Sobranie sochinenii*, vol. 4, pp. 5-12.

21. Akhmatova here has compiled Gumilyov's Don Juan list. Gumilyov dedicated his book *The Quiver* (1916) to Tatyana Adamovich (1892-1970), the sister of the poet and critic Georgy Adamovich (1894-1972). Nadezhda Mandelstam devotes a brief chapter to the writer and revolutionary Larisa Reisner (1897-1926) in

her *Hope Against Hope.* Olga Arbenina (1899-1980), an actress at the Alexandrinsky Theater, was Gumilyov's mistress in 1919-20.

22. See Gleb Struve's introduction to his edition of Gumilyov's *Sobranie sochinenii*, vol. 1, p. xxi.

23. A slip of the pen. The mistake in numbering is Akhmatova's.

24. Vera Nevedomskaya and her husband lived on the Podobino estate, not far from Slepnyovo, the Gumilyov family home. This paragraph and the next are Akhmatova's furious reaction to Nevedomskaya's memoir, which is quoted in N. Gumilev, *Sobranie sochinenii*, vol. 1, pp. xvii-xviii.

25. Vladimir Shileiko (1891-1930), Orientalist, poet, translator and Akhmatova's second husband.

26. Mikhail Zenkevich's unpublished autobiographical novel *(Muzhitskii sfinks)* dates from the 1920s.

27. Akhmatova's dislike for Georgy Ivanov and his *Petersburg Winters* is given more rein in her "History of Acmeism."

28. Quotations from poems in *The Pyre* (1918) and *Pillar of Fire.*

29. "To the Memory of Annensky" (*BP*, pp. 211-13) is a student's moving tribute to his mentor. It opens Gumilyov's book *The Quiver.*

30. Akhmatova quotes the fourth quatrain from Gumilyov's "The Tsarina" (*BP*, pp. 122-23).

31. See Gumilyov's "Margarita" (*BP*, pp. 178-79).

32. Quotations from Gumilyov's "That Other One" (*BP*, p. 164) and "The Eternal" (*BP*, pp. 164-65). According to Akhmatova, both poems are about her.

33. I have inserted this short section from a recent publication of Akhmatova's autobiographical prose *(Literaturnoe obozrenie*, no. 5 [1989], p. 13), since it continues the theme of the previous fragment.

34. Akhmatova's note refers the reader to two early poems: "And when we had cursed each other" (1909) and "They came and said" (1910). *Complete Poems*, vol. 1, p. 281, vol. 2, p. 497.

35. The first publications from the cycle now known as *Northern Elegies* appeared under the title *Leningrad Elegies.* "It was dreadful to live in that house" is the opening line of the "Third Elegy."

36. Gumilyov, unfortunately, is often still remembered for his exotic, romantic adventures in the manner of "The Captains" (1908, *BP*, pp. 152-56). An extract from "The Captains" in prose translation is available from Dimitri Obolensky, *The Heritage of Russian Verse* (Bloomington, Indiana, 1976), pp. 293-95. The other poems Akhmatova refers to are "The Lake of Chad" (*BP*, p. 105) and "The Giraffe" (*BP*, p. 103).

37. These three poems, all from Gumilyov's *Pillar of Fire*, are available in English translation in *Russian Literature of the Twenties. An Anthology*, ed. Carl Proffer, et al. (Ann Arbor, 1987), pp. 385-89. The Russian texts are "Pamiat'" (*BP*, p. 309), "Shestoe chuvstvo" (*BP*, p. 329), and "Zabludivshiisia tramvai" (*BP*, p. 331). The last two poems are available in prose translation in Obolensky, op. cit., pp. 299-303.

38. The "old man" in Gumilyov's 1916 poem "The Worker" (*BP*, p. 260) has nothing in common with the image of the worker in Russian literature of the Revolution. A prose translation is available in Obolensky, op. cit., pp. 297-98.

39. "The Magic Violin" (*BP*, p. 114) opens the collection *Pearls*; Gumilyov's drama in verse *Gondla* (1917) is set in ninth-century Iceland.

40. "Iambic Pentameters" (*BP*, pp. 220-22), a poem of disillusion and missed opportunities.

41. *Letters on Russian Poetry* is available in English in: Nikolai Gumilev, *On Russian Poetry*, trans. David Lapeza (Ann Arbor, 1977).

42. Akhmatova uses the English word "best-seller."

43. No edition of Gumilyov's poetry appeared in the USSR after 1923, a situation that did not change until 1988 when *Izbrannye stikhotvoreniia* (Moscow: Ogonek, 1988) appeared, soon followed by a number of collections.

Boris Pasternak

Akhmatova's diary entry for February 8, 1966 includes the sentence: "I know that after I finish writing about Lozinsky, I should write about Boris." However, the fragment translated here is the only known sketch of Pasternak.

Boris Pasternak (1890-1960), best known in the West for his *Doctor Zhivago* (1957) and the ensuing scandal that erupted when he was awarded the Nobel Prize the following year, is one of Russia's great lyric poets of the twentieth century. The diary in verse *My Sister—Life* (1922), Pasternak's best-known collection of the early period, earned him a reputation as one of the leading poets of the day. (The work has been expertly translated by Mark Rudman and Bohdan Boychuk [Ann Arbor, 1983].) Christopher Barnes' *Boris Pasternak. A Literary Biography* (New York, 1990–) will no doubt be the standard work when it is completed.

Akhmatova always regarded Pasternak highly—see her "Work in Progress" (1936), where she singles out Pasternak and cites her poem addressed to him. However, the relationship occasionally became strained, partly because Akhmatova suspected that Pasternak did not really know her poetry (see Chukovskaya's memoir of Akhmatova for frequent references to and discussions of Pasternak).

1. Pasternak's verse collection *Second Birth* (1932).

2. No new collection of Pasternak's poetry appeared until the 1940s, no doubt due in part to the repressive and terrifying times. During the thirties Pasternak made a number of poetic translations.

Marina Tsvetaeva

The eighteen-year-old Marina Tsvetaeva, who had been writing verse for a dozen years, published her first collection of poetry, *Evening Album*, in 1910. Though published privately, the volume attracted the notice of some of the leading poets of the day. Tsvetaeva, a gifted and original versifier in her early books, attained her mature poetic voice in the 1920s and 1930s. Two of her best collections, *Craft* and *After Russia*, were published in emigration in 1923 and 1928 respectively; Tsvetaeva left Russia in 1922 to be united with her husband, Sergei Efron. Returning to Russia in 1939, Tsvetaeva was unable to find suitable employment, much less publish her poetry. Finally, on August 31, 1941, she hanged herself in Yelabuga, a provincial town to which she had been evacuated from wartime Moscow. Simon Karlinsky's *Marina Tsvetaeva, The Woman, Her World and Her Poetry* (Cambridge, 1985) provides the best introduction to Tsvetaeva's life and work; see also Maria Belkina's *Skreshchenie sudeb* (Moscow, 1988) for a detailed account of Tsvetaeva's last two years.

The relationship between Akhmatova and Marina Tsvetaeva, the other woman in the quartet of Russian poets, was complicated. Tsvetaeva addressed a number of poems to Akhmatova, beginning with "To Anna Akhmatova" (1915), but the best known are the eleven poems in the cycle *Poems for Akhmatova,* written over the short period of June 19 to July 2, 1916 (four of them are translated by Elaine Feinstein in *Selected Poems of Marina Tsvetaeva* [New York, 1986], pp. 15-17). As the title of Akhmatova's "Belated Reply" (1940) suggests, Akhmatova was slow with her response. Akhmatova chose the opening line from the first poem in Tsvetaeva's *Poems for Akhmatova*—"Muse of lament"—as an epigraph to her poem "The Four of Us" (1961). Jane Taubman discusses Tsvetaeva's *Poems for Akhmatova* in her *A Life Through Poetry: Marina Tsvetaeva's Lyric Diary* (Columbus, 1989).

1. The meeting between Akhmatova and Tsvetaeva took place just a few months before the latter's death. Akhmatova frequently stayed with the Ardovs when she was visiting Moscow. For information on Nikolai Khardzhiev, scholar and friend of Akhmatova, see Akhmatova's letters to Khardzhiev.

2. Akhmatova refers to Tsvetaeva's highly developed sense for the dramatic and the ability to transform seemingly everyday events into Poetry.

3. Akhmatova's *A Poem without a Hero.* Akhmatova did not read the recent "Belated Reply" or *Requiem.* In the fall of 1940 Tsvetaeva records her assessment of Akhmatova's *From Six Books:* "It's old and weak... What had she been doing between 1917 and 1940?" (quoted in Viktoriia Shveitser, *Byt i bytie Mariny Tsvetaevoi* [Paris, 1988], p. 473).

4. Zaum—literally, "beyond the mind." A poetic language promoted by the Russian Futurists.

5. Tsvetaeva presented Akhmatova with a copy of her *Poem of the Air* (May 1927).

6. *Antony and Cleopatra:* "His delights were dolphin-like: they show'd his back above the element they liv'd in" (Act V, scene 2).

Titsian Tabidze and Paolo Yashvili

Titsian Tabidze (1897-1937) and Paolo Yashvili (1895-1937), were major Georgian poets of their generation. As the dates of death indicate, both were repressed (Yashvili committed suicide) and were posthumously rehabilitated.

1. Boris Pasternak made his first trip to Georgia in 1931 at the invitation of Yashvili. This initial trip laid the groundwork for a series of translations from the Georgian. See Lazar Fleishman, *Boris Pasternak. The Poet and His Politics* (Cambridge, 1990).

PROSE ABOUT THE POEM

Prose About the Poem

1. Mikhail Lermontov's romantic drama in verse written in 1835. Associations from this work are found throughout *A Poem without a Hero* (i.e., Petersburg, life as masquerade, tragic passion, and death).

2. Olga Glebova-Sudeikina (1885-1945), a famous ballerina, singer, and actress. In the early 1920s she shared an apartment with Akhmatova; she emigrated in 1924, leaving behind her belongings: pictures, icons, china, antique tiles, etc.

3. Akhmatova's paraphrase of Pushkin's epithet.

4. Vsevolod Knyazev (1891-1913), a young poet and cornet who was in love with Olga Glebova-Sudeikina. This unrequited love led to his suicide in 1913, which is a central leitmotif in *A Poem without a Hero*.

5. *Enuma Elish* was an unfinished play in verse and prose that Akhmatova burned in 1944. The title is taken from the opening words of an Assyrian epic about Creation. During the 1960s she intended to reconstruct and finish it, but it was never completed. Contrary to Akhmatova's assertion, excerpts in verse were published during her lifetime under the title: "From the Tragedy: Prologue, or a Dream within a Dream."

6. This letter, like the one that follows, does not have a real addressee. The epistolary form is used as a literary device. In several variants of *A Poem without a Hero* it was intended for a section of comments by the author.

7. Amanda Haight has speculated that this may be Nikolai Khardzhiev (*Anna Akhmatova: A Poetic Pilgrimage*, p. 155).

8. Akhmatova's note: "Why the 'second'—I prefer odd numbers, why not the 'third' or the 'seventh'. How about the 'seventh'?"

9. Akhmatova's note: "The schemes of Belkin."

10. Tr. "On the better side of forty."

11. V. V. Cherdyntsev (1912-71). These lines are from a poem dedicated to Akhmatova.

12. V. A. Komarovsky (1881-1914), the author of a single book of poetry, *First Haven* (1913). Nikolai Gumilyov remarked that in this poet's work there was "not only a Tsarskoe Selo landscape but a Tsarskoe Selo sphere of ideas."

13. S. Z. Galkin (1897-1960), a Soviet Jewish poet with whom Akhmatova was acquainted in her later years and several of whose poems she translated.

14. Akhmatova lived here from 1924-26.

15. A hemistich from the final, unpublished portion of Pushkin's poem "Remembrance" (1828).

16. Tatyana Vecheslova (b. 1910) was a soloist with the Kirov Ballet when Akhmatova became acquainted with her in 1944. In 1946 she dedicated to her the poem "Inscription on a Portrait."

17. A dance performed by Olga Glebova-Sudeikina.

18. From 1935 Akhmatova kept her papers and some of her books in an old narrow trunk which had a hinged lid decorated with bas-relief carvings. Kashchei is a figure from Russian legend who captures wayfaring strangers.

19. A line frequently quoted by Akhmatova from a poem that has not survived.

20. The words of a curse on Petersburg uttered by Eudoxia Fyodorovna Lopukhina (1669-1731), the first wife of Peter I who was banished to Pokrovsky Monastery in 1698.

21. The title of Igor Stravinsky's opera based on Pushkin's *Little House in Kolomna*.

22. Peter Viereck (b. 1916), American poet and historian.

The Ballet Libretto

1. The altar of Zeus, striking for the bas-relief figures on its frieze that depict the battle of the gods against the Titans.

2. A reference to works of art from the beginning of the century that celebrated pre-Christian Russia: Sergei Gorodetsky's first book of poetry *Spring Corn* (1907) and *Perun* (1907); Igor Stravinsky's ballet *The Rite of Spring* (1913), A. N. Tolstoy's collections of verse *Lyrics* (1907) and *Beyond Blue Rivers* (1911), and motifs from ancient Slav mythology in the early works of Velimir Khlebnikov.

3. "An Evening of Dances from the Eighteenth Century by Tamara Platonovna Karsavina" was held on March 28, 1914 at The Stray Dog, a bohemian café in Petersburg frequented by Akhmatova and her friends. The event spawned a poem by Akhmatova dedicated to Karsavina.

4. This is taken from an epigram about Osip Mandelstam which was composed in the Poets' Guild. Akhmatova adds: "As he smoked, Osip would try to flick the ashes over his shoulder, but a little mound of ashes would always collect there."

5. A reference to Marina Tsvetaeva's prose memoir of 1936 "An Otherworldly Evening," which describes a literary evening arranged, in part, for her arrival from Moscow in 1916. The focus of the memoir is the poet Mikhail Kuzmin who published a collection of verse entitled *Otherworldly Evenings* in 1921. Akhmatova was not present at this literary soirée.

6. The pseudonym of theater director Vsevolod Meyerhold (1874-1940), under which he staged several productions at the beginning of the century and published the journal *Love for Three Oranges*. In 1914 Blok and Akhmatova published poems dedicated to each other in Meyerhold's journal.

7. Viktor Khlebnikov (1885-1922), renowned Futurist poet who changed his first name from the Latin "Viktor" to the Slavic equivalent "Velimir." Akhmatova nicknamed him Velimir I because his fellow Futurist poets had elected him the "King of Time" in 1915; in 1917 Khlebnikov himself had organized The Society of the Chairmen of the Globe which admitted poets, artists, sculptors, and scholars.

8. Vasily Rozanov (1856-1919), philosopher, literary critic, and publicist.

9. Akhmatova is referring to the early period of Mayakovsky's life and artistic development before his acquaintance with Lili and Osip Brik in 1915.

10. Vaclav Nijinsky (1889-1950), leading dancer with Diaghilev's Ballets Russes. On September 26, 1917 he danced the lead roles in Stravinsky's *Petrouchka* and the ballet *Spectre of the Rose* for the last time—soon after he became mentally unwell and never returned to the stage.

11. Vsevolod Meyerhold died in prison in 1940 after his arrest the previous year. A detailed account of his arrest and execution was published in *Ogonyok*, no. 15 (April 1989), pp. 10-12.

ABOUT PUSHKIN

In the section **About Pushkin,** the majority of the notes belong to Akhmatova and are marked [A. A.]. Commentary by Emma Gershtein from her edition of *O Pushkine* is marked [E. G.]. The notes done by the editor of this volume are marked [Ed.].

A Word about Pushkin

"A Word about Pushkin" was first published in *The Star* (1962, no. 2) to commemorate the 125th anniversary of Pushkin's death.

1. Pavel Shchegolyov (1877-1931), author of *Duel' i smert' Pushkina*, (1916-17). [Ed.]
2. Idaliya Poletika, one of Pushkin's major enemies in society. [Ed.]
3. The influential courtier, G.A. Stroganov, who was related to Pushkin's wife (her mother's cousin), patronized by d'Anthès. [Ed.]
4. Countess Maria Dmitrievna Nesselrode (1786-1849), wife of the Minister of Foreign Affairs, was one of Pushkin's bitterest enemies. Her salon was distinguished by its conservative snobbery. [Ed.]
5. A citation from Horace's "Exegi monumentum aere perennius," the source of Pushkin's famous "I have erected unto myself a monument, not made by hands" (1836). [Ed.]

Pushkin's Last Tale

1. V. Sipovsky's reference to Klinger's tale *Le coq d'or* as a source for *The Golden Cockerel* is completely unfounded (V. Sipovskii, *Pushkin. Zhizn' i tvorchestvo*, St. Petersburg, 1907, p. 470). [A. A.]
2. *The Alhambra, or the New Sketch Book* by Washington Irving (Paris: W. Galignani, 1832). [A. A.]
3. *Les contes de l'Alhambra précédés d'un voyage dans la province de Grenade;* traduit de Washington Irving par m-lle A. Sobry (Paris: H. Fournier, 1832, 2 vols.). [A. A.]
4. No. 1019, "cut, no markings" (see: D. Modzalevskii, *Biblioteka Pushkina* (St. Petersburg, 1910). [A. A.]
5. M. P. Alexeyev has demonstrated that Pushkin's *A History of the Village of Goryukhino* and Irving's *A History of New York* belong to the same genre (see "K istorii sela Goriukhina" in *Pushkin. Stat'i i materialy* [Odessa, 1926, vyp. 2]). [A. A.]
6. The following tales from the *Alhambra* cycle were published: "The Rose of the Alhambra" *(Son of the Fatherland,* no. 70, 1835) and "Governor Manco" *(Forty-One of the Best Short Stories by Foreign Writers,* part 9, 1836). A complete translation of *The Alhambra* was published in 1879: Vashington Irving, *Putevye ocherki i kartiny,* per. s angl. A. Glazunov (Moscow, 1879). See also: *Nasledstvo Mavra i arabskii astrolog. Ispanskie legendy.* Soch. V. Irvinga (Moscow, 1889). [A. A.]
7. Irving's letter from Alhambra, dated March 15, 1828: "I received from my poor devil guide many most curious particulars of the superstitions which circulate among the poor people inhabiting the Alhambra respecting its old, mouldering towers. I have noted down these amusing anecdotes, and he has promised to

furnish me with others. They generally relate to the Moors and the treasures they have buried in the Alhambra, and the apparitions of their troubled spirits about the towers and ruins where their gold lies hidden!" *(The Life and Letters of Washington Irving* [London, 1862, vol. 1, p. 435]).

One of Ximínez's lesser-known "stories" (with a reference to Irving) put forth as a "folk tale" is to be found in V. P. Botkin's *Letters about Spain* (Pis'ma ob Ispanii [St. Petersburg, 1857, p. 412]). Cf. V. Irving, *Putevye ocherki i kartiny* (Moscow, 1879, p. 266). In Irving's book this story represents the kernel of the legend about the Arabian astrologer. [A. A.]

8. On October 19, 1830, Irving writes from London: "I have finished three of the *Alhambra* tales, and worked upon three others. Dolgorouki, who has read those finished, speaks in the most encouraging terms of them, and from his knowledge of the country, and the places and the people, he is enabled to judge of their local verity" *(The Life and Letters of Washington Irving,* vol. 1, p. 521).

Prince Dmitry Ivanovich Dolgorukov (1797-1867), son of the poet I. M. Dolgorukov, was then secretary at the Russian Embassy in London. Dolgorukov and Irving became friends in Madrid, where the former was an attache of the Russian Embassy. Before his diplomatic career, Dolgorukov wrote poetry and was a member of The Green Lamp society, where he would meet with Pushkin. From April 4, 1820 Dolgorukov was an official at the Russian Embassy in Constantinople (with S. I. Turgenev and D. V. Dashkov). He returned to Petersburg in 1821. In Pushkin's letter to S. I. Turgenev (written in Kishinyov and dated August 21, 1821) there is a reference to Dolgorukov: "Regards to Chu [D. V. Dashkov], if Chu remembers me, but Dolgorukov has certainly forgotten me." Dolgorukov's correspondence from abroad was published in *The Russian Archive* in 1914-15. There is not a single reference to either Irving or Pushkin. [A. A.]

9. *The Arabian Nights* also has a magical horseman, but there it has a different function (see "The Story of the Porter and the Three Maidens"). I am indebted to I. Yu. Krachkovsky for this reference. [A. A.]

10. According to a communication from Professor Azin-Palaciosa of Madrid University, nobody in Spain has studied the sources of Irving's *The Alhambra*. [A. A.]

11. The sketch is found in Pushkin's drafts between *Yezersky* and the beginning of a translation of *The Odyssey* (notebook no. 2374, page 7). It was first published with the title "An Experiment in Children's Verse" (Opyt detskogo stikhotvoreniia *[Russkii arkhiv,* no. 3, 1881, p. 473]). A more complete text is printed in Pushkin, *Polnoe sobranie sochinenii* (Moscow-Leningrad, 1931, vol. 2, p. 257). [See also: *Pushkin, Polnoe sobranie sochinenii* (Moscow-Leningrad: AN SSSR, 1949, vol. 3, p. 304).] [A. A.]

12. Akhmatova here and elsewhere quotes Irving in French. I have substituted Irving's original in all of these instances, using the text found in *The Complete Works of Washington Irving,* vol. 14, ed. W. T. Lenehan and A. B. Myers (Boston, 1983). [Ed.]

13. The English translation of *The Golden Cockerel,* here and elsewhere, is from Alexander Pushkin, *Collected Narrative and Lyrical Poetry,* trans. Walter Arndt (Ann Arbor, 1984), pp. 415-21. [Ed.]

14. Single combat between rival sons is a very widespread motif in European folklore. See, for example, "Lord Ingram and Chiel Wyet" [Child, *The English and Scottish Popular Ballads* (Boston, 1882-91)], where the brothers who have killed each other are described exactly as in *The Golden Cockerel.* [A. A.]

15. It should be noted that the denouement in *Tsar Saltan* also differs from the denouement of its source and the fact that the Tsar out of joy pardons the evil sisters is, according to Sumtsov, a feature that is "totally alien to folklore variants." [A. A.]

16. See the listing on the verso of the last page of the fair copy. [A. A.]

17. The rough drafts have still not been systematically analyzed. I am using the transcriptions made available to me by S.M. Bondi, for which I wish to acknowledge my gratitude. [A. A.]

18. In 1832 N. M. Komovsky wrote Yazykov: "As a teller of fairy tales Zhukovsky shaved his head and adopted new clothes, but Pushkin sports a beard and is dressed in a peasant coat" (*Istoricheskii vestnik*, 1883, no. 12, p. 534). [A. A.]

[Akhmatova presents five examples of Pushkin's lexical changes here; they have been omitted in this translation.—Ed.]

19. "In the open field stands a man leaning on his spear, in a white cloak, his hat from Sorochinsk, and he is dozing standing up" (*The Tale of Yeruslan Lazarevich*); see also the stanza about the "Roman Pope" in the draft of *The Tale of the Fisherman and the Little Fish* [...]. [A. A.]

20. "He saddles that good steed [...] and cinches twelve girths of Shamakhanian silk..." (*The Tale of Ivan the Bogatyr*). And in Radishchev's poem *Bova*: "Covered in rugs of soft Shamakhanian silk." [A. A.]

21. Yu. Tynianov, *Arkhaisty i novatory* (Leningrad, 1929), p. 269. [A. A.]

22. These allusions, as well as the ironic treatment of the central character, Tsar Dadon, have led to the hypothesis that *The Golden Cockerel* is a "concealed political satire." See A. Pushkin, *Skazki*, ed. A. Slonimsky (Moscow-Leningrad 1930), pp. 25-29; Pushkin, *Poln. sobr. soch.* (Moscow-Leningrad 1931), vol. 6, p. 331. [A. A.]

23. In all editions of Pushkin's works after the word "hint" (namek) there is a comma (which follows the notes in his diary) or an exclamation point, but not a colon, as in the fair copy. [A. A.]

24. See the drafts of Pushkin's essay on Voltaire (1836), which have been studied by Yu. G. Oksman. [A. A.]

25. *Letters of Alexander Pushkin*, trans. J. Thomas Shaw (Madison, 1967), p. 643. [Ed.]

26. Compare "But with tsars it is bad to squabble" in *The Golden Cockerel*. [A. A.]

The lines from Pushkin's "My Pedigree" are from Walter Arndt's translation in *Collected Narrative and Lyrical Poetry* (Ann Arbor, 1984), pp. 101-3. The italics are Akhmatova's. [Ed.]

27. *Letters of Alexander Pushkin*, p. 670. [Ed.]

28. Letter to Pletnyov (July 22, 1831): "The Tsar has taken me into service—not into the government office or the court of the military. No, he has given me a salary, has opened the archives to me, so that I may hole up there and do nothing. That is very kind of him, isn't it?"

Letter to Nashchokin (September 3, 1831): "The Tsar [...] has taken me into service—i.e., has given me a salary and permitted me to burrow in the archives, to compile a history of Peter I. God grant the Tsar health!" (Ibid., pp. 517, 526.) [Ed.]

29. L. Maikov, *Pushkin* (St. Petersburg, 1899), p. 208. [A. A.]

30. When he describes his presentation to Princess Yelena Pavlovna, Pushkin does not forget to mention that she "talked with me about Pugachev." [A. A.]

31. Pushkin refers to his quarrel with the tsar two more times: (1) in a letter to his wife (July 11, 1834): "A few days ago I came within a hair's breadth of committing a disastrous thing: *I came within a hair's breadth of quarreling with him.* And how I had to show the white feather! And I became depressed. *If I quarrel with this one*—I won't live to see another. But I can't be angry with him long—even though *he's not in the right*" [*Letters of Alexander Pushkin*, op. cit., p. 670]; (2) in his diary: June 22nd. "The past month has been stormy. I barely escaped quarreling with the court—but everything came right in the end." [A. A.]

32. Ibid., p. 694. [Ed.]

33. Ibid., p. 695. [Ed.]

34. *Istoricheskii vestnik*, 1883, vol. XIV, no. 12, p. 539. "The Genealogy of the Pushkin Family" for A.S. was always to some degree oppositional, or at least, *polemical.* [A. A.]

35. Cf. also: "Another... I'm afraid to name him, though he's known by all of society" (Griboyedov, *Woe from Wit*). [A. A.]

36. Akhmatova cites four lines from the unfinished chapter 10 of *Eugene Onegin*, here translated by Vladimir Nabokov *(Eugene Onegin*, vol. 3 [New York, 1964], pp. 315-16). The variant Akhmatova quotes, however, differs in the fourth line. Nabokov's translation reads: "our tsar in *congress* said." [Ed.]

37. The 1829 quatrain that describes a bust of Alexander I is titled "On the Bust of the Conqueror." In *The Age of Bronze* Byron describes Alexander I as the "coxcomb tzar" and "imperial dandy"—both phrases connote the Russian word *shchegol'*. [A. A.]

38. Compare "Dadon returns" with "The return of Alexander I" ("To Alexander"). [A. A.]

39. Golitsyn, Tatarinova, Krüdener and others. On the eve of the Battle of Austerlitz, Alexander I had a prolonged discussion with the eunuch Kondraty Selivanov, who, according to rumors in Petersburg, predicted defeat. [A. A.]

40. Alexander I was a European figure. Pushkin may have suspected a conscious desire on the part of the satirist and hoaxer Irving to depict Alexander I in the Spanish tale (Alexander I's suppression of the Spanish Revolution). [A. A.]

41. The location of these lines on the notebook's cover in itself indicates that the piece was composed intermittently. [A. A.]

42. It was written after the poem "He lived among us," dated August 10, 1834. [A. A.]

43. An attempt to completely remove the Shamakh element is evident in the fair copy:

The tent opened... and a maiden
[Dark-browed and round-faced]
[The Shamakhanian Queen]

The last line was changed to "Dark-browed and round-faced" but was then reinstated. [A. A.]

The Tale of The Golden Cockerel. Commentary

1. This manuscript, as is the case with all of Pushkin's manuscripts, is in the collection of the Manuscript Division of Pushkin House, Institute of Russian Literature, USSR Academy of Sciences. [E. G .]

2. See B. L. Modzalevskii, *Biblioteka Pushkina:* "No. 1019. W. Irving, *Les contes de l'Alhambra...,*" "cut, no markings." [A. A.]

3. The fragment "God sent me a wonderful dream" can be traced to the Spanish romance cycle about Rodrigo (see N. V. Iakovlev's article "Pushkin i Sauti" in the collection *Pushkin v mirovoi literature* [Leningrad, 1926]). [A. A.]

4. See *The Telescope,* 1832, IX (September). [A. A.]

5. See, for example, the review of *The Alhambra* in *Revue de Paris,* 1832, 5-6, pp. 263-66. [A. A.]

6. The decoding of the political meaning of *The Golden Cockerel,* as well as an analysis of the devices Pushkin employed for the transformation of a pseudo-Arabian legend into a Russian folk tale is dealt with in my article "Pushkin's Last Tale" *(Zvezda,* 1933, no. 1). [A. A.]

7. See the list of "folk tales" on the verso of the last sheet of the autograph of *The Golden Cockerel.* [A. A.]

8. An interesting example of the utilization of folklore in a work of political satire, which Pushkin may have known, is the separate edition of a tale recorded by the Brothers Grimm—"Der Fischer und seine Frau," which, owing to the events of 1814, was interpreted as an allegorical biography of Napoleon (the book was subtitled "Eine moralische Erzählung"). As has now been established, Pushkin utilized the variant recorded by the Brothers Grimm for his work *The Tale of the Fisherman and the Little Fish.* [A. A.]

9. See Pushkin's essay "Alexander Radishchev" (1836). [A. A.]

10. We know that the first four lines of this tale belong to Pushkin, who, according to Smirdin, thoroughly analyzed the entire tale. [A. A.]

11. "And he rode into an open field towards a white tent, in which sat three beautiful maidens, the daughters of Tsar Bugrigor. The world has never seen maidens as beautiful as these." [A. A.]

12. See, for example, the English ballad "Lord Ingram and Chiel Wyet" (Child, *The English and Scottish Popular Ballads* [Boston, 1882-91]). [A. A.]

Benjamin Constant's *Adolphe* in Pushkin's Works

The essay on *Adolphe* and Pushkin, the best-known of Akhmatova's Pushkin studies, first appeared in *Vremennik pushkinskoi komissii,* vol. 1 (1936). Sharon Leiter's translation of this essay, which was first published in *Russian Literature Triquarterly* (no. 9, 1974), has been extensively revised for this volume. [Ed.]

1. N. P. Dashkevich, *Pamiati Pushkina* (Kiev, 1899), pp. 184-95; N. O. Lerner, newspaper *Rech',* Jan. 12, 1915; N. Vinogradov, *Pushkin i ego sovremenniki* (Petersburg, 1918), vyp. 29, pp. 9-15. [A. A.]

2. See *Causeries du Lundi* (Paris, 1868), vol. II, pp. 432-33. [A. A.]

3. Thomas Moore, *The Life, Letters and Journals of Lord Byron* (London, 1830), p. 309. [A. A.]

4. *Ostaf'evskii arkhiv kniazei Viazemskikh* (St. Petersburg, 1899), vol. 1, p. 60. [A. A.]

5. In the 1870s, Vyazemsky, recalling this period, wrote: "We were disciples and followers of the doctrine proclaimed from the tribune and in political polemics by such teachers as Benjamin Constant, Royer-Collard and many other of their associates" *(Polnoe sobranie sochinenii,* vol. 10, p. 292). Karamzin, the Turgenevs and the Vyazemskys read *La Minerve Française,* Constant's political

journal. For the influence of Constant's political views on Pushkin, see the articles by B.V. Tomashevsky: "Frantsuzskie dela 1830-31 gg. (Pis'ma Pushkina k E. M. Khitrovo)" (Leningrad, 1927); "Iz pushkinskikh rukopisei," *Literaturnoe nasledstvo*, 1934, nos. 16-18, pp. 254, 286, 288). In the foreword to his translation of *Adolphe*, Vyazemsky attempts to link the novel with Constant's political tracts. Vyazemsky says the following about Constant: "The author of *Adolphe* is strong, eloquent, caustic, moving.... In creation as well as expression, in understanding as well as style, all his strength, all his power is in truth. He is the same in *Adolphe* as he is on the orator's platform, in contemporary history, in literary criticism, in the loftiest considerations of spiritual speculations and in the dust of political pamphlets." For the influence of Constant's political tracts on the Decembrists, see V. I. Semevsky's book *Politicheskie i obshchestvennye idei dekabristov* (St. Petersburg, 1909). [A. A.]

6. In his foreword "From the Translator," Vyazemsky writes that in Constant's autobiographical confession we see "the imprint of the author's ties with a renowned woman, who attracted the attention of the entire world to her work." [A. A.]

7. *Rukoiu Pushkina* (Moscow-Leningrad, 1935), p. 184. [A. A.]

8. *Starina i novizna* (1902), book 5, p. 47. The similarity between this comment about *Adolphe* and the definition of *Adolphe's* language in Pushkin's note about the forthcoming publication of *Adolphe* is obvious. It is likely that Vyazemsky informed Baratynsky of the contents of this note, which had not yet been published. [A. A.]

9. In his foreword, Vyazemsky writes: "My love for *Adolphe* has been vindicated by public opinion." Vyazemsky did not translate the last paragraph of Constant's foreword to the third edition of *Adolphe*. He probably chose this course of action because it is there that Constant renounces *Adolphe* and writes: "The public probably has forgotten it, if it ever knew it." Constant's retraction contradicts Vyazemsky's assertion that *Adolphe* is a story "which so strongly affected public opinion." Moreover, it could have harmed *Adolphe* in the eyes of Russian readers. [A. A.]

10. *Russkii arkhiv* (1895), book 11, p. 110. Pletnyov checked Vyazemsky's translation against a copy of *Adolphe* that belonged to E. M. Khitrovo. [A. A.]

11. *Zven'ia* (Moscow, 1951), vol. 9, p. 175. [A. A.]

12. "A few days ago I read with pleasure Constant's renowned novel, *Adolphe*. It analyzes the workings of the human heart and depicts a man of the present age whose egotistical feelings are spiced with pride and weakness, with high spiritual transports and insignificant actions" (V. Nikitenko, *Dnevnik v trekh tomakh* [Moscow-Leningrad, 1955], vol. 1, p. 102). [A. A.]

13. *Moscow Telegraph* [Moskovskii telegraf], 1831, nos. 1-4. Judging by the review *(Moscow Telegraph*, 1831, part 41, pp. 231-244) of Vyazemsky's translation, Polevoi was acquainted with French critical articles on *Adolphe*. In his review of the translation of *Adolphe*, Bulgarin wrote: "The worth of *Adolphe* has long been appreciated by this author as well as by all people of refined taste *(Northern Bee* [Severnaia pchela], 1831, no. 273). [A. A.]

14. See S. I. Rodzevich, *Predshestvenniki Pechorina vo frantsuzkoi literature* (Kiev, 1913). [A. A.]

15. *I. S. Aksakov v ego pis'makh* (Moscow, 1888), vol. 1, 307-8. [A. A.]

16. B. L. Modzalevskii, *Biblioteka Pushkina* (St. Petersburg, 1910), no. 813. [A. A.]

17. Pushkin also mentions Constant's name in the rough draft of chapter 1, stanza V of *Eugene Onegin*. Onegin could conduct an argument: "On Benjamin...." In 1817-18 Turgenev and Vyazemsky often call Constant simply Benjamin (*Ostaf'evskii arkhiv kniazei Viazemskikh*, vol. 1). [A. A.]

18. The influence of Chateaubriand on Pushkin is an established fact. Pushkin called *Melmoth* "Maturin's brilliant work." D. P. Yakubovich led me to the search for Constant's name in the rough drafts of *Eugene Onegin*. [A. A.]

19. *Literaturnaia gazeta*, 1830, vol. 1, no. 1, p. 8. [A. A.]

20. Foreword to the translation of *Adolphe*. However, this is incorrect: *Adolphe* was published in 1815, that is, after two cantos of *Childe Harold* (1812), *The Giaour* (1813), *The Bride of Abydos* (1813), and *Lara* (1814), and Byron did not read *Adolphe* until the summer of 1816. Pushkin's and Vyazemsky's error is probably explained by their having read *Adolphe* prior to becoming acquainted with Byron. However, they could have known, from periodicals or from persons who knew Constant, that *Adolphe* was written long before its publication. In an extremely hostile review of Vyazemsky's translation (*Moscow Telegraph*, 1831, part 41, pp. 231-44) Polevoi notes this chronological error, saying that it demonstrates the inaccuracy of "truths that *are heard, but not felt*." By this, he is no doubt hinting that Vyazemsky had repeated Pushkin's words. We know that Pushkin became acquainted with Byron around 1820. The first mention of Byron in the correspondence between Turgenev and Vyazemsky occurs in 1819. [A. A.]

21. "And meanwhile, in a few days, I will send you two supplements to my translation: a letter to Pushkin and a few words from the translator," wrote Vyazemsky to Pletnyov on January 12, 1831 (*Izvestiia Otd. Rus. iaz. i slov. Ak. Nauk*, 1897, vol. 2, book 1, p. 92). The dedication is dated "Meshcherskoye (Saratov Province), 1829." Vyazemsky apparently wished to establish the primacy of his translation by indicating this date. [A. A.]

22. In Vyazemsky's *Staraia zapisnaia knizhka*, there are the following notes: "June 16, 1830: Now I must look over my *Adolphe* and write a foreword to the translation." "June 22: I have been rereading several chapters of *Adolphe*." "June 25: Today I finished looking over *Adolphe*." "December 24: So Benjamin Constant is dead; and I had thought to send him my translation of *Adolphe* with a letter. However, Turgenev had told him that I was his translator." [A. A.]

23. In the letter cited above, Vyazemsky tried to bring pressure on Pletnyov: "My *Adolphe* has disappeared without a word and in the meantime Polevoi, always ready for any dirty trick, is printing his *Adolphe* in *The Telegraph*. Has my manuscript been sent to the censors?" The extent to which Vyazemsky was irritated by Polevoi's behavior is demonstrated by his subsequent strange request: "Check *The Telegraph*'s translation against my translation. May God forgive and save us if there is any similarity. I will gladly change everything, even if I spoil my translation—just as long as it doesn't resemble the other one." Vyazemsky repeats this request in a letter dated January 31. [A. A.]

24. January 19, 1831 (in a note containing the news of Delvig's death). Pushkin may also have conveyed his remarks to Vyazemsky personally. They saw one another on the 25th and 26th of January 1831 (see N. O. Lerner, *Trudy i dni Pushkina* St. Petersburg, 1910, p. 235). On January 31, Vyazemsky, via Tolmachevoy, sent Pletnyov the "Dedication" and "Foreword," copied by V. F. Vyazemskaya, which had received Pushkin's sanction ("Neskol'ko pisem kn. P. A. Viazemskogo k P. A. Pletnevu," *Izvestiia otd. rus. iaz. i slov. Ak. Nauk*, 1897, vol. 2, book 1). N. K. Kozmin's commentary to Pushkin's notes on *Adolphe* (*Sochineniia Pushkina*, published by the Academy of Sciences, vol. 9, part 2 [Leningrad, 1929], p. 163 note),

asserts that Vyazemsky sent Pushkin for his perusal the entire translation of Constant's novel. [A. A.]

25. Ibid. [A. A.]

26. Bulgarin cites this statement and ironically adds: "very likely those who don't know the French language" (*Northern Bee*, 1831, no. 274) [A. A.].

27. We know that Pushkin called "metaphysical" that language capable of expressing abstract ideas. However, when Pushkin speaks of the metaphysics of the character of Nina Baratynsky or of the metaphysical language of *Adolphe*, he obviously has in mind the psychologism of these works. It is this sense of the word Vyazemsky has in mind when he calls *Adolphe* a representative of the "worldly, that is to say, practical metaphysics of our age" (Foreword to *Adolphe*). [A. A.]

28. *Ostaf'evskii arkhiv* (1899), vol. 2, p. 280. [A. A.]

29. "With us it's not the same as it is in Europe—here tales are a rarity," wrote Pushkin to Pogodin on August 31,1827. And again in 1831: "In prose we have only Karamzin's *History*. The first two or three novels appeared only two or three years ago" (*Roslavlyov*). [A. A.]

30. *Starina i novizna* (1902), book 5, p. 50. (Italics mine, A. A.) [A. A.]

31. Vyazemsky wrote that he wanted "to analyze, to feel our language, to perform experiments on it, if not tortures, and to find out to what extent it can approximate the foreign language" (Foreword). Complaints about the crudeness of the Russian language are very often encountered in Vyazemsky's *Notebook*. For example, "We complain about the correctness of establishing foreign words in the Russian language. But what is to be done when our minds, having borrowed several concepts and nuances from other languages, do not find the necessary words at home for their expression. How, for example, are we to express in Russian the concepts which the words "naive" and "serieux" awaken in us? Purehearted, simplehearted, open *(chistoserdechnyi, prostoserdechnyi, otkrovennyi)*—none of these expresses the meaning of the first word; important, staid *(vazhnyi, stepennyi)* do not express the concept peculiar to the other. And therefore we must unwillingly say *naivnyi, ser'eznyi*. The latter word has entered general usage. We must not lose sight of the fact that the Western languages are the heirs of the ancient languages and their literatures, which attained the highest level of refinement, and we must assimilate all the tones, all the nuances of refined society. Our language springs, if you like, from noble but poor parents, who could not bequeath their descendant the literature of a refined society which was unknown to them. The Slavic language is good for church services. You can pray in it, but you can't write novels, or political and philosophical dissertations." At about the same time (1830), Pushkin called Vyazemsky's poems metaphysical: "You as easily divine Glinka in his elegiac psalms *as you recognize Prince Vyazmesky in his metaphysical stanzas*" (Italics mine, A. A.). (See *Karelia or the Imprisonment of Marfa Ioanovna Romanova*). [A. A.]

32. *Corinne*, livre VII, ch. 1, "De la littérature italienne." In her book *Dix années d'exile*, de Staël wrote on the absence among the Russians of a language capable of expressing abstract ideas. See B. V. Tomashevsky's article, "'Kinzhal' i m-me. de Staël," *Pushkin i ego sovremenniki* (Petersburg, 1923), vypusk 36. [A. A.]

33. For example: "Almost always, when we want to be in harmony with ourselves, we turn into accounts and rules our weaknesses and inadequacies. Such a ruse satisfies in us *that half which, so to speak, is the spectator of the other.*" [A. A.] [Here and elsewhere Akhmatova cites *Adolphe* in Vyazemsky's translation. Ed.]

34. "In this need there was undoubtedly much vanity; but there was not only vanity in it; it is quite possible that there was even less of it than I myself supposed." [A. A.]

35. "I succeeded in restraining myself and I locked in my breast the slightest signs of dissatisfaction and all the powers of my mind strove to create for myself an artful gaiety. This labor had an unexpected effect on me. We are such unstable creatures that in the end we experience those very feelings which in the beginning we manifested out of pretense." [A. A.]

36. Stendhal, *Rome, Naples et Florence*. Note of January 4. Vyazemsky likely knew of Stendhal's comment on *Adolphe* when he wrote to A. I. Turgenev (1833): "I have loved Stendhal since I first read *The Life of Rossini*" (*Ostaf'evskii arkhiv*, vol. 3, p. 233). *La Vie de Rossini* appeared in 1823; 3rd edition, *Rome, Naples...* in 1826. [A. A.]

37. "I cast myself upon the earth; I want it to open and swallow me forever; rest my head on the cold stone so that it may calm the ardent fever which is devouring me...." [A. A.]

38. "Such is the capriciousness of our feeble heart that we leave with a horrible torment those with whom we abide without pleasure." [A. A.]

39. This is said by a female representative of Petersburg high society which leads us to believe that her ideal was Adolphe. In this same "Novel in Letters," the scene of the lovers' meeting in the midst of a large social gathering is very reminiscent of a similar description in *Adolphe* (chapter 3). In *Dubrovsky* (1832), the description of the conduct of a "man of the world," Prince Vereysky, who is visiting Troyekurov, also recalls *Adolphe*: "...the Prince was enlivened by her presence; he was gay and succeeded several times in attracting her attention by his interesting stories." Compare this with *Adolphe*: "I... tried a thousand means of attracting her attention. I led the conversation to subjects that were entertaining for her... I was inspired by her presence: I succeeded in gaining her attention...." [A. A.]

40. We can identify the kind of novels that Vyazemsky called "drawing-room novels": "I have finished reading *Le Moqueur amoureux by* Sophie Gay: weak, thin, but good enough, a drawing-room novel" (Viazemskii, *Polnoe sobranie sochinenii*, vol. 9, p. 126; July 6, 1830). "I have finished reading *Granby, roman fashionable*. When you read this novel, you really think you are going from drawing-room to drawing-room" (Ibid., p. 142). In his crushing analysis of Vyazemsky's translation, Polevoi wrote that "Constant's novel is a true record of the non-fictitious scene of high society—and nothing more" (*Moskovskii telegraf*, 1831, vol. 41, p. 235). [A. A.]

41. *Putevoditel' po Pushkinu, Polnoe sobranie sochinenii* (Moscow-Leningrad, 1931), vol. 6. [A. A.]

42. The dating of this fragment presents certain difficulties: the plan of the story (notebook 2282, page 23) is found amidst the drafts of "Gasub" and side by side with the poem, "Let us go, I am ready..." (December 24, 1829). The draft of the beginning of the first chapter is found in the former "Onegin Collection." It is written on two sheets which the police numbered (64 and 76). As L. B. Modzalevsky has established, Pushkin tore these sheets from notebook 2371, in which is found (almost contiguous with the Onegin draft) the continuation of the first chapter and a well-known part of the second chapter (pages 86, 87, 88, 89). They could not have been written earlier than the year 1830. (See B. V. Tomashevsky, "Pushkin i romany frantsuzskikh romantikov," *Literaturnoe nasledstvo*, nos. 16-18, p. 947.) In notebook 2286 we find (pages 13 and 50) a fair

copy of the text of the first chapter, dated "February 24," as G. O. Vinokur pointed out to me. Both manuscripts bear traces of several stages of work. All this speaks for the fact that Pushkin wrote this fragment intermittently; he began it in 1830 (or perhaps even during the last days of 1829), and in 1832 (February 24), he copied and corrected it, apparently intending to continue it. [A. A.]

43. The epigraph to the first chapter: "Your heart is a sponge, sated on bile and vinegar," serves, of course, as an additional characterization of the hero. One should note as well that the phrase: "In these moments I must stay at home..." originally looked like this: "In these moments I must stay at home and not vex you with my spleen." [A. A.]

44. "I find this type of success the pleasure of egotism" *(Adolphe)*. Adolphe is speaking of his social successes: "You will see him in various circumstances and always as the victim of that mixture of *egotism* and sentimentality which flowed together in him." In 1836, Pushkin wrote: "Today's [writers] like to represent sin as always and everywhere triumphant and in the human heart they see only two strings: *egotism and vanity.*" This makes it clear why, in the late 1820s, Pushkin considered Adolphe to be a contemporary hero. [A. A.]

45. Zinaida's predecessor in Pushkin's work is Countess Leonora D. in "The Moor of Peter the Great," who "was not in the first flower of youth, but was still famous for her beauty." [A. A.]

46. In the manuscript the second chapter begins with the underlined phrase: "Zinaida possessed him." Apparently, Pushkin originally intended to give a more detailed account of the preceding events. In *Adolphe* the sentence quoted above corresponds to the following passages: "I was only a weak, grateful and enslaved man...." "I submitted to her will." [A. A.]

47. Originally it read: "On Vasilyevsky Island." Both correspond to the third floor in *Adolphe.* [A. A.]

48. Originally it read: "from whence she sent Volotsky a small page." Constant has: *billet*, i.e., a small sheet of paper, a little letter, a note.

49. See also: "She never let me go without trying to detain me" *(Adolphe).* "'You're leaving already?' said the lady with agitation. 'You don't want to dine here?' 'No, I gave my word.' 'Dine with me,' she continued in a sweet and shy voice" ("In a Corner of the Little Square"). [A. A.]

50. Notebook 2371, page 68. [A. A.]

51. The hero's surname in the Pushkin fragment reveals his social position. The *Princes Volotsky*, a family which was dying out in Pushkin's time, traced its lineage back to Ryurik and ruled the city of Volok Kamsky or simply Volok. Pushkin, who took such a lively interest in his own genealogy, naturally knew the ancient Russian families and in 1830 remarked on the extinction of many of them: "As I look around me and when I read our ancient chronicles, I deplore the way the ancient noble families are being destroyed...." (See also: "I am sorry that the Princes Pozharsky are no more/ And that of others there is no longer even hearsay" ["Yezersky "]). In the preparatory notes for *Boris Godunov*, the branches of the house of Ryurik are copied from Karamzin: "Princes Ryurik, Shuisky, Sitsky, Vorotynsky, Rostovsky, Telyatevsky, and so on"; several of these are named in the tragedy itself: *Shuisky, Vorotynsky, Sitsky, Shastunov* (as well as Kurbsky—"the highborn heir." Compare this with chapter 10 of *Eugene Onegin*: "But a highborn versifier"—about Prince Dolgorukov); the surname *Sitsky* is repeated in "Yezersky": "And he died, after having demoted the Sitskys." In "The Moor of Peter the Great," we find the name Rzhevsky, of whom it is said that he sprang from an ancient boyar family: his father-in-law is *Lykov*; the proposed

suitors of Rzhevskaya—*Lvov, Dolgorukov, Troyekurov, and Yeletsky*. (Pushkin wrote about Yeletsky's origins in the fragment "In Spite of Great Advantages," 1830.) Rzhevskaya appears again in the plan of the story, "About the Strelets and the Boyar's Daughter." Of course, it is not coincidental that many Pushkin heroes in the non-historical works of 1829-34 bear surnames of the house of Ryurik, which no longer existed in the nineteenth century or whom it was possible to name without offending anyone, e.g., *Yeletsky*. *Minsky*, the hussar-aristocrat ("The Station Master") and *Minsky* ("Guests Gather at the Dacha"), the self-recommending member of the house of Ryurik, *Muromsky* ("Mistress into Maid"), the anglophile who ruins himself. Prince *Gorsky* (the draft of "In a Corner of the Little Square"), *Troyekurov* again (*Dubrovsky*) of whom it is said that he came of an eminent family, and Prince *Vereysky* (same work), and Princess *Yeletskaya* ("Queen of Spades")—are registered in Dolgorukov's *Book of Russian Genealogies* as tracing their family from Ryurik. Pushkin also mentions surnames descending from his ancestor, Radsha. See Pushkin's *The Genealogy of the Pushkins and the Hannibals: Buturlin*—one of Shuisky's guests, and *Buturlin*—who, together with Dolgoruky, contended with Peter in the senate ("The Moor of Peter the Great") and the Muscovite matron Povodova ("A Romance on the Caucasian Waters"). Also descending from Radsha, the Moscow nobleman Rozhnov is mentioned in *Boris Godunov*. Thus, we see that the semantics of these surnames provide additional material for framing questions about Pushkin's relationship to the old aristocracy. [A. A.]

52. Fuflygina is not mentioned in the former Onegin collection or in the continuation of the Pushkin fragment in notebook no. 2371. The character was probably introduced by Pushkin only in 1832, when he rewrote the tale (notebook 2386): this is supported by the corrections in this passage of the manuscript. In 1832, Pushkin was living in Petersburg and his relations with Countess Nesselrode had already been defined. Nashchokin tells us about the conflict between Pushkin and Nesselrode. This conflict apparently dates from the early 1830s. (See P. I. Bartenev, *Rasskazy o Pushkine*, Moscow-Leningrad, 1925, pp. 42, 111.) [A. A.]

53. One paragraph after the word "*bonheur*" written by Pushkin in the margins of *Adolphe*, there follows Adolphe's discourse on his independence and his regret for its impending loss: "It has been so pleasant to feel myself free, to go, come, absent myself, return without worrying about anyone." Pushkin (1830): "I am sacrificing my independence, my carefree, capricious independence.... In the morning I rise when I wish, I receive whom I please...." [A. A.]

54. "I did not lament for any one calling; having tasted none, I lamented for all callings"; "I felt the keenest impatience to acquire again in society and in association with my equals a position belonging to me by right." [A. A.]

55. N. P. Dashkevich notes that Onegin's letter to Tatyana echoes several ideas from Adolphe's explanation to Ellénore (see chapter 3), but gives no examples of this similarity, which, as we shall see further on, is important in connection with *The Stone Guest*. [A. A.]

56. Compare this with "The Snowstorm": "I acted carelessly, giving myself up to the sweet habit of seeing and hearing you every day." Pushkin refers the reader to Rousseau's *The New Heloise* ("Marya Gavrilovna recalled St. Preux's first letter"). However, the expression "sweet habit" does not appear in St. Preux's first letter. [A. A.]

57. Not long before this, apparently in September, Vyazemsky's *Adolphe* came out. In *Trudy i dni Pushkina*, N. O. Lerner erroneously claims that Vyazemsky's translation came out in March 1831 (N. O. Lerner, p. 238). [A. A.]

58. Compare "Mistress Into Maid": Alexei entreated Liza "*not to deprive him of his one joy*—seeing her." Remember that Vyazemsky finished the revision of his translation of *Adolphe* in 1830. In August, he saw Pushkin and traveled with him from Petersburg to Moscow, leaving his translation in the care of Zhukovsky and Delvig. It was probably then that Vyazemsky gave Pushkin his translation of *Adolphe*. [A. A.]

59. Compare Pushkin's letter to an unknown woman (1823): "*Je ne demande rien*"; in the same letter he writes about hopeless love: "*Si j'avais des espérances*"; compare, too, the lyrical poem "Confession" (1826): "I do not dare to ask for love." [A. A.]

60. Adolphe says that he lavished on Ellénore, who had agreed to see him alone, "a thousand assurances of his tenderness, devotion, and eternal respect." [A. A.]

61. It is to be found next to the phrase in which Adolphe's characteristics are given: "You are familiar with my position, with this character which is considered strange and wild...." (The words printed in italics are underlined in Pushkin's copy of *Adolphe*.) Compare the manuscript of *Eugene Onegin*, chapter 8, after stanza XXX: "Having overcome his wild nature." [A. A.]

62. In the beginning of the novel, Adolphe characterizes himself as a seducer. See, for example: "In the home of my parent, I formed a sufficiently immoral manner of thinking about women...." "My heart demanded love, but my ego demanded vain successes. Ellénore seemed worthy of my seductive efforts...." "I did not think that I loved Ellénore, but could no longer reject the thought of being liked by her.... I invented thousands of ways to conquer... my imagination, my desires, a kind of science of social self-advertisement arose in me." [A. A.]

63. This phrase sounds like a quotation. Compare *Eugene Onegin* (chapter 3, stanza IX): "Malek-Adhel, and de Linar," and also Pushkin's notation: "Malek-Adhel, the hero of a mediocre novel by Mme. Cottin. Gustave de Linar, the hero of a charming tale by Baroness Krüdener." Pushkin speaks twice about the lack of verisimilitude in Cottin's novels: in chapter 3 of *Eugene Onegin* (stanza XI, the characteristics of the heroes of the old novels) and in the article, "The Opinion of M. E. Lobanov on the Spirit of Literature" (1836). [A. A.]

64. In the same fragment of the tale ("In a Corner of the Little Square"), which repeats the plot of *Adolphe*, the influence of Balzac as well is undoubtedly present. I have in mind the discourse on how a deceived husband must conduct himself. In December 1829, Balzac's celebrated *Physiology of Marriage*, which Pushkin mentions in *Egyptian Nights*, was published (anonymously). This book treats the question of the conduct of a deceived husband in great detail. For example: "*Quelle doit être la conduite d'un mari en s'apercevant d'un dernier symptôme, qui ne lui laisse aucun doute sur l'infidélité de sa femme*" (p. 287, 1868 edition). Compare Pushkin's fragment: "X. soon became convinced of his wife's infidelity. He did not know which course to take: to pretend to have noticed nothing seemed stupid to him." Compare this with *The Physiology of Marriage*: "*Paraître instruit de la passion de sa femme est d'un sot, mais feindre d'ignorer tout est d'un homme d'esprit*" (p. 229). And on the same page: "*Le grand écueil est le ridicule*." Balzac also gives a number of examples of husbands who laugh "at so common a misfortune" (p. 288), which Pushkin calls "contemptible." In the Pushkin fragment, one simile is taken from this same book by Balzac: "He left the room, like a schoolboy

leaves a classroom" (draft). "*Elle s'évada comme un écolier qui vient d'achever une pénitence.*" Compare also "The Station Master": Dunya, dressed in the full luxury of fashion, sat on the arm of his chair, like a rider on her English saddle." Compare this with Balzac's: "*J'aperçus une jolie dame assise sur le bras d'un fauteuil, comme si elle eût monté un cheval anglais*" (p. 115). In a letter of April 12, 1831, Count V. S. Golitsyn, to whom Pushkin was constantly loaning books, wrote: "I am sending you a depraved book (*Physiologie du mariage*)..." (*Literaturnoe nasledstvo*, vols. 16-18, p. 610). [A. A.]

Pushkin's *Stone Guest*

Akhmatova's third Pushkin article, devoted to the little tragedy, *The Stone Guest*, is dated 1947. More than ten years had passed since the publication of her work on Pushkin and Benjamin Constant (1936). The essay, however, did not appear in print until 1958, though Akhmatova had read her new work to a number of the leading Pushkin scholars soon after its completion. Her analysis of *The Stone Guest* bears witness to her increasing interest in Pushkin's biography, to which she would turn in the 1950s. In the late 1950s Akhmatova returned to her essay on *The Stone Guest* and wrote a number of extended insertions. These interpolations were never fully integrated into the final text.

1. S.M.Bondi pointed this out in his study "Stat'i Pushkina o Baratynskom" (see his book: *Novye stranitsy Pushkina* [Moscow, 1931], pp. 123-24). [E. G.]

2. In his diary Vyazemsky coldly lists *The Little Tragedies* as new things Pushkin had brought from Boldino (P. A. Viazemskii, *Polnoe sobranie sochinenii*, St. Petersburg, 1884, vol. 9, p. 152), and Zhukovsky wrote to Pushkin in 1831: "There's no need for you to get angry at *The Plague*: it is scarcely better than *The Stone Guest*." Belinsky's raptures date from 1841 ("... Pushkin's greatest creation is his (play) *The Stone Guest*" (V. G. Belinskii, *Polnoe sobranie sochinenii*, Moscow, Publications of the Academy of Sciences of the Soviet Union, 1954, vol. 4, p. 424). [A. A.]

3. Alexander Pushkin, *Collected Narrative and Lyrical Poetry*, translated by Walter Arndt (Ann Arbor, 1984), p. 410. [Ed.]

4. Here and following the English translation of the final version of *The Stone Guest* is from *The Little Tragedies*, translated by Antony Wood (London: Angel Books, 1982), pp. 45-72. [Ed.]

5. "Sit still, write, write poetry" (P. A. Vyazemsky to Pushkin, May 10 1826); "All in all, it would be more prudent for you to stay *quietly* in the country" (V.A. Zhukovsky to Pushkin, April 12, 1826). [A. A.]

6. If it is natural for all the discourse of Leporello and Laura to be based on popular speech, then the expressions of the Commendador's widow—"I'm dying of curiosity" and "No, I've never seen the likes of it"—are often explained by Pushkin's expressed conviction that popular speech is an absence of affectation and a sign of good breeding. Let us recall that in the sketch "Concerning All Sorts of Writing," Pushkin notes that in romantic tragedy the "blend of the comic and tragic sometimes necessitates expressions of popular speech for tension and refinement." [A. A.]

7. The Escorial is a royal palace, hardly a suitable location for a duel. Pushkin is probably alluding to the fact that the quarrel took place at the palace, thus em-

phasizing yet again Juan's closeness to the court. Does not Juan speak just as casually about the king: "The King still loved me when he banished me." [A. A.]

8. It seems to me that the much debated issue of whether Don Carlos was the Commendador's brother must be answered in the affirmative: it is difficult to imagine that Juan had two duels with two Spanish grandees and killed both, but for some reason he is afraid of only one family's vengeance and the King's anger about only one of these murders. Pushkin's laconicism again creates a certain reticence here. Moreover, any attempt to make this more concrete would have led to an additional confession by Don Juan in the concluding scene with Doña Anna, who at this time should be mourning the death of her brother-in-law. [A. A.]

9. See da Ponte: "Here I await vengeance against the godless one who killed me." Da Ponte's Don Juan (as well as Leporello) addresses the statue with the formal "you." Pushkin's Don Juan addresses the statue in the familiar form straight away. This is not high style, but a remnant of their good relations in their lifetimes. It is the same with Carlos, too: Juan uses the familiar "you" straightaway. [A. A.]

In Pushkin's tragedy there is one more phrase that represents a literal translation of the libretto: "L'ho voluto"—"he wanted that himself." In da Ponte, Juan says this about the Commendatore whom he has murdered, but Pushkin's Juan—about the murdered Carlos.

10. It is even more terrible in the draft: "To your wife." [A. A.]

11. "Tipsy fiddler"—because the customers hired musicians to serenade and it was customary to treat the musicians to drink afterwards (see Le Sage's Le Diable boiteux). [A. A.]

12. See my article on Adolphe. Adolphe was the alter ego of Onegin and thus, to a certain extent, of Pushkin himself. [A. A.]

13. Alexander Pushkin, Collected Narrative and Lyrical Poetry, translated by Walter Arndt (Ann Arbor, 1984), p. 99. [Ed.]

14. Alexander Pushkin, Eugene Onegin, translated by Walter Arndt (New York, 1981), p. 67. [Ed.]

15. In spite of this, the theme of the wounded conscience appears in Pushkin's lyrics in the late 1820s: the mighty "Remembrance" (1828) and "A Georgian Song" ("Don't sing, my beauty, in my presence..."), which was written a few days later, where the "fatal" image of the "distant poor maid" resembles poor Inez. [A. A.]

16. The variant lines from Pushkin are translated by Vladimir Nabokov in his monumental Eugene Onegin, translated from the Russian with commentary (New York, 1964), vol. 3, p. 80. [Ed.]

17. Eugene Onegin, translated by Walter Arndt, p. 220. [Ed.]

18. Let us recall that Pushkin wrote this letter right after he had received the consent of the bride's parents to his marriage to N. N. Goncharova, when these words sounded, to say the least, unexpected. Pushkin foretold his own fate with complete accuracy: he really did die because of Natalya Nikolayevna and left her a radiant young widow, free to choose a new husband. [A. A.]

Pushkin's Death

"Pushkin's Death" was first published in the journal Voprosy literatury, no. 3 (1973), pp. 207-36. One typescript of the manuscript bears the following note in Akhmatova's hand: "This work was completed a long time ago, for the most part before the war. Afterwards, I had only to enter new pieces of information (Fiquelmont's diary, d'Anthès's visit to Alexandra Nikolayevna, the Karamzin family correspondence, etc.), which did not contradict my original conception even a single time. From the beginning I often described my work, and later read it. Therefore, some things may seem familiar. There is only one truth."

The circumstances leading to Pushkin's duel and death are so well known to the Russian reader that Akhmatova does not insult her audience with a retelling of basic facts. The following short summary may be of use to the non-Russian reader. Alexander Pushkin, Russia's national poet, died on January 29, 1837, as the result of a duel with Georges d'Anthès (1812-95), which had taken place two days earlier. D'Anthès, an Alsatian gentleman and former page to King Charles X, arrived in Russia in 1833, where he was adopted by the Dutch ambassador Baron Louis de Heeckeren (1791-1884) in 1836. The relationship between d'Anthès and Pushkin's wife, Natalya Nikolayevna (née Goncharova, 1812-63), one of the great beauties of St. Petersburg society, became the subject of gossip in 1836. Things came to a head in November, when Pushkin received an anonymous letter informing him of his induction into the Most Serene Order of Cuckolds. A duel between d'Anthès and Pushkin was averted by the marriage of d'Anthès to his beloved's sister, Yekaterina Goncharova (January 10, 1837). The calm was short-lived and Pushkin sent the elder Heeckeren an insulting letter (January 26) that could only be answered by d'Anthès's challenge.

In her essay Akhmatova makes frequent reference to Pavel Shchegolyov's *Pushkin's Duel and Death*, which is both a study and compilation of materials about Pushkin's last days. One of the more comprehensive studies in English is Walter Vickery's *Pushkin. Death of a Poet* (Bloomington, 1968). See also Ernest J. Simmon's *Pushkin* (New York, 1964) and D. S. Mirsky's *Pushkin* (New York, 1963).

References to E. G. Gershtein's commentary to the volume *O Pushkine* (2nd edition, Gorky, 1984) will be cited in the notes as *OP*.

1. Idaliya Poletika (ca. 1807-1890), the illegitimate daughter of Count Grigory Stroganov (1770-1857) and a Portuguese countess. After the death of his legal wife, Stroganov did marry his mistress, but did not adopt Idaliya. The second cousins Idaliya and Natalya Goncharova were initially friendly, but there was a falling out between Idaliya and Pushkin, the exact nature of which has never been precisely identified. Idaliya became one of Pushkin's bitterest enemies in society, an attitude which she maintained even after the poet's death.

Prince Alexander Trubetskoi (1813-89), comrade-in-arms of Georges d'Anthès. His memoirs, *Rasskaz ob otnosheniiakh Pushkina k Dantesu* (1887), should be treated with extreme caution.

A. P. Arapova (née Lanskaya), daughter of Pushkin's widow from her second marriage, penned an unreliable and hostile memoir of Pushkin, supposedly based on information supplied by her mother and Aunt Alexandra. [Ed.]

2. Charles Maurice de Talleyrand (1754-1838) and Clemens Metternich (1773-1859), illustrious statesmen, represented France and Germany at the Congress of Vienna (1814-15). Heeckeren's career, though certainly not as brilliant as those with whom Akhmatova compares him, was nevertheless respectable. He received an ambassadorship to Vienna, even after the Pushkin affair. [Ed.]

3. Alexander Karamzin (1815-88), son of Nikolai Karamzin (1766-1826), author of "Poor Lisa," a classic of Russian Sentimentalism, and *The History of the*

Russian State. The Karamzin salon was an important center of Petersburg cultural life for almost a quarter of a century. [Ed.]

4. Andrei Karamzin (1814-54), son of Nikolai, was abroad from the period May 1836 to October 1837 for health reasons. The correspondence between Andrei and the Karamzin family during this time, an important document of the era, has been collected in the volume *Pushkin v pis'makh Karamzinykh. 1836-1837 godov,* edited by N. V. Izmailov (Moscow-Leningrad: AN SSSR, 1960). [Ed.]

5. Countess Dolly (Darya) Fiquelmont (Fikel'mon, 1804-63), wife of the Austrian ambassador, was hostess to one of the most brilliant salons in Petersburg. Pushkin made her acquaintance in 1829 and became a frequent visitor. An excerpt from her diary, dated January 29, 1837, recounts the events leading up to the duel ("Iz dnevnika grafini D. F. Fikel'mon," *Pushkin. Issledovaniia i materialy,* vol. 1, 1956, pp. 343-50). Akhmatova is probably referring to the following: "His [Pushkin's] trust in her knew no bounds, moreover, she reported everything to him and relayed d'Anthès's words" (*OP*, p. 250). [Ed.]

6. Sofia Karamzina (1802-56), Karamzin's eldest daughter. [Ed.]

7. Yekaterina Nikolayevna Goncharova (1809-43), Pushkin's sister-in-law, married d'Anthès on January 10, 1837. [Ed.]

8. Yekaterina Zagryazhskaya (1779-1842), lady-in-waiting at court and aunt to the Goncharova sisters. [Ed.]

9. See d'Anthès's letter, written while he was under arrest, to the presiding judge. The mysterious tone in A. I. Turgenev's diary is now easily explained (December 19, 1836): "Evening at Princess Meshcherskaya's (Karamzina): About Pushkin: everybody is attacking him because of his wife, I stood up for him. Sofia Nikolayevna's compliment regarding my civility." That is what was taking place (probably not all that seldom) behind Pushkin's back in the home of his "friends." [A. A.]

10. Fyodor Tyutchev's poem "January 29, 1837." [Ed.]

11. Count Alexander Benckendorf (1783-1844), head of the Third Section (the secret police), was the suspicious intermediary between Pushkin and Nicholas I. After Pushkin's exile, the poet was required to submit all new compositions to Benckendorf. [Ed.]

12. Alexander Turgenev (1784-1845), member of the Arzamas society and friend of the Pushkin family, presided over Pushkin's burial alone, except for the police escort. [Ed.]

13. Countess Maria Nesselrode (1786-1849), wife of Karl, the Minister of Foreign Affairs, belonged to Heeckeren's inner circle and was one of Pushkin's most powerful enemies. Her salon was distinguished by its conservative snobbery.

Sofia Bobrinskaya (1799-1866), wife of Alexei (1800-68), grandson of Catherine II. Bobrinskaya was one of d'Anthès's supporters during his trial.

The "counterfeit note" is Shchegolyov's term for an undated note written by Heeckeren to d'Anthès, while the latter was standing trial for his part in the duel. Shchegolyov characterizes the note as a "counterfeit document, written with a specific aim that only the addressee can comprehend." In the note Heeckeren describes the appearance of the anonymous letters, and then writes that "Madame de N. and Countess Sophie B. send you their very best wishes. Both are taking a great interest in us" (*OP*, pp. 252-54). [Ed.]

14. Vasily Zhukovsky (1783-1852), poet, translator and one of Pushkin's closest friends, was appointed tutor to the Tsarevich in 1825, a post that enabled him to intercede on behalf of Pushkin, among others. In his letter to Benckendorf

(February-March 1837) Zhukovsky writes: "Pushkin was driven out of his wits, lost his head and paid for it dearly. On his part there was only the fury of insane jealousy; on the other, to the contrary, there was a debauchery that was both empty-headed and malicious" (*OP*, p. 254). [Ed.]

15. Prince Pyotr Vyazemsky (1792-1878), poet, critic and friend of Pushkin. Vyazemsky writes Countess Emilia Musina-Pushkina (1810-46), one of the great beauties of the day, that "if there had been on his part passion or at least honest courting, then as I mourned Pushkin I would not be blaming his opponent. In this regard I am not rigorous. Mercy should be granted for every sin, but not for every baseness" (February 16, 1837, *OP*, p. 255). [Ed.]

16. In his letter of January 26, 1837 to Heeckeren, Pushkin writes: "And so I am obliged to address you to ask you to put an end to all these intrigues *[mettre fin à tout ce manège]*" (*OP*, p. 255). [Ed.]

17. I am not in the least asserting that d'Anthès was never in love with Natalya Nikolayevna. He was in love with her from January 1836 until the autumn. In his second letter *"elle est simple"*— a fool nonetheless. [A slip of the pen. Akhmatova has in mind the second mention in Dolly Fiquelmont's diary ("she, out of naivete, or more likely, her astounding simplicity..."), and not d'Anthes's second mention (*OP*, p. 255)—Ed.] But by summer Trubetskoi was already under the impression that this love was a rather shallow love: when it became clear that it threatened d'Anthès's career, he quickly sobered, became cautious, in conversation with Sollogub called her *mijaurée* (an affected person) and *Närrin* (a foolish woman), at the envoy's request he wrote a letter in which he relinquishes her, and towards the end he probably even hated her, because he was unbelievably rude and there was not a trace of remorse in his conduct after the duel. [A. A.]

18. That is, that she loves him, has never loved like this, that she wanted him to love her, but that she is faithful to her duty, i.e., she answered like Tatyana. [A. A.]

[The heroine Tatyana from Pushkin's novel in verse, *Eugene Onegin*—Ed.]

19. I thought this earlier. However, from the Karamzins' correspondence it becomes clear that N.N. did meet with d'Anthès at the Karamzins' home, where everybody knew that he was in love with her. [A. A.]

20. On July 9th Pushkin writes: "I am in mourning and do not go anywhere." Is it not then that Natalya Nikolayevna goes out alone, for which Dolly [Fiquelmont] reproaches Pushkin? [A. A.]

21. Pushkin's sisters-in-law, Yekaterina and Alexandra (1811-91) had moved in with the Pushkins in 1834. [A. A.]

22. "You would murmur to her, 'Give me back my son'"—from Pushkin's letter to Heeckeren (November 17-21, 1836, *OP*, p. 256). [Ed.]

23. "Like a shameless old woman, you would lie in wait for my wife in every corner *[dans tous les coins]* to speak to her about your son" —ibid. [A. A.]

24. Maria Merder (1815-70), lady-in-waiting, records the following scene in her diary (January 22, 1837):

D'Anthès was talking animatedly with an elderly woman, who, as far as I could ascertain from what I overheard, was reprimanding him for the loftiness of his behavior. [...] He answered:

"I understand what you wish to convey, but I'm not at all certain that I've been foolish."

"Prove to society that you are capable of being a good husband... and that the rumors that are circulating are groundless."

"Thank you, but let society judge me." (*OP*, pp. 256-57). [Ed.]

25. See Vyazemsky's letter to Prince Mikhail Pavlovich: "To those who congratulated him on this wedding, Pushkin answered so that everyone could hear—'*Tu l'as voulu, George Dandin.*'" The reply, from Molière's *George Dandin*, was used in the sense "you got what you wanted." And, of course, the similarity between the names d'Anthès and Dandin was not lost on Pushkin's audience (*OP*, p. 257). [Ed.]

26. Fiquelmont's diary: Pushkin did not wish to be present at his sister-in-law's wedding, nor to see them after it, but common friends very ill-advisedly hoped to bring about a reconciliation or at least a rapprochement and brought them together almost daily" (*OP*, p. 257). [Ed.]

27. Pushkin challenged Count Vladimir Sollogub (1813-82) to a duel in February 1836, but the duel did not take place. [Ed.]

28. See *Rukoiu Pushkina*, p. 348. Her address is written on Osipova's letter of January 9th [1837]. [A. A.]

Yevpraxia Vrevskaya (1809-83), daughter of Praskovya Osipova (1781-1859), a neighbor from Trigorskoye. In his letter of February 1837, A. I. Turgenev writes his brother: "Now we know that on the eve [of the duel] Pushkin confided in a certain lady, the daughter of the same Osipova with whom I stayed in Trigorskoye, that he was going to duel. She did not know how or could not intervene and now his wife who has learned of this is reproaching her" (*OP*, p. 257). [Ed.]

29. See the essay "Alexandrina" for Akhmatova's interpretation of "Pushkin's friend." [Ed.]

30. This meeting between Natalya Nikolayevna and d'Anthès has not been verified. [Ed.]

31. Pushkin's widow married Pyotr Lanskoi (1799-1877) in 1844. [Ed.]

32. See, for example, the note in A. I. Turgenev's diary (January 21) that d'Archiac had shown him the November documents relating to the duel. For what reason? When everything apparently was so successfully settled. [A. A.]

[Viscount Auguste d'Archiac (1811-51), attaché at the French Embassy and d'Anthès's second.—Ed.]

After the December peace, in connection with the wedding the Heeckerens started to pull the marionettes' strings: "The rumors in the city have resumed" (Vyazemsky). "Everyone has started talking again about his love" (N. Smirnov). [A. A.]

33. Pushkin's note of March 6, 1834: "In the city there's a lot of talk about the relationship between the young Princess Suvorova and Count Wittgenstein.... Suvorova's indiscreet behavior is attracting general attention. The Tsaritsa summoned her and scolded her, the Tsar even more" (*OP*, p. 261). [Ed.]

34. We know that Natalya Nikolayevna did not know how to conduct herself in society not only from Countess Fiquelmont, but also from Vyazemsky's letters to Natalya Nikolayevna herself after Pushkin's death (unpublished). [A. A.]

35. Vyazemsky to A. Bulgakov (February 5, 1837): "Much of this affair remains murky and mysterious even for us"; and to Musina-Pushkina (February 26, 1837): "This affair is shrouded in so much mystery, even for those of us who followed it close at hand" (*OP*, p. 262). [Ed.]

36. Pushkin was summoned to the Winter Palace on November 23, 1836. N. Edelman argues that Pushkin did *not* send the November 21st letter to Benckendorf and that the audience was engineered by Zhukovsky. See

Edelman's *Pushkin. Iz biografii i tvorchestva 1826-1837* (Moscow, 1987), pp. 385-95. [Ed.]

37. The Siberian city of Nerchinsk was the site of a group of prisons where political prisoners were sent (for example, the Decembrists and participants in the Polish uprisings and the populist movements in the 1860s). [Ed.]

38. Prince Hohenlohe-Langenburg-Kirchberg (1788-1859), the Württemberg ambassador in St. Petersburg (1829-48), writes in his "Note about Pushkin" (Zametka o Pushkine): "There are two opinions about the anonymous letters. The one that enjoys the public's greater confidence points to O... [i.e., Ouvaroff-Uvarov]. The other opinion, the government's opinion, based on the identity of the placement of the punctuation, on the peculiarities of the handwriting and the similarity of the paper, accuses H [Heeckeren]" (*OP*, p. 262). [Ed.]

39. A. Ammosov recorded the account of Pushkin's second, Danzas: "Pushkin, judging by the handwriting, suspected the elder Heeckeren to be the author of these notes and even wrote about this to Benckendorf" (*OP*, p. 263). [Ed.]

40. The source of Zhukovsky's fairy tale is his letter to Pushkin (November 14-15, 1836). See *Perepiska A.S. Pushkina*, vol. 1 (Moscow, 1982), p. 130. [Ed.]

41. Cf. Zhukovsky's description of d'Anthès in his letter to Benckendorf: "On the other hand, there was a debauchery that was both empty-headed and deliberate." [A. A.]

42. Zhukovsky's letter to Pushkin: "I know what you are planning to do." Pushkin really was planning to gather his neighbors and lasso the Heeckerens, and this was the revenge with which Rayevsky's Odessa "victories" were nothing in comparison, and which the Tsar, and not Zhukovsky as Sollogub thought, forbade Pushkin. [A. A.]

[In his memoirs, Sollogub writes that Pushkin read him the letter to Heeckeren and that he immediately sought out Zhukovsky to advise the poet not to send the letter (*OP*, p. 264).—Ed.]

[D. S. Mirsky summarizes the Rayevsky affair in his *Pushkin:* "It would seem that Pushkin was made a dupe of his cynical, clever, and immoral friend Alexander Rayevsky (1795-1868), who was himself in love with the Countess (Vorontsova) and who used Pushkin as a decoy and as a screen...the Countess became so intimate with Pushkin that Rayevsky found it easy to 'open the eyes' of Count Vorontsov... Pushkin's removal from Odessa in August 1824, was the result of this quarrel."

According to Vyazemsky, after Rayevsky himself was requested by the same Vorontsov to leave Odessa, he met the Countess on a busy street and shouted so that all could hear "Take care of our daughter" (*OP*, p. 263).—Ed.]

43. Benckendorf's mention of Thibault, the French tutor who lived at the Karamzins (as a possible author of the diploma), after the disclosure of the *bande joyeuse* becomes interesting. He, too, could have been one of *mes drôles*. The chief of police evidently knew that the Karamzins' Frenchman was somehow connected to d'Anthès. And, in general, all our hatred for Benckendorf notwithstanding, we should not underestimate his information. For this reason Shchegolyov entirely out of place speaks ironically of Benckendorf's request for d'Anthès's handwriting. This is the result of the conversation in the Winter Palace (November 23rd), the result of Nicholas I having believed Pushkin. [A. A.]

44. Pushkin's January letter to Heeckeren is largely a reworking of the November letter that was not sent. [Ed.]

45. The unseemly role of Nicholas I in this affair probably figured in this same story: he demanded Pushkin's pledge not to undertake anything himself, while promising that he would take measures, and he did nothing. [A.A.]

46. Prince Pyotr Dolgorukov (1816-68), not an individual known for his principles, certainly was capable of writing the letter. However, N. Edelman (among others) disagrees with Akhmatova on this point. It should be noted that Dolgorukov's candidacy as author of the letter was most forcefully endorsed in the 1860s, when Dolgorukov, a political émigré, was particularly active. [Ed.]

47. See the memoirs of Prince Lobanov-Rostovsky as published by E. G. Gershtein (Ogonek, no. 31, 1951). [Ed.]

48. The son of Mikhail Vorontsov (1782-1856) took Dolgorukov to court for slandering his late father. The scandalous proceedings found Dolgorukov guilty. See Shchegolev, Duel' i smert' Pushkina (Moscow, 1987), pp. 414-22. [Ed.]

49. The philosopher Pyotr Chaadayev (1794-1856) was declared insane and put under house arrest after the publication of his first "Philosophical Letter." [Ed.]

50. Count Matvei Dmitriyev-Mamonov (1790-1863), minor poet, pamphleteer and social activist, was put under house arrest in 1823. In 1826 he was declared insane for his refusal to bend to Nicholas I's will. Dmitriyev-Mamonov, subjected to forced "treatment," did finally and truly become insane. [Ed.]

51. The Messenger of Europe (1871, no. 9, pp. 48-49). N. I. Khardzhiev brought this article to my attention, for which I most heartily thank him. [A. A.]

52. Praskovya Osipova's letter to Pushkin (January 6, 1837). [Ed.]

53. "He has some secret motive that has induced him to adopt the young man and to give him his name and fortune"—Count Fiquelmont to Prince Metternich (February 14/2, 1837, OP, p. 266).

Many, not unreasonably, have suggested that the relationship between Heeckeren and his adopted son was a homosexual one. Akhmatova is clearly hinting at that, but the subject, with rare exceptions, was not allowed in print. [Ed.]

54. In his letter dated June 26, 1837, Andrei Karamzin describes his meeting with d'Anthès in Baden-Baden. Andrei scolds his brother Alexander for abandoning d'Anthès, whom he—and his family—had earlier been fond of. [Ed.]

55. Vrevskaya writes about the same thing when she reports that when she met Pushkin in the theater, she implored him not to send the challenge and to pity his children. "The Tsar will take care of them, he knows everything about my case," Pushkin answered. In saying this, Pushkin evidently had in mind his visit to the Winter Palace and the Tsar's reaction to his communication. In the letter to his sister, Nicholas I repeats all the facts as if they had been dictated by Pushkin. [A slip of the pen. Nicholas I's letter (February 3, 1837) is addressed to his brother Mikhail Pavlovich and not his sister. (OP, p. 270).—Ed.] He says then several times, meaning November, i.e., the day of the meeting in the Winter Palace. [A. A.]

56. In his letter to Count Tol (January 26, 1837), Pushkin, thanking the Count for his warm response to The History of the Pugachev Rebellion, especially remarks on the unjustly maligned General Mikhelson. The letter closes with the sentence: "Genius uncovers the truth at first glance, and truth, as the Holy Bible says, is more powerful than the Tsar." [Ed.]

Alexandrina

Akhmatova's essay on Pushkin's sister-in-law, Alexandra Goncharova, appeared posthumously (*Zvezda*, no. 2, 1973, pp. 208-13).

Akhmatova recorded the following in connection with her work on "Alexandrina":

> In March 1962 Alexander Avdeyenko interviewed me for APN [Novosti Press Agency] (Komarovo). I said: "I have written a work on Pushkin's death. Apart from that piece, I have a separate chapter about his wife's sister and her role in the tragedy."
>
> In early 1963 I outlined my Pushkin research in more detail for M. Dolgopolov, a correspondent for *Izvestiya*. [...] I read "Alexandrina" many times (to V.V. Vinogradov, V. M. Zhirmunsky, I. M. Semenko, Oksman, [...], Karaganova, who wanted it for *Novy mir*. Basalayev wanted it for *Zvezda*).
>
> Therefore, what Yashin writes in this connection seemed particularly strange (*Zvezda*, nos. 8-9). (Quotation.) "Now we know"—and you expect a reference to my work. There, however, is no reference. Therefore, I am venturing to publish "Alexandrina," which has long been in my desk, all the more so since it is not the facts that are interesting, but the method, which is somewhat novel.
>
> As far as the *bande joyeuse* is concerned, nobody has yet touched upon it. [The quotation to which Akhmatova refers is from Yashin's article "Khronika predduel'nykh dnei" (*Zvezda*, no. 9, 1963, p. 173)—Ed.].

1. See S. N. Karamzina's letters: "He insists that he will never allow his wife... to receive her married sister." Further it is said that Pushkin's decision "will set all of Petersburg's tongues wagging," (*Pushkin v pis'makh Karamzinykh* [Moscow-Leningrad, 1960], p. 148). Even more important is the fact that Pushkin stresses this prohibition even in his challenge. It is worth noting that this motif is absent from the November letter, but we must remember that in November Heeckeren was truly afraid of Pushkin, who was threatening to expose him as author of the diploma. The Tsar had forbidden him to speak about the diploma, and so in the challenge there is instead the prohibition of contacts between the two households. [A. A.]

2. See Heeckeren's letter to Baron Verstolk, dated January 30, 1837: "We have carefully avoided visiting the house of M. Pushkin (writes the Dutch ambassador who was twice in the month of January refused entry into the house—A.A.), since his gloomy and vengeful character is only too well known." (P. E. Shchegolyov, *Duel i smert' Pushkina*, 3rd ed., [Moscow-Leningrad, 1928], p. 325).

I should like to draw attention to the fact that in the biography of d'Anthès, written by his own grandson, Metman, the situation is described in very different terms: "After the wedding, relations between the two households remained correct, though cool" (Shchegolyov, p. 360). [A. A.]

3. Trubetskoi twice mentions that he heard the version of Pushkin's liaison with Alexandrina from Idaliya Poletika. Trubetskoi's source allowed that Alexandra was a "very homely but quite intelligent girl" and that even before she met Pushkin, "she knew by heart all of her future *beau frère*'s poems and was in love with him from afar." [E. G.]

4. A. I. Kirpichnikov wrote the following about the episode when d'Anthès and Natalya Nikolayevna kiss in Trubetskoi's narrative: "The story of the denun-

ciatory kiss is a 'wandering tale,' with a venerable lineage that is encountered in various cultures, and here was probably taken from some French collection of *contes poétiques*" (*Russkaia starina*, 1901, vol. 106, p. 79). Similar episodes are found in Boccacio's *Decameron*. [E. G.]

5. Let me remind the contemporary reader that the Horse Guards were the foremost regiment, that they served at the palace and that only sons of the most important and richest families could become officers of the regiment. [A. A.]

6. The story of this lady is difficult and complicated. She did not belong to the Karamzin-Vyazemsky *bande joyeuse*, her husband was a friend and regimental colleague of d'Anthès, and she was Natalya Nikolayevna's best friend, although she is not mentioned among those who were with her in January. [A. A.]

7. Akhmatova is mistaken—the anonymous January letters are mentioned in the record of the court proceedings convened to investigate the duel. [E. G.]

8. "Poletika, with whom I have frequently recalled this episode... has recently died in Odessa. The episode is very clear in my mind" (Shchegolyov, p. 424). [A. A.]

9. Yes, a new epoch had dawned, and Bartenev (in his old age) and P. E. Shchegolyov unearthed Poletika's fabrication and readily accepted it. I need not even mention the twentieth-century reader. He is simply delighted: "She understood him better, she loved his poetry." As if it were such a rarity or virtue to love Pushkin's poetry. [A. A.]

10. I have mentioned above the tale, which belongs to world folklore, and which was adapted to the Pushkin family tragedy and playfully recounted by Trubetskoi on the basis of d'Anthès's own words. [A. A.]

11. Sofia Karamzina in a letter to her brother Andrei (February 2, 1837): "I am glad that d'Anthès did not suffer at all and, since Pushkin was already fated to become the victim, that he was the only victim." [E. G.]

12. In her nonsensical memoirs Arapova announces to the amazed reader that before her wedding Alexandrina had a long conversation with Natalya in which the sisters attempted to find the least awkward way of informing the groom that she was no longer a virgin and that Pushkin was her lover. [A. A.]

13. It is said that until recently the chain decorated the Friesenhof home. Knowing this, is it still possible to seriously claim that it was proof of a criminal relationship between *la châtelaine* (the mistress of the castle) and her brother-in-law? [A. A.]

14. In the summer of 1836 Koko (Yekaterina Nikolayevna), who was in love with d'Anthès, helped arrange meetings between him and her sister so that she, too, could see him (Shchegolyov, p. 72). [A. A.]

15. See Zhukovsky's notes (Shchegolyov, p. 308). [A. A.]

16. See the Karamzins' description of the flirtation with A. Rosset (*Pis'ma Karamzinykh*, p. 120). I may be taking too much liberty by comparing this with Arapova's description of family life in the d'Anthès house, where Yekaterina is described as suffering because her husband loves Natalya, yet I am doing so, because Arapova's source was most probably also Alexandrina. [A. A.]

17. See Pushkin's letter to Bobrinsky, where he asks which one of his sisters-in-law is invited to the ball. [A. A.]

18. Katerina Ivanovna Zagryazhskaya—Stroganov's cousin and sister of Pushkin's mother-in-law, Natalya Ivanovna Goncharova, was also, as we know, not kindly disposed to Pushkin. Not much has been said so far about her attitude to Pushkin, but it has been assumed that she was rather friendly towards him (he was careful to "kiss her hand" in letters, etc.). This assumption is unfounded.

After all, she dresses Koko for her wedding (see *Pis'ma Karamzinykh*, p. 159), she was also at the apartment on the Moika during the poet's final hour and did not enter the study (*this is very significant*). We can, at any rate, be quite certain that she was not on Heeckeren's side (see Heeckeren's letter to d'Anthès in which he says that he has forbidden Koko to correspond with her aunt and offers a general characterization of her). She was neither on Pushkin's, nor on d'Anthès's side, but was merely protecting the interests of Natalya Nikolayevna. It is very likely that Alexandrina did the same.

People see what they want to see, and hear what they want to hear. [A. A.]

19. The late M. G. Solomina told me in 1924 that she used to meet Arapova in society and that Arapova eagerly told her that her mother, N. N. Lanskaya, was much happier in her second marriage. [A. A.]

20. The coat in which Pushkin was shot. [E. G.]

21. Yekaterina Heeckeren died in 1843 in a post-labor fever. [E. G.]

Pushkin and the Shores of the Neva

First published in the almanac *Prometei*, no. 10 (1974), pp. 226-34. The translation is of the text as published in *O Pushkine* (Gorky 1984), pp. 151-62.

1. "The Solitary Hut or Vasilyevsky Island" (Uedinennyi domik na Vasil'evskom) is reprinted in .A. S. Pushkin, *Polnoe sobranie sochinenii*, vol. 9 (Moscow, 1965). This is a record of an oral story by Pushkin, which was made by his acquaintance V. P. Titov. It was first published under the signature Tit Kosmokratov in the almanac *Northern Flowers* (1829). Akhmatova newly interprets this tale in the incomplete "Pushkin in 1828." [E. G.]

2. This is Golodai Island. Its name comes not from the Russian word "golod" (hunger), but from the English "holiday" and is a result of the fact that English merchants visited it on Sundays. "Or a clerk / When he takes a boat ride on a Sunday / Will visit the deserted island." [A. A.]

3. In his article "Peterburg v tvorchestve Pushkina" (*Pushkinskii Peterburg* [Leningrad, 1949], p. 27), B.V. Tomashevsky compares the landscape in "The Solitary Hut" with the topography of the house where Parasha lives in *The Bronze Horseman*, and not with the topography of the place where Eugene is buried. [E. G.]

The translation of *The Bronze Horseman* is from *Collected Narrative and Lyrical Poetry*, trans. Walter Arndt (Ann Arbor, 1984), p. 438. [Ed.]

4. "Recurrent dream" points to the fact that the image appeared to Pushkin with great frequency. [A. A.]

5. In a draft to this article, which concerns the line from the rough copy of Pushkin's "fragment," Akhmatova wrote: "There are many other small islands besides Golodai off the Neva shores. There really are sea birds there (seagulls, ducks); the fishing nets are hung out to dry, sometimes a boat full of holes passes by, the charred remain of campfires can be seen. At least that's how it was in the early twentieth century, when I often visited those places." [E. G.]

6. *Collected Narrative and Lyrical Poetry*, p. 454. [Ed.]

7. *Eugene Onegin*, trans. by Walter Arndt (New York, 1963), p. 25. [Ed.]

8. See note 8 to chapter 1 of *Eugene Onegin*. [E. G.]

9. See, for example, on Petersburg ladies: "Oh, you wives of the North." [A. A.]

10. After Akhmatova's death N. I. Khardzhiev brought to my attention a publication on the burial of the executed Decembrists on Golodai Island, which had eluded the notice of specialists: L. Zhemchuzhnikov, *Moi vospominaniia iz proshlogo* (Moscow, 1926), vyp. 1, p. 133. [E. G.]

11. Akhmatova is referring to two poems by Pushkin: "In the depths of Siberian ore" and "October 19, 1827," from which she cites the closing line. [E. G.]

12. Akhmatova is not completely accurate in her chronology of Pushkin's notes and drawings: the news of the execution of the Decembrists reached Pushkin on July 24, 1826; the poet was still finishing chapter 6 of *Eugene Onegin* in August 1827; the first two drawings of the gallows were done in November 1826, and later repeated in 1828 in the drafts of *Poltava*. [E. G.]

13. See T. G. Tsiavlovskaia, "Novye autografy Pushkina na russkom izdanii *Aivengo* Val'tera Skotta," *Vremennik Pushkinskoi komissii* (Moscow-Leningrad, 1966), p. 7. [E. G.]

14. *Russkii arkhiv*, 1866, column 1464. [E. G.]

15. Pushkin does not forget about the oaks "planted by friends," "To this day they have gravely chanted / To grandsons of the wrongly slain."
This is Pushkin reminding the "present-day" Kochubeis that they ought to be proud of an ancestor who perished under such horrible circumstances. [A. A.]
Quotations from Pushkin's *Poltava* are from *Collected Narrative and Lyrical Poetry*. [Ed.]

16. See the draft: "The heart finds a secret nourishment." [A. A.]

17. N. V. Izmailov, "Liricheskie tsikly v poezii Pushkina 30-kh godov," *Pushkin. Issledovaniia i materialy*, vol. 2 (Moscow-Leningrad, 1958), p. 38. [E. G.]

18. Significantly, Tatyana is not recalling the family grave of her father ("Dmitri Larin, God's servant and brigadier"), but the humble cross of her nurse. It is possible that the poet was recalling his own Arina Rodionovna, whom he had buried at the Okhtinsky cemetery (where the cook in his "Little House in Kolomna" is also buried: "Her coffin was taken to Okhta").
See also the enigmatic notation of 1829: "I visited your grave—but the place was crowded: *les morts m'en distraient...*" (the dead distracted my attention...) (III, p. 477). [A. A.]
Eugene Onegin, p. 219. [Ed.]

19. In the third (incomplete) copy of the typescript of "Pushkin and the Banks of the Neva," Akhmatova has indicated a footnote. On the verso of the previous page (page 6), there is a pencilled note in Akhmatova's hand which may be intended for this note: "The ballad 'The Drowned Man' was written in the same year (1828). We believe that the peasants' terrifyingly punishing refusal to give a grave and a cross to a man who came to his death by drowning is not a coincidence in Pushkin's work. And we should not be misled by the subtitle—'a folk tale.' A poet takes only what suits him and what he needs from the treasures of folklore." [E. G.]

20. See the drafts where the word "society" [svet] is written three times. We know something about the nature of conversations concerning the Decembrists from the "immortal" remark of Countess Nesselrode whose salon was one of the best in Petersburg. She is reported to haved said: "What a misfortune it is to have such a man in one's family." [A. A.]

21. This reference has been proven wrong. [E. G.]

22. See T. Zenger, "Iz chernovykh tekstov Pushkina. Novye strofy *Evgeniia Onegina*," *Pushkin—Rodonachal'nik novoi russkoi literatury* (Moscow-Leningrad, 1941), pp. 36-43. [E. G.]

23. Two years later he wrote for Poltoratskaya: "When God will forgive us, / When I will not be hanged." [A. A.]

REVIEWS & PUBLIC ADDRESSES

On Nadezhda Lvova's Poetry

The review of Nadezhda Lvova (1891-1913) marked Akhmatova's prose debut (*Russkaia mysl'*, 1914). Lvova's only collection of verse (she committed suicide in 1913) was published posthumously in 1914 under the title *An Old Tale*. The book appeared with an introduction by the influential Valery Bryusov, who had dedicated his *Verses to Nelly* (1913) to Lvova.

1. Karolina Pavlova (née Janisch, 1807-93), who published her verse in Russian in the 1830s and 1840s, also wrote poetry in French and German (she translated Pushkin and others into German). For more information on Pavlova see Barbara Heldt's Introduction to her translation of Pavlova's *A Double Life* (2d ed., Oakland, CA., 1986), as well as Heldt's *Terrible Perfection. Women in Russian Literature* (Bloomington, Ind., 1987).

Work in Progress

"Work in Progress" appeared in *Literary Leningrad* on September 29, 1936.

1. These two Pushkin studies are included in the present volume.
2. The Academy (Jubilee) edition of Pushkin's *Complete Works* was published without extensive commentary. Akhmatova's commentary to *The Golden Cockerel*, translated in this volume, was published in *Rukopisi Pushkina* (Moscow, 1939).
3. Daniel Vorouzhan (1884-1915), Armenian lyric poet.
4. Eghishe Charents (1897-1937), the foremost Armenian poet of his generation. One of Akhmatova's translations of Charents, "To My Mother," was printed with the following notice: "I request that my honorarium for the translation of this poem be paid to the fund to aid the wives and children of the heroic Spanish nation, which is so valiantly fighting the fascists for the freedom and independence of its country." The most complete selection of Charents in English is *Land of Fire. Selected Poems*, edited and translated with an introduction by Diana der Hovanessian and Marzbed Margossian (Ann Arbor, 1986).
5. Akhmatova's *From Six Books* (1940).
6. "The Poet (Boris Pasternak)" was first published in 1940 (in *Zvezda*).
7. Nothing came of Akhmatova's plan to translate Shelley's verse tragedy, *The Cenci*.

Radio Broadcast "This is Radio Leningrad"

Akhmatova's wartime appeal to the women of Leningrad was first published by Olga Berggolts in her *This is Radio Leningrad* (1964). Berggolts (1910-75)

Anna Akhmatova

worked for Leningrad Radio during World War II and witnessed the taping of Akhmatova's speech.

Radio Broadcast on the Anniversary of Pushkin's Birth

1. A quotation from Alexander Pushkin's 1821 poem "To Chaadayev."
2. Akhmatova's "In Tsarskoe Selo III" is quoted here in Walter Arndt's translation (*Selected Poems*, pp. 8-9).

Notes in the Margin

Akhmatova's review of E. G. Gershtein's *Sud'ba Lermontova* (Moscow, 1964) was first published in *Literaturnaia gazeta* on March 16, 1965. Gershtein's study makes significant use of archival materials to document the last years of the poet's life (1837-41). For a good overview of Lermontov's life and works, see William Edward Brown's *A History of Russian Literature of the Romantic Period* (Ann Arbor, 1986), vol. 4.

1. Akhmatova traveled to Italy in 1964—the 400th anniversary of Shakespeare's birth and the 150th anniversary of Lermontov's birth.
2. Prince Vladimir Golitsyn (1794-1861), Lermontov's commander in the Caucasus, recommended the poet for the Golden Sabre for his bravery. Lermontov met with Golitsyn again in the summer of 1841 in Pyatigorsk, where the poet had come to take the cure.
3. General Alexei Yermolov (1777-1861) is mentioned in the opening pages of Lermontov's novel *A Hero of Our Time*.
4. The poet Lensky is killed by Onegin in a duel in Pushkin's *Eugene Onegin*. The Russian titles of the Lermontov poems Akhmatova refers to are "Opravdanie" and "Son" (both dated 1841).
5. Gershtein proposed that Lermontov's "Valerik," which described military life and the battle Lermontov participated in on the River Valerik on July 11, 1840, and "The Captive Knight" were both written in 1841. The authoritative *Lermontov Encyclopedia* (Moscow, 1981) lists the dates of composition of the poems as 1840.
6. In his "Hussar" poem "To N. I. Bukharov" (1838?) Lermontov paraphrases lines from Alexander Pushkin's "My Pedigree" (1830). *The Tambov Treasurer's Wife* (1837-38), a satire of high society in a provincial town, was composed in the Onegin stanza.
7. Prince Pyotr Vyazemsky (1792-1878), brilliant observer and letter writer, outlived his friend Pushkin by forty years. Though Vyazemsky wrote poetry until his last years, he is remembered for the verse written in the twenties and thirties, and for his letters and journals.

Pushkin and Children

First published in a slightly abbreviated form in *Literaturnaia gazeta* (May 1, 1974), which omits the references to Yershov and the fatherless children, that is, fathers who disappeared during the Great Terror.

1. See Pushkin's letter to Vladimir Odoyevsky (December 1836): "Saints alive, Your Highness! Have some fear of God: I am neither kith nor kin to Lvov, Ochkin, or the children. Why should I play the fool for *The Children's Journal?* As it is, they're already saying that I am falling into my second childhood" (*The Letters of Alexander Pushkin*, trans. J. Thomas Shaw [Madison, 1967], p. 814).

2. "The learned cat" is from the introduction to Pushkin's *Ruslan and Lyudmila;* "the weaver and the cook" from *Tsar Saltan*. Both are superbly translated by Walter Arndt in Alexander Pushkin, *Collected Narrative and Lyrical Poetry* (Ann Arbor, 1984).

3. Pyotr Yershov (1815-69)—author of *The Little Humpback Horse*, a classic Russian fairy tale in verse.

4. The one-hundredth anniversary of Pushkin's death was celebrated with extraordinary fanfare.

A Word About Dante

Akhmatova delivered her "A Word About Dante" at the celebration marking the 700th anniversary of Dante's birth, held in Moscow's Bolshoi Theater on October 19, 1965. This was Akhmatova's last public appearance.

1. Akhmatova has taken her epigraph from Dante's *The Purgatorio*. The lines in John Ciardi's translation (New York, 1961) read: "A lady came in view: an olive crown / wreathed her immaculate veil, her cloak was green, / the colors of live flame played on her gown."

2. Akhmatova quotes the last quatrain of her 1924 poem "The Muse," here translated by Walter Arndt (*Selected Poems*, p. 87).

3. Akhmatova cites the concluding lines from Nikolai Gumilyov's poem "Florence." See his *Stikhotvoreniia i poemy* (Leningrad, 1988), pp. 397-98.

4. Osip Mandelstam's *Conversation about Dante* was written in 1933, but not published in the USSR until 1967. See Osip Mandelstam, *The Complete Critical Prose and Letters*, edited by Jane Gary Harris (Ann Arbor, 1979) for an English translation.

5. The lines from Mandelstam's "I hear, I hear the early ice" (1937) are from David McDuff's translation of Mandelstam's *Selected Poems* (New York, 1975), p. 145.

6. See Akhmatova's tribute to Mikhail Lozinsky.

7. The translation of Akhmatova's poem "Dante" (August 17, 1936) is from *Complete Poems of Akhmatova*, vol. 2, p. 117.

LETTERS

The first major compilation of Akhmatova's letters appeared in *Sochineniia*, (Paris, 1983) vol. 3, edited by Gleb Struve et al. The Struve edition, which includes letters to eighteen addressees, made use of previous periodical publications, adding to the canon some letters that had not appeared earlier. A number of letters have surfaced since that time and are available in M. M. Kralin's edition of Ahkmatova's works *(Sochineniia*, vol. 2 [Moscow, 1990]).

Consideration of space dictated that a selection be made from Akhmatova's letters. The editor and translators have attempted to present a representative range of addressees.

The letters to Anatoly Naiman are translated in his *Remembering Akhmatova*, trans. Wendy Rosslyn (London, 1991) and, therefore, have not been included.

The editor gratefully acknowledges his debt in the compilation of the notes below to the Struve and Kralin editions, as well as the separate journal publications cited.

To Sergei von Shtein

The ten letters to Sergei von Shtein (1882-1955), professor, poet, translator, and the husband of Akhmatova's elder sister, Inna, are the only letters surviving from the period before Akhmatova's marriage to Nikolai Gumilyov in 1910. These letters document Akhmatova's early literary enthusiasms (Alexander Blok and Valery Bryusov), the decision to marry Gumilyov, even though she was in love with another man, her weak health, and a romantic outlook on life. By the time of this correspondence, von Shtein was already a widower—Akhmatova's sister Inna died July 15, 1906 of tuberculosis. Von Shtein remarried, which may account for the less intimate tone of the last letters.

E. G. Gershtein's publication of this correspondence first appeared in *Russian Literature Triquarterly*, no. 13 (1975), accompanied by an English translation by Edith Stevens. The Stevens translation has been revised for this volume.

Letter 1

1. Valeria Sreznevskaya (née Tyulpanova, 1888-1964), was Akhmatova's friend from childhood until her death. Akhmatova dedicated two poems to her: "Instead of wisdom—experience" (1913, *Complete Poems*, vol. 1, p. 382) and "To the Memóry of V. S. Sreznevskaya," written on the day of the addressee's death (1964, *Complete Poems*, vol. 2, pp. 318-19).

2. Akhmatova's older brother, Andrei Gorenko (1886-1920).

3. Vladimir Golenishchev-Kutuzov (b. 1879), was a student at Petersburg University. The lyrical novella "Confusion" (1913, *Complete Poems*, vol. 1, pp. 300-303) contains echoes of Akhmatova's unrequited love for him.

4. The meaning of this incomplete sentence has eluded the commentators of these letters.

Letter 2

1. Alexander Fyodorov (1868-1949), minor poet and prose writer, addressee of the poem "I walked with you over the black abyss" (1904, *Complete Poems*, vol. 2, pp. 486-87).

Letter 3

1. Anna Vakar (née Stogova), the elder sister of Akhmatova's mother and the wife of Viktor Vakar.

Letter 5

1. A line paraphrased from Alexei Tolstoi's "In the midst of a noisy ball, by chance."
2. The concluding stanza of Bryusov's poem "In the Torture Chamber."
3. Lines from Bryusov's cycle "The Eternal Truth of Idols."
4. Iolanthe—heroine of the eponymous opera by Tchaikovsky.

Letter 7

1. Akhmatova's cousin, Maria Zmunchilla, who later married Andrei Gorenko, is the addressee of the poem "Delusion I" *(Selected Poems,* p. 5).

Letter 8

1. Leonid Andreyev's play *The Life of Man.*
2. The publication of the poem "There are many glittering rings on his hand" in the second issue of Gumilyov's journal *Sirius* (1907) marked Akhmatova's debut in print. No poems by her appeared in the journal's third and final issue.

Letter 9

1. The elder sister of Akhmatova's father, Andrei Gorenko.
2. After graduation from the Fundukleyevskaya School, Akhmatova went on to law school in Kiev.

To Valery Bryusov

Akhmatova's two letters to Valery Bryusov (1873-1924) were first published by Gabriel Superfin and Roman Timenchik in *Cahiers du monde Russe et soviétique,* 15, 1-2 (1974), pp. 183-200. The extensive commentary to the letters superbly documents the Akhmatova-Bryusov literary relationship, which underwent a gradual cooling on both sides. According to V. A. Beer, Akhmatova's classmate, Bryusov's *Fiery Angel* was one of Akhmatova's favorite books. The letters to von Shtein attest to her familiarity with Bryusov's poetry. Though Bryusov hailed Akhmatova's *Evening* as the most interesting book published by the Poets' Guild, his reviews of *Plaintain* and *Anno Domini* were sharply negative, perhaps influenced more by the polemic with Acmeism than by the poetry.

Letter 1

1. Akhmatova sent the following poems: "Do you want to know how it was?" (1910, *Complete Poems,* vol. 1, pp. 224-25); "For you, Aphrodite, I'll compose a dance" (1910, *Complete Poems,* vol. 2, pp. 498-99); "The Old Portrait" (1911, *Complete Poems,* vol. 2, pp. 504-7); "The wind blows stifling hot" (1910, *Complete Poems,* vol. 1, pp. 232-33).
2. Bryusov became head of the literary section of *Russian Thought* in the summer of 1910.

Letter 2

1. Akhmatova enclosed three poems: "Insomnia" (1912, *Complete Poems*, vol. 1, pp. 330-33); "I dream of him less now, thank God" (1912, *Complete Poems*, vol. 1, pp. 484-87); "Intertwined in my dark braids" (1912, *Complete Poems*, vol. 1, 350-51); "Insomnia" appeared in *Russian Thought* (no. 2, 1913).

2. Lev Gumilyov was born on October 1, 1912.

To Alexander Blok

This is the only known letter written by Akhmatova to Blok. See V. A. Chernykh, "Perepiska Bloka s A. A. Akhmatovoi," *Aleksandr Blok. Literaturnoe nasledstvo* (1987), vol. 92, book 4, pp. 571-77. See also Akhmatova's memoir of Blok.

1. Akhmatova describes this incident in her "Reminiscences of Alexander Blok."

2. Akhmatova sent her poem "I visited the poet" (*Complete Poems*, vol. 1, p. 362) in reply to Blok's "'Beauty is frightening,' they will tell you" (quoted in full in note 10 to "Reminiscences of Alexander Blok"). Both poems were first published in the inaugural issue of Vsevolod Meyerhold's *Love for Three Oranges* (1914).

To Pavel Shchegolyov

Pavel Shchegolyov (1877-1931), literary critic and Pushkin scholar. Author of the compendium, *Pushkin's Duel and Death*, to which Akhmatova frequently makes reference in her Pushkin studies. The text appears in *Sochineniia* (1983), vol. 3, p. 336.

To Nikolai Gumilyov

Only two letters from Akhmatova to Gumilyov have been located. The text is printed in *Sochineniia* (1990), vol. 2, pp. 188-89.

Letter 1

1. I. Yasinsky's review "New Books" appeared in *New Word* (no. 7, 1914).

2. Akhmatova is probably referring to a Russian translation of the French poet F. Jammes (1868-1938) that appeared in 1913 (*Stikhi i proza*).

3. E. A. Znosko-Borovsky (1884-1954), writer, theater critic and secretary of the editorial board of *Apollon*.

4. Georgy Chulkov (1879-1939), Symbolist writer and friend of Akhmatova.

5. Two poems were enclosed: (1) "All year you've been inseparable from me" (*Complete Poems*, vol. 1, pp. 398-99) and (2) "Last Will and Testament" (*Complete Poems*, vol. 2, pp. 538-39).

Letter 2

1. The poem "To My Sister" (*Complete Poems*, vol. 1, pp. 442-45).

2. Valery Bryusov's review "The Year in Russian Poetry" appeared in the July issue of *Russian Thought*.

To Georgy Chulkov

The Symbolist writer Georgy Chulkov (1879-1939) and his wife Nadezhda were friends of Akhmatova for many years. The two letters to Chulkov are printed in *Sochineniia* (1990), vol. 2, pp. 189-90.

1. Akhmatova's first narrative poem, *At the Edge of the Sea*.
2. The trip to Switzerland did not take place because of the outbreak of the war.
3. Chulkov's wife.
4. The Pushkin scholar, Pavel Shchegolyov.

To Anastasia Chebotaryevskaya

Anastasia Chebotaryevskaya (1876-1921), writer and wife of Fyodor Sologub. The text is printed in *Sochineniia* (1983), vol. 3, pp. 336-37.

1. Akhmatova's "Prayer" and "Comfort" *(Complete Poems, vol. 1, pp. 435, 433)* were published in the almanac *War in Russian Poetry* (1915), which was compiled by Chebotaryevskaya and Sologub.
2. "July 1914" *(Complete Poems, vol. 1, pp. 427-29)*.

To Fyodor Sologub

The Symbolist prose writer and poet Fyodor Sologub (1863-1927), best known for his novel *The Petty Demon*. Akhmatova's letters to Sologub are published in *Sochineniia* (1983), vol. 3, p. 337.

To Anna Gumilyova

Akhmatova's letters to her mother-in-law, Anna Gumilyova, are printed in *Sochineniia* (1990), vol. 2, p. 191.

Letter 1
1. Lyova—Akhmatova's son, Lev Gumilyov.

Letter 2
1. P. N.—Pavel Nikolayevich Luknitsky (1900-73), friend of Akhmatova and biographer of Nikolai Gumilyov, with whom the young Lev was in correspondence. See Luknitsky's *Vstrechi s Annoi Akhmatovoi* (Paris, 1991) for his account of his meetings with Akhmatova in the years 1924-1925.
2. Shurochka—Alexandra Sverchkova, Nikolai Gumilyov's half-sister.

To Vladimir Shileiko

Many of the letters to Vladimir Shileiko (1891-1930) survive in copies Pavel Luknitsky made before sending them to the addressee. *Sochineniia* (1990, vol. 2) prints sixteen letters. Akhmatova and Shileiko were married in December 1918 and separated in 1921. The letters, however, attest to the couple's continuing good relations.

Letter 1
1. Akhmatova and Shileiko somehow managed to feed and keep their St. Bernard, Tapa (also called Tushin, Tapusya, Taptan), despite the hunger of the early 1920s and their general inability to cope with daily life. Tapa's health and illnesses emerge as a central theme in these letters.
2. Akhmatova's nickname translates as Evil Spirit.

Letter 2
1. Pavel Luknitsky visited regularly during this period and often ran various errands for Akhmatova. See his *Vstrechi s Annoi Akhmatovoi* (Paris, 1991).
2. Shileiko's wife, Vera Konstantinovna (née Andreyeva).

Letter 3
1. The two-volume collection of Akhmatova's poetry was not published. A volume did not appear until 1940.

Letter 5
1. Shileiko's family nickname.

Letter 6
1. Nikolai Punin, the art historian, was Akhmatova's third husband.

Letter 7
1. Akhmatova enclosed a childhood photograph of Shileiko.
2. Shileiko's wife, Vera Konstantinovna.

To Ioanna Bryusova

Ioanna Bryusova (1876-1965), the widow of the Symbolist poet and theoretician Valery Bryusov (1873-1924). The text of Akhmatova's letter is published in *Sochineniia* (1983), vol. 3, p. 338.

1. Pavel Luknitsky, under Akhmatova's supervision, had undertaken the task of collecting Gumilyov's archive.

To Nikolai Khardzhiev

Akhmatova became acquainted with the literary scholar and art historian Nikolai Khardzhiev (b. 1903) in the summer of 1930 and the two remained on friendly terms until Akhmatova's death. The most comprehensive edition of Akhmatova's letters to Khardzhiev, which also includes inscriptions on books and photographs and other letters to Khardzhiev containing mention of Akhmatova, was edited with an introductory essay and extensive commentary by E. Babayev: "A. A. Akhmatova v pis'makh k N. I. Khardzhievu (1930–1960-e gg.)," *Voprosy literatury*, no. 6 (1989), pp. 214-47.

Letter 1

1. Irina Punina (b. 1921), Nikolai Punin's daughter by his previous marriage to Anna Arens.

Letter 2

1. Vera Rumyantseva, mutual friend of Akhmatova and Khardzhiev, worked as a bibliographer at the Tretyakov Museum.

2. Akhmatova's son, Lev Gumilyov, was away on an archaeological expedition.

3. Akhmatova's husband, Nikolai Punin.

4. Osip and Nadezhda Mandelstam.

Letter 3

1. Akhmatova's essay on Pushkin's *The Golden Cockerel* was published in 1933 as "Pushkin's Last Tale."

2. Nikolai Punin.

Letter 4

1. Caesar Volpe (1904-41), critic and literary historian.

2. Khardzhiev's friend, the literary critic Mikhail Matveyevich Nikitin, was imprisoned from 1933 to 1936. He died at the front in 1942.

3. Nikolai Punin.

4. Khardzhiev collaborated with Viktor Shklovsky on the publication *Chulkov and Levshin* (Leningrad, 1933).

5. The writer Boris Pilnyak (1894-1941), best known for the novel *The Naked Year*.

6. Sofia Tolstaya (1900-57), granddaughter of Leo Tolstoy and widow of the poet Sergei Yesenin.

7. Viktor Borisovich Shklovsky.

Letter 5

1. Vera Fyodorovna Rumyantseva.

2. Lev Gumilyov.

3. Mikhail Matveyevich Nikitin.

4. Vladimir Bonch-Bruyevich (1873-1955), director of the State Literary Museum. Akhmatova declined the offer.

Letter 6

1. Khardzhiev had presented Akhmatova with an antique album, which she used to record the final versions of her poems. At present this album is in the possession of Irina Punina.

2. Osip Mandelstam was arrested in Moscow on May 14, 1934.

Letter 7

1. The literary critic, Lidia Andreyevskaya and her husband, Boris Engelgardt. Both perished during the Leningrad blockade.

2. The Leningrad critic Lidia Ginzburg (1902-90).

Letter 8

1. Khardzhiev arrived in Alma-Ata in November 1941, the same month Akhmatova settled in Tashkent.

2. *A Poem without a Hero.*

3. Shklovsky, Zoshchenko and Khardzhiev had sent a collective letter to Akhmatova from Alma-Ata. Lili Brik was living in the city of Molotov at the time.

Letter 9

1. Viktor Shklovsky visited Tashkent in spring 1942.

2. Akhmatova met Nikolai Punin and his domestic entourage (first wife, daughter, granddaughter, and third wife) at the train station in Tashkent as they made their way to Samarkand. In his letter written in the hospital in Samarkand, dated April 14, 1942, Punin writes his former wife about how much she and her poetry mean to him. The text of this letter is published in *Anna Akhmatova. Stikhi. Perepiska. Ikonografiia* (Ann Arbor, 1977).

3. Vladimir Georgiyevich Garshin (1887-1956) remarried in Leningrad during the blockade. His relationship with Akhmatova dated from the late 1930s.

Letter 10

1. "Don't lose your despair" was Nikolai Punin's favorite saying, often quoted by Akhmatova.

Letter 11

1. Konstantin Paustovsky's adopted son, S. Navashin.

Letter 12

1. Akhmatova had been seriously ill with typhus.

2. Khardzhiev returned to Moscow in December 1942.

Letter 13

1. Valeria Sergeyevna Poznanskaya, a friend of Akhmatova.

2. One copy of *A Poem without a Hero* is dated: "August 18, 1942. Tashkent."

3. Nikolai Punin was professor at the Academy of Fine Arts, which had been evacuated to Samarkand.

4. Alexei Kruchenykh (1886-1968), Futurist poet.

5. Osip Brik (1888-1945), critic and LEF theoretician, and his wife Lili (1891-1978) are best remembered for their association with Vladimir Mayakovsky.

6. Khardzhiev lived in Marina Grove during the thirties and forties.

Letter 14

1. Nadezhda Mandelstam.

2. Akhmatova read her "Mayakovsky in 1913" at one of the evenings held to commemorate the thirteenth anniversary of Mayakovsky's death.

Letter 15

1. Akhmatova is alluding to the ending of Chekhov's *Cherry Orchard.*

2. Kruchenykh had composed a variation on Akhmatova's "Muse."

3. Akhmatova moved to the house on Zhukovskaya St., 54, in May 1943, which she shared with Yelena Bulgakova, widow of Mikhail Bulgakov. Akhmatova's poem "The Hostess," (1943) dedicated to Yelena Bulgakova, draws on motifs from Bulgakov's novel *The Master and Margarita*, known to very few people at this time, and which would not be published for another twenty years.

4. Akhmatova's collection *Selected Poems* (Tashkent, 1943).

5. Kornely Zelinsky (1896-1970), editor of the Tashkent publication of Akhmatova's selected works.

6. Yevgeny Khazin (1893-1973), Nadezhda Mandelstam's brother.

Letter 16

1. The actress Natalya Vishnevskaya was known for her readings of Lermontov's poetry.

2. Asya Sukhomlinova, Akhmatova's Tashkent friend.

3. The *Selected Poems* volume published in 1943 in Tashkent.

4. Akhmatova is referring to successful maneuvers by the Allied Forces in the Mediterranean.

Letter 17

1. Khardzhiev had secured an invitation for Akhmatova from the State Publishing House, which would allow her to return to Moscow.

2. Nadezhda Mandelstam.

Letter 18

1. Nikolai Punin's first wife, Anna Arens-Punina.

2. Pasternak's letter has not survived.

Letter 20

1. The suprematist artist, Nikolai Mikhailovich Suetin (1897-1954), pupil of Kazimir Malevich and Khardzhiev's friend.

2. Akhmatova published poems from the cycle "In Praise of Peace" in *Ogonyok* (October 1950)—an attempt to secure the release of her son.

Letter 21

1. Khardzhiev's wife, Lidia Vasilyevna Chaga.

Letter 22

1. Akhmatova's memoir of Amedeo Modigliani, for which she had asked Khardzhiev to write a short note about the portrait. Khardzhiev's text was published as an afterword *(Den' poezii, 1967)*.

Letter 23

1. Marc Chagall's daughter, Ida.

2. Anatoly Naiman collaborated with Akhmatova on the volume of Leopardi *(Lirika, 1967)*.

3. Akhmatova's dacha in Komarovo.

To Osip Mandelstam

Akhmatova's letter to Mandelstam first appeared in *Vestnik Russkogo khristianskogo dvizheniia*, no. 116 (1975); reprinted in *Sochineniia* (1983), vol. 3, pp. 338-39.

1. Akhmatova visited the exiled poet in Voronezh in February 1936.

2. Boris Pasternak attended an international writers' congress in Paris in the summer of 1935.

3. Akhmatova's collection did not appear in 1935.

4. The poet's wife, Nadezhda Mandelstam.

To Emma Gershtein

Emma Gershtein (b. 1903) met Akhmatova in 1934 at the Mandelstams' apartment and they remained friends until the end of Akhmatova's life. The letters translated here attest to a relationship that was reinforced by mutual friends (for example, the Mandelstams) and scholarship (Pushkin and Lermontov). One of Akhmatova's few published reviews was written on Gershtein's Lermontov study (*Sud'ba Lermontova*). Gershtein's numerous publications of Akhmatova's writings include many of the Pushkin studies, as well as Akhmatova's letters to von Shtein. Her book on Mandelstam (*Novoe o Mandel'shtame* [Paris, 1986]) includes numerous references to Akhmatova. A second book of memoirs is forthcoming. The selection of Akhmatova's letters to Gershtein was published by the addressee in *Voprosy literatury* (no. 6, 1989) with a memoir of Akhmatova in the thirties and an afterword.

Letter 1

1. In August 1936 Akhmatova spent 10-12 days at Gershtein's.

2. In fact, not an article on Lermontov, but a bibliography of Nikolai Gumilyov.

3. Akhmatova had been awarded a pension for her contributions to Russian literature, but this pension was cancelled and reinstated more than once.

Letter 2

1. This short note was a postscript to Nadezhda Mandelstam's letter to Gershtein.

Letter 3

1. Nadya—Nadezhda Mandelstam.

2. Yelena Mikhailovna Fradkina, wife of Nadezhda Mandelstam's brother, Yevgeny Khazin (1893-1974).

3. Sergei Borisovich Rudakov met the Mandelstams in Voronezh, where he was also living in exile. He became a frequent visitor at the Mandelstams and embarked on a detailed commentary of Mandelstam's poetry, based on their frequent discussions. Akhmatova and Gershtein made Rudakov's acquaintance in Voronezh through the Mandelstams. Finding an ardent admirer of Gumilyov in Rudakov, Akhmatova gave him part of her Gumilyov archive for study and safekeeping. Nadezhda Mandelstam also entrusted Rudakov with some of her husband's manuscripts and other materials. Rudakov was killed at the front in January 1944. The fate of these archives remains unknown. It appears that Rudakov's widow supplemented her income by trading in Gumilyov manuscripts, although she alternately claimed that the archive had been confiscated by the secret police and that she had destroyed the archive not wishing to be compromised by holding materials of two politically suspect poets. In any case, the archives were never returned. As this letter attests, during his lifetime Akhmatova was concerned about Rudakov's well-being. She presented Rudakov with an inscribed copy of *From Six Books* and dedicated to him the 1945 poem "To the Memory of a Friend." See E. G. Gershtein, *Novoe o Mandel'shtame*.

4. The artist Alexander Osmyorkin and his wife Yelena.

5. Akhmatova's son Lev Gumilyov completed serving his sentence on March 10, 1943.

Letter 4

1. This note was a postscript to a letter from Nadezhda Mandelstam.

2. Gershtein's father passed away on November 14, 1943.

3. Akhmatova left Tashkent in early May 1944.

Letter 5

1. Lev Gumilyov, who had been working in an industrial complex exempted from the draft, secured permission to be sent to the front.

2. Nikolai Gumilyov's mother, Anna, died on December 24, 1942.

3. Nikolai Ivanovich Khardzhiev first met Akhmatova in 1930 and remained a friend for life. See Akhmatova's letters to Khardzhiev.

Letter 6

1. Gershtein had received a letter from Lev Gumilyov, written on the outskirts of Berlin, in which he shared his thoughts on life after demobilization. Gershtein had sent a copy of this letter to Akhmatova.

2. The Leningrad critic Lidia Ginzburg (1902-90), author of studies on Russian poetry, the psychological novel, and memoirs. Ginzburg's reminiscences of Akhmatova were published in her *Literatura v poiskakh real'nosti* (Leningrad, 1987).

3. At the time Gershtein was not officially affiliated with any institution and had difficulty publishing her work on Lermontov.

4. Akhmatova's close friends, the writer Viktor Ardov and his wife Nina Olshevskaya. The planned trip did not take place.

Letter 7

1. Boris Eikhenbaum (1866-1959), Formalist critic par excellence, author of one of the first books on Akhmatova's poetry *(Anna Akhmatova. Opyt analiza,* 1923), and eminent Lermontov scholar (see his *Lermontov: A Study in Literary-Historical Evaluation,* trans. Ray Parrot and Harry Weber [Ann Arbor, 1981]). Gershtein had begun her work on Lermontov under Eikhenbaum's direction.

2. These plans did not materialize.

Letter 8

1. Akhmatova's translation of Hugo's "To L" was printed in Hugo's *Collected Works* (Moscow, 1953).

2. N. I. Khutsishvili.

Letter 9

1. Akhmatova lived with Irina Punina and her daughter Anna Kaminskaya in Leningrad.

2. Nikolai Khardzhiev's *The Fate of an Artist* (1954).

3. The art historian Vsevolod Petrov (1912-78).

4. Akhmatova became acquainted with Tatyana Konshina and Natalya Ignatova in 1952 at the Bolshevo sanatorium.

Letter 10
1. This telegram is dated by the Moscow postmark.

Letter 11
1. Akhmatova's letters to Irina Tomashevskaya, wife of the eminent critic Boris Tomashevsky, are published in *Ob Anne Akhmatovoi* (Leningrad, 1990).
2. Gershtein's twenty-eight-year-old nephew had died as the result of a helicopter accident.

Letter 12
1. The date of the telegram has been set by the Moscow postmark.

Letter 13
1. Nadezhda Mandelstam.
2. Akhmatova refers to her extremely difficult and complicated family and living situation.

Letter 14
1. Mikhail Zoshchenko died on July 22, 1958.
2. Maria Petrovykh (1908-79), poet and translator.
3. The unnatural fear of correspondence is a result of the consequences that may be meted out to the sender, addressee, or their families.

Letter 15
1. The actor Roman Albertovich Rubinstein, Irina Punina's second husband.
2. Akhmatova's translation from Hindi was published in Sumitranandan Pant, *Izbrannye stikhi* (Moscow, 1959).
3. Boris Ardov (b. 1940), the Ardovs' youngest son, was keen on drawing, but went on to acting school, while Gershtein's nephew Pavel Bochkov (b. 1940) pursued art.
4. The prominent linguist and literary scholar Viktor Vinogradov (1895-1969) authored an early study of Akhmatova's poetry (*O poezii Anny Akhmatovoi*, 1925).
5. Valeria Sreznevskaya (1888-1964), lifelong friend of Akhmatova. See Akhmatova's autobiographical prose.

Letter 16
1. Akhmatova's telegram refers to Pyotr Vyazemsky's letters to E. Musina-Pushkina, which Gershtein had discovered in a Moscow archive during her Lermontov research. Akhmatova cites these letters in her study "Pushkin's Death."

To Nadezhda Mandelstam

The letters to Nadezhda Mandelstam (1899-1980), the poet's widow and Akhmatova's close friend, were published in *Sochineniia* (1983), vol. 3, pp. 339-41; reprinted in *Sochineniia* (1990), vol. 2, pp. 226-28.

Letter 1
1. Eduard Babayev and Nina Olshevskaya.

Letter 2
1. M. M. Kralin corrects the date, which is given as 1945 in the Paris edition of Akhmatova's works, to 1952.
2. Akhmatova's translation of Victor Hugo's *Marion De Lorme*.
3. Akhmatova moved from the House on the Fontanka to her apartment on Krasnaya Konnitsa in 1952.

Letter 3
1. Nothing came of Akhmatova's plan to live with Nadezhda Mandelstam.

Letter 5
1. Akhmatova may be referring to her memoir of Osip Mandelstam.
2. Nadezhda Mandelstam's brother, Yevgeny Khazin.

To Vladimir Garshin

Vladimir Garshin (1887-1956), medical doctor, professor, and nephew of the Russian writer, Vsevolod Garshin, was instrumental in Akhmatova's leaving Nikolai Punin. Akhmatova demanded that her letters to Garshin be returned to her after the dissolution of their relationship. The letters were destroyed by Akhmatova, with the exception of this short note.

To Irina Tomashevskaya

Akhmatova's letters to Irina Tomashevskaya (née Medvedyeva, 1903-73), literary critic and close friend, are printed in *Sochineniia* (1990), vol. 2, pp. 217-21 and in *Ob Anne Akhmatovoi* (Leningrad, 1990), where they are part of Z. B. Tomashevskaya's account of her parents' friendship with Akhmatova ("Ia—kak peterburgskaia tumba," pp. 417-38).

1. *Selected Poems*, published in Tashkent in 1943.
2. Vladimir Garshin (1887-1956).
3. The Pushkin scholars Mstislav and Tatyana Tsyavlovsky.
4. The Leningrad critic Lidia Ginzburg.
5. Iosif Orbeli (1887-1961), director of the Hermitage.

To Boris Pasternak

The text of these two letters was first published in *Sochineniia* (1990), vol. 2, pp. 225-26.

Letter 1
1. Pasternak's *On Early Trains* (1943).
2. The actress Natalya Vishnevskaya.

Letter 2
1. Nina Olshevskaya.
2. Akhmatova was hospitalized after her first heart attack in 1951.

To Vera Sutugina

Vera Sutugina (1892-1969), a member of the editorial staff of *World Literature*, became acquainted with Akhmatova in 1919. The letters are printed in *Sochineniia* (1983), vol. 3, pp. 366-67.

1. Alexander Tikhonov (1880-1956), author of the memoir *Time and People*.

To Lev Gumilyov

Akhmatova's three letters to her son, Lev Gumilyov (b. 1912), were first published in *Sochineniia* (1990), vol. 2, pp. 228-29.

Gumilyov was arrested on November 6, 1949 and not released until 1956. Evidently the first two letters here are all that survive from Akhmatova's voluminous correspondence with her son during his imprisonment. In his own right, Lev Gumilyov is a respected historian, Orientalist, and ethnographer (see Akhmatova's second letter and the references to the Huns).

Letter 1
1. The artist and former professor, Alexander Osmyorkin, died in poverty on June 25, 1953.

Letter 2
1. Gumilyov was born on October 1, 1912.

Letter 3
1. Probably Alexander Surkov, the editor of Akhmatova's *Poems* (1958).

To Aleksis Rannit

The poet, literary critic, and art historian, Aleksis Rannit, who was writing an article on Akhmatova's poetry, had sent her a Russian translation of his poems as well as several questions regarding her biography. Three of Akhmatova's letters to Rannit were published in *Sochineniia* (1968), vol. 2, pp. 304-7.

Letter 1
1. Akhmatova did not realize that Rannit wrote poetry in Estonian. His poetry has been translated by Igor Severyanin, Georgy Adamovich and others.
2. In his *The Three Worlds of Boris Pasternak* (1961), Robert Payne makes the absurd claim that he had met with Akhmatova in Paris in 1938. Rannit called him on this in a letter to the editor published in the *New York Times,* but Payne stuck to his story.
3. See Akhmatova's autobiographical prose for her criticism of Georgy Ivanov's *Petersburg Winters* and Leonid Strakhovsky's *Craftsmen of the Word. Three Poets of Modern Russia. Gumilyov. Akhmatova. Mandelstam* (Harvard University Press, 1949).

Letter 2

1. Akhmatova thought that Rannit's poem "Blue" was addressed to her.

2. Akhmatova answered seven of the ten questions sent by Rannit. The questions to Akhmatova's answers are: (2) When did you begin to write verse and when were your first poems published? (3) Who in your family encouraged your literary endeavors? Who inspired you? (4) Who was your favorite poet as a child and whom do you place higher today among Russian poets? (5) Who among Russian poets was your teacher in both the structural and linguistic sense? (8) Have you given your poems to friends and poets prior to publication for technical criticism and did you follow their advice and criticism? Who were your advisors? (9) How long is the process of creating your poetry? Are most of your poems written in the course of one day, one week, one month? (10) What in your opinion is your particular technical or thematic contribution to poetry? What in your opinion was first introduced by you into Russian poetry, which has still not been noticed by the critics?

3. Akhmatova's "Latest Poem," the first line of which reads "One, like an anxious thunderbolt" (*Complete Poems*, vol. 2, pp. 160-63).

Letter 3

1. The artist Alexander Tyshler (1898-1980) executed several portraits of Akhmatova in the 1940s in Tashkent.

To Kornei Chukovsky

Akhmatova's letter to the children's writer and critic Kornei Chukovsky (1882-1969), published in *Novyi mir* (no. 3, 1987), is reprinted in *Sochineniia* (1990), vol. 2, pp. 233-34.

1. Chukovsky's article "Reading Akhmatova," an analysis of *A Poem without a Hero*, was published in the journal *Moskva* (1964).

To Semyon Weinberg

Semyon Weinberg (b. 1905), doctor by profession and amateur translator, primarily from Russian into German. The letters to Weinberg were first published in *Sochineniia* (1983), vol. 3, pp. 353-54.

To Georges Nivat

Sergei Makovsky's sketch of Nikolai Gumilyov had been translated by the French Slavist, Georges Nivat (b. 1935). See Akhmatova's negative appraisal of Makovsky's work in the autobiographical prose. The letter to Nivat was published in *Sochineniia* (1983), vol. 3, p. 354; reprinted in *Sochineniia* (1990), vol. 2, p. 236.

To Viktor Gorenko

Viktor Gorenko (1896-1979), Akhmatova's younger brother, moved to Sakhalin in 1918, and later emigrated to China and then to the U.S. in 1947. Akhmatova's letters to her brother, as well as an interview with him, are published in *Anna Akhmatova. Stikhi, perepiska, vospominaniia, ikonografiia* (Ann Arbor, 1977).

To Fyodor Malov

The letter to Fyodor Malov, an agricultural worker, is one of Akhmatova's few responses to her readers. Akhmatova supposedly was intrigued by Malov's naivete and his earnest style. Malov had written Akhmatova that he had wanted to write sooner, but chores and work prevented him. Malov's letter and Akhmatova's response were first published in *Sochineniia* (1990), vol. 2, pp. 250-51, 380-81.

1. "Midnight Poems" (*Complete Poems*, vol. 2, pp. 266-77).
2. This fragment does not appear in the final text.
3. The publication in *Day of Poetry* (1964) appeared without the third poem and epilogue of the final text.

To Joseph Brodsky

On February 18, 1964 the future Nobel Laureate, Joseph Brodsky, (b. 1940) was sentenced to five years forced labor for parasitism, a sentence that was reduced after massive protests both in the USSR and abroad. Brodsky belonged to the group of poets affectionately (and sometimes ironically) called Akhmatova's boys (along with Dmitry Bobyshev, Yevgeny Rein and Anatoly Naiman). For more information on the Akhmatova-Brodsky friendship, see Anatoly Naiman, *Remembering Akhmatova* (London, 1991), Solomon Volkov's interview with Brodsky (*Kontinent*, no. 53, 1987) and Brodsky's "The Keening Muse" in his *Less Than One. Selected Essays* (New York, 1986), pp. 34-52.

The texts of Akhmatova's letters were published by Yakov Gordin as "Dialog poetov (Tri pis'ma Akhmatovoi k Brodskomu)" in *Akhmatovskii sbornik*, vol. 1, ed. Serge Deduline and Gabriel Superfin (Paris, 1989); they are also included in *Sochineniia* (1990), vol. 2, pp. 253-55.

Letter 1
1. A quotation from *The Way of All the Earth* (*Complete Poems*, vol. 2, p. 377).
2. The line is taken from "From the Diary of a Traveller" (*Complete Poems*, vol. 2, p. 715).

Letter 2
1. Anna Kaminskaya, Punin's granddaughter.
2. Brodsky's poem on T. S. Eliot's death is dated January 12, 1965.

Letter 3

1. Yakov Gordin dates this letter as July 10, 1965 by Akhmatova's reference to St. Peter's Day.

2. Tolya—Anatoly Naiman.

3. The eighteenth-century Smolny Cathedral was erected according to the designs of Bartolomeo Rastrelli.

4. Brodsky's friend, G. Ginzburg-Voskov.

AFTERWORD

Akhmatova's Prose

E. G. Gershtein's "Akhmatova's Prose" is translated from the text published in Akhmatova, *Sochineniia* (1986), vol. 2, pp. 367-77. Unless marked otherwise, all notes below belong to E. G. Gershtein; the translator's notes are indicated by [Tr.] at the end.

1. Nadezhda Lvova's *An Old Tale,* with a foreword by Valery Bryusov, had been published the previous year in Moscow by Halcyon Press. Akhmatova's brief review, entitled "On Nadezhda Lvova's Poetry" is translated in this volume.

2. Artur Lourié (1893-1966) was A. K. Glazunov's pupil at the Petersburg Conservatory. He emigrated in 1924.

3. From Kornei Chukovsky's diary. *Literaturnoe nasledstvo,* vol. 92, part 2 (Moscow, 1981), p. 258.

4. In the former Marble Palace, Akhmatova lived in the official apartment of her second husband, Vladimir Shileiko. Akhmatova touches on the topic of Chénier and Pushkin in her "Marginalia."

5. L. A. Mandrykina, "Nenapisannaia kniga," *Knigi. Arkhivy. Avtografy* (Moscow, 1973), p. 67.

6. *Voprosy literatury,* 1978, no. 1, pp. 185-228.

7. E. G. Gershtein and V. E. Vatsuro, "Zametki A. A. Akhmatovoi o Pushkine," *Vremennik pushkinskoi komissii,* pp. 30-44.

8. For an English translation of *Requiem,* see Robin Kemball's version in the collection edited by Walter Arndt, Anna Akhmatova, *Selected Poems* (Ann Arbor, 1976), pp. 125-33. Hereafter the collection is identified as *Selected Poems.* [Tr.]

9. *Kul'tura i zhizn',* 1957, no. 1.

10. Akhmatova's commentary on Pushkin's wife, as well as Tsvetaeva's view of her, receives an ironical fictional treatment, in its turn, in Andrei Bitov's novel *Pushkin House.* [Tr.]

11. For a signal instance of a hagiographical approach to Pushkin's wife, see I. Obodovskaia and M. Dement'ev, *Natal'ia Nikolaevna Pushkina* (Moscow, 1985). [Tr.]

12. *Duel' Pushkina s Dantesom-Gekkernom. Podlinnoe voenno-sudnoe delo 1837 g.* (St. Petersburg, 1900), p. 146.

13. *O Pushkine,* ed. E. G. Gershtein (Leningrad, 1977; 2nd edition, Gorky, 1984).

14. Akhmatova's reminiscences of Modigliani and Blok are translated in the present volume. [Tr.]

15. See Akhmatova's memoir of Mandelstam in the present volume. [Tr.]

16. In her reminiscences Akhmatova calls this novel *Riddles and Enigmas*. The title *Riddles and Enigmas (Mysteries)* appeared on the front title page of the ninth volume of *The Complete Collected Works of Knut Hamsun*, published by V. M. Sablin (Moscow, 1907).

17. *Victoria* (1898) and *Pan* (1894) are two of Hamsun's most popular novels. [Tr.]

18. For a translation of "A Dark Veil...," see *Selected Poems*, p. 7; see also *Poems of Anna Akhmatova*, trans. Stanley Kunitz and Max Hayward (Boston, 1973), p. 43. [Tr.]

19. Selections from the cycle are rendered into English in *Selected Poems*, pp. 90-92. [Tr.]

20. The reference here is to the lines of the seventh poem in Akhmatova's cycle *Wildrose Blooming*: "The wildrose emitted such a fragrance,/That it was transformed into a word," and to the lines in the seventh stanza of Pushkin's poem "There was a time—our youthful play":

> You recall how suddenly
> These orchards, these live waters, came to life...

21. Cf. the commentary of V. M. Zhirmunsky in *Anna Akhmatova, Stikhotvoreniia i poemy*, Biblioteka poeta, Bol'shaia seriia, 2nd ed. (Leningrad, 1977), p. 511. (The correct date of publication is 1976, Tr.)

22. Michal was Saul's younger daughter (I Samuel 14:49), who married David (18: 20-27). [Tr.]

23. See Akhmatova's *Pages from a Diary*.

24. The opening lines of *At the Edge of the Sea (Complete Poems*, vol. 2, p. 357). [Tr.]

25. The premise of Pushkin's poem is the divine origin of poetic creation, whereby the poet receives and fulfills the word of God, Who transforms the poet into a seer. That view gained ascendency during the Romantic period. (On the topic, see Victor Erlich, *The Maker and the Seer.*) [Tr.]

26. Akhmatova first saw the famous altar at the exhibit of the treasures of Pergamum, on loan from the Berlin Museum and shown in the Hermitage in 1958.

27. N. Il'ina, *Dorogi i sud'by* (Moscow, 1985), pp. 298-99.

28. Carl Proffer's annotated, unrhymed version of this masterpiece appears in *Selected Poems*, pp. 137-82. [Tr.]

SELECTED BIBLIOGRAPHY

Akhmatova, Anna. *Sochineniia v dvukh tomakh*, volume 2 (Proza, perevody), edited by E. G. Gershtein, L. A. Mandrykina, V. A. Chernykh, N. N. Glen (Moscow: Khudozhestvennaia Literatura, 1986). [Comprehensive collection of Akhmatova's prose.]

——. *Sochineniia v dvukh tomakh*, volume 2 (Stikhotvoreniia raznykh let, proza, pis'ma), edited by M. M. Kralin (Moscow: Pravda, 1990). [The most complete compilation of Akhmatova's letters with commentary.]

——. *Sochineniia*, edited by B. A. Filippov and G. Struve, volumes 1-2 (Washington, D.C.: Inter-Language Literary Associates, 1967-68), volume 3 (Paris: YMCA Press, 1983). [The first effort to collect all of Akhmatova's poetry and prose.]

——. *O Pushkine*, edited by E. G. Gershtein, 2d ed. (Gorky, 1984); 3d ed. (Moscow: Kniga, 1989). [The definitive text of Akhmatova's Pushkin studies. Extensive commentary.]

Gershtein, E. G. and V. E. Vatsuro, "Zametki A. A. Akhmatovoi o Pushkine," *Vremennik Pushkinskoi komissii*, vyp. 8 (1970), pp. 30-44.

Liamkina, E. I., "Vdokhnovenie, masterstvo, trud (Zapisnye knizhki A. A. Akhmatovoi)," *Vstrechi s proshlym*, 2d. ed. (Moscow: Sovetskaia Rossiia, 1980), pp. 380-420.

Mandrykina, L. A. (ed.), "Listki iz dnevnika. Vospominaniia. Novella ob O. E. Mandel'shtame," *Zvezda*, no. 6 (1989), pp. 20-38. [Commentary by L. A. Il'iunina and Ts. T. Snegovskaia.]

——. "Nenapisannaia kniga," *Knigi. Arkhivy. Avtografy* (Moscow: Kniga, 1973).

Suvorova, K. N. and V. A. Chernykh (eds.), "Samyi neprochitannyi poet. Zametki Anny Akhmatovoi o Nikolae Gumileve," *Novyi mir*, no. 5 (1990), pp. 219-23.

Timenchik, R. D. and V. A. Chernykh (eds.), "Avtobiograficheskaia proza," *Literaturnoe obozrenie*, no. 5 (1989), pp. 3-17.

Vilenkin, V. (ed.), "Listki iz dnevnika (O Mandel'shtame)," *Voprosy literatury*, no. 2 (1989), pp. 178-217.

INDEX